January 16, 2000

Peggy,

Days of Harvest
Glory.

Love,

Ruth

Harvest Glory

I Ask for the Nations

Visas

AMBASSADE DE COTE D'IVOIRE ADDIS-ABEBA

NOM: HEFLIN
Prénoms: RUTH WARD
1. Numéro de visa: 8167
2. Genre de visa: court séjour
3. Date de délivrance: 9 mai 1967
4. Date d'expiration: 3 août 1967
5. Nombre d'entrées autorisées: une
6. Durée autorisée du séjour: un mois

R L'Ambassadeur

ADDIS. ABEBA

HIGH COMMISSION OF INDIA
LONDON

IMMIGRATION OFFICER
(94)
EMBARCEn
17 APR 1968
LONDON AIRPORT

CCCP
Таможня

ENTRADA
PUNTA CAUCEDO
Aeropuerto Internacional
Republica Dominicana

IMMIGRATION
565 DEPARTED
9 JUN 1996
A
565 SINGAPORE 565

...SSY OF PAKISTAN
...ABUL

8 MAI 1967

L'Ambassadeur

IMMIGRATION DIVISION
BANGKOK THAILAND
A 280 DEPARTED
SIGNED 29 DEC 1991

EMBASSY OF THE REPUBLIC OF THE SUD...
CAIRO

ENTRY / TRAN...

No. of Visa
Date of Issue 11. 3. 1967
Validity 11. 3. 67
Period of Stay ..... Two weeks
Purpose of Visit ..... Tourism
Fees Collected ..... L.E.2.—
Receipt No. 15292

CONSUL GENER...

Visas

T.C. VILAYETI
17-2-67
ÇIKIŞ-1

3315 ...

-3 MA 1967
BÖLGE-4

T.C. VILAYETI
4-2-67
GIRIŞ
EDIRNE VILAYETI

中华人民共和国
1984.5.14

中华人民共和国
1984.5.17 出境签证
ENTRY-EXIT VISA
有效 第 L3315 号
GOOD FOR JOURNEY
有效期至 1984年6月15日
VALID UNTIL
入境后前往
DECLARATION
中华人民共和国外交部驻香港签证办事处
1984年4月30日

IMMIGRATION
ARRIVED
29 DEC 1991
MELBOURNE AIRPORT
04 TP

IMMIGRATION & ETHNIC AFFAIRS
DEPARTED
11 JAN 1992
SYDNEY 356
AUSTRALIA

EMBASSY OF
ADDIS ABABA

SENEGAL
50
FRANC

RANGPO P.S.
SIKKIM
16-2-1999

CESKOSLOVENSKÉ VIZUM
NÁVRATNÉ - VSTUPNÍ
na 02 dni
cestám po _____ dnech
Spolucestují _____
_____
Použití viza do 3 měsíců
Ve Vídni dne 6 XII. 1967

RÉ...
No.
Nom...

ROYAL NEPALESE EMBASSY

AMBASSADE D...
ADDIS

Harvest Glory

I Ask for the Nations

by
Ruth Ward Heflin

Harvest Glory
Copyright © 1999 by Ruth Heflin

All Scripture references are from the Authorized King James Version of the Bible, unless otherwise indicated.

McDougal Publishing is a ministry of The McDougal Foundation, Inc., a Maryland nonprofit corporation dedicated to spreading the Gospel of the Lord Jesus Christ to as many people as possible in the shortest possible time.

Published by:

McDougal Publishing
P.O. Box 3595
Hagerstown, MD 21742-3595

ISBN 1-884369-81-2

Printed in the United States of America
For Worldwide Distribution

Dedication

To my nieces and nephews, grandnieces and grandnephews and great-grand-
nephews:

Michael, Pat, Katherine Austin "Katie" and Anne Elizabeth Heflin
Edith Ann, Jim, Mary, James and Arthur Douds
Willard Henderson
David, Gail, William, Sharon, Michael and Kimberly Henderson
Helen Ruth, Naomi, Krystle, Joseph and Jeremiah Medina

To Sally and Bill Galbraith

To Bette Lewis

To Senator Stewart Greenleaf

Acknowledgments

Those who helped me put this book together:

Harold McDougal
Connie and Bill Wilson
Debbie Kendrick
Ruth Kendrick
Shoshannah Kendrick
Patricia Grant
Susan Weatherby

Foreword

My earliest recollection of a conversation with Ruth Heflin was in the Spring of 1975 in Jerusalem. Having just heard for the first time many of the earlier accounts of this book, I approached her and offered, "Should you ever decide to do a book of your life, I would be so pleased to help you." She graciously answered in her 'very Ruth' way, "Thank you, honey, that's so sweet of you, but we couldn't tell these stories just yet. We need to protect what God is doing." She perceived the Lord's timing and preferred to remain hidden for the time being to be more effective.

She and her associates were going into Russia, believing for the release of Soviet Jewry, planting a prayer ministry in Jerusalem to bless Israel and the nations, and calling forth prophets and sending them to the four corners of the Earth. These 'releases of the Spirit' were the normal course of their activities. Ruth made herself available to God to be His messenger in many unusual, difficult and delicate situations. How she allowed the Holy Spirit to instruct and lead her will surely challenge and enthrall the reader.

Because I was privileged to hear many of these accounts when they just occurred, my recollection of the circumstances may lend a greater insight to the reader. First, these remarkable incidences were the result of much prayer and fasting, and rarely was the financial provision apparent at the onset. As Solomon so wisely proffered, *"Before honour is humility"* (Proverbs 15:33).

Certainly there were enough challenges to have deterred any but the most tenacious, but Ruth would cleave to the very word of God — whether it came through prophecy, a whisper from His throne or a passage from the Bible. She rejoiced in the message and the messenger.

After we had been in Jerusalem a year or so, we met a man who told us that God had spoken to him several years before to go to Jerusalem and establish a ministry of praise and worship on Mt. Zion. Not only had he not answered the call, but he knew of yet another individual who had not either. As far as we knew, Ruth Heflin was God's third choice for the vision. Through the years I observed that when the Lord called, the response of many was, "Why me?" while Sister Ruth was always asking God, "Why not me?"

Twice Ruth went to nations, believing that she would be there for a lifetime — Hong Kong in 1958 and Israel in 1972. Her wholeheartedness is compelling. Twice she anointed men to be Prime Minister of their respective countries. She stood personally before Bob Hawke in Australia to anoint him, and she stood

before the Lord in a prayer meeting in Jerusalem to anoint Yitzhak Rabin to return to the position of Prime Minister of Israel after many years. Her
singlemindedness prevailed for both situations.

It is impossible to know Ruth Ward Heflin and not be affected by the realm
of endless possibilities that have set her apart. Those who meet her for the first
time through the pages of this book will have to agree with me — there is no
one quite like her. Her breadth of vision, her perception and her understanding of spiritual matters will allow her to reach beyond the printed page. The
grasp of the reader will be tightened on the purposes of God in the heavens.

Lastly, this book is much too short. There are so many wonderful stories that
have not been told and many that are yet to happen. Sister Ruth needs to com-
mence work on volume two as soon as possible.

Deborah Kendrick
Ashland, Virginia
June 1999

I Ask for the Nations

In the name of Jesus,
In the name of the Lord,
I come to Thee, Oh God,
In the name of the Lord.
I ask not for riches.
I ask not for fame.
I ask for the nations,
In Jesus' name.

May they not be naked.
May they not be ashamed
To stand before Thee, Oh God,
On that Great Judgment Day.
Oh, may they be spotless.
And may they be clothed.
Oh, may they know Jesus
That day at Thy throne.

CHORUS:
I ask for the nations.
I call them by name.
I present them to the Father,
In Jesus' name.
I ask for the nations.
I call them by name.
I present them to the Father,
In Jesus' name.

Birthed in the prayer meeting in Bethlehem in 1977

Ask of me, ...

And I shall give thee the heathen for thine inheritance,

and the uttermost parts of the earth for thy possession.

Psalm 2:8

Introduction

When I was a little girl, my mother said to me, "When you grow up, I believe that you will be a missionary." I did not want to be a missionary, so I would stomp my feet and throw a temper tantrum. She was very wise and didn't mention it after that, but I'm sure that she prayed.

I do not think the Lord ever asked me to be a missionary, but in my teens I think I asked Him. I remember saying to the Lord one day at a prayer meeting, "Isn't there something I can do for You somewhere in the world?" The rest of my life has been composed of that "something" that I could do for the Lord "somewhere in the world."

Ruth Ward Heflin
Ashland, Virginia
July 1999

≥ 1 ≤

"You Look Like A Chinese"

Our early campmeetings were very simple. We met in a small tabernacle that was later used for the children and now has been taken down to make way for the greater thing God is doing. The dirt floor of that small tabernacle was covered with sawdust. When the people would begin to dance and praise the Lord, a cloud of dust would rise up from the floor. But there was another cloud that was equally visible in that humble setting. It was a cloud of God's glory. A visible presence of the Lord was with us in those days.

When Polaroid cameras first became available, one lady wanted to take my picture. I posed inside the Tabernacle just after preaching and praying for people. When the photo developed in a few minutes it was filled with bright light. She adjusted the camera and tried again, only to have the same thing happen. Although Polaroid film was considered to be very expensive in those days, she tried several more times. Each time was with the same result. I finally realized what was happening; she was getting a picture of the glory of God in our midst.

I suggested that she take a picture of something else to test the camera, and that picture turned out just fine. Feeling that she finally had the adjustment of the camera right, she insisted that we try one more time and turned to take my picture again. But when the film developed, it was the same as before — filled with bright light. That glory was what formed my early life.

I was born in the glory one Sunday after the evening service. My parents were Pentecostal pioneers. At the time I was born, they were living in a couple of the Sunday school rooms of the church they founded in Richmond, Virginia. I was born in those rooms in the glory of God that was manifested in their ministry.

When I was a young girl, I went directly from school to the church on Wednesday afternoons. The faithful of the church were gathered in prayer from one to four. I attended most of those prayer meetings.

During the first two hours they had been making their petitions and interceding before God. During the last hour they would just bask in His presence. Those were the best times. Every petition they could think of had been made. Now the Holy Ghost took over. Sounds of glory, dropped into my spirit from those years, have kept me as I traveled all over the world in ministry.

15

I have been in thousands of meetings and heard thousands of sermons, but the greatest influence in my life has been those glory sounds that came forth in the latter hours of those prayer meetings where God's people touched the eternal realm.

One evening when I was fifteen I was kneeling in the glory, moved by the Spirit of God and what He was doing in the midst of the people, and a very simple vision came to me. Since I don't recall having visions before that time, this may have been the first one. It certainly was life-changing.

It didn't seem to be a very spiritual vision. I saw myself eating with a group of Chinese people. I was holding a bowl and chopsticks, like they were. The vision only lasted a few seconds, but in that moment I fell in love with the Chinese people.

That vision was all-encompassing. It was not so much what I saw but what I experienced. When I came out of the service, I felt different; I felt Chinese. I even felt as if I looked Chinese.

As I left the Tabernacle, one of a group of young students from Beulah Heights Bible School in Atlanta, Georgia was standing there. "My, I feel strange tonight, Jim," I said to him.

"You look strange," he answered.

"Now, don't tease me," I protested.

"I'm not teasing," he replied, "I mean it. You do look strange."

I was sure that he could not know what had just happened to me, so I asked him, "Well, what do I look like?"

His answer was astonishing: "You look like a Chinese." That's how life-changing the vision was for me.

Until that moment, I didn't know a single Chinese person, but now I wanted to know them, and I wanted to go anywhere they were to be found.

We didn't go out to eat much in those days, except on birthdays or other special occasions, but from then on, I only wanted to go to Chinese restaurants. Later, when saying good-bye to me in New York, my father joked, "I'm so happy you're going. Now we can go out and have a good steak on birthdays and won't have to eat Chow Mein or Chop Suey every time."   ✳

⩙ 2 ⩙

"I Will Give You My Knowledge"

Because I was able to skip several grades in school, I was scheduled to graduate early from high school. The Thanksgiving before my graduation, I was trying to decide which college I would attend. My personal desire was to go to Wheaton College where my Uncle Bill had done some graduate work, but I wanted to know God's thoughts on the matter. We were having special meetings during the holiday weekend, and I was praying seriously, seeking God's will.

That same group of Bible school students from Georgia was with us, and one day while I was praying at the altar, the principal of the school, Rev. Robert Lichty, prayed for me. He had no way of knowing what was on my mind, yet he began to prophesy: "Desire not earthly knowledge and earthly wisdom. If you will seek My face, I will give you My knowledge and My wisdom." With that one sentence, I knew that I would not be going to college. I would seek the face of the Lord and gain wisdom and knowledge from Him. I never questioned God about the subject again, and it has been amazing through the years to see the knowledge and wisdom He has given me supernaturally.

This word from God freed me to pursue the ministry immediately. After I graduated from high school, I began to believe Him to open doors of ministry for me. It was a busy fall in many ways. As a family, we were busy in our church and camp activities, and when we didn't have services of our own, we traveled somewhere to be blessed in the services of others.

My most memorable experience of that fall, however, was my first revival. A pastor from the mountains of Virginia invited me to preach a two-week revival in his church. I was only sixteen. I had been helping my father with his daily radio broadcasts for some time and in the church and the campmeetings, but this was my first time to minister away from home.

Before I left, Daddy sat me down and gave me a very good piece of advice. "Remember that every church has a different order," he said. "They all do things differently. It's not your responsibility to change the way a particular church does things. Your only responsibility, when they turn the service over to you, is to bless the people." That piece of advice has saved me a lot of trouble through the years.

I realized how important his advice was when I got to the church where I had

17

been invited to preach and saw how truly different their services were from anything I was accustomed to at the time. For one thing, I wasn't accustomed to such extensive dancing in the service. In that little mountain church the people danced before the Lord for about an hour every night.

They also looked different. The ladies wore high-top boots and high-collared dresses with sleeves that came to their wrists. I thought my father was a strict holiness preacher, but these people were even more strict.

Mother had decided to accompany me to that first meeting, and I was happy to have her with me. After a few days, however, she became very sick. That was unusual because Mother was never sick. She was so ill that we had to call my father to come and get her. No sooner did she know that Daddy was on the way to get her than Mother began to get better, and by the time he arrived, she was feeling well. I kidded her about it and said that she just missed Daddy and that's why she had become sick. Looking at it in retrospect, I believe that the Lord wanted Mother to remove her hands from my ministry. He knew that in the future I would be going to many places where she would not be able to accompany me. From the very beginning He wanted to establish His order concerning my life.

I went to the revival with a single navy-blue dress that I would wear each evening when I preached, and I had three different white collars that went with it. There was a round one and a v-necked one. I don't recall what the third one was like, but it was different. I wore that dress to church, preached in it, then came back to where I was staying and hung it up so that it could be ready for the next service.

Every day I worked hard and prayed hard at preparing my sermon for that evening. I memorized certain passages that I felt I wanted to emphasize and searched out others that agreed and tried to line them up in a way that would be pleasing. I am so grateful for the ease that we have since learned in the Spirit. It would have served me well back then.

There were many things about the life of the mountain people that I found new and exciting. I was especially interested in the process of making apple butter. For several days I sat with the women peeling bushels of apples. When enough apples were ready, they were placed in the big iron kettle, and we took turns stirring the pot over the open fire with a long wooden paddle. All day long the apples cooked. Then the sugar, cinnamon and other spices were added, and the mixture was cooked some more until the apple butter was just right. My, it was delicious on biscuits.

It was one of those mountain places famous for its family feuds. Everyone came to church from miles around. Some came for God, and some came for other reasons, but it was an exciting gathering, nevertheless. It was not until eighteen years later that I learned that those had been the best revival meetings they had ever experienced in that place. God helps beginners in amazing ways. I surely could have used that encouragement as a teenager, but I never heard it until much later.

Every night, after the people had been dancing around the church for about an hour, the music would stop, the offering would be taken, and the service would be turned over to me. Just as I was getting started, however, I noticed many families beginning to get their children together, looking to make sure they had all their belongings and then slipping quietly out of the church. Before long, half of the crowd was gone. It was a terrible experience for a sixteen-year-old preacher. Why were so many people walking out just when I was getting started? They were not even giving me a chance. Were they not even interested in what I had to say?

When it happened the first time, I had no idea what was going on, and it concerned me. I remembered my father's words, however, and reached inside my spirit and made every effort to bless the people. Several nights later I learned why so many were getting up and going out when I began to preach. Nobody had thought to tell me that many members of the church were on shift work. They didn't want to miss the whole revival, so they came to church for the worship service — even though they had to get home and get ready to work the midnight shift. It was a good experience for me. Now, when anyone walks out of a service while I am preaching I am sure that it is because they are on shift work.

What a wonderful revival! I was so excited when I got back home because I had received my first offering. It was huge — $80. That was a lot of money for a young person in those days, and I used it to finance a trip for our whole family to a conference in Atlanta, Georgia. I was able to pay the gasoline and the food for the entire trip.   ✳

"Stop Talking in Chinese and Go To Sleep"

Later that fall, the Lord sent Sister Beulah Watters to our church. She had been a missionary to Hong Kong before and during the Second World War and was now preparing to return to Hong Kong. I found the prospect of life among the Chinese so compelling that I asked her if I could go back with her and live with her in Hong Kong. She said she would be very happy to have me living with her, but she wondered if my parents would be willing to let me go that far away at such a young age. When I asked my parents if they would be willing, they did not hesitate. As it turned out, they had known God's plans for my life by the Spirit.

Mother later admitted that she had felt a slight reservation in her spirit about my going out to Hong Kong. She was sure that in the future God would use me all over the world, but she wanted to be sure that Hong Kong was the first place God wanted me to go.

In the midst of her hesitancy, she prayed, "Lord, of all the countries in the world, the only place that I have a little trepidation about is the very place You are now calling my daughter. Is this really the first place You want her to go? If it is, please give us a sign."

I had developed a habit of reading late at night and, because my bedroom was across the hall from Mother and Daddy's, she would call out before she went to sleep, "Ruth, stop reading, turn out the light, and go to sleep." She said it every night. One particular night, I had already gone to sleep and both she and Daddy heard me speaking fluent Chinese in my sleep. Without thinking, she called out, "Ruth, stop talking in Chinese and go to sleep." No sooner had she said it than it dawned on her that this was the sign she had asked the Lord for.

Her call had awakened me, and I answered her, "I'm not talking in Chinese; I'm asleep."

God had heard the cry of a mother's heart.

After Sister Watters went back to Hong Kong, I began to look for a way that I could join her. In those days young ladies never traveled alone, so I needed to find someone who was going to that part of the world. That fall, when we were attending a convention in Philadelphia, we learned that a couple who had lived in Hong Kong would also be in the convention. I felt that this was my answer to prayer, and I rushed to meet them. They were Dr. and Mrs. Ralph Phillips, and they told me that they would be returning to Hong Kong in January. "May I go with you?" I asked.

"Well, we're going by ship," they answered. "If your parents agree, it's fine with us."

When I excitedly approached my parents with this news, Mother said, "If you can pray in the money for your inoculations and your passport, we'll accept it as God's confirmation that this is the time to go."

In those days, the required inoculations cost only $2.00 each, and a passport application was only $10.00, but that still seemed like a lot of money to a young girl. The next time I went out to preach a revival, however (this time in Bristersburg, Virginia), somebody gave me $10.00 and told me it was to get my passport. Each step of the journey was proving to be very exciting and rewarding.

The Phillips were planning to travel by merchant ship. The ship would leave from New York City, travel through the Panama Canal and make a stop in California. Since the Phillips were from the West Coast, they would board there. As we neared the departure time, however, they called one day to say that something had come up that prevented them from traveling just then. I was disappointed to hear that. I already had my passport and my inoculations, and I felt that it was time for me to go. Would my parents agree for me to travel alone? That was a big question. I prayed fervently that they would and, in the end, they agreed for me to go on the ship anyway.

Not only was it rare for young people to travel apart from their families in those days, but I was, as it turned out, the youngest evangelist who had ever gone out to Hong Kong alone. Other ministers in Hong Kong had children who traveled with them, but I was going strictly on my own.

One of the greatest miracles God did was to provide my boat ticket. The cost from New York to Hong Kong was $575.00 — a lot of money for our humble church. The monthly missionary offering, received with great effort, was $30, and $10 of that came from my parents. As we prayed about it, Mother had a dream. In her dream she saw someone go to the bank and borrow $500 to complete my fare. She didn't tell anyone about that dream.

My brother, who was assigned by a local company to cover sales in the New England area, came to Richmond for a company meeting. He wasn't saved at the time, but he was interested in what was happening with his little sister. When he came by the house he asked Mother if I had been able to raise my fare. "No," she told him, "she's still lacking $500."

Later that evening, after his meetings were finished, my brother came by the church where we were concluding our service, and he handed me a check for $500. "Where did you get this?" I asked.

"I went to the bank and borrowed it," he told me.

I was elated. I had known that God would answer our prayers, but how He would do it I could not imagine.

Mother was standing a little behind my brother when he gave me the check, and she motioned for me to pray for him and mouthed the words "Pray for him." She was always anxious for us to take any opportunity we had to bless my brother, and this seemed like a perfect one.

I prayed and asked God to bless my brother for the sacrifice he was making to help me get to Hong Kong, and I prayed for his prosperity — spiritual and physical.

He was a little naughty in those days and, after I finished praying, he looked up and said, "Where's my change?" as if to insinuate that my prayer had not been worth the entire $500 he had given. Later, however, after the Lord had saved him, he was able to travel all over the world himself. I think he got a very good return from the Lord on that initial $500 investment. He was blessed and blessed abundantly, and through his gift I had moved one step closer to the realization of my vision.   ✳

$\rightslice$ 4 $\leftslice$

"Faraway Places With the Strange Sounding Names"

I had no idea what an exciting city Hong Kong was. It is one of those places that you have to be called *from*, not called *to*. I also didn't know that Hong Kong, after the War, had become the shopping capital of the world. Because of its base of manufacturing and trade and the absence of customs duties, people came to Hong Kong from all over the world to shop. It was a duty-free port. Beulah Watters was also behind the times in this regard. Since her memory of Hong Kong was from the period just before and during the war, she gave me a long list of things I should take with me on the ship.

Besides clothing and personal items, I took a five-year supply of such things as thumb tacks, Kleenex, soap and toilet tissue. I took a hammer and nails. I took several musical instruments, including a violin, an autoharp and an accordion. I took my own bed, a folding cot. I took all the things one would need if living on the back side of the desert somewhere. When it was all packed, there were twenty-seven pieces of luggage, some of them quite large.

Because of our many travels around America, Daddy had become adept at packing the car in an amazing way. He somehow extended the back of the car, loaded all that luggage into the space he had created and then tied it all down tight. It was an amazing sight to behold. With everything in place, we set out for New York City. It was the beginning of February, 1958, and I had just turned eighteen.

My brother met us in New York City, and we had a wonderful time together as my many belongings were loaded aboard the ship, the *S.S. Pioneer Mist* of the United States Lines. I settled into my cabin. Leaving home and embarking on such an unknown journey was a big step for me, but I don't remember shedding a single tear when it came time to say good-bye to my family.

After my family departed, the ship still didn't sail for two days. Mother later told me what happened as they were leaving the city. My brother was going back to New England to his work, and my parents were returning to Richmond. He said to them, "Follow me, and I'll lead you out to the highway. When we get there, we'll say good-bye. Then, I'll go north, and you go south." Daddy was pleased with that idea because he didn't know his way around New York City very well.

When they got to the main highway, and my brother turned north, Mother suddenly began to cry, and she cried and cried. Daddy said, "Aren't you something! You just saw your daughter off at the ship; you don't know if you'll ever see her again; she's going ten thousand miles away; and you never shed a tear. But now, when your son is just going up to New England, you're crying."

"Oh," Mother replied, "my daughter knows the Lord, and if something happens and she dies, I'll meet her in Heaven. My son doesn't know the Lord, so if something happens to him, I wouldn't have that privilege of ever seeing him again." Thank God that my brother was later saved and had many years of fruitful ministry.

At Christmas time he and I had sung two secular songs brought to mind by my pending journey: *Far Away Places* and *Slow Boat to China.* That exotic trip I had dreamed of for so long was about to begin.   ✻

⩗ 5 ⩘

"My Heart Was Pounding"

Spending forty days on an oceangoing freighter was a wonderful experience. After leaving New York, we stopped in Charleston, South Carolina, then went on to Panama City, Panama. We stopped in Hawaii for a day or two and then proceeded on to the Philippines and, from there, to Hong Kong. The ship had cabins for a dozen people, but there was only one other passenger on board for the first part of the journey, a young Filipina, Nina Abad.

Coming from a small town like Ashland, Virginia, and being raised in church, I had a rude awakening in store for me on board that ship. Every day Nina and I sat at the captain's table and ate with him and the chief engineer, and it quickly became apparent that our captain was not at all holy. Ship's captains, I was to learn, were not known for their uprightness, but this captain surely was more unholy than most. Every day at mealtime he delighted in taunting me and making fun of my faith. After each mealtime, I would return to my cabin and pray that I would have more grace and wisdom in dealing with the captain, and the next mealtime I would be there at his table.

I never failed to show up at mealtimes, even when it got stormy. I wasn't about to let his taunting get the best of me. Forty days of mealtime conversation with an ungodly ship's captain was an education, to say the least. God was preparing me for Hong Kong.

When the ship stopped in Manila, something very interesting happened. Nina told me about a special party to which she said I was invited. As it turned out, it was a birthday party for President Carlos Garcia, and all the local dignitaries were present. It was my first time to see the Filipino people in their formal attire made of pineapple fiber (called piña cloth) — the men in their elegant *barong Tagalogs* and the women in their equally elegant *sarongs*, formal dresses with the butterfly sleeves. While we ate tropical fruits that I had never seen or tasted before, the wonderful Filipino music played in the background. It was an exotic setting, like something from a storybook.

I was seated next to a lady who was a direct descendant of our President Harrison, a fellow Virginian, and all around us sat the prominent politicians of the Philippines. How we enjoyed that celebration! Little did I realize at the time that God would, in the future, give me opportunities to minister to important politicians all over the world. It was a sign of things to come.

After leaving Manila Bay, the ship stopped at another Philippine port to load pineapples. We were able visit a pineapple plantation and have dinner there.

We spent Palm Sunday on board the ship in the South China Sea, celebrating with other Americans by singing hymns while I played my accordion.

As we neared Hong Kong, and I saw the islands coming into view, my heart was pounding. What a thrill!

My first glimpse of Hong Kong was awe-inspiring, and that scene became embedded forever in my memory. Hong Kong Harbor was exquisitely beautiful. I had never before, nor have I since, seen a view to equal it.

On one side of the boat was the island of Hong Kong, with the town of Victoria (commonly called Hong Kong) built on the hillside. There were no skyscrapers. Most of the buildings were only two or three stories high. However, the city was compacted together, even at that time.

On the right of the boat was the peninsula of Kowloon that was attached to the mainland of China. I could see the clock-tower that was part of the Kowloon Railway System that went as far as the border of China.

In the harbor were Chinese junks, the large wooden boats that Chinese fishing families used and lived on, the smaller sampans that the people, mostly Haaka, rowed from a standing position, as well as the larger oceangoing ships, freighters, tug boats and ferry boats that made up the traffic in a busy, thriving harbor.

As I was looking out over the amazing scene before me, I saw a small boat approaching, and in it was Beulah Watters, coming to meet me. It had all begun in that Little Tabernacle in Ashland, Virginia, with the simple vision of me eating with the Chinese people, and now here I was. Words fail me to describe how happy I was at that moment! It was March 25, 1958.

Eating with the Chinese people, as I had seen myself doing in the vision, was what I did most in those first days. The Chinese Christians held several welcoming feasts to celebrate my arrival. I was also invited to afternoon teas in the British tradition and other special occasions. Having seen this in vision before it happened taught me that I could trust the Holy Spirit. When He drops something into our hearts, it is bigger than the moment, and we can entrust our lives to it without fear.

To this day, I have a great love for the Chinese people. In later years, God was to give me the opportunity to see an enlargement of that vision, but it all began with a simple call in the heart of a fifteen-year-old girl.   ❋

~6~

"Dong, Dong, Dong; Dong, Dong, Dong; Dong, Dong, Dong"

I was very excited by the strangeness of the world into which I was suddenly thrust and I was awake far into the night. At midnight someone at Radio Hong Kong (Rediffusion, as it was called locally) decided to play *Carry Me Back to Old Virginia*. Actually they played this song every night at midnight as they signed off the air. As a teenager far from home this might have played on the emotions of some, but I had prayed long and hard to get where I was, and I was not sorry to be there. The only tinge of homesickness I felt came several days after I arrived. On Easter Sunday I received a corsage of flowers sent to me by my brother. Other than that moment, I can honestly say that I was delighted to be there. I knew that God had sent me, and I was determined to make the best of my opportunity.

I was taken directly from the boat to Beulah Watters' tiny two-room apartment on Temple Street, which I later discovered to be the most infamous street in Hong Kong. She lived in that area of the city because it was near the church.

Temple Street was lined with open street markets and small dwelling places. I had come from the country and was unaccustomed to the noises of the city, but I found the noise of the hawkers calling out their wares and the other noises of a busy Chinese society to be utterly charming.

Not everything in my new life was pleasant. Even though we were not well off in America, we definitely had more than I now had in Hong Kong. Beulah, her adopted Chinese daughter, Beulah Mae, and I lived in a very tiny apartment. When I put out my cot at night to sleep, my feet had to go under the table, for there was no other space available.

Sister Beulah took it as a great responsibility that my parents had entrusted me to her care, and she was very cautious about letting me out of her sight. After all, she didn't want me to get lost in Hong Kong.

She served a lot of oatmeal and bread. At first, I imagined that she must have some stomach problem as a result of her life under the Japanese occupation during the Second World War, but I was to learn that it was just her lifestyle. She had never married, had lived in Bible schools where someone else had done the

28

cooking. Thus, she had never learned to cook well. With the rest of the household, I was soon looking forward to our meals of oatmeal and bread.

The thing that bothered me most about my life in Hong Kong, however, was something quite different. I had come from a very busy church life, and I missed that blessed activity. Although Beulah was very good to me, we were just not as busy as I was accustomed to being back home. We had gone to church somewhere every single night as I was growing up, and the little Pentecostal Church at 37 Jordan Road (where Pastor and Mrs. Tseung had a great heart for God and for His people) had services only on Wednesday night and Sunday morning.

I threw myself into the young people of Hong Kong. They were very excited about a young person from America coming to live with them and had given me a very warm welcome to the colony. It had been quite a thrill to see my name written in Chinese for the first time on the large welcome banner they created in my honor and to share with them in a wonderful welcome banquet. They were very warm and friendly, and I sensed that I would find a home among them. So, despite, the strangeness of my surroundings, I quickly settled into Hong Kong life.

One of the greatest challenges I faced in those early years was learning the language. I didn't have enough money to take the normal four-hour-a-day official course. An hour was the most I could afford.

We lived in Tsim Sha Tsui, only about three blocks from Nathan Road. I learned that there were Chinese courses available at the European YMCA and that I could walk along Austin Road to Nathan, then down Nathan Road, and, cutting through the Peninsula Hotel, easily get to the European YMCA. So I joined those classes.

The first day I went to my Chinese language class, the teacher, Mr. Wong Kwok Man, started by repeating the nine Chinese tones: *"dong, dong, dong; dong, dong, dong; dong, dong, dong."* Each of these *dong*s had a different tone, but they all sounded alike to me, and I wondered if I would ever learn such a difficult language. For the entire hour the man did nothing but repeat those tones over and over, and I was unable to make any distinction between them.

The next day the teacher began by repeating the Chinese tones, and I found that my hearing had not improved overnight. I was still unable to distinguish between the sounds. At one point this study seemed so futile that I thought to myself, *I might as well pack my bags and go back to America.* I didn't think very long or very seriously on this idea, however. I had a father whose favorite saying (outside the Bible) was: "A quitter never wins, and a winner never quits." I knew that I could not go home. I had to stay and persevere, so I simply had to learn the Chinese language.

I had done well in Latin in high school, but Chinese was a tonal language.

When my hearing had grown sensitive to the variations between the Chinese tones, the rest would come.

While I was struggling to learn the language, Mother often wrote and reminded me: "Remember, if you are there the rest of your life, you will never speak better Chinese than your Daddy and I heard you speak by the Spirit in your sleep." That was a special encouragement that I very much needed at the time.

I have often compared my experience with learning the Chinese language to our need to have ears sensitive to the voice of God. Once we learn to hear His voice, then we can move on very quickly to the important things He wants us to do.

The real key to my learning the Chinese language was a miracle the Lord did for me. He told me that if I would find an anointed Chinese person who didn't speak any English and would pray with that person, He would quicken the language to me. The language of prayer is the language of the Bible, and that was the language I needed to know in order to preach. I found such a person in Faith Paau, and we began to pray together.

At first, my Cantonese prayers were very limited. I learned a few words of praise and would use them to worship the Lord in Chinese, but the rest of my prayer had to be in English. As my anointed friend prayed, however, I began to catch bits and pieces of what was being said and to join in with her. In this way, I learned the language — from hearing it in prayer. By the end of the first year, I was praying fluently in Cantonese myself and beginning to teach a Sunday school class. By the end of two years, I was preaching in Chinese. Until that time, I preached using an interpreter.

The need I quickly noticed in many of the local churches was for the members to receive the baptism of the Holy Spirit. I began to preach on that subject and lay hands on the people to be filled, and soon I was being invited to many different churches, up to fifteen different churches each month. Many of these churches were made up of recent refugees from the mainland of China. They were, for the most part, very simple people, not yet acclimated to their new surroundings. Because they were from various provinces of China, sometimes I needed two interpreters to make the message understandable to everyone. I would speak a line in English; one interpreter would repeat that line in Cantonese; and a second interpreter would repeat the same line in one of the mainland dialects, such as Swatowese. Amazingly, the message would find its mark.

The limitations placed on one by the inability to communicate taught me a valuable lesson. One Sunday afternoon, when I was preaching in a very small chapel in Wong Tai Sin, where Rev. and Mrs. Wong were pastors, their son was serving as my interpreter, and he seemed to be having a very difficult time of it.

I Ask for Hong Kong, Japan and Taiwan

That, of course, affected my ability to preach with liberty. *Oh,* I thought, *if I could only speak their language!* It was not the first time I had entertained this thought. Anyone who has ever had to preach for any period of time through an interpreter will understand the limitations one feels when doing it that way. Yet the Lord spoke to me very plainly at that moment and said, "Even if you could speak their language like a king, it would still be up to Me to open their spiritual understanding."

I prayed, "Oh, Lord, forgive me for thinking that it is all in the language. You open their understanding."

It was easy to see the bewilderment on the faces of many of those refugees. They had come from small villages and had suddenly been thrust into the teeming masses of Hong Kong. They were trying to find their way. Suddenly the Holy Spirit began to turn on light bulbs in each of them. I could see it on their faces. With all their limitations, suddenly the Spirit of revelation began to break forth, and I could see the light of the glory of God upon their countenances.

How glorious that experience was! It changed my life and ministry. From that time forward I have known that I must depend upon the Holy Spirit to bring understanding to those who are listening to me as I preach. It is not by language, but by the Spirit. No matter how eloquent a speaker may be, it takes the revelation of the Holy Spirit in the lives of the people who hear to make Jesus real to them.

I had many unusual and humorous experiences in those early years. One night, for instance, I was speaking in a church in the New Territories of Hong Kong, just on the border with China. A spotlight from the border went back and forth over the church building as I spoke that night and my two interpreters, Cantonese and Swatowese, forwarded the message. In the middle of my message, a man stood up and came down the aisle toward me. I was excited by the thought that even before I had given an altar call, someone was responding to my message. When he got to the podium, however, it quickly became apparent that his intention was very different.

In true Chinese style, a nice cup of tea or hot water was always placed at the podium for the speaker. The man had spotted it and, feeling thirsty and not realizing that the cup was there for my use, he picked it up and proceeded to drink it all down. It was a long and very dramatic process. Since the cup had a cover (as Chinese tea cups commonly do) he first removed the cover, drank all the contents, then replaced the cover, and, finally, returned the cup to its place. Once he was finished, he turned and went back to his seat. I never forgot that experience. It seemed very typical of the new things we were all experiencing. I was loving every moment of life in Hong Kong.

While I was living in Hong Kong, I had the privilege of knowing Gladys Aylward. A book was written about her life, *The Small Woman* by Allen Burgess, and later a movie was made from it called "The Inn of the Sixth Happiness," in which Ingrid Bergman played the lead part. Gladys was short, and when we walked down the street together in our *Cheong Sams*, people greeted her with *"Ai Goo Neung,"* meaning 'the short one,' and they called me *"Go Goo Neung,"* 'the tall one.'

Gladys was living in Taiwan when the movie came out, and I later learned that many of her supporters in England dropped her as a result. They were offended by the movie, which portrayed her as having a romantic alliance, which was absolutely not true. That part of the story was thrown in by the scriptwriters to make the movie interesting. Gladys' supporters imagined also that she had received a lot of money from the film. Evidently Allen Burgess made money from the movie rights, but the whole affair hurt Gladys rather than help her.

Thankfully, Bob Pierce, the founder of World Vision, asked her to travel and promote the mission. She did well for them. She was such a dramatic person that she could easily have played her own part in the film, and they would not have needed Ingrid Bergman.

When a reporter went to her house to interview her, he saw a sign that said:

> *For consider him that endured such contradiction of sinners against himself,*
> *lest ye be wearied and faint in your minds.*   Hebrews 12:3

Although she was going through such a difficult time, she refused to *"be faint in [her] mind."* Gladys was a wonderful woman, and I was blessed to know her.

I did not fully realize it yet, but God had placed the nations in my spirit many years before, and my ministry would soon reach far beyond the borders of Hong Kong. It was the custom in those days for a missionary to dedicate an entire life to just one place, and I was willing to do that, but God had a different plan for me. My ministry to other places was about to begin.

Every year most ministers in the colony took time off in August for vacation or, as it was called there, "holiday." My parents had never taken vacations, so I wasn't looking forward to a vacation. What should I do with the time available to me? As I prayed about it, I felt that I should go and preach in Japan and Taiwan.

I took a boat to Japan. Someone had given me the addresses of churches in Yokahama and Tokyo and in Naruo, a little town near Osaka. More people were filled with the Spirit during those meetings, I was told, than had received over the period of many years.

In Taiwan I preached outdoors in a park in Taichung (with Gloria Wine as my interpreter). Three thousand Taiwanese gathered to hear and to respond to the Gospel.   ❋

⚐ 7 ⚐

"A Soldier in a Foxhole"

After I had been in Hong Kong for about two years, Mother and Daddy invited me to come back to Ashland to speak in our summer campmeeting. Daddy was very perceptive. Although I had never once called home in those two years (long-distance calls, especially international long-distance calls, were still a luxury that we could not afford), he sensed that I was getting a little cool spiritually. I was not as "on fire" for God, as *yit sam* (hot-hearted) for God, as the Chinese would say, as I had been when I left home.

Often, when we are around people who are not really on fire, we begin to perform without realizing that we are performing, and our zeal, our zest for the Lord, is not present in the same measure. For the past two years I had been in church services where I did not understand what was being said. I was still learning the very difficult Chinese language. After a while you get tired of asking someone to interpret what is being said, and you just withdraw into yourself. I needed a good campmeeting.

It was quite an honor for a twenty-year-old to speak at camp, and there, in the little tabernacle, God gave me a fresh touch of His Spirit that summer and set my soul on fire for Him once again. I promised God that I would never again lose the fire of the Lord and, from that time to this, I never have.

During campmeeting a man from the Richmond area attended the meetings. He was very friendly. After listening to me preach, he suggested that I try to be a little more "ladylike" in my presentation. That sort of criticism can be devastating to a twenty-year-old. When I went to the platform, my mind was in a turmoil.

How am I going to preach tonight? I wondered. Then someone gave a word of prophecy in which the Lord reminded us of our status as soldiers on the battlefield for Him.

That's it! I suddenly realized. *When a soldier is in a foxhole, he really doesn't care what he looks like to other soldiers. He is intent upon protecting himself and defeating the enemy.* When the time came to preach that night, I was able to do so with complete abandon. It was such a freeing experience that it affected me for years to come. I was not to be concerned about what the person in the next foxhole thought. I was just to concern myself with winning for the Lord. ✳

8

"We'll All Go to India"

That fall Daddy attended a conference in Hagerstown, Maryland, and was asked to give a testimony. He had been having some outstanding miracles of healing in his tent meetings. It was his habit to pitch his Gospel tent each year just as soon as the weather would permit in some area that needed the Pentecostal message and to preach there every night until he had established a church. Many churches were established in this way. He was a great pioneer in church planting, often one each summer. He always had great miracles, but that summer had been unusually wonderful.

When he was asked to testify in the Hagerstown conference, he told about some of those healing miracles. Pastor P.J. Thomas, a brother from South India who had many churches under him, was attending the conference. When he heard my father tell such great stories, he went to him and said, "We need you in India. We need these kinds of miracles for our people."

Daddy didn't want the man to feel that he had misrepresented himself, so he said to him, "I don't have a very big tent. It's quite small, as a matter of fact."

Pastor Thomas answered, "You may not have a big tent, but you have great miracles, and we need your ministry in India." He gave my father his card and insisted that he wanted him to come have meetings in India. They spoke at length about a possible time that such meetings would take place.

When Daddy got back home, he was very excited about the possibility of ministering in India, and when he told Mother and me about his invitation, we got excited too. He had been to Jamaica a time or two for conventions, but this was his first major foreign invitation. Mother and I both said, "We're going too."

I'm not sure Daddy knew what such a trip would cost, but I remember him answering, "Well, I'll tell you what we'll do. You pray in your money, and I'll pray in my money, and we'll all go to India."

Mother had prepared to go to India with her mother and brother when she was sixteen. Grandmother Ward had applied to a mission board, but was rejected as she was over thirty-five. Now, as we thought of the possibility of standing on Indian soil to minister, I could sense a great excitement in Mother's spirit.

34

I Ask for India and Hong Kong

A trip for three to India was very expensive, more than four thousand dollars in airfares alone. Daddy went to the bank and borrowed the money. One of the members of our church owned a printing company and offered to co-sign the note. It was a great miracle. After they returned home, Mother and Daddy prayed in the money over the coming months and paid it all back.

Our round-the-world tickets were written through London, Paris, Rome, Jerusalem and Cairo, then to Bombay and other cities of India, before going on around the world through Southeast Asia and back home again. I would be left in Hong Kong.

In London, Paris and Rome, we took a couple of days to see the usual tourist sites. In London we saw Buckingham Palace and the Tower of London for the first time, and we ate fish and chips and Yorkshire pudding.

We were amazed at how small the elevator was in our hotel in Paris. By the time the three of us squeezed into it, it was full. We saw the sights of Paris. It was a wonderful time because God was enlarging our vision and giving us a greater understanding of the world around us.

In Rome we saw the Catacombs, St. Peter's Square at the Vatican, the Cathedral and some of the museums.

From Rome, we flew directly into the small Jerusalem airport and got a room in the YMCA. Brother Paul Kopp, who had had a great healing meeting in Jerusalem, was staying in the YMCA as well, and we were able to meet and have fellowship with him.

It was our first time in the Holy City, and we had a wonderful time seeing all the holy sights in and around the city. We rode camels and did all the rest of the usual tourist things.

From Jerusalem, we went on to Cairo, Egypt. There the waiters wore the long *jalabeas* with turbans, and they bowed low and served beautifully. One gentleman who served in the hotel where we stayed in Cairo was particularly gracious in serving Mother. For years afterward Daddy always teased her that what she needed was the care of that particular servant.

From Cairo, we flew on to Bombay. There we took Indian Airlines to Cochin in the south of the country and were met and taken by car to Thiruvella, where we began the wonderful Indian meetings that would change all our lives forever.

While we were in Paris, I couldn't help but notice the many wonderful French perfumes for sale. (Every young girl loves perfume.) "Mother," I ventured, "couldn't we buy just one little bottle?" Daddy had given us a little talk before we left home about how we had to be careful and stretch our money so that they could complete the round-the-world trip that included so many countries.

"It would be wonderful to have some perfume from Paris," Mother answered me, "but we have only a little money for the whole trip, so we can't spend on anything we don't absolutely need." I understood what she was saying, but I couldn't help but tell the Lord how much I would love to have some of that perfume.

Several services a day were conducted in Thiruvella in the courtyard of the church compound under a shelter woven from palm leaves. The Indians called it a *pundal*. Between services we would sometimes sit on the porch of the pastor's home. A large tree shaded the area, and it was cooler there, so our meals were served to us there as well.

One day, just as we were finishing our lunch, a taxi pulled into the compound. The Indian compounds had such high walls that you usually could not see into them from the street. The driver of the taxi obviously knew this church compound, and had driven past the front of the house and into a side entrance some distance away and now pulled around to the front of the house. He had two lady tourists in his car and he wanted to ask if they could eat their lunch under the shade of our tree.

"Let me go ask the pastor," I said, and I went to find him. Pastor Thomas said it would be fine, so the three of them proceeded to eat their lunch there under the shade of the tree.

After they had finished eating, the two ladies came up on the porch to speak with us. They were from France, had completed their stay in India and were on their way back home. Just before they left, one of the ladies reached into her purse, pulled out two bottles of French perfume and handed them to me. I found it to be a very amazing experience. The Lord had been so concerned about showing me His love that He had sent tourists all the way from France to South India to bring me some French perfume.

Mother and Daddy were just as touched by the incident as I was. They had wanted to be able to buy perfume for their daughter, but they could see that God was taking care of me, even providing the desires of my heart. It helped them during the years ahead not to worry about me as I was traveling in other countries.

Several great miracles happened in that compound. Early one morning Pastor Thomas came to say that someone had arrived with a hundred rupee note for me. It was a huge sum of money at the time. He was amazed and said, "In all these years, no one has ever done this for me. I have had other foreign guests as speakers, but this is the first time someone has brought such an offering." God was revealing to us His faithfulness.

I Ask for India and Hong Kong

There were many new and wonderful experiences on that trip, new sights and smells and new foods. Sleeping on an Indian bed took a little getting used to. The beds in the south are made of boards covered with pads that could not be much more than half an inch thick. My father was a big man, and he said that he never knew he had so many bones in his body until then. With all the new experiences, we were excited to be in India to minister.

That first night as we stood in the convention, Mother cried and cried. The vision God had placed within her heart when she was just sixteen (and she was now fifty) had come to pass. Amazingly she had kept the vision alive in her heart all those years. First Grandmother, then Mother and Daddy, had supported missionaries in India and other countries, as well as hosting them in their homes throughout the years.

My father loved to preach, and he preached with great anointing and inspiration. He enjoyed it so much that sometimes it was difficult for him to stop. Because of this, he was known to be a little long-winded. We had heard that the people of South India loved to sit for hours in their services, and that if a preacher didn't preach at least an hour, they sometimes were reluctant to give him a second chance. I teased Daddy that he would feel right at home among these people.

Surprisingly, the first night Daddy got up to preach through an interpreter in South India, the interpretation broke his stride, and he suddenly didn't have anything to say. After only a few minutes, he looked back to me and, because I had been preaching now for several years through an interpreter in Hong Kong, called me to come finish the sermon.

It didn't take Daddy long to adjust, however, and he had a wonderful time preaching to the people of South India. They expected him to preach long sermons, and he didn't disappoint them. One service started at eight in the morning and didn't finish until four or five in the afternoon. The congregation never stood up once during all that time.

India was full of need and thus was a ripe place for miracles. This was my father's meat and drink, so he delighted in praying for the Indian people. He would get totally lost in the Spirit. One night, he was so lost in God that he was not even conscious that he was praying for a leper who had open sores all over his body. He wore nothing but his *dhoti,* so his entire torso was exposed, and my father was so anointed that he moved his hands around over every sore the man had. If he had been conscious of what he was doing, he might have thought better of it.

The next night, the pastor came leading a nicely dressed man. He said, "Do you remember this man?" We didn't. He didn't look like the same man at all. He opened his shirt to show us that his skin was like baby's skin. There was not a single open sore remaining anywhere on his body. He was wonderfully healed by the power of God.

My father had great success praying for crippled children, a gift my brother later displayed as well. He would take the child, pray for him, and then step back four or five paces from the mother. Invariably, when Daddy put the child down, he ran to his mother. This electrified the crowd and people suddenly came from every direction to join in the excitement. Many were saved as a result. The next night, many more crippled children were brought for prayer.

We traveled extensively throughout the state of Kerala preaching in one large convention after the other. The crowds were always in the thousands. In one meeting, we ministered to fifty thousand people. All three of us were able to preach in that place.

Years before, during the revival of the fifties, servants of God had been sent to our city and had been used to lay hands on my parents and prophesy over them that they would reach multitudes for the Lord. Their church in Richmond was still quite small at the time, and they averaged only about thirty-five to fifty in each service. The promise of the Lord, that they would reach multitudes, had seemed impossible, but God was bringing it to pass.

After several weeks of rich ministry in Kerala, we got a train to Madras and there had to transfer to another train for Vijayawada in Andhra Pradesh. It is difficult to describe the huge crowds that throng the Indian train stations. You would have to be there to appreciate it. There is never enough room on the trains for all those who want to travel, and those who don't get on first have to stand up for days or even hang off the steps of the cars, so everyone is pushing to get on first. We nearly got separated in that great surging crowd. It was like being swept away with the strong current of an overflowing river.

Later my father said that he suddenly realized, in the midst of all the shoving, that I was carrying all the money and Mother was carrying all the passports. We had left him with all the coats. It had been very cold, with snow on the ground, when we left America, but we certainly didn't need our coats in the one-hundred-and-twenty-degree heat of India. If we had been separated, he would have been left with no money and no passport, and the coats would not have done him much good. He didn't even know the exact address of the place where we were going.

When we got to Vijayawada, we found that the local believers had rented railway cars parked in a station siding as housing for their foreign guests. They showed us to our car, and we found it to be more than adequate. It had seats with thick cushions on them. Compared with what we had experienced sometimes in South India, these new accommodations were like staying at the Hilton Hotel. We were thrilled.

When mother stood up and began to dance in the Spirit in those meetings, the crowd was enthralled and tried to mob her. They had never seen the glory of God upon a person in this way. As we were trying to get her out through the crowd of thirty thousand Indians that night, the people kept forcing their way in around her, trying to honor her, as the Indian custom is, by touching her feet. Mother was greatly moved by this experience, by the fact that the people had felt the presence of the Lord and by their reaction to that presence.

While we were in South India, we traveled all the way to Cape Comorin and dipped our feet in the place where three great bodies of water meet: the Bay of Bengal, the Arabian Sea and the Indian Ocean. Mother brought home a film box full of the colored sands from that place. We recently found it in a small box of mementos she had kept all these years.

We flew back to Bombay, then on to New Delhi. From there, we went to Agra to see the world famous Taj Mahal. We returned to New Delhi and flew to Calcutta and on to other parts of Asia.

We made stops in Bangkok, Thailand; Manila, Philippines and Saigon, South Vietnam; then Mother and Daddy accompanied me back to Hong Kong. It was wonderful to have them there, to introduce them to all my friends and to have them preach in the churches of Hong Kong.

One of our wealthy Chinese friends gave a wonderful feast in honor of Mother and Daddy. It had many courses, all of them were exotic, and every course was more sumptuous than the previous one. One course, for instance, consisted of a complete roasted pig.

The Chinese custom at feasts is that while you are waiting for the food to come, you eat watermelon seeds. There is a great art to eating the seeds, and for the Westerner, who is not accustomed to eating watermelon seeds, it can seem like an impossibility. Just the right amount of pressure must be applied to the seed at just the right angle in just the right place to crack it open without destroying its contents.

When my father wasn't doing very well with his watermelon seeds, our hostess began to crack them with her own teeth and then hand them to him. She did it so well that her teeth never touched the meaty portion he would eat.

As she held the delicate seed between her thumb and her forefinger and inserted it between her teeth, her other fingers — one adorned with a gorgeous diamond ring, one adorned by a gorgeous pearl and diamond ring, and the other adorned by a gorgeous jade and diamond ring — was what stood out to him. Her nails were beautifully manicured and polished and the rings that adorned them were exquisite. She herself was impeccable in her tailored Chinese *cheongsam*. The whole ambiance of that evening in a luxurious Chinese restaurant with lovely people and delicious food seemed like something from a fairy tale, and he never forgot that experience.

Both Mother and Daddy were deeply moved by the things God had done on that trip and they took home a lifetime of memories. After about a week in Hong Kong they flew back to America. They had been absent from the church for about a month and needed to get back home, but they were never the same again. After that first trip, they made another, even more extensive, trip the following year. In that trip, they took in some of the places they had gone the year before and other new places as well. It was the beginning of greater things for them both, and after that they both traveled extensively.

Daddy traveled until the Lord took him home. Mother has traveled to more than eighty countries, many times to China, many times to Jerusalem and many times to Russia. It took them many years to make the first trip, but the other trips came in quick succession. Their going opened the nations up to them.

After my parents had gone back to Virginia, I soon got back to my daily routine in Hong Kong. This time, there were some new elements. ❋

9

"Oh, Jesus, I Didn't Know
That You Loved Me So Much"

When I returned to Hong Kong that year, I was so on fire for God that people later told me they came to the prayer meetings I was attending just to see someone on fire for God. I wept for the Chinese people and sought God for revival among them. Many years later, when I was in China and a group of visitors from Hong Kong came, one lady approached me and asked, "Would you happen to be that young lady who always wept in prayer for the Chinese people many years ago in Hong Kong?" She had never forgotten.

My "fired-up" spirit was not universally appreciated, however. The head of one Pentecostal denomination called me to his office to complain. "When we get to the meetings," he said, "you're already in the Spirit. I know how you folks from the South are, but it would be so much better if you waited until we all got in the Spirit before you show such exuberance."

"There are many Southerners who are not on fire for God," I told him. "When I went back home and God reignited the flame in me, I promised Him that I would never again let it go out, and I want to keep that promise." He criticized me so severely, however, that it gave me a headache, and I cried to the Lord most of the night.

About that time, God was dealing with me concerning knowing His voice. I thought I knew it, He told me, but I really didn't, and it was important for my future ministry. He wanted to speak to me, and I needed to hear clearly what He was saying. Like many Christians, I questioned, wondering if I was really hearing from God. How could I be sure? God told me that He wanted me to know His voice as well as I knew the voice of my earthly father.

One day, as I was praying, the Lord spoke to me and gave me a message for the head of that Pentecostal denomination, a message concerning his son. I argued with the Lord. How could I go to a man who had been so critical of me? How could I tell him that I had a message for him from God?

In the end, I could not resist the Spirit of God, so I went and knocked very cautiously on the man's door. When he appeared, I told him that God had spoken to me while I was praying that morning and gave me a message for him. I was about to tell him what God had said when he began to weep. Tears streamed down his cheeks as he said, "Ruth, I would give anything just to be able to say that God had spoken to me. He has used me in many parts of the world, but I can't say that I ever heard His voice and knew it."

Before I had even begun to deliver the message God had given me, He had already given the man a heart that was tender toward me. When I delivered the message, he was ready and received it well. In this way, the breach between us was healed.

The Lord sent me to another Pentecostal leader with a message, and this began a pattern of similar experiences. Each time it concerned something the person had been needing to hear from God. This particular Pentecostal leader said, "Ruth, all my life I've waited for that word from God."

This was the beginning of God speaking to me in a new dimension and sending me to pastors and other church leaders all over the world. The gift would greatly expand in later years, but it was birthed in my spirit during those days of revival in Hong Kong.

I made many close friends among the missionaries of Hong Kong. One of the closest of those friendships (and one that continues until the present) was with Sister Gwen Shaw. We did many things together. One of those things was to preach in the rooftop schools of the colony.

The government was building dozens of new high-rise buildings to accommodate the constant flood of refugees from Mainland China, and they always reserved the rooftop for a school. They gave the churches and mission groups the privilege of organizing these schools and placing qualified teachers in them. This was a wonderful opportunity for presenting the Gospel to the children and, at night, the schools could be used for churches. Most of those schools were on the eighth floor or higher, and none of the buildings had elevators, so it was a challenge to walk up that many stairs, but it was always worth the climb.

Easter weekend of that year Sister Gwen and I were invited on Friday to speak to a gathering of local Assembly of God young people. About sixty young people had gathered when, suddenly, the Holy Spirit was outpoured upon them. One by one, they began to fall out under the power of God and speak in tongues. Most of the older people present had never seen anything like this before, and one little pastor went quickly to get a thermos of hot tea to try to revive the young people. We had to explain to him that the young people were fine and that this was a work of the Holy Spirit, nothing to be worried about.

The meeting was so blessed that we were invited to return for another meeting on Saturday night, and that meeting was so blessed that I spoke every Saturday night there until several hundred young people were saved and filled with the Spirit.

One of the current crazes among young people in the colony was collecting cards featuring the top movie stars of the day. No one preached against that, but as they were slain in the Spirit, many of these young people got up to say that they had seen visions and that they were going home to get rid of their movie star card collection. No one preached on the sufferings of Jesus, but some young people had visions of Jesus on the cross and actually felt His suffering. One young lady not only saw the suffering Savior in vision, but she also acted out the experiences of Christ's passion on the cross. She writhed in agony as her hands were seemingly being nailed to the cross. As she experienced this, she said, "Oh, Jesus, I didn't know that You loved me so much." The Lord was faithful to teach the Chinese young people in the Spirit.

The revival among the young people of Hong Kong was so wonderful that the Assembly of God established a high school for them. I believe that high school, born out of revival, still exists today. This revival was noised abroad. Lester Sumrall flew in from the Philippines to see this great move of the Holy Spirit.

Another revival fire broke out in Hong Kong that year, this one among a totally different class of people. S.K. Sung, the Hong Kong millionaire and leader of the Full Gospel Businessmen's Fellowship in the Far East, had gone to the annual convention in Miami, Florida, that summer and had come back with a new touch of God on his life. When we saw each other on the street one day, I could sense his excitement.

"I want to begin inviting speakers to come from America to minister to our businessmen," he told me. "My wife and I will invite prominent local business leaders to dinners in our penthouse, and then we can minister to them. Please help me by inviting many of the missionaries and other Christian leaders from the historic churches so that they can be blessed too."

I had always loved people and had made the acquaintance of all the denominational missionaries in Hong Kong. I was now able to invite them to these penthouse dinners on the Peak. The result of our efforts was wonderful — revival among the wealthiest business people and the denominational missionaries.

The missionaries especially were shy about this experience, and we often could not pray for a couple together. Although they had been married for years, they were too shy to receive this experience in the presence of the other. Some of us would pray for the husband in one room, and others of us would pray for the wife in another. This became a wonderful training ground for me, training that was later put to use among many people in other parts of the world.

Some of the prominent speakers whom God would use in that revival were Ed Stube, David DuPlessis and Harald Bredesen. The meetings in Brother Sung's house were very successful. Many were baptized in the Holy Spirit and spoke in tongues. This was a new and unfamiliar atmosphere for me. I had learned, long before, how to be bold in church, but now I learned how to prophesy in ballrooms and banquet halls, and I learned it from the Episcopalians and the Dutch Reformed. I learned how to lead people to the Lord at social events and how to help them be filled with the Spirit on their yachts.

During this period, we were able to say to the wealthy Christian businessmen of Hong Kong, "You have a spiritual responsibility to the staff and employees of your factories and offices." Many of them took this to heart and began to gather their employees and staff during working hours for prayer and Bible study, and wonderful revival resulted from these meetings.

I was still quite young, but now the words of the Lord spoken over me when I was just fifteen came back to me loud and clear. He had promised to give me wisdom and knowledge, and He did just that in those days. Often I would find myself sitting with successful businessmen, most of them already millionaires, and they would be asking me questions related to business as well as to spiritual matters. I had been raised in Richmond, Virginia, in the humble home of pastors, and I had seldom held more than fifty dollars in my hand at any one time. The questions these men posed involved thousands and even millions of dollars. I kept reminding myself of the Lord's promise. God was faithful to give me wisdom to answer these men, and the answer He gave me was always exactly what that individual needed.

Sometimes, when I was asked a question, it seemed as if I was looking on as someone else gave the answer. I was listening to myself answer, and I was hearing the answer for the first time, just like the person to whom I was speaking. I certainly could not take credit later for what was said. I was learning that the wisdom of God covers the lack of experience and training of a young person, and He will help us at any age to excel.   ❋

◿ 10 ◺

"One Day by One Day"

After living with Beulah Watters for awhile, I had been able to get my own rented place in the Literature Department of the Assembly of God at the corner of Argyle Street and Kadoorie Avenue. My Canadian friends, Rev. and Mrs. Spence, were in change of the bookstore and lived upstairs. Most of the apartment was used by the mission as an office in the daytime, but I had one private room, and I could use the entire apartment in the evenings. I continued to rent that space when I went home for campmeeting.

I had left my return to Hong Kong open so that I could take advantage of any invitations to preach while I was home for the summer, so with summer campmeeting, speaking engagements at home and the trip to India, I had been away for quite a few months. Not knowing that I was due back, the missionaries in charge loaned my apartment to a visiting family just a few days before I got there. When I got back unexpectedly and found them occupying the space, I didn't have the heart to move them out. I was just one person, and it was easier for me to find a place to spend the night in overcrowded Hong Kong than it would be for them. My friend Gwen Shaw kept my parents with her in her house, but I had to find a place to stay. For a time, I stayed one night with one family and another night with another family. Most of my friends didn't have any extra room, so it was always a sacrifice for anyone to accommodate me for the night.

After a while, the pressure of finding a place to stay each night began to get to me, and I began to feel a little sorry for myself. One night, during that great revival among the young people, I was telling the Lord about my plight. "I have a place to stay tonight, Lord," I prayed, "but what about tomorrow night?" Suddenly a Chinese girl who had just been filled with the Spirit and who didn't know a word of English began to speak in fluent English. I never forgot what she said: "Sister, do not worry about tomorrow. Follow Me one day by one day." If that were not enough, she said it a second time, "Sister, do not worry about tomorrow. Follow Me one day by one day."

I went to the piano and began to sing as the words and music came to me:

45

Harvest Glory

One day by one day, I'll walk with the King.
One day by one day, His praises I'll sing.
One day by one day, I'll follow my Guide.
One day by one day, I'll walk by His side.

It was probably the first song God gave me. From that time on, I have tried to follow the Lord one day at a time. ✱

11

"I Have Called You To a Ministry Around the World"

Something else was happening in my life during these months. The previous fall, I had become engaged to a young man we had known for many years, and we decided to be married in Hong Kong. He thought he would accompany us on the trip to India, and that way my parents could be present at the wedding. Things didn't seem to come together for him to make the trip, but he encouraged me to go ahead with my parents. He knew that it would be much better for them if I could accompany them, and they were so excited about the whole venture that he hated to disappoint them.

We did take along all the clothes we would need for the wedding, however, and when I got back to Hong Kong, I kept expecting him to come. When days passed and then weeks and months, and he still hadn't come, I was torn inside about what God was saying to me.

That fall, when God sent Ed Stube to Hong Kong, it was as much for me as for anyone else. Ed was an Episcopalian from Montana, and God had done such an amazing thing in his life and ministry that he had gained considerable media attention. Every Episcopalian priest he had approached over the past few years had been filled with the Spirit. He was also instrumental in founding an Episcopalian magazine that was used as a voice for the revival.

He spoke at the first dinner party Brother and Sister Sung arranged, where so many business people and missionaries had been filled with the Spirit. He was also invited to speak at a prayer meeting at the Peninsula Hotel. This particular prayer meeting was held every Friday afternoon, and people from various missions around town attended. I was very impressed with his ministry there, especially with the fact that he was bold enough to prophesy in those surroundings. We Pentecostals prophesied, but we usually did it in church. This was something new for me, although it would later become quite common.

Ed teased me about this. When he was saying one night that Pentecostals had stopped with the experience of speaking in tongues and had not allowed the gifts of the Spirit to operate in real-life situations, he suddenly looked my way and added, "Oh, I mean every other Pentecostal group except Ruth's."

That same night some of us were together in the roof-garden restaurant at the European YMCA, and I decided to ask his advice about the confusing feelings I had been having over the past few months about getting married. I said, "Brother Stube, I have something I want to discuss with you."

"Wait a minute," he said, "don't tell me the problem yet. I feel the Spirit of prophecy coming over me. Let's just bow our heads a moment." And with that he began to prophesy. Through him the Lord said: "I have called you to a ministry around the world. It was not that you doubted My word, but you doubted that I could do it for you. If you will make the consecration, I will prove to you that I am able to do it." In that moment, I knew that the Lord was requiring me to leave my own desire behind for the ministry. It was already November, and I wasn't about to spoil my fiancé's Christmas by telling him that I had decided not to marry him, so I said nothing.

Then something very unexpected happened. A few days before Christmas I got a call from my fiancé in America saying that he was coming to Hong Kong the next week to marry me. When I hung up the phone, my head and my heart were pounding. I had just told the Lord I would not marry, but I was already rationalizing, *Surely the Lord only wanted me to be willing to give him up. Now that I'm willing, He is going to let me marry him after all. He is going to give him back to me, as He gave Isaac back to Abraham.* Having justified my decision, I announced to all my friends that I was getting married the following week.

On Christmas morning, I went to church for a holiday service. It was a rather usual Christmas service, and I felt that I had heard the sermon dozens of times. The pastor spoke on the gold, the frankincense and the myrrh that the wise men had brought to the Christ-child. When the minister came to the myrrh, he said that myrrh represented our willingness to deny ourselves for the sake of the Gospel. In that moment, the Lord spoke to me very plainly. He showed me that when I had said, after the prophecy in November, that I would give up my fiancé, it was because I did not think he was coming to Hong Kong anyway. "Now, if you give him to Me," the Lord said, "you will be giving Me a gift." This became my Christmas gift to the Lord, and I am still single today.

This decision was not as easy or as clear-cut as it may sound. For some time after that, I experienced a struggle within, and I was not at all sure that I was doing the right thing. I was vacillating between the will of God and my own will, and I was quite miserable. Then one night I had a dream. I saw myself in a beautiful house with a lovely mural on the wall. I was holding a beautiful red-haired baby boy in my arms. (My fiancé had red hair.) I heard myself saying, "Everything is wonderful. It couldn't be better. There's only one thing that bothers me, that I can never work for God again." I was so struck by the dream that I wrote to my fiancé and told him what I had seen. "What about it?" I asked. "Would you be in agreement for me to continue my ministry?"

He wrote back, "How do we know what the future will hold?" I had hoped he would say, "No matter what the future holds, we will always put God first." If he

I Ask for Hong Kong

had said that, I probably would have continued considering our marriage. When he answered the way he did, I knew that I had to obey God and stay single. It was one of the most difficult things I ever did, but I have never had a regret.

As I was choosing to move into a worldwide ministry, in the natural, there were a number of things that hindered me. The fact that I had gotten as far as Hong Kong as a young person was quite an amazing thing. In those days, a missionary spent a lifetime in the same country. I had planned to spend the rest of my life right there in Hong Kong.

The fact that I was in Asia where the elderly were revered and I was a young person was another strike against me. I was also in a part of the world where women had few opportunities outside of the home, and that was a third strike. Also I was from a small independent church in Virginia, with no real worldwide connections.

It was about this time that I remembered something the Lord had said to me when I was eleven years old. A visiting minister had laid his hands on my head and said that I would be used of God all over the world. I had entirely forgotten that incident.

Mother had also told me of a time when I was a child and another visiting preacher had been speaking one night in our church. He was drawn by the Spirit to leave the platform and walk down one aisle. He said, "Somebody on this side of the church, somebody in this area right here, is going to be used of God to bless the nations of the world." Then he went back to the pulpit, picked up his Bible and resumed his sermon. He did this several times.

Mother and I were sitting together in the part of the church he indicated. She later remembered that I was fidgety and not listening very well to what was being said, but she sensed that God was talking about the two of us. The Lord had His hand on my life at a very early age to make me an emissary to the nations.

I remembered now her story and thought of it in the light of what God was saying, "It's not that you doubted My word, but you doubted that I could do it to you." I had apparently dismissed those two experiences from my mind as being implausible, but now the Lord had re-awakened that vision within my spirit, and I knew that He would do what He had spoken.

Most of us know that God can do anything, but we are not sure He will do it through us. The Lord had given me the key that day when He said, "If you will make the consecration, I will prove to you that I am able to do it." Every enlargement of ministry requires a further consecration on our part. I said yes to the Lord that day and very quickly He showed me what He could do.

He had said that if I would make the consecration, He would use me around the world. I knew that He meant it and that He would remove every obstacle and make a way for me to do His work. I'm not sure if I knew how quickly it would all begin to unfold. By January, I was ministering in India to ten thousand people a night and rejoicing in the miracle of God's grace!

☙ 12 ☙

"God's Eternal Purposes for My Life"

Because of the previous trip with my parents, India was not totally new to me, but this time was different, mainly because I was on my own. It was a very exciting time because I had a sense of God's eternal purposes for my life, and I knew that it was a beginning of His launching me into the nations in a fuller sense.

One of the great lessons I learned while traveling in India on this occasion (and there were many) was a result of being alone much of the time. Although I was with large crowds, I had no one to speak with except an interpreter. One pastor was always assigned as my interpreter, and often he would be the only person who could speak English. My interpreter was with me at meeting times, but between meetings he was busy with other necessary arrangements or was resting, so I had no one with whom to carry on a conversation.

There were many long bus trips, train trips and airplane trips alone, but I quickly learned that God was with me and that the challenge of the Holy Ghost never left me. I am determined to be among those at the forefront of what God is doing in the world. His Spirit lives within me, and that is a permanent challenge. I have an intimate relationship with the Lord, and He is able to whisper "well done" into my ears — even when there is no one else to talk to. Thank God for those early experiences in India that taught me so much.

I was in India several weeks, and when I got back to Hong Kong and Gwen heard about the great meetings I had there, she began to seek God seriously for India. In later years, God used her mightily there as well.

At the same time that I was looking forward to getting back into the revival in Hong Kong, I was also excited to see what God had for me next. ✳

⚞ 13 ⚟

"Tell Her That Her Prayers Are Answered"

In the late spring of 1962 Brother Sung was invited to go to Zurich, Switzerland, for the first European Convention of the Full Gospel Business Men's Fellowship. When he couldn't go because of business, he sent me in his place. The convention was held in Congress House in Zurich. It seated several thousand people, and it was filled with people from everywhere. It was a great convention.

It was very exciting for me to be part of what God was doing around Europe and other parts of the world. I met believers from many countries. Among them was an old friend, Minor Argenbrite, part of the Executive Board of FGBMFI, and Bob Guggenbuhl, President of the Zurich Chapter and Director of the FGBMFI in Europe. The finest officers of the FGBMFI were present, for example, and the special speakers were all leaders in their respective areas in the exploding Charismatic Movement. As the delegate from Hong Kong, I was given a lot of deference, and I was able to meet and speak with the leaders present.

The evening speaker was Dr. Samuel Doctorian, an Armenian born in Jerusalem (on Prophet's Street), but living in Beirut, Lebanon. He had traveled extensively in the States and had brought with him to the conference a tour group made up of American believers. After the conference they were going on to the Middle East, and Brother Doctorian invited me to accompany them.

We flew from Zurich to Beirut for our first meetings in the church of Samuel Doctorian. Many things about my Middle Eastern trip deeply moved me, but one of the things that most stuck in my spirit was the dedication of the poor Armenian believers in his church. They had determined to put up a church building in Beirut to glorify the Lord. They did not know where the funds for such a project would come from, since both land and building materials were expensive in Beirut, but they were believing God for a miracle. When I heard about it, I somehow felt that S.K. Sung might be able to help them.

In my ministry, both public and private, I often spoke about people who had given sacrificially to God. Sacrificial giving had been instilled in me since childhood, and my parents and the members of our church were wonderful examples,

51

as they were constantly giving in a sacrificial way for the sake of the Gospel. One day when we had gotten to know each other better, Brother Sung had said to me, "You know, I have never given sacrificially. In any given meeting, I have always given more than anyone else. My offering has always been the largest. Still I have never given sacrificially. I love what you are saying. Please pray that God might give me the opportunity to do that someday."

The Armenian believers were ready to sacrifice for the Beirut project themselves. One lady got up and said that she didn't have any money to give, so she wanted to give her wedding ring so that the church could be built. A man got up and said that he also did not have money to give, but he wanted to offer his son to work on the building. Others responded in similar ways. The more I listened, the more I was moved by their love for the Lord.

In the midst of these spontaneous offers of love to the Lord, I remembered what Brother Sung had said to me, and I felt that this might be the perfect opportunity for him to do what he had been wanting to do for a long time. I determined to tell him about this opportunity when I next saw him.

When we finished our meetings in Beirut, we took a bus for Damascus, Syria.

When we got to the Syrian border, Samuel Doctorian got off the bus to process all the papers, and the rest of us waited on the bus. After he had been gone for a very long time, I felt that something was wrong. "Excuse me," I said to the others, "I'm going to go and see what's happening." I was just an invited guest of the tour group, but I sensed that the Lord could use me to help resolve whatever was wrong.

When I found Samuel Doctorian, he said, "They're not going to let me into Syria. I was in the north not long ago and had a great meeting, and someone has blacklisted me. I tried to explain to them that I have this American group and I need to take them on, but they won't listen." When he said that, I began to pray for a miracle.

When the head immigration officer came out and saw me there, he asked, "Who is she? What is she doing?"

Samuel Doctorian said, "She is one of the members of our tour group, and she is sitting here praying that God might move on your heart to allow me to go into Damascus."

"Tell her that her prayers are answered," the man said, placing into Dr. Doctorian's hands the necessary permits.

When we got back to the bus, everyone was very excited about this great miracle. That night there was great rejoicing in the Christian and Missionary Alliance Church where we preached in Damascus.

I Ask for Switzerland, Lebanon, Syria, Jordan, Egypt, Israel and Italy

In Amman we preached in several Arab churches, then we went on to have meetings in Jerusalem. We stayed in the American Colony Hotel. It was near the Garden Tomb and Samuel Doctorian knew the Keeper of the Tomb, Brother Solomon Mattar, and Brother Mattar allowed us to go into the tomb one night to pray. It was a wonderful experience.

During our prayer that night Brother Samuel Doctorian gave a prophetic word. The Lord said, "Just before I return, I have something important for you to do in the Holy City." Since the "thee" or "you" of prophecy can mean either singular or plural, it was not immediately apparent to whom the message was addressed. I was still quite young and had been serving the Lord abroad for just a few years, so I assumed, as many of us do, that what God was saying was for Samuel Doctorian, the mature minister among us. It wasn't until years later that I realized that God had been speaking to me as well.

In those days, there was such a small handful of believers in Jerusalem that it was difficult to conceive of the great thing that God was saying He would do in later years.

After the meetings in Jerusalem, we went back to Beirut. We were scheduled to fly from there to Cairo. Samuel Docktorian told me that his wife Naomi didn't want him to go on to Cairo. He had conducted such powerful crusades there that he was also on an Egyptian blacklist. I encouraged him to go. "God gave you the miracle at the border of Syria, and I believe He will do the same thing in Cairo." After considering it for a time, he decided to go.

When we got to Cairo, Samuel Doctorian was singled out and taken aside, and the identical scene that we had witnessed at the Syrian border was replayed. When I knew what was happening, I went inside where he was being questioned and began praying for a miracle of God's favor. Again an immigration officer came out and asked Samuel Doctorian who I was and what I was doing. He answered as before, that I was a tour member who was praying that God might give him favor.

"Tell her God has answered her prayer," the man said, and handed over all the required papers.

When we got to the meeting in the Heliopolis area of Cairo that night, word had spread that Samuel Doctorian was in town, and more than four thousand people had gathered. What a great meeting we had that night!

From Cairo, we flew to Rome. We toured the city, and from there I was able to get a flight to Seattle. I would be attending the FGBMFI World Convention in that city, and Brother S.K. Sung would be there too. When I had a chance to speak with him, I was moved to tell him what I had seen in Beirut and to encourage him that this was his opportunity to give sacrificially. I was surprised to see that this made him visibly nervous. When I asked him why, he told me that his former partner's widow had just recently approached him and told him that she wanted him to buy out her share of the business. He had always kept large amounts of cash available, but he had used all of his cash reserves to buy the widow's shares. Now, for the first time in his life, he was experiencing a cash flow crisis, and it made him understandably nervous.

He did want to make a sacrificial offering, however, and just as soon as he could, he sold something and sent $20,000.00 to Beirut, a considerable gift for that time.

That next January, Samuel Doctorian and I paid a visit to the owner of the land the people wanted to buy. He was Mr. Sami Sohl, the former Prime Minister of Lebanon, and we were able to negotiate with him for the land. With Brother Sung's gift the believers bought the land for their church.

Many years later, during the Lebanese war, when the country was experiencing extreme difficulty, the church building these people put up was one of the few to remain open, and quite a number of congregations used it, staggering their meetings so that they could all benefit. To this day, that church building in the city of Beirut is used by multiple congregations.

Since we had arrived in Seattle a day before the convention was to start, we were invited by some of the leaders of the Full Gospel Business Men's Fellowship to go with them to Portland, Oregon, to dedicate a new chapter of the organization.

That afternoon we were sitting together beside the hotel pool having a soft drink and sharing what God had been doing. Several people had been swimming in the pool, but I had not paid any attention to them. Suddenly my eyes were drawn to a man who was getting out of the pool. He seemed to be heading our way. The Lord spoke to me and said, "Invite him to Hong Kong."

I had no idea who the man was, but I stood up as he approached and found myself saying, "The Lord spoke to me to invite you to come to Hong Kong." He was Harald Bredesen, the well-known Dutch Reformed minister, whom God was using so mightily among denominational people. He had never yet been abroad, but he had received a prophetic word that he would be traveling to other countries. He told me that he had come to the convention with one thing in mind, to hear from the Lord when he would be going to the foreign countries and

I Ask for Switzerland, Lebanon, Jordan, Egypt, Israel and Italy

which countries he should go to first. Even before the convention had begun, he now had an invitation to Hong Kong.

S.K. Sung instantly stood up to say, "I'll pay your way." In just a few moments the matter was thus sealed, even before we had a chance to be formally introduced. I spent some time getting to know Harald Bredesen personally during that convention.

Not long after I returned to Hong Kong, I got a letter from Harald Bredesen asking when I thought he should come. I told him that I felt God had something else for him to do in America first, and when that was done, he should come. This released him to accept invitations to Princeton and Yale where God used him for the wonderful revival that followed. He arrived in Hong Kong later.

Two more very wonderful things happened in the conference in Seattle. S.K. Sung had invited my wayward brother and, because the World's Fair was being conducted in Seattle that year, he had accepted the invitation. Little did he know that he would be saved and filled with the Spirit there and would begin his own fruitful ministry.

Pastor Constance Klotz of Red Bluff, California prophesied over me in the Seattle convention, and the Lord said that whereas I had been going behind the reapers, gleaning in a corner of the field, I would now glean in the middle of the field among the reapers. I knew that God's hand was upon my life, and I could sense great increase for the future.　　　　　　　　　　　✳

⩗ 14 ⩘

"Go Anyway!"

By now, I had fallen in love with India, with the Indian people, with the Indian food and with the exquisitely beautiful Indian countryside, and I was thrilled that fall when the Lord spoke to me to spend more time in India. I had scheduled some meetings with Pastor P.J. Daniel for January of 1963, but God spoke to me to go two weeks early. I said, "Lord, they don't even know I'm coming," but my direction was clear: "Go anyway!"

I flew into Bombay and caught a flight to Cochin. There I got on a local bus and went down to Mavelikera. I wasn't sure if I could remember the road leading up to Pastor Daniel's house where I had to get off the bus. I did remember that there was a little kiosk situated at that point along the main road. When I got there, I recognized the place and signaled the driver to stop and let me off. It was night, and there was only a little light from a lantern in the kiosk. As I stepped off the bus with my luggage in hand, I was wondering, *How will I get down this dark road?* Just then a hand reached out of the darkness to me. When I looked, I recognized Pastor Daniel's hearing and speech impaired servant. He had come down to the road to buy something and was standing right there at the moment I happened to arrive. He was very excited to see me and joyfully escorted me down the dark road, through the tall coconut palm trees, with only the moon as the light, until we arrived at Pastor Daniel's house. Needless to say, I was also thrilled to see him.

Brother Daniel was, of course, surprised to see me. "We were not expecting you for two weeks."

"I know," I said. "God told me to come early."

We sat and had a delicious cup of Indian tea and discussed the possible reasons God had sent me early. He said to me, "I have a friend over in Kottayam who is starting a conference tomorrow. His name is Pastor P.M. Philip. If you would like, I can take you there for the opening service tomorrow." I agreed.

Out of politeness for a foreign guest, Pastor Philip asked me to say something that first night in the conference. There were other foreign guests as well, some Finnish missionaries. He had plenty of speakers. After he had heard me, he asked if I would stay and be the main speaker for the conference.

The meeting was held in the Town Hall of Kottayam. It was in this place that

I Ask for India

I had a most unusual experience. After I had spoken one Sunday morning, communion was served, and then all the people were given an opportunity to greet each other. Locally, they called it a "love feast." I knew the Indian custom of the brothers greeting each other with a kiss on each cheek and the sisters doing the same with the sisters. I was shy about kissing anyone, much less people I had never met. *What should I do?* I wondered.

The platform was quite large, and I thought at first that I could surely not be expected to go all the way over to where the sisters (known as Bible women) were gathered to greet them. Perhaps I would be excused from this part of the service. Then I noticed that everyone was looking at me, wondering what I would do, and I sensed that my future ministry in India depended on how I responded in that moment. As I made my way toward the ladies' section, I found myself praying the prayer I would often pray: "Jesus, help me."

When we look up to Him and call out for His help, He is always there. When we cannot show love, He can. When we are not sufficient in ourselves, He is. When we are not able, He is able. If we are only willing, He will do the work for us.

Just at that moment, as I prayed, "Jesus, help me," it seemed like a great bucket of honey from Heaven had been tilted over and began to flow down on me. By the time I reached those sisters, I was weeping and feeling more love for them than I had ever imagined possible and found it easy to embrace and kiss each of those sisters, one by one.

Pastor Philip, who was loved by many and was considered to be the most outstanding Pentecostal evangelist in India at the time, fell in love with my preaching and, after my meetings with Pastor Daniel were over, he took me to many other parts of India. He arranged meetings for me, accompanied me and became my interpreter. It was a great privilege. He was such a great preacher in his own right that to have him promoting me was a humbling but wonderful experience. During that period he became a real father figure for me.

He took me to all the great conventions of India, and because he was so highly respected, I was well received everywhere we went. He too ministered in those conventions and still often interpreted for my preaching. Later that year I had the highest honor in India, of being invited on my own to speak in the All India Pentecostal Convention. It was held that year in Jabalpur.

At Easter time that year Pastor Philip took me to New Delhi and introduced me to another pastor, M.K. Chacko, a man who also became a great friend. I preached several Easter conferences for him after that. It was a wonderful time.

57

God was putting me into a whole new situation, placing me among people who provided my every physical and financial need.

I had determined early in my Indian experience to show respect for the Indian people by wearing a *sari* when I was in India. They responded by giving me many beautiful *saris* to wear. Wearing the *sari* and eating Indian food was never a burden for me. I found something about the whole subcontinent, and later the whole Himalayan region, to be very captivating.

The opportunities I was afforded in India were rather unique to women. Neither before or since has a woman been so openly received there. This was not without its downside. At some of the conventions, Pastor T.G. Oomen, who could quote the Bible from cover to cover, would introduce me. At others, Pastor Philip would do it. I would not usually ask what was being said, but for some reason one night I was curious. I turned to one of the pastors who spoke English and asked, "What is he saying?"

I'm not sure what I expected to hear in reply, but what I did hear was that Pastor Oomen was relating how God had used the donkey to speak to the prophet. "And remember," he said, "it was a she donkey."

It was just that rare to have a lady minister in India, and night after night I was duly humbled with comments like that one. By the time I spoke, I knew it had to be the power of God that was ministering through me, not any of my own strength. God helped me, and I became known in those years as "the Lady Billy Graham of India."

It was the time of the great Charismatic Renewal all over the world, and I was preaching a lot on the Holy Spirit wherever I went. Thousands needed to be filled with the Spirit, and it was often my privilege to help them receive this blessing. I did preach salvation, and I did pray for people to be healed, but others were doing this, so I felt my special place was to help people be filled with the Spirit. One brother, after he heard me speak on some other subject, looked at me very seriously and said, "I didn't know you could preach on anything but the Holy Spirit."

I was ministering to people who desperately needed the outpouring of the Holy Spirit, so message after message was concerning the Holy Spirit — the infilling of the Spirit, the empowerment of the Spirit, the ministry of the Spirit, the comfort of the Holy Spirit, etc. When the Lord sends a ministry to us, it is to fill in the gaps, to stir us up in the area of our need. That doesn't mean God isn't saying anything else and we can throw away everything else we believe. These days that man would probably think I could only speak on the glory, for I find much of my ministry time consumed with that subject. I like to flow with the revelation of the hour, and I never make apologies for what I am preaching at the moment.

Traveling so much in India was a great challenge. For the most part, we moved about by third-class train. When we were traveling from Kerala to New Delhi, for instance, it took us three days and three nights on the train. The trains were always very crowded, but this one was especially crowded. When we would stop at a station, people waiting there would throw their luggage in through the window so that they could get aboard. Luggage was piled high in the aisles.

I made the mistake of going all the way into the carriage to be seated, and when it came time to use the rest room, there was no way for me to get through the aisle. Pastor Philip announced to all the people in the car in Hindi that *Memsahib* needed to use the rest room, and at the next station everyone backed out onto the platform so that I could get through the car. When I returned to my seat, they all came crawling back over the luggage to resume their seats. This happened over and over again as we crossed the countryside.

We were blessed. I have known people who traveled for three days and three nights on Indian trains standing up, and sometimes they have had to stand in the very rest room itself, because there was no other available spot.

There were other humorous experiences in our travels. Once, when I was traveling with Pastor Daniel, we took a long bus ride to visit a pastor's home. When we got to his house, I told Pastor Daniel that I would like to visit the rest room, and he went out to tell our hosts. He came back a few minutes later to say, "Just a moment."

Before long I heard some pounding outside. After an interminably long wait, the hammering stopped and Pastor Daniel came back to say, "You may come now." What I discovered when I went outside was that the family had built an outhouse just for me — while I was waiting. The Indian people have always been gracious to do their very best for me, even when it is not required of them.

In one convention where I was speaking, they used a sheet strung on wire to block off a small room for me in the corner of a church building. That night I went into the little room and got into the bed they had prepared for me. When I woke up the next morning, I discovered that there were at least fifty other women sleeping in the same room, and I was the only one with a curtained-off private area. I had always been able to sleep well, and I had slept straight through the night without knowing that anyone else was even present.

India was not without its dangers. It was, after all, a Hindu nation, and sometimes the Hindus became militant against Christians. Once, when I was preaching in a tent meeting in Chandigarh, in the Punjab, a group of young men from the same militant Hindu sect that had run T.L. Osborn out of India, rose up and tried to shout me down. Chandigarh was their headquarters. A school teacher authority suddenly came on me, and I pointed my finger at them and said in a stern voice, "You sit down. I am a guest of the Indian government, and you will treat me as a guest." Every last one of them sat down like little boys in a classroom, and we had no more problems.

Another time, when I was preaching in New Delhi, a group of them came to the *shamiana* (tent) and threatened that if we didn't close down the meeting they would do us harm. I encouraged all the believers to join me at the pastor's house for an all-night prayer meeting. Some of the believers were quite fearful, and I sensed that we had a decision to make: trust God and go on or be fearful and turn back. After we had prayed all night, however, we went on with the meeting and never had another moment's trouble.

The enemy tried in other ways to stop my ministry. When I was with Pastor Matthew at Kariamplave in Kerala, we walked several miles one day to the river for a baptismal service. Several hundred people were baptized that day, and then we walked several miles back in the hot sun. My parents had been there before, although it was a rather primitive place.

Later that day, I was scheduled to speak at the Women's Convention. My head was pounding, and I found myself holding on to the table for support. It soon became apparent that I had suffered a sunstroke.

I was able to get through my message, but when I got back to my room, I collapsed onto the bed and could not get out of it when time came for the service that evening. Suddenly all the liquid in my body seemed to drain out. I was totally dehydrated and began drifting in and out of consciousness. When I came to, there was no one with whom to speak English to ask what was happening to me. Pastor Philip was preaching in the service.

I was to learn that most people who suffer a sunstroke that serious die. During that evening and night, the pastor's wife was determined that I would live. She spoke no English, but God understood her prayer. She never left my bedside, but stayed there praying, believing God to spare my life.

The next morning God said to me, "Would you be willing to stay in India?"

I said, "Lord, I never once considered that You didn't want me to go back to Hong Kong." I had just assumed that Hong Kong would always be my base, and I had a return ticket to Hong Kong. I had arranged it to end there, but if God wanted me in India, why not?

"Of course I'll stay," I answered the Lord. "I would be glad to live here."

I never used that Hong Kong portion of my ticket, staying some six months

I Ask for India

in India. I didn't live there the rest of my life, but just as soon as I said that I was willing to, I was instantly healed.

Hong Kong has always remained my first love, for there is something wonderful about the first place to which God calls a person. The Chinese people have also always been special to me.

Those early years in Hong Kong were the formative years of my adult life, and I was blessed to spend them among the Chinese people. I learned many wonderful things from them, special courtesies that I try to incorporate into my life even to this day.

Other than Jerusalem, Hong Kong is still my favorite city in the world. Jerusalem has to be my favorite because of its spirituality, but I love Hong Kong for its exciting cultural difference, for its delicious Chinese food and for the wonderful Chinese people.

I have always been grateful for God's call to Hong Kong. When I go back, I always ride the Star Ferry across the bay from Kowloon to Hong Kong. It is a thrill just to feel the breeze blowing on my face and to be able to look out on the varied junks and sampans and the majestic oceangoing ships. I could ride that ferry all day long. Sometimes I ride to one side of the bay, then turn around and ride back. Then, when I have walked along the waterfront to the place I'm staying, I feel the desire to do it all over again. Hong Kong is truly an exotic place.

Now, however, I had a new love. India had captivated my heart, and for several years afterward, I would spend half my year in India and eventually was able to minister in every state in the nation.

There is something unique about the church in every nation, and the thing that impressed me about the Indian believers at that time was that they knew the Word of God to a degree that I had not seen in any other nation. They knew it by book, by author, by subject and in many other ways. I met men in South India who could quote the Bible from cover to cover. If you mentioned any two words from the Bible, they could tell you where those words were found — without looking. They not only have a gift of knowing the Word of God, they have the gift of imparting it as well. The Indians have the greatest Christian conferences.

I have often said that the Korean church is known for its prayer. This is not just something that Dr. Cho has made known. It was already a characteristic of the Korean church when he was still a boy. In the great Presbyterian gatherings of Korea, everyone was up at five in the morning praying and seeking the face of God, and God gave them great and miraculous answers to prayer. The Koreans have raised up prayer mountains all over the world, places to come aside and seek the face of God.

India has its place in God's heart, and in mine.   ✳

≍ 15 ≍

"I'm Staying One More Night"

In 1964, my brother made his first trip to Israel. He went with Kash Amburgy of Ohio, a man who was used of God to get Americans to travel to the Holy Land. He was one of the first who showed people that they could travel on credit, and this opened the door to millions of poor and middle class people to see the lands of the Bible.

After a trip or two with Kash, my brother began taking his own tours and did so, not only to Israel, but to other countries as well, until he died. He always recognized the debt he owed to Kash Amburgy for getting him started in that ministry.

Kash Amburgy's group would be taking a few days to tour Rome on their way back to America and, since I was on my way to India, it was decided that I would join them in Rome. Some other people from our church were also with the tour, and I stayed with them in their hotel room. We were all in service together that first night in Rome. Then the tour was to leave the next day.

I was unable to get a flight that same day on to India, so I would have to stay one more night in the hotel. I had told the desk clerk that I would be staying one more night, although I only had $26.00 with me and I was planning to spend several months in India.

When everyone came down to the lobby and the group was checking out, the clerk said to me in a rather loud voice, "So, you're staying one more night?"

"Yes," I answered, "I'm staying one more night." I thought the fact that I was staying one more night had already been understood and I wondered why he was asking me again. I came to the conclusion that the Lord let him do it so that Brother Kash Amburgy could overhear, for when he heard it, he said, "Put that on my bill," and my need was met.

Two other young ministers who had been on that tour were staying behind because they had a desire to preach in Rome. Pastor John McTernan, an American who had a wonderful church in Rome, was there seeing everyone off that day, and he said to me now, "Would you like to come to our service tonight?"

"I would love to," I answered him.

The two young men and I were picked up later that day from the hotel by Rev. McTernan and taken to the church. Brother McTernan was a good friend of

62

I Ask for Italy

David DuPlessis, and they had been working together in connection with the Vatican Council and with the outpouring of the Holy Spirit in the various areas of Rome. On the way to the church that night, Brother McTernan said to me, "I want you to preach tonight."

I was caught off guard. "Oh, brother," I answered, "I didn't even bring my Bible. It's packed in my suitcase. I just came by Rome to see my brother. And besides, these two brothers have a burning desire to preach in Rome, where Paul preached. I don't have an overwhelming desire to do that, like they do."

"You're preaching because God told me to have you preach," he said, and that settled it.

I didn't know at the time that a woman had never preached in this church before. I only found that out later.

At the end of my sermon that night, the Lord said to me, "Yield to Me."

I said, "Well, Lord, that's what I've been doing all evening long."

He said again, "Yield to Me," and I knew that He wanted more than I had been giving. I lifted up my hands to show my surrender to the Spirit, and as I did, I was slain in the Spirit.

When I came to myself, I was concerned. I hadn't given an altar call. I hadn't prayed for anyone. That did not seem like the proper way to end a period of ministry. Rather sheepishly I raised myself up on one elbow to see what everyone else was doing at the moment, and I was amazed to see that everyone else had been slain in the Spirit as well. When I had allowed that wind of the Spirit to sweep over me, it had swept over the entire congregation and slain them all. It had never happened in that church before.

The next day when Pastor McTernan came to get me and take me to the airport, he told me, "We couldn't go to bed last night. All we could do was talk about the service. The thing we kept saying was, 'And to think, that God would use a woman to bring revival to Rome.' " He had a hard time believing that it was possible.

"There are always many preachers wanting to preach in my church because of this desire to preach where Paul preached. I also want to do a little preaching in my church. That's why God has me here. But I want you to know that any time you want to come to Rome, you have an open invitation." ✶

⚞ 16 ⚟

"I Am Jodi"

While I was at Pastor Philip's place in Kottayam that January, I was told that another American was arriving by bus. I walked out to the street to the bus stop to greet him. He was Harold McDougal, a young Spirit-filled Methodist minister from West Virginia. Over the coming weeks Harold and I were scheduled in many of the same conventions. We had opportunity to speak during mealtimes and after meetings, and we became close friends. I found that he shared my love for India and its people, so much so that he was seriously thinking about spending the rest of his life there.

We were both fascinated by the spiritual hunger of the Indian people. They would come from many miles around to the various conferences, carrying their little bundles over their shoulders and would camp out, sleeping on mats on the ground, and cooking in their huge common rice pots.

The meetings themselves were held in a *pundal*, a covering made by placing woven palm leaves over a bamboo frame. There were no seats and the people sat on mats on the ground, sometimes for hours at a time. The majority of the people slept on the same mats under the same *pundal.* Such was their desire for God.

In other areas, where people came just for a specific service, they were a sight to behold as they made their way back through the darkness to the homes. It was always a moving experience to be part of these great processions. Hundreds or sometimes thousands of people would be making their way through the trees, across the streams, and up the hillsides, with only their homemade torches to light the way.

As they went, they sang, and we sang with them all the Indian choruses we knew. We also enjoyed singing together many of the American hymns of consecration we had not heard for such a long time. Those were wonderful days, as we were continually being challenged by the Holy Spirit to give more of ourselves to Him.

Through the coming years Harold and I worked together in many countries. Neither of us could have imagined at that time, however, that he would one day become my editor and publisher.

I Ask for India

One of the things that blessed me most about my years spent in India was to see many young Indian men challenged to full time service for the Lord through my ministry. When they saw that I was young and did not have a large organization behind me but that God was miraculously providing my needs, they were challenged to resign their jobs to take up the life of faith.

This was a big step for men and women living in such a poor country. The Indian Christians were not accustomed to giving toward the Lord's work. The unusual thing about my own life that spoke to so many was that Indians, in general, were never expected to give anything to foreigners. Instead, they expected to receive when foreigners were present. My needs, however, were always completely supplied and usually through local people.

Among those who made a decision to live the life of faith because of my ministry there were two young men who had wonderful jobs in New Delhi. One of them was Samuel John. Brother John had a wonderful position with the catering department of Indian Airlines. Not only did he have a good salary and good benefits, but he could fly home to Kerala free each year from North India with his family, and he could take home leftover food to his family every week night. That seemed like a lot to give up, but I told him that if he would step out by faith, I knew that God would support him and his family. I offered to preach his first series of meetings for him. He made the decision to obey God and started a work in Chandigarh. As I had promised him, I went and preached his first series of special meetings for him.

Some years later, we bumped into each other in a shop in Hong Kong. He was so glad to see me and to tell me how the Lord had blessed his work. "You must come and see the work now," he said excitedly. "We have one hundred and twenty-five churches."

Later, I did go preach for Pastor John in Chandigarh and saw what a wonderful work God had done through him. While I was there in Chandigarh, I noticed something new in their services. I knew many of the Indian choruses, but they were singing something altogether new. In fact, it didn't sound like Hindi at all. It sounded heavenly, eternal. I tapped Pastor John on the shoulder and asked him, "Where does this chorus come from?"

"One of the Indian brothers was carried away to Heaven," he explained, "and this was the song that he heard the angels sing. He brought it back to us in our language."

How wonderful it was to see these precious people moving in heavenly realms.

The other young man who gave his life to full time service in New Delhi was Claude Roberts. He had worked for an international pharmaceutical company and had traveled for them as a salesperson. It was a wonderful position, and he and his family enjoyed a very nice house.

Claude Roberts, too, became willing to give up his job, and he went to Jaipur in Rajastan and established the church there. Since then he too has raised up more than a hundred churches and more than one hundred and thirty preachers.

These were two good examples of what God did, but there were many more. Some years later, when I was already living in Jerusalem, I was told one morning that an Indian couple had come to attend our service. When I went to greet them, the brother said, "Sister Ruth, don't you remember me?"

"I'm sorry," I answered, "but I don't believe I do."

"I'm Jodi," he responded. "I was your interpreter in South India when I was just a young man. You didn't know it, but soon after you left, I went North because of the challenge of your ministry." He had raised up more than a hundred churches and a hundred workers as well.

This scene was repeated again and again through the years and became our greatest legacy in India.   ✳

My grandmother, Sophia Evans Ward, is the second woman on the left. Grandfather William Arthur Ward is standing behind her left shoulder, 1909.

Grandfather Ward, noted evangelist and orator, with his Bible.

Grandmother Ward with Mother, Edith Mary Ward, 1910.

Standing: Wallace Harrison Heflin, Jr., William Arthur Ward, Daddy holding me, my sister Mary Elizabeth, and Grandmother Ward holding John Robert (Bobby) Ward,1945.

The Heflin Family: Daddy (Wallace Harrison Heflin), his brother Irving, his sister Avalene, Grandmother Heflin (Ruth Blanche), brother Lester and brother Leroy.

W.H.H. Sr. and Edith Ward Heflin, 1930.

My sister Betty and her husband, Willard. She is holding David. Edith Ann is standing with Willard Jr. (Willie).

The church in which I was born, Rowland and Greyland Avenue, Richmond, Virginia.

Mother and Grandfather Ward when he was 94.

My brother (whom we called Sonny) Mother, Betty, Daddy and me.

Standing: Joe Medina, Jim Dowds, Willie Henderson, me, David Henderson, second row: Rev. Wallace Heflin, Jr., Edith Heflin, Helen Medina, Naomi Medina, sitting: Edith Ann Dowds holding Mary, Gail Henderson holding Kimberly, William, Sharon and Michael Henderson.

Practicing preaching at 9 years old, June 6, 1949.

In the famous blue dress, 1956.

Hong Kong Harbor.

On the boat headed for Hong Kong, 1958.

In the middle, with Beulah Watters and Rev. and Mrs. Wong at his church at Wong Tai Sin.

Welcome dinner upon arrival to Hong Kong, with Beulah Watters, Pastor and Mrs. Tseung and Mr. Fong.

Teaching at a rooftop school in Hong Kong.

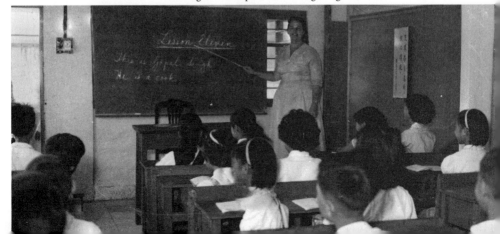

Park Meeting, Tai Chung, Taiwan, 1959. I was 19 years old.

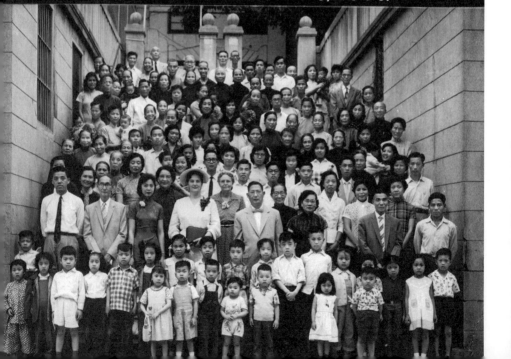

CHRISTIAN PENTECOSTAL CHURCH HONG KONG WELCOME MISS RUTH WARD HEFLIN TO OUR CHURCH ON APRIL 6, 1958.

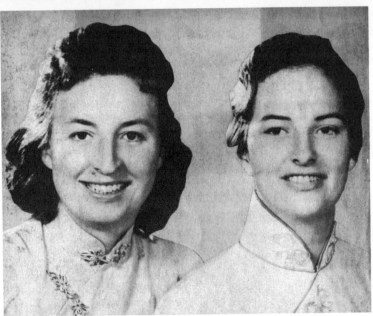

Gwen Shaw and me. This photo appeared on the song sheet cover of our first Gospel song, which I wrote in Hong Kong, 1961.

On the China border with my brother, Christmas, 1959.

Mother, Daddy and Mr. S.K. Sung, 1961.

With Faith Paau, my chinese prayer partner and friend.

☙ 17 ☙

"I Will Change Your Ministry"

That summer, during our summer campmeeting, I took another giant step in my spiritual development. I believed in dancing before the Lord, but I was very happy to let other people do it. I made sure that I was always busy, either playing the organ or in some other aspect of the service, when others were dancing. I had never really come into a liberty in worshiping in this way. The Lord spoke to me at the beginning of the campmeeting that it was important for me to dance before Him. He showed me how David, after he had danced before the Lord as the Ark made its way back into the Holy City, was able to feed the people. In fact, he had given them all a triple portion:

And he dealt among all the people, even among the whole multitude of Israel, as well to the women as men, to every one a cake of bread, and a good piece of flesh, and a flagon of wine. So all the people departed every one to his house.
2 Samuel 6:19

I was familiar with the story of Jesus feeding four thousand on one occasion and five thousand on another, and there were other references in Scripture to men of God miraculously feeding large groups, particularly the miracle of Moses feeding the children of Israel in the wilderness. As far as I could see, however, David had been the only person in Scripture to ever feed a triple portion or to feed an entire nation. If I wanted to feed nations, the Lord was showing me, I had to be willing to worship Him in the dance.

This was a great revelation to my spirit. I did want to feed nations. I had already preached to large numbers of people overseas, and I knew what it was to give men and women bread and meat, but I wanted to feed the wine of revival. I wanted to offer Spirit and life to the multitudes of hungering men and women that I knew were awaiting the wine of the outpouring of the Holy Spirit in the last days.

The Lord did not tell me I had to dance to be saved, or I had to dance to be filled with the Spirit, but He was giving me a greater challenge concerning the nations. I wanted to obey Him, and I made up my mind that every day during our month-long campmeeting, I would dance before the Lord.

It didn't happen easily or all at once. To begin with, I only wiggled my toes in my shoes. Then I progressed to the place that I was able to shift my weight from one foot to the other. Gradually, however, I became more and more free, until finally I could actually dance before the Lord in every service.

Nobody else knew what God had been saying to me, and no one else could have understood the struggle I was having to obey Him. The wonderful thing about campmeeting, however, is that there is so much happening in every service, and God is dealing with so many people individually, that nobody is really paying any attention to what is happening to you. The others are preoccupied with what God is doing in their own lives. So I did "my own thing," and I was able to move into a new place in God.

Toward the end of campmeeting that summer, Mother prophesied over me: "I am going to change your ministry. I am going to send you to kings and queens, potentates, people of position, and you will speak to them of me." She saw in vision the name of the first place I was to go. She did not know how to pronounce it, so she just spelled it out: K-A-T-H-M-A-N-D-U. "You will go to K-A-T-H-M-A-N-D-U," the Lord said.

Although I had preached extensively in India, I did not recognize the name of the capital of the little Himalayan kingdom of Nepal, which lies just north of India. From that day on I began reading all that I could find out about the area.

Nepal, I learned, was a Hindu kingdom which, both because of its strict religious beliefs and because of its location in the mountains, had kept itself closed to foreigners. The country was considered to be a hundred years behind other countries in the region in development, and it was still difficult to get permission to travel there.

I learned that some people were in Nepali prisons for converting to Christianity or converting others to Christianity. One brother, Prem Predhan, won nine people to Christ and was sentenced to nine years in prison, one year for each person he had baptized. The nine people whom he had brought to Christ were also imprisoned for a time.

One night in our service in the Richmond church a very simple brother had a wonderful vision concerning Nepal. He saw a crown, and he described it perfectly. It had teardrop emeralds around the base and the top and diamonds and a cluster of teardrop rubies around the side. It was topped by feathers.

One day I drove to Washington, D.C., to visit the Nepalese Consulate. It was on Leroy Place (and still is today). By mistake I knocked on the wrong door. Instead of entering the chancery, I was attempting to enter the embassy itself. The son of the ambassador answered the door and invited me to come in. As I entered the hallway of the embassy, I was amazed to see a painting of the King of Nepal. He was wearing the crown the brother had seen in his vision and had described in such detail. How exciting it was to see that!

76

I Ask for Nepal

I told the ambassador's son about the vision. When he learned that I was interested in a visa, he showed me next door to the chancery. I had been in the hallway long enough to see the confirmation of the vision, and the painting would not be forgotten.

That summer a Filipino businessman attended the summer camp. Afterward he went to New York, and we had been in frequent contact with him by phone to see how his affairs were developing. My parents felt that we should drive up to New York and spend some time with him. He needed some encouragement. We did this. There were six of us in the car, my parents, my brother and I and Harold and Diane McDougal. They had been with us during camptime and had stayed over to help do some building on the campground.

After we had prayed for the Filipino brother and God had given him an encouraging word, we decided to pass by the United Nations' headquarters. We looked around the building and grounds and ended up in the viewing gallery, looking into the U.N. Chamber itself. A meeting was in progress, and we could see the various ambassadors at their respective tables with their identifying name plates. Suddenly my eyes were drawn to the representative from Nepal, and just about that time he got up, gathered up his papers, and started leaving the Chamber.

I knew that I must meet him, so we all rushed out of the viewing gallery, wondering how or where we might find the man. Most of the ambassadors, it turned out, left by a private underground exit where they could board their limousines and depart unnoticed by the crowd on the street. The Nepalese Ambassador, however, because his office was nearby, came out of a street-level exit.

We didn't actually see him come out. In fact, there were so many people milling about that it was difficult to see anyone. When I did see him, he had stepped off the curb and was about to cross the street. I ran and caught his attention and spoke to him of my desire to visit Nepal. He invited us back to the Nepali Embassy nearby, and there he issued my visa to enter the Kingdom of Nepal.

I cannot describe how excited I was in that moment! I was twenty-four years old, and I was on my way to a fairy-tale kingdom to meet the Royal Family. I had a visa. Now all I needed was an airline ticket. ✸

⚔ 18 ⚔

"He Said You Would Know What to Do with It"

Our family had developed a habit of faith that God always honored. When He told us to go somewhere for Him, we packed a bag by faith that He would make the provision for the journey. I already had my bag packed and waiting.

The first summer I was home from Hong Kong, I met a lovely lady by the name of Mrs. Bruce Crane Fisher. A Baptist pastor from Charles City, Virginia, met me and, wanting to encourage a young person who was serving the Lord, he invited me to speak in his church. That night, at the close of his service, Mrs. Fisher came and introduced herself to me. She asked if I would like to come home and spend the night in her home. I thanked her for her invitation but told her that I was driving my father's car and that he would need it the next morning.

After I said good-night to the pastor and his people, I got in the car to leave, but it would not start. I was still turning the motor over, trying to get it to start, when I looked up to see the lovely lady standing there. She said, "Well, I guess you'll have to go home with me now. You can call your parents and let them know what happened, and I can send someone tomorrow to see what's wrong with your car."

I thanked her and got in her car to go home with her. On the way I learned that she was an Episcopalian who supported other local churches with her presence at special events.

When we had driven several miles, she pulled into Westover on the James River. The house, one of the finest examples of Georgian architecture in America, was built in 1730 by William Byrd II, founder of the City of Richmond. That night I climbed up the steps of a beautiful antique bed and lay down feeling like a colonial aristocrat and enjoying every moment of it.

The next morning, I was pleasantly surprised when a maid brought me breakfast in bed. This was something new for me. I had never received such wonderful treatment. Mrs. Fisher sent one of her staff to look at Daddy's car, and when he put the key into the ignition, the car started immediately. It was one of those divine interventions that has no explanation. God had arranged our meeting, and Bruce Fisher and I became close friends.

Now, as I was preparing to go to Nepal, I had a dream about Bruce Fisher and

I Ask for Nepal

saw her adjusting a pink dress on me. She was saying, "This is for your trip to Nepal." I also saw her rolling up some carpets and she was saying something about what a bother it was. I didn't know exactly what the dream meant, but I knew that God was going to use her in some way in connection with my trip to Nepal. I made a point of not calling her in the days that followed. God was going to do it, and I would let Him do it in His own way.

In the meantime, I went to North Carolina to preach, and a sister in the church there offered to make me a dress. The dress she made was beautiful and it was pink. I was wearing it a week or so later back in Virginia when my brother called from Richmond and said, "Put your suitcase by the door. You'll be leaving soon. I'm on the way home to tell you the rest."

"What is it?" I asked excitedly.

"You got a letter from Mrs. Fisher," he said. "I held the envelope up to the light, and I could see that it has a check in it. I think it's enough for you to go to Nepal." When he returned home and I was able to open the letter, I saw that he was right. The check was for more than $1,200.

I called Mrs. Fisher immediately to thank her. I was curious. The amount was so exact that I wondered how she had arrived at the precise fare to Nepal and back. Had her travel agent used Calcutta as a turnaround point for the around-the-world fare? Or had he used New Delhi?

As it turns out, I had assumed too much. She had not thought of Nepal at all. "Let me tell you why it's such an odd amount," she offered. "I really don't like to open my house to the public, but I do it once a year for a week for the prestige of the local garden club. In return, they give me a part of the receipts. Since the money comes to me in this way, I like to do something with it that is meaningful to me. I was praying about it, and God spoke to me to send it to you. He said you would know what to do with it."

We talked for a while, and I told her about the dream. Somehow in the conversation she used the word bother and I said, "That reminds me. In my dream, I saw you rolling up your carpets and saying what a bother it was. "

"Yes," she laughed, "I always roll up the carpets when they have the open house because I don't want the women's heels to ruin them."

God had miraculously supplied my ticket to Nepal. Her offering was almost to the penny the amount I needed. For about thirty years afterward I received the same annual surprise gift from Mrs. Bruce Fisher. The money was always used for *Harvest Glory*. Especially in the years when I was traveling and living very simply, sleeping at times in airports, train stations or in the mountains in a tent without a home of my own, it was always a comfort to know that God used funds from such a gracious house to finance my journeyings.   ✸

⚜ 19 ⚜

"Greet the Brigadier"

I made stops in Hong Kong and Manila on my way to India to connect to Nepal. On the flight from Manila to Calcutta, I spoke with a gentleman who was sitting across the aisle from me. He was from Whitehall, the British equivalent of our Pentagon, and when he learned that I was going to Nepal, he said, "Please give my greetings to a dear friend. He is The Brigadier, and we have known each other for many years." He gave me the man's name, and I promised to pass along his greeting.

As I was waiting to change to the Nepalese airline in Calcutta, I started to take a picture of the Nepalese plane. It had a beautiful Nepalese flag painted on the side of it, and I was so excited about going to Nepal that I wanted the remembrance. At that moment, a British gentleman stepped up to me and said, "If I were you, I wouldn't take a photo of that. A tourist was prevented from boarding his plane recently because he had been seen taking photos at the airport. They're very sensitive about it." I was glad that he had told me in time. How terrible it would have been to get so close and be denied entrance to Nepal for something so foolish!

Most British gentlemen are very reserved, but because this man had rescued me in this way, he felt free to speak with me. He was Major Guy Potts, and when we got on the plane, he politely asked, "May I sit here beside you?" I welcomed his company. I learned that he was a major with the British military and that he was posted to Nepal.

When he told me this, I mentioned the British man I had met on the former flight and the fact that he had sent his greetings to "The Brigadier." "If you have an introduction to The Brigadier," Major Potts said to me, "then I must look after you." And he did. When we got to Kathmandu, he whisked me through customs and immigration.

In Hong Kong the Lord had spoken to me to check at the PanAm office to see what the major hotel in Kathmandu was and to make a reservation to stay there. I had made a reservation at the Hotel Royal, and now I learned that Major Potts would be staying there, too.

After Major Potts had seen me safely to the hotel, he disappeared for awhile. When he came back, he said, "I hope you don't mind, but I have taken the lib-

I Ask for Nepal

erty of arranging an invitation for both of us to the British Embassy tonight to meet the British climbers who have just conquered one of the major peaks of the Annapurna Mountain Range [a section of the Himalayan Mountains]." I spent a very enjoyable first evening in Kathmandu, meeting the British Ambassador, the members of the British expedition and others whom the Ambassador had invited to this special reception.

The next afternoon, the major said to me, "I have to fly to our headquarters in Dharan, the eastern part of Nepal [where the famous Gurkhas were stationed], but I didn't want to leave you without knowing some Americans here. I went over this morning and spoke with the secretary at the American Embassy. They are giving a party tonight for several senators who are in town. The First Secretary will pick you up," and he gave me a time to be ready.

At the party at the home of the First Secretary that night, I met my first Nepalese official. He asked me what brought me to Nepal, and I told him that I had come to see the King. "Oh, all you Americans want to see the King," he said. "Why do you want to see him?"

I answered that I had recently read a poem the King wrote, and because I wrote a little poetry myself, I wanted to discuss the poem with His Majesty. I had indeed seen a poem the King had written in which he expressed his search for God. His Majesty King Mahendra, considered by his people to be a god himself, was willing to write of his own search for God.

The gentleman was a little tipsy, and he asked me how I had arrived at the reception. When I told him the First Secretary had been kind enough to pick me up at my hotel, he said, "Well then, I'll take you home." I silently prayed that if this was not supposed to be, something would intervene to prevent it. I later saw that a very sophisticated New York woman was drawing him deep into conversation. I heaved a sigh of relief that the Lord was taking care of me.

Toward the end of the evening, however, the man returned, intent on taking me home. He had been drinking steadily throughout the evening, and I was dreading a scene. "Are you ready to go?" he asked.

Before I could answer, the First Secretary appeared and, slapping the man warmly on the back, said, "How is the Chief of Protocol tonight?" I knew in that moment that God had arranged the meeting. This man was important to my stay in Nepal, just how important I would soon learn.

Because the officials of Nepal desired to keep the kingdom closed to the outside world, visas were only issued for six days. Even my visa, issued by the Nepali Ambassador to the United Nations, was only valid for that short time. The Chief of Protocol was the only man in the nation who had the authority to extend visas. The Lord had been good to me to allow me to meet him the second night I was in Nepal.

81

The following evening, I had dinner with the Chief of Protocol. During the course of the evening, I said to him, "You need to know the Lord."

"I've seen Him," he said.

"You've seen Him?" I asked.

"Yes," he answered. Then he thought better of it and shook it off. "No, no, no!" He was upset with himself for saying as much as he had.

I wasn't about to let him off the hook that easily. "When did you see Him?" I insisted. "Please tell me." After some coaxing he finally told me his story.

Big-game hunting is one of the popular sports in the Himalayan Mountains, and hunters from all over the world commonly fly to Nepal to hunt. This man, a cousin to the King, had been on a hunt with the King and other members of the royal family when he was lost in treacherous mountain terrain. When he realized that he was hopelessly lost, he called out to God for help, and a Shepherd, holding a lamb in His arms, appeared to him, taking him by the hand and leading him to a place of safety. He did not know that our Scriptures call Jesus the Good Shepherd, yet he looked at me as he said, "The thing that bothers me about you is that you look like Him."

I told him that night about the brother in our church who had the vision of the King's crown and how I had seen it in the painting in the Nepalese Embassy in Washington, D.C. He seemed very touched by that. "I know the painting," he said. "I was the one who gave it to the Embassy."

God had been preparing all the details. My mistake in entering the Embassy in Washington had probably happened just so that I could retell the story and touch this man's heart, thus opening him up to God. My visa was extended, and I ended up staying in Nepal, not six days, but six months.

From the day I arrived in Kathmandu, I was invited to one embassy function after another. I was in a different embassy nearly every night. I was not immediately aware of all the reasons God was doing this, but I later came to the conclusion that He was teaching me how to handle myself in social situations. I had no background for diplomatic circles, yet before long I had met all the various ambassadors in Kathmandu. ✳

⚓ 20 ⚓

"Four Thousand Feet Above Sea Level"

The Hotel Royal was a very interesting place indeed. For starters, it was located in the Kathmandu Valley, one of the most beautiful spots in the world. The valley lies at about four thousand feet above sea level, and is a place where people of many Himalayan regions gather.

Since the Royal was the finest hotel in town, people from many nations visiting Nepal, for hunting and climbing, as well as diplomats, businessmen, and even visiting royals from other countries, stayed there. There was a large fireplace in the hotel around which guests gathered to tell their most interesting hunting and mountain-climbing stories.

One of the highlights of the early part of my stay in the country was meeting and speaking with a large team of National Geographic explorers brought over to do research and filming in Nepal. They all stayed in the Royal and I was able to listen to them share their experiences in the Nepali mountains.

Besides being one of the last remaining Shangri-las in the world, Nepal drew people looking for fine Tibetan rugs. There was a large community of Tibetans living in Kathmandu, and many people came to the country just for that.

Boris, the Russian manager of the hotel, was quite a personality. He had been written up in many magazines for his many adventures. When he was young, he had danced in the Diaglev Ballet. Afterward, he had lived for many years in France. He married a Danish lady named Inger. She had gone back to Copenhagen for a visit, and was not there at the time, but her mother (whom everyone called Ma Scott) was there. She liked me and looked after me like a daughter.

Since he ran the most important hotel in town, Boris had entertained many famous people, including Her Majesty Queen Elizabeth and Prince Philip. He arranged exotic picnics as they rode on the back of elephants through *The Terae*, the jungle area of Nepal. He had many friends among the royalty of other countries as well, especially among the Europeans.

On many evenings I was invited to special parties in Boris' penthouse. His mother-in-law made sure I was included on the guest list, so I met many well-known personalities from Europe and other parts of the world, and heard them tell their wonderful stories. One of the people I met through Boris' mother-in-law, was the famous Peter Aufschnsfter. The book, *Seven Years in Tibet,* had been written about his adventures. He was a very private person and didn't attend any receptions, but I met him on several occasions while I was there. He was a good friend of Ma Scott and Boris, and would stop by to see them. After she had introduced me to Aufschneider, I saw him again one day when I accompanied Boris down into *The Terai,* the lower area of Nepal, to see his pig farm. Aufschneider was there, and I got a picture of him that day. An Austrian, Aufschneider had met a Tibetan woman and was living in the Tibetan style. After that, when he was near the Royal, he sometimes came by to say hello.

The hotel served wonderful Nepali food. It was similar to Indian food in many ways, but it had its own little touches that made it unique and special.

This was going to be an interesting stay.

Time sped by very quickly and before I knew it Christmas had arrived. It was the first time I could ever remember not being with other believers at Christmas time. On Christmas Day, I came down to the dining hall, only to find it totally empty of guests. Everyone else in the hotel had been up late the night before partying and had not yet gotten up. The menu was fabulous — wild boar and turkey and ham and everything to go with it, and there were many waiters hovering near ready to serve me, but suddenly I was no longer hungry. Christmas is people, and without people, I couldn't enjoy the special Christmas meal. I quietly pushed my seat back, got up and went to my room. I didn't eat that day. Such was the atmosphere of Nepal.   ✻

⚔ 21 ⚔

"Walk, As It Were, On Tiptoes"

Nepal was not really open to the Gospel. Although there were more than one hundred missionaries (one hundred and twenty-six to be exact) living in various parts of the country, they were "silent missionaries." To gain entry into Nepal, they had signed a pledge stating that they would never speak of Jesus. Their hope was that through their smiles and their demonstration of love as they cared for the sick, fed the hungry or taught someone to speak English, Christ would be revealed to the people.

I knew this fact before arriving in Nepal and realized that what I was about to do might be considered illegal and might anger some people. Soon after I arrived I went to speak to the president of the United Mission to Nepal and told him that I had come to speak to the Nepalese Royal Family about Jesus Christ. I said that he would not be seeing me again until just before I left the country because I did not want to jeopardize the position of the missionaries and their organization.

That first week Nepal had been so enjoyable that it somehow seemed to me to be a very "normal" place. The Lord had told me before I left to be careful, to "walk, as it were, on tiptoes," but that hardly seemed necessary now. How little I knew!

There really were no churches to speak of in Nepal. A few Christians met for Sunday morning service in a building belonging to the USAID program. The British ambassador and several others attended these services, and I started attending the first Sunday I was in Nepal.

That first week I met Stephanie Vernon from Pennsylvania. She had been living in Nepal for several years, teaching English and the Bible to monks in the Tibetan monasteries in Kathmandu. She was living at Bodhnarth, a Tibetan temple complex, but she had another small apartment elsewhere in the city. She invited me to go with her to her apartment for lunch. She was very interested in Christian fellowship, and she hoped that we could spend some time together in prayer.

After lunch we started to pray. In the midst of our prayer, a young Nepali boy interrupted us to say that the police were coming. I was twenty-four years old, and suddenly I was facing the prospect of years in a Nepali prison.

Before she went to answer the door, Stephanie showed me a place to hide. I hid there and waited until it seemed that everyone had gone. When I came out, I found that they had taken Stephanie away. I later learned that they had taken her to the border with India and were planning to put her out of the country. Before they could do that, God intervened for her, and she was able to come back to Kathmandu. Having had this experience my first Sunday afternoon in town, I suddenly understood what God had meant, and I got back up on my tip-toes and was more careful from then on. This was serious business.

On New Year's Eve, I was with the other guests in the hotel dining room. When I returned to my room it was on fire. I could not, at first, tell how bad the fire was because of the dense smoke. The only thing I was really concerned about was my Bible and I went dashing through the smoke to get to it. It was laying on the bed, and the bed was on fire. Flames had totally surrounded the Bible and had even burned part of the bookmark that was hanging out of it, but the Bible itself was untouched. I grabbed it and rushed back out of the room, my clothes saturated with smoke. The next day, when I went to church, I had to go in the same beaded sweater I had worn the night before. All my other clothes were lost in the fire. Obviously, it had been some type of attack on my life and my possessions, but God was protecting me.

At one embassy party, I met the Indonesian ambassador, and said something to him about being a Christian. "Well, I am too," he said.

"Why haven't I ever seen you at church?" I asked.

"I didn't know there was a church here," he said. After that, he would pick me up and take me to church. He was a very sincere Christian and befriended me in those difficult times. ✳

﹏ 22 ﹏

"On January Twenty-first"

I arrived in Nepal in November, and by the time my birthday rolled around, on January 21 of the following year, I still had not met any members of the Royal Family. I knew that God had sent me, but I needed to have some sign from the Lord. I said to the Lord that day, "Lord, I want You to do something today that will bring to pass this word You have given. I have met many ambassadors and other important people, but I haven't met any immediate member of the Royal Family." Still, several days went by, and nothing apparently had happened.

I was invited to the Indian embassy to attend their National Day celebrations on January 26. That evening I met the First Secretary of the Indian Embassy, and he invited me to dinner several nights later. When I arrived at his house for dinner, I was introduced to His Royal Highness Prince Basundhara, the brother of the King. It was a small dinner party and quite formal because the First Secretary was meeting the prince for the first time. There were only five of us there that night.

In the course of conversation, the First Secretary said, "And Your Royal Highness, when did you decide to leave London to return to Nepal?"

The prince answered, "It was only recently, on January twenty-first, that I decided to come back to Kathmandu to attend the wedding of Princess Shanti [his niece and the king's eldest daughter]." When he said January 21, I knew that he was the answer to my prayer.

During the course of the evening I slipped into the rest room and asked one of the ladies in attendance just how I should *namaste* or curtsy to the prince, and I stayed there a little while practicing my *namastes*, low bows with hands folded in front of my face. Later, when the prince was leaving, I approached him, bowed and said, "Your Royal Highness, I know you must be very busy, and I understand that you have come home to attend the wedding of Princess Shanti, but if you have a few minutes, I would like to speak with you about an important matter." He acknowledged that he had heard me with a slight nod, and then he got in his limousine and was driven away.

The next night I was sitting by the fireplace in the Hotel Royal when all the men suddenly jumped up and begin to bow. I had been staying in the hotel for going on three months, but I had never seen guests acting like this. I looked in the direction everyone was bowing, and saw, coming down the corridor of the hotel, His Royal Highness Prince Basundhara.

The prince came directly to me and said, "Are you ready to talk about that important matter?" I said that I was, and he told me to get my coat, that he would take me back to his palace. Although he had been living in London for years, he had several palaces in Nepal, all of them fully staffed.

In the car on the way to the palace, we made small talk about the country, but when we were seated in his palace, the prince turned to me and got right to the point. "Now, what was so important?" he asked.

I explained to him that I had not even heard of his country and knew nothing of it until my mother had received a vision from God and had prophesied that I should come to Kathmandu and speak to the Royal Family about Jesus Christ. "Since you are a member of the Royal Family," I said, "I want to speak to you about Jesus." He told me to speak on, and for the next four hours I spoke to the prince about the Lord. Before the night was over, God did something wonderful in his heart.

The next night, I was invited to dine in the palace. "Last night was the happiest night of my life," the prince told me. Although he had been in the mission hospital with two coronaries, the nurses there, because of their legal commitment to silence, had not spoken to him about Christ.

"What can I do to help you?" he asked.

"Help me meet the other members of the family," I answered.

The Royal Family of Nepal was large and some of its members had not been in Kathmandu for ten years, since the coronation of the King. Some of them lived in the hill stations of India, and others lived in Europe. Now they were all gathering again for the wedding of Princess Shanti. "You know them all," I told him. "I trust you to know whom I should meet. Whatever you want to arrange is fine with me."

In the coming weeks, Prince Bashundara arranged something every day. If the King was having a breakfast or lunch, the prince would have a dinner at his palace. If the Grand Palace was having a dinner, he would have a breakfast or lunch to which I was invited with several members of the Royal Family that I had not met yet. The very next night, in fact, I was having dinner with several brothers-in-law of the King and was able to tell them about the Lord.

I had flown in some beautiful leather-bound New Testaments from India, gift boxed, for me to present to the members of the Royal Family. They were all in English because all the members of the Royal Family spoke English well.

The Lord used Prince Basundhara, and one after another, I met and witnessed to most of the members of the Royal Family.

I Ask for Nepal

Prince Basundhara's life also came under attack. Soon after the night I laid my hands on him and prayed, I was awakened one night and sensed that he was in danger. I prayed until I felt the assurance that he was safe. The next day he came to the hotel early. "I want to tell you what happened last night," he said.

"No," I interrupted. "Before you tell me what happened to you, I want to tell you what happened to me." I told him how I had gone to bed earlier than usual and how the Lord had awakened me to pray for him.

"Oh, you saved my life," he said. "You saved my life." He was driving home from the king's palace after dinner, when he came to a spot where road crews had been repairing the road, and his tire struck a round rock that had been left on the surface. He lost control of his car and was headed over a deep embankment when the car suddenly lunged sideways and struck a pole, saving him. Otherwise his car would have gone into the river.

"Did you think to pray?" I asked.

"Ruth," he answered, "all night long I could feel your hand on my head praying for me." That and other experiences like it through the years let me know how important it is to lay hands on people as we pray for them. In times of need they remember the weight of glory that they felt and the presence of God that comes through the laying on of hands and the ministry to an individual.

Within a few short weeks, I was able to meet every member of the Royal Family, except the King and Queen, and one brother, Prince Himalaya.

One evening Prince Basundhara and I were speaking about the problem of the Nepali constitution prohibiting conversion. "Well, remember," he said to me, "you're going to have lunch tomorrow with my nephew." It took me a moment to realize what he was saying. I had forgotten that his nephew was the crown prince and would one day become the King. Of course, he was the one with whom I should be talking.

At lunch the next day, I spoke with the crown prince about the need for the constitutional ruling to be changed so that Nepali men and women could have a right to choose the god they wanted to serve without the fear of being imprisoned. I quoted to him the words of Jesus:

And this gospel of the kingdom shall be preached in all the world for a witness unto all nations; and then shall the end come. Matthew 24:14

"I believe that the Lord allowed your grandfather, King Tribhuwan, to overthrow the power of the Ranas so that this scripture can be fulfilled," I told him. For some one hundred years, the family of the Prime Minister of Nepal, the Rana family, had controlled the politics of the kingdom. It was only around 1955 that the king's family had regained control over the government. This happened during the rule of King Tribhuwan, the grandfather of the crown prince with whom I was speaking.

The crown prince dropped his head and said, "Perhaps you're right." That crown prince is the present-day King of Nepal, His Majesty King Birendra. We played ping pong together.   ✸

≈ 23 ≈

"What Do You Suggest That I Read First?"

Spiritual people in Richmond had been very excited about my trip to Nepal, and right up until the day I had left, Mother and I were receiving phone calls from those who had visions or dreams to tell us. One of those was a Lutheran lady who called to say she had seen me in a vision in Nepal and saw that I came to a very narrow place, a place of danger, and didn't seem to know which way to go. Then she saw a man with a ruby in his hand come, take me by the hand and lead me to safety. The fact that he had a ruby in his hand made her think that he was a member of the Royal Family. I knew that at some point, when my life was in danger, someone would appear to lead me out of danger.

Besides my visits with the Royal Family, I was busy with receptions and other embassy events. In Kathmandu I met for the first time officials of the Israeli Embassy. While I was there, in fact, President Zalman Shazar came to Nepal for a visit. His niece Shulamith Katznelson later became my friend in Israel. My life was broadened in many ways during this period of time.

Soon after my arrival in Nepal, I met Prem Predhan, the man who had only recently been released after spending nine years in prison for baptizing nine converts. I was able to strengthen him and help him in the faith. Later, I invited him to come to America and paid his way so that he could come.

During that first trip to Nepal, I also became familiar with another Himalayan Kingdom, Bhutan. The brother of the Prime Minister of Bhutan and his wife came to live in Kathmandu for a season. I was so anxious to get a glimpse of him. When you love a region as much as I did the Himalayan region, everything about it is exciting to you. When I finally saw him one day in one of the hotels, he cursed, using the Lord's name in vain. I spoke up and said, "Oh, I'm so glad to see that you know His name!" This relationship only enhanced our desire to visit Nepal.

I met people I was not expecting to meet. One night, during a reception at the Hotel Royal, I was speaking with a man I had just met. I wasn't yet sure just who he was. I asked him if he had read the New Testament, and he said yes, he had read it when he was a young boy in school, but he hadn't read it since. I asked him if he would like to read it again, and he said he would, but he didn't have a Bible. "I have an extra one in my room," I said. "If you like, I'll go and get it for you." He was pleased, so I excused myself, went to my room, got the New Testament and brought it back to him. It was a beautifully bound leather edition in a special gift box.

Just as I was presenting the New Testament, a lady reporter with Reuters News Service walked by. For some reason, she had taken a dislike to me and would often say unkind things about me. When she saw that I was giving a New Testament to this man, she said in a loud voice for everyone to hear, "My God, what will this girl do next?"

I ignored this, thinking that it was nothing more than her usual bad humor.

"What do you suggest I read first?" the gentleman asked.

"You appear to be a man of action," I answered him. "I suggest that you read the book of Acts. It speaks about the early church and the acts of the Apostles in those beginning days."

"Will you find it for me?" he asked.

I took the lid off the box, opened the New Testament, turned to the book of Acts and put a marker there. Then I put the New Testament back in the box, closed it and handed it back to him.

"I promise you I will read it," he said. "I want to give you my card. Please come and see me so that we can discuss the New Testament together."

When I looked at his card, I learned that he was the Russian Ambassador to Nepal. Those were still Cold War days, and I immediately understood why the lady with Reuters had reacted as she had. If I had known who the man was, I might have been more hesitant to speak with him. Thank God I wasn't, because his heart was hungry for the things of God.   ✳

⚹ 24 ⚹

"Lest I Sleep the Sleep of Death"

I was in regular communication with home and my family knew, in general, what was happening with me in Nepal. They were praying, as a family and as a church, for my safety and my success. One night Mother, who has knelt every night beside her bed and read a Bible passage and said her prayers since she was a small child, came upon a verse that troubled her spirit:

> *Consider and hear me, O LORD my God: lighten mine eyes, LEST I SLEEP*
> *THE SLEEP OF DEATH;*
> *Lest mine enemy say, I have prevailed against him; and those that trouble me*
> *rejoice when I am moved.*
> *But I have trusted in thy mercy; my heart shall rejoice in thy salvation.*
>
> Psalm 13:3-5

Those words, *"lest I sleep the sleep of death,"* kept going over and over in her spirit. She was sure that God was showing her that I was in danger of sleeping the sleep of death and she prayed for my safety in Nepal. After praying, she felt confident that God had answered her, and she went to sleep.

The next night, when Mother was saying her prayers before going to bed, she opened the Bible to the exact same portion of scripture again. This alarmed her, and she woke Daddy up and told him about it. They prayed and believed God together for my safety.

When this same thing happened the third night in a row, she woke Daddy again, and this time she suggested that maybe they should bring me home from such a dangerous place. My father's answer was: "Well, we might as well find out right now if the Lord has called her. If He's called her, He'll take care of her."

When I went into the hotel dining hall one morning, I noticed that everyone was looking at me in a strange way. "Where have you been?" someone asked. "We've been missing you the last few days."

"I just saw you yesterday," I said.

"No you didn't," they answered, "we haven't seen you for several days."

When I checked to see what day it was, I discovered that they were right. Somehow several days of my life had mysteriously disappeared. I came to the

93

conclusion that I had been poisoned and had slept for several days. The amazing thing was that when I did wake up, I felt fine. I would not have known that anything was wrong at all if it were not for those who had missed me. God had done a wonderful miracle to preserve my life. Without knowing it, I had taken on some new enemies. ✳

⚑ 25 ⚑

"Auntie, May I Walk on Your Back?"

I made friends with many of the local Christians. That first Sunday, when I went to church in Kathmandu I met Betty Mendies and her two sons, Charles and Thomas. Betty and her husband Tom were operating a local hotel, the Everest. She was Canadian and he Anglo-Indian. They had met in Calcutta where she was a missionary with the Salvation Army. Later, after they were married, she and Tom had decided, both for the sake of business and the sake of the Gospel, to move to Kathmandu. Betty often brought the boys to the hotel and had a meal with me.

Charles, who is so well-known these days in evangelical circles worldwide, especially after his own time of imprisonment in Nepal for the Gospel, was just a boy then. He would say to me, "Auntie, may I walk on your back?" He thought he was giving me the greatest massage in the world. He was a very loving and caring person. Later, he came to Virginia and lived with my brother in his house for a year, and my brother became like a father to him.

When my brother died, Charles wanted desperately to get to the funeral. He had been planning to bring his whole family to the United States, but it was difficult for him to make all the necessary connections in such a short time. In the end, we had to arrange for a private plane to fly him and his family from New York to Richmond so that they could get to the funeral service before it was over.

Betty Mendies is still in Nepal, looking after children, and blessing the Body of Christ there. Charles and Susan Mendies and their family have a wonderful ministry in New Delhi that blesses politicians in the Indian Parliament as well as those in other countries.

Everywhere Charles goes he is known for his spirit of excellence and his deference to others. He clearly has a servant's heart and, because of it, God has raised him up to serve in higher and higher places.

When Mother Theresa died, Charles was asked by her order to coordinate the details of the funeral with the Indian government and military. It was a very ticklish situation because she was a beloved Christian in a Hindu state. The night before the funeral the Indian general in charge of the funeral arrangements told

95

Charles he wanted someone carrying the cross just ahead of the government officials. Charles replied that it would not be necessary to do this, that Mother Theresa would not have required it, nor would her order. The general replied that the government of India wanted a cross. It was the symbol of Christianity, and it should be there before this great Christian lady.

What a great gesture that was! Not only did the Indian government give Mother Theresa a state funeral, but with all the honors accorded to a Christian.

As in her life, so in her death, Mother Theresa was used to bring down the caste system. Wealthy businessmen and people of high degree stood in line to pass her bier, next to former lepers and untouchables. Together they felt the bonding of the moment, as they grieved for one whom they fondly called "Mother." Charles humbly assisted them all.   ✳

≈ 26 ≈

"I'm Taking You to My Palace"

As we moved toward spring, I was scheduled to meet the King and Queen of Nepal. Just about that time there was an assassination attempt on the king's life, and all appointments were cancelled. Prince Basundhara arrived unexpectedly and unannounced at the hotel early that very morning. A waiter knocked on my door to say that the prince was in the lobby, waiting to see me. Aside from the fact that I was not expecting him, knowing that he was there so early seemed highly unusual, for he was not a morning person.

Asking a prince what he was doing and why, was not proper, so when I went down to the lobby, I greeted him as always and asked him how he was. "Get your coat on," he said. "I'm taking you to my palace."

I didn't ask any questions. I got my coat, and we left.

When we got to the palace, a servant brought us breakfast beside the pool, and we ate. Still nothing was said about why I was there.

I finally came to the conclusion that the Lord was just giving me another opportunity to speak with him about spiritual things. "Why don't you have a servant bring your Bible," I suggested. I had given him a lovely Thompson Chain Reference Bible. It was now brought, and we sat by the pool for several hours more going over some of the Scriptures together.

When lunchtime arrived, we were still talking, so again we were served beside the pool. We finished eating, but still the Prince did not seem inclined to terminate our session. By late afternoon, we were still sitting there talking about the things of the Lord. Then the Prince was summoned to take a telephone call. When he returned, he sat down again, and we talked for a little while more. Finally, he asked me if I was ready to go back to the hotel. I told him I was, and someone was sent to accompany me.

That night I learned that there had been an assassination attempt against the King. The prince had obviously known of the unrest and had decided to protect me. He never offered an explanation, and I never asked for one. I did remember the vision the Lutheran lady had received about a man with a ruby in his hand who would come and take me to a place of safety.

When all the king's appointments were cancelled, I was disappointed. I had been in Nepal already six months and, although I had met many members of the Royal Family, nothing could replace meeting the King himself. I had become good friends with Prince Basundhara (who had come for the wedding and had stayed all this time). I had become good friends with Lendrup Dorji, brother of the Prime Minister of Bhutan, and his wife, Glenda. As I prayed about whether to stay longer, the Lord said to me, "Go back to America, and you will meet the King with greater honor."

As I prepared to leave Nepal, it was with great awe. God had been so good to me. At first, because my visa was only for six days, I had been staying in the hotel on a daily rate. After I received my visa extension, however, I was able to switch to a monthly rate, and they moved me to the top floor. That floor had an outside courtyard, and there were steps leading to it from the outside. A person could actually ascend those steps without going through the hotel. At night, when I was returning to my room, that part of the hotel was never well lit. When I looked back on it, I was amazed to realize that during six months in Nepal, I had never once felt fear. Although I had been in some very awkward situations, I had always felt the peace of God. What a miracle!

When I first went to Nepal, the number of Christian believers in the country was reckoned at something less than one hundred. Now, I understand, there are more than one hundred thousand believers in Nepal.

When I got back home to America after six months, I was greeted by my very thin mother. She had promised God when I left for Nepal that she would fast the whole time I was away. Because I had a visa for only six days, she was not expecting my stay to be so long. Still, she had remained faithful to her promise to God, taking only some liquid nourishment all during those six months and believing God for the accomplishment of His purposes and for my safety. ✳

⚓ 27 ⚓

"A Broadtailed Sheep"

The summer after I came home from Nepal, I was preaching one afternoon at summer campmeeting from Psalm 47:

> *He shall subdue the people under us, and the nations under our feet. He shall choose our inheritance for us, the excellency of Jacob whom he loved. Selah.*   Psalm 47:3-4

As I was preaching that day, I said to the people, "Since coming back from Nepal, I have had a great desire to go to South America. I purposely am not reading anything about that part of the world right now, because if I were to choose where I would go, I would choose some exciting place like Rio de Janeiro, Brazil, or Buenos Aires, Argentina, or one of the other well-known places. I prefer to let the Lord choose for me."

After I finished preaching, I was kneeling at the altar when my father came and laid his hand on my head. I fell out under the power of God and began to speak in tongues. Like most Americans, I knew only a few words of Spanish, but somehow I knew that I was speaking in tongues in fluent Spanish at that moment. After a while I heard myself saying, *"Tarata, Tarata, Tarata,"* and I sensed that this was the name of a place in South America where I was to go.

I got up from the altar very excited and started toward my parents' house, where I was still living, to find an atlas and look up the name *Tarata*. As I was crossing the campground, I met a young woman who was attending the campmeeting. I had seen her sitting in the services drawing sketches of everyone and making notes. She said to me now, "I would like to draw a picture for you."

At that moment, I had my mind on this word *Tarata*. I politely suggested that she walk with me to my parents' house, and she agreed to accompany me.

When we got to the house, I got the atlas and sat at the kitchen table preparing to look for a place called *Tarata*, while the young lady took a piece of paper and a pencil I gave her and began to sketch. I excitedly opened the index to the T's. No *Tarata* appeared on the first page. I was about to turn to the second page when she said, "There's a river that goes this way. Then it goes that way. Here, in the middle, is a broadtailed sheep."

I looked at her a little askance and asked, "Did you have a vision?"

"Look," she answered, "Just let me draw this for you." But I sensed that there was something to what she was saying.

"What else did you see?" I asked. As I began to prod her, she told me more. "Bark canoes" and "Indians" and "broadtailed sheep" were among the things she proceeded to describe to me.

While she had been talking, my fingers had been turning the pages of the atlas trying to find Tarata. I had found the name in the index. Tarata was in Peru. I turned to the specified page, and when I looked down at it now, I saw the exact same map this young lady had just finished drawing. There was a river that came one way; then it went the other way; and in the middle stood a broadtailed sheep.

When she saw this she was suddenly uncomfortable. She was afraid that I would go to South America based on her map, and if I failed she would be responsible.

I said to her, "Don't worry about it. You heard the story about my six-month trip to Nepal. When I went there to witness to the Royal Family, I didn't even have a map, and God kept me by miracles. He is sending me to South America now, and there is nothing to worry about."

I had a word, the name of a place, and I had a map.

During that final week of campmeeting, my father took an offering for me to go to Peru. I would fly into Lima, then take another flight from Lima to Tacna, the closest airport to Tarata. Tarata, it appeared, was a very small place — just how small I was soon to learn.

I found a gentleman in the Tacna airport who spoke English and said to him, "Excuse me, sir, could you tell me how to get to Tarata?"

He said, "Why do you want to go to that God-forsaken place?"

Normally, I would have just said I was a tourist, but since he said it was a God-forsaken place, it didn't sound like a tourist spot, so that reason was out. I was momentarily dumbfounded and left mumbling. Then I blurted out, "Well, God spoke to me to go to Tarata."

Then he remembered, "There's a missionary who goes there once a month. I'll take you to his house."

I knew I wasn't lost. I had traveled, led by the voice of God and by vision and revelation, for many years now, and I didn't feel like I was on unfamiliar territory. All I needed to know was how to get to Tarata.

I was always careful not to make local missionaries feel that I was just another Pentecostal on a wild goose chase, and that they had to feel obligated to look after me because I was stranded. "No!" I protested, "Just tell me how to get there. Do I go by donkey? Do I go on a truck? Is there a bus? How do I get there? Do I go by train? What is the manner of transportation to get to Tarata?"

I Ask for Peru

He thought a while longer and finally, shaking his head, said, "Lady, I'm sorry, but I don't know how to get to Tarata. This missionary I'm telling you about goes there once a month. I think it's best if I take you to his house." Well, it seemed like I had no other option at this point, so I consented.

When he knocked on the door of the missionary's house, a gentleman came to the door, and my new-found friend spoke to him in Spanish. He explained to him the gist of our conversation, that I was from America, was saying that God had told me to go to Tarata and, because he didn't know how to get there, he had brought me to this house.

As he heard this news, a broad smile began to break upon the face of the missionary, and, although I didn't know why, he seemed as glad to see me as if I were some long-lost relative. I was welcomed with open arms.

I soon learned that they were part of a group of Irish Baptist missionaries who had been working in Tacna and other parts of southern Peru for more than thirty years. They also had a work in Tarata, a small, tribal mountainous village. Recently their work in that village had come under spiritual attack, and they had met in Tacna for an entire week to decide what to do with the church in Tarata.

One of the most serious problems was that one of their missionaries had developed a severe heart condition and, because Tarata lay at such a high altitude, his doctors had advised him against going back there. The other missionaries had tried to get someone from Lima or from other areas of Peru to help out, but they had been unsuccessful. Now they were faced with the decision to close the church until help could be found. They hated the thought of closing it, but they didn't know how to keep it going.

Being good Baptists, each day they would read from some book of devotions. They regularly read Oswald Chambers' *My Utmost for His Highest*, selections from Amy Carmichael's devotions and Mrs. Cowman's *Streams in the Desert*. The past week they had noticed something very interesting about their devotions. They kept coming across the same passage about God sending Philip to the Ethiopian eunuch. After this had happened several times, they began to get the message and prayed, "God, if you could send Philip to the Ethiopian eunuch, you can send somebody to help us! Send somebody from somewhere. Send anybody from anywhere." When I arrived, they knew that I was the answer to their desperate prayers.

"We didn't think God would send someone all the way from North America," they said. They were too polite to say, "We didn't think that God would send a woman," and "We didn't expect that God would send a Pentecostal." I just happened to be the person available at the moment.

I prayed for that sick missionary, and the Lord healed him. He was thrilled and agreed to take me to Tarata. There we had such wonderful success in the short time I had available that many of the other problems of Tarata were also resolved.

As it turned out, one of the missionary families had become so discouraged over this whole matter that they had decided to leave Peru after thirty years of service. Now they were encouraged to stay on and to complete their assigned work.

Tarata was just as the young woman had described it, an Indian village built high in the Andes Mountains at the bend of a river. Most of coastal Peru is inhabited by Spanish-speaking people, but God had shown her Indians and bark canoes, and the people of Tarata had them.

I had never been in a sheep-raising community before, so I knew nothing of the various types of sheep. The sheep raised in Tarata, it turned out, were of the broadtail variety, just as God had shown her. That experience proved to be very important. We were moving into something new in God.　　　※

⚜ 28 ⚜

"Someone to Carry My Books"

That fall we fixed up and moved into a church building our congregation in Richmond had purchased on Hull Street, and after moving in we all spent much time in fasting and prayer, seeking the face of God and rejoicing in the goodness of the Lord for giving us the new facility. During this time God began to give us a series of visions and revelations.

One night, for instance, I was awakened by the Lord and He said to me, "Chad." I didn't know where Chad was, so I looked it up in the atlas and found that it was a country in West Africa. I knew that Chad would be part of my next trip.

Sometimes the names the Lord gave us were of people rather than places, and I filed those away in my memory, knowing that their importance would become clear with time.

One day a friend had a vision of a house, and God made her to know that the house was in Ireland. It was a great house, with unusual chimneys and unusual windows. It was architecturally interesting. Every window in the house seemed to be shaped differently, for instance, and all the chimneys in the house were different as well.

In the vision she saw the two of us entering the house, and when we turned through a doorway, we were facing the music conservatory. As we went on into the conservatory, she saw a lady seated in a wheelchair. We prayed for her, and the Lord healed her.

The house she had seen in the vision was so unusual that she decided to go to the library of Randolph Macon College in Ashland and look through some books on special houses to see if she could find it. She found a wonderful book called *Great Houses of Ireland* and came back with the book, very excited to show me that it contained an actual photograph of the house she had seen in her vision and described to me. It was known as the Rostrevor House and it was located in Rostrevor, Ireland. I knew that I must include Ireland in my next itinerary.

Later that year, God told me to take the young lady who had the vision with me on my next trip. When the time came and we were packing, she said to me, "I'll put all your Bibles and things in this attaché case, and I'll carry the books."

When she said that, I suddenly remembered a word of prophecy God had given me some time before. He said that He would give me "someone to carry my books." That had seemed like a very strange word because I never traveled with books. My Bible and a concordance were usually all that I had along. Occasionally I took a small atlas, but nothing more. Books are heavy and make travel difficult. Now I understood the word. The Spirit of God is faithful in fulfilling every word that He has spoken unto us — even when we don't perceive at the time what He is doing.

Little by little, God had dropped important revelations into our spirits, and by the time we got ready to go, we had ten or twelve major revelations to work on. We were learning that you can travel for God without an address, but you don't dare go without a revelation.

I had been traveling for the Lord now for a number of years, usually alone, and I had gone from initially living very simply in each place to a higher level of existence. Now, however, as I took someone along, God dropped us back to the bottom so that she could experience all the joys of living very simply and trusting the Lord moment by moment. I was also reduced, because if I had had money I would have given it to her, and she would not have had the opportunity to cultivate and develop her faith. For this trip, God gave us only enough to buy our tickets to Belfast, Ireland, with very little left over for daily expenses.

✳

29

"This Is the Conservatory"

When we got to the Rostrevor house, we learned that it had been given to a Catholic religious order, and the sisters of that order were now occupying it. As one of the nuns was showing us around, we came to one of the rooms, and she said, "This is the conservatory." It was the room that had been seen in the vision. We told the sister about the vision and about the lady that had been seen in the wheelchair. "That would be the former owner," she said. "She is in the hospital because she has fallen and broken her hip." She gave us the name of the lady's niece and a visit to the niece led to our going to the hospital to pray for the woman in the wheelchair, and God healed her.

It has never ceased to amaze me how concerned the Lord is for each of us. He loved that woman so much that he gave the detailed vision that brought us to the hospital to pray for her.

It had not been very long since I returned from Peru and worked with the Irish Baptists, so I thought we should stop by their headquarters in Ireland and get to know their staff there.

We flew into Belfast and went to visit the Irish Baptist Mission Board. The leaders of the Irish Baptists in Ireland were very happy to meet me. They had received reports of God's supernatural intervention in Tacna and Tarata, and those reports had now been widely circulated among the Baptist churches in Northern Ireland. While we were sitting and talking with them, the Lord reminded me of a name He had dropped into my spirit before leaving America: McCullough. I turned to one of the leaders and said, "Excuse me, but would you know anybody by the name of McCullough?"

"Oh, yes," the man answered, "that's the name of the only board member who's not present today. He's our treasurer."

I said, "Well, God gave me his name before I left America, so I would like to meet him." The meeting was arranged.

God wanted to have us meet all the board members so that they could all hear firsthand the many stories of victory from Peru, and they rejoiced that their efforts were bearing fruit.

We preached for the Baptists of Belfast and, through that ministry, God began to open other doors. One of the places we were invited was called

Cookestown. My associate had had a vision before we left America and had seen a town that was just one long street. She had said to me, "Ruth, it's the strangest thing I've ever seen. Can you imagine a town that has only one long street? Behind that street I saw nothing on either side. There were no other streets. That seems very strange." When we arrived at Cookestown, it was exactly as she had seen in her vision.

In Cookestown, we were taken to pray for a lady who had cancer, and the Lord wonderfully healed her. We preached in the Baptist church there, and the Lord brought a great stirring of revival. The ease of it amazed both of us. God was doing the work.

We had many other wonderful experiences in Northern Ireland.   ✳

$\mathbf{30}$

"How Delicious It Smelled"

From Ireland we went to London, England and from London we went to Paris, France. Although I had been in London and Paris before, I had never taken time to visit the great museums and to enjoy the culture of Europe. My friend, because of her background in art and because of having lived in London, knew the museums and taught me aspects of art that have only blessed and enriched my life through the years. Later, when I would repeat some obscure fact about art, she would say, "Where did you hear that?"

"You taught me," I answered. She was always amazed that I had remembered, but it was the faithfulness of the Holy Spirit that brought these things to my remembrance when I needed them.

In each place God was giving us just enough for the next leg of the journey. That was not as horrible as many might imagine. It was a blessing in many ways. Trusting the Lord for daily provision is always a wonderful experience. Having little money was not a hindrance to our doing the Lord's work. We were blessed to believe Him for miracles as we went.

This kept us looking for the cheapest way to travel. I didn't mind that because I had always loved overland travel and found that travel by local transportation was a rewarding way of seeing places up close and of getting to know the people and their culture. Because of time constraints, I was not able to do much of that type of travel in later years, and I missed it.

From Paris we took the Orient Express. These days it has become very fashionable, but we traveled on it when it wasn't nearly as luxurious. We traveled on it third class.

On the way to Istanbul, there were some Eastern Europeans on the train. They carried along their big salamis and their long baguettes of bread. As they cut off big chunks of salami and began to devour it, the smell of it made us drool. How delicious it looked and smelled! ✳

⋙ 31 ⋘

"Hey, I Know You"

We arrived in Istanbul with six dollars and had to hunt for a very inexpensive place to stay. We settled on a student hostel, a place for university students. It was occupied by young people preparing for the professions. The rooms were unheated and, since it was snowing in Istanbul, it was freezing in the rooms. I took the mattress from another bed and the rug from the floor and put them both on top of me to try to stay warm through the night.

The little restaurants in that part of town each had one particular soup that they cooked each day and served with bread. We quickly learned the specialty of each place, so if we wanted something different on a particular day, instead of changing the soup, we changed the restaurant and had our different bowl of soup and slice of bread.

Each evening, before bedtime, we gathered with the other students around a tiny potbellied stove and had petite cups of hot tea. I'm not sure you could actually call it a potbellied stove because the pot was so small, but it was better than nothing. The delicate glass cups we drank from were only a few inches tall and about as big around as a silver dollar, so they didn't hold much. The idea was to hold the cup of hot liquid in your hands and get the warmth from it. Wonderful stories were told around that fire, and we were able to tell our share of them.

It was January or February of 1967, and we were able to tell the Turkish Muslim young people of Istanbul that very soon all of Jerusalem would be in the hands of the Jewish people. This sparked some argument and harsh comments, but at least we got our blood flowing. A few months later, during the Six-Day War, in June of 1967, the city of Jerusalem was returned to Jewish sovereignty for the first time in two thousand years.

Years later I was in New Delhi, India, and went to the Australian Embassy to get a visa. While I was waiting for my visa, a young man shouted to me from across the room. I turned to see a redheaded Turk. "Hey, I know you," he shouted. "You're the one who prophesied that the Jewish people would soon have Jerusalem, and they did!"

I remembered having seen him around the fire. "What are you doing here?" I asked.

108

I Ask for Turkey

"I'm going to be immigrating to Australia," he answered, and we had a wonderful reunion right there in the embassy of Australia in New Delhi. Our prophesy had made a great impact on him, and I couldn't help but wonder about the other young people we had met in Istanbul that winter.

In Istanbul we enjoyed going to Topkapi, the famous palace museum. We enjoyed Hyia Sophia, the famous Church of St. Sophia. We enjoyed seeing the Blue Mosque and its beautiful tile work. After a lovely time in the city, we left by local bus south to Izmir.

Making such a trip in winter was quite an experience because none of the buses were heated and it was so COLD! The frost on the inside of the windows was at least a quarter of an inch thick. It was so thick that we couldn't see out, and we sat huddled in our winter coats trying to keep warm. Many of the passengers got sick, and the Turkish conductor periodically sprinkled a lemony-scented toilet water throughout the bus in an effort to keep everyone well.

Izmir is the biblical Smyrna, and to be able to reach out and touch the people there and speak with them was a wonderful experience. Along our way, we visited other sights of the seven churches mentioned in the book of Revelation. We spent one night, for instance, in Efes, the biblical Ephesus. I remember well the little garden hotel we stayed in. Although one could hardly call it a hotel, it did have a little garden. The proprietor was kind enough to give us a fairly private area where we slept on the floor Turkish style. There was a tiny, open clay stove in the room. It was much like a campfire, but it kept us from freezing. The eggs he fixed for us the next morning were some of the best I have ever eaten. I can still picture him and remember his kindness to us.   ❋

⚜ 32 ⚜

"A Box of Oriental Sweets"

From Turkey, we crossed over the border into Syria. Border crossings were always a very exciting part of our travels. Many Americans never have these experiences because we have such a large territory with open borders. The rest of the world, however, knows the importance and the treachery of borders and border crossings. It is difficult to imagine the red tape involved in leaving one country and entering another. It has to be experienced to be appreciated.

The border of Turkey with Syria is located on a high mountain and, when we left one side and entered the other, we had to carry our luggage through a sort of no-man's land. The wind was whipping over the top of the mountain so strongly that, if it had not been for the intervention of a Syrian major who accompanied us, I might have been blown off the side of the mountain.

When we reached the Syrian Immigration and Customs area, we saw that the customs officials were trying to make a Syrian businessman pay a duty on the pistachio nuts he carried. Instead of paying the required taxes, he opened the nuts and shared them with all of us in the room. My, they were delicious!

When we finally got through Syrian Immigration and Customs we started our journey to Damascus, and the same major accompanied us. Americans are blessed in that everywhere we go, the people of other countries want to talk with us, and many times the talk is of politics. The major wanted to discuss the whole Middle East situation, and it was a very enjoyable trip.

We arrived in Damascus late, and after we checked into a small hotel, we found that everything was closed, and we could get nothing to eat. Aside from the pistachios, we hadn't eaten during the journey, so we were very pleased when the major came back carrying a box of the most delicious sweets we had ever eaten. That was my associate's introduction to the honey-rich pastries of the Middle East known as *baklava*. He had brought us a great variety to try. They were of different shapes and sizes and flavors.

We each wanted to taste everything, so we split each piece, each of us eating half. In this way, we devoured an entire box of oriental sweets between us. To this day, I love *baklava*.   ✳

110

≥ 33 ≤

"Just Wait Till We Get to Jerusalem"

From Damascus, we traveled overland to Jerusalem. My colleague had traveled extensively. When she would tell me about some of the things she had seen, I would say to her, "Just wait till we get to Jerusalem. It's different from anything you've seen anywhere in the world."

"I know Oriental marketplaces," she would answer. "I've been to Marrakech in Morocco." She wasn't expecting Jerusalem to be anything new.

"Just wait till we get to Jerusalem," I would say.

She would answer, "I've been in many ancient capitals. I know walled cities," and she would mention one or two of the walled cities she had visited.

I was sure that she was wrong and, no matter what she would say, I would always answer, "Just wait till we get to Jerusalem." Even in those days there was something very special to me about Jerusalem, and I knew that when she got there, she would experience it too.

When we got to Jerusalem, she quickly discovered that the Holy City was more than just an Oriental marketplace, more than just a walled city, more than just a Middle Eastern town. Many times after that, when we would converse with people in different parts of the world, and they would ask us what part of the world we considered to be the most wonderful, she would invariably answer Jerusalem. To this day, Jerusalem is totally in my heart and in my spirit.

We were blessed to be the guests of Brother Solomon Mattar, the Keeper of the Garden Tomb. There were some cottages on the grounds of the Garden Tomb, and he let us stay in one of them for more than a month. This afforded us sufficient time to begin to absorb the life of Jerusalem and its environs, both holy and secular.

This was Jerusalem, before the Six-Day War, and when we stood at the Intercontinental Hotel on the Mount of Olives with our Arab guide, looking west, we asked him, "Can we see any part of Jewish Jerusalem from here?"

"Oh, no," he said, "it's not possible to see Jewish Jerusalem from here." When we got to know Jerusalem better, we discovered that half of what we were seeing from that point had indeed been Jewish Jerusalem.

The hospitality of the shopkeepers in Jerusalem was exceptional. While we were looking around their shops, they would offer us tea with mint. Since we

111

wanted to learn all we could about Oriental rugs and other Oriental artifacts, we accepted these invitations, and someone would quickly go out and bring back hummus and pita bread or kabob and shashlick, pieces of lamb meat on a skewer, cooked over coals of fire. Sharing with the people in this most personal way quickly gave us a feel for the city and its people. I had no idea then that I would eventually come back there to live and to have a part in what God was doing there. ✸

≤ 34 ≥

"Tutankhamen, Disrobed and Petrified"

From Jerusalem, we went down to Aqaba and boarded a boat that was taking phosphate from the Dead Sea. Passing through the Suez Canal, we arrived at Cairo.

Cairo has many charming family hotels, and we stayed in one called the Carlton, just off of 26th of July Street.

Egypt was delightful, but hot. It was a good time to be there because there were few tourists. From Cairo, we took a train to Luxor.

We rented bicycles, so that we could see as much as possible on our limited budget, and aside from the fact that I got exhausted from the heat and exertion once in a while and keeled over, we had a wonderful time. We saw Karnak and Thebes.

One day while we were visiting the Tomb of Tutankhamen (commonly called King Tut) in the Valley of the Kings we saw an open door and decided to see what was behind it. What we found was a group of scientists from the University of Liverpool in England all gathered around a table examining a mummy. They had removed the wrapping and had the black body under a bright light, examining and measuring it from every angle. At first they were so engrossed in their work that they didn't notice us. When they became aware of our presence, an eery silence descended over the room, and everyone turned to stare at us. It was obvious that we had wandered into a place we did not belong, so we quickly excused ourselves and left. But we had already seen the body of the famous King Tut, disrobed and petrified.

We worked our way down through Egypt to Aswan, and there we boarded a paddle boat and started up the Nile River toward the Sudan. Two American travelers that we had bumped into several times along our way got on the same boat. We had seen them at the Valley of the Kings and at Luxor. One of them was a high school principal from Washington, D.C., and the other was a Fulbright Scholar from Baltimore, Maryland. We had sometimes stayed in the same hotels, and we had seen them ordering their proper meals while we searched for the cheapest items on the menu so that we could stretch our funds. Now, on the plodding trip up the Nile, we all became close friends.   ✳

≥ 35 ≤

"There Was No Visible Highway"

When we boarded a train to cross the Sudan, none of us had any local money, and we were all hungry. Our friend from Baltimore had some crackers and a small can of sardines. "How about doing the multiplication of the loaves and the fishes," he said. We prayed over the food, and everyone in the coach was given a little. If it didn't multiply on the outside, it did seem to multiply on the inside. We all felt better after that.

We arrived in Khartoum at Easter time, and on Easter Sunday, we went to church at the Anglican Cathedral.

When our time in Khartoum was finished, we took a desert bus on the overland route heading for Ethiopia. The bus was packed. The wheels of that bus were as tall as I am, and the tires were huge in circumference, desert tires. There was no visible highway. The bus headed straight into the desert. How the driver knew which way to go was a mystery. Perhaps he followed the sun. We never knew just how he was guided. We were on our way to Kassala, a small town on the border between the Sudan and Ethiopia.

We had never seen such a lot of flies as covered the meat in the market place of Kassala. We survived on Coca-Colas for the several days we were there. We quickly discovered, as did all the other travelers, that it was "impossible" to get across the border into Ethiopia. There was a war going on between the two nations, and no one was being allowed to cross the border.

Many of those who had made this trip were desperate to cross. They sent telegrams to the emperor in Addis Ababa, urging him to open the borders. Others picketed the office of the Ethiopian consulate, trying to force him to grant permission to cross. Nothing seemed to be working. We were all told that we would have to go back to Khartoum and fly to Addis. We didn't have enough money to do that, so while the others picketed and wondered what to do next, we began to pray, believing God for a miracle. We didn't know how He would do it, but He was our only hope.

While we were speaking one day with the chief of the Sudanese police, he invited us to his home for afternoon tea on Friday. On Friday, we went, and while

114

we were having tea, it came time for him to pray his afternoon prayers. He excused himself, got out his prayer rug and said his prayers toward Mecca. When he was finished, he came back, and we continued our visit.

Seeing the unabashed sincerity of this man, we thought we had discovered how to get across the border. We told him that we were very religious people, too, and that since there was no church in Kassala, we simply had to be in Ethiopia by Sunday morning so that we could go to church. This touched him, and he said, "I'll see what I can do to help you." After thinking for a while, he came up with an idea. "I have a group of prisoners I'm sending back to Ethiopia tomorrow in a truck," he said. "If you are willing, I will arrange for you to go with the truck. You must get some kind of permission from the Ethiopian consulate, or I can't do it."

We went to see the Ethiopian consul, but he said that he could not grant us a visa. "Could you just prepare something with your typewriter that says something simple like this," and we suggested these words: "Kindly help these ladies in any way possible." He agreed and typed it out for us and signed it. It was not official, but we wondered, with the present chaos, if the people at the border would even read it. If they saw the Amharic writing with the signature of the consular official, they might just let it pass. And that is exactly what was about to happen.

We took that note back to the Sudanese chief of police, and the next day he put us in a car and sent us to join a waiting truck that would transport us into Ethiopia. The truck, it turned out, was more like a paddy wagon. The back of it was fitted out like a jail cell, and it was filled with young Ethiopian prostitutes who had come across the border illegally to ply their trade in the Sudan.

We were placed in the front seat of the truck, beside the driver. A guard, armed with a machine gun, rode on the front of the vehicle, and we set off for the border. When we got to the border, we showed our little note, and the guard motioned for us to go on through. So far, so good. We were experiencing favor with God and man. ✳

≥ 36 ≤

"We Can't Go Back"

When we got to Tessenei, the first town in Ethiopia, an official there took one look at our paper and told us that we would have to go back. We could not enter Ethiopia without a visa.

"We can't go back," we said, "we have to go to church tomorrow. It's Sunday."

"Very well," he said, "I will permit you to spend the night tonight and go to church here tomorrow, but you must come back here tomorrow after church, and we will send you back to the border."

That night we found some local missionaries and they invited us to stay with them. They were very happy to see someone from abroad, and we were very happy to see them as well. My associate had been wanting tomatoes, and they served us tomatoes that evening for supper.

The next morning we went to church in Tessenei and, after church, as we had agreed, we went back to the police officer who was so intent on sending us back across the border into the Sudan. We tried again to convince him to let us go on, but he had not changed his mind overnight. "I have to send you back," he said. "I have my orders." Just at that moment, a big tear rolled out of the corner of my eye. It seemed to move in slow motion, and when it finally plopped on his desk, I was sure that I had never heard a tear make so much noise.

The Ethiopian officer was horrified. "Oh, please," he pleaded, "don't cry. Don't cry. Oh, please don't cry. Okay, stop crying. I won't send you back. I will send your passports back with a message to the consul there to place a visa in them and send them back here. Okay? Please don't cry." We had to wait a couple of days as the passports were sent back to Kassala for processing and returned, but God had performed the miracle, and we didn't have to go back.

I have always marveled at that great miracle. I have never been one to cry much, but God knew how to wring a huge and noisy tear out of me that day, and it was most effective.

We stayed in Tessenei a few days, and when it came time to go, the missionary ladies sent a couple of young men early in the morning to claim seats for us on a local bus bound for Asmara and hold them for us until we got there. This

I Ask for Ethiopia

proved all important. People were climbing in through the windows to take the best seats, and we would have had difficulty claiming one on our own.

It was quite a ride across the northern part of Ethiopia to Asmara. Once inside the city, we stayed at the Hamashien Hotel. There we met a Mr. Habashi, an Ethiopian who lived in Egypt and belonged to Coptic church. Several times the Emperor had stayed with him in Egypt. We sat in the garden of the hotel among the most beautiful bougainvilleas I had ever seen and talked about Mr. Habashi's friendship with the Emperor of Ethiopia.

I had been very excited about going to Asmara and knew that we had something important to do there. Whenever God has quickened something to my spirit, it has always thrilled me and I have immediately been off and running with it. Sometime before this, however, when God had given me a word for one of the brothers in our church in America about Asmara, he had been very slow to respond. The northern part of Ethiopia was in political and military turmoil and, since that time, the area has broken off into a separate country called Eritrea. When I saw that this brother didn't really want to go, I said to the Lord, "If he doesn't want to go, send me. I'm willing." That is how I found myself in delightful Asmara. In addition to finding the most delicious Italian coffee anyone could ever ask for (right there in the Hamashien Hotel), God used us to bring revival to that place as we ministered in the local church.

Asmara had gained prominence during the Second World War, when it was occupied by the Germans. After the war, an American base had been established in the city. We went there and met some of the chaplains and officers and spoke with them about what God was doing in that day.

From Asmara we moved on south to Gondar. Before we left home, the Lord said to us, "Halfway into your journey, you will meet people who have only held to the five books of Moses." We were not sure just where all our journey would take us or how long we would be gone. So we could not determine where the halfway point would be. As it happened, Gondar turned out to be the halfway point of our journey, both timewise and distance wise. That is where we met Sally Teel, prayed for her, and she was baptized in the Holy Spirit. Sally was a missionary with the church Mission to the Jews, an Anglican group out of England. This was the first time I met missionaries working with the Jewish people. Gondar, it turned out, was home to thousands of Ethiopian Jews. There were Ethiopian Jews scattered throughout other parts of Ethiopia and in the capital, Addis Ababa, as well.

When Sally told us about the Ethiopian Jews — who only held to the five books of Moses — I suddenly remembered the prophetic word given in our church: "Halfway into your journey, you will meet a people who have only held to the five books of Moses." It would be some time before our own vision for the in-

117

gathering of the Jewish people would fully develop, but the Lord was giving us a foretaste of that coming ministry by allowing us to be a blessing to the Jewish people of Gondar. Years later, Professor Kassa, who was governor of Gondar at that time, came to Jerusalem and was our guest in the Holy City as well as in Tiberius.

This was also the first time we met a representative of the Israeli Aid Program and of the Israeli people abroad. He was sent to do special aid projects on behalf of the Jews.

From Gondar, we went to Addis Ababa. On a future trip to Ethiopia, we would experience sweeping revival there. This trip was more a time of orientation and personal witnessing and getting an overview of the nation. ✳

﹏ 37 ﹏

"A New Tribal Witchcraft"

From Addis, we flew to Nairobi, Kenya, and from Nairobi we went overland to Jinja. The Lord had told us to go to the place where the Nile flows out of Lake Victoria. We knew that Lake Victoria was in Uganda, but the maps we consulted in America showed no name for the spot where the lake met the Nile. We did not actually learn the name of the town we were to visit at the confluence of these two great bodies of water until we got to Nairobi. There we were able to secure a more detailed map. We had been traveling now for several months, heading for a place we didn't even know the name of: Jinja.

When we got to Jinga, we met David and Mary Clark. Her father, Rev. Bob Lichty, had been the first African missionary I met as a girl (and the man who laid hands on me the day I received my call to the nations). Hearing him preach and tell his stories of Africa had arrested my spirit. Now here we were at a mission station where his daughter and son-in-law were serving. What a thrill!

The Clarks had been very successful in raising up churches all around Jinja, but they had not been as successful inside the town. Many had accepted the Lord in the street meetings in Jinja, but somehow the fruit had not remained. Jinja, they told us, had become semi-industrialized, and people of many different tribal backgrounds had come there to live and work. Each group brought with it a new tribal witchcraft, so Jinja was a town dominated by the influence of witch doctors. We preached on the streets of Jinja with the Clarks, and when people responded, we took them back to the church and immediately prayed for them to be filled with the Holy Spirit. They would need this power to resist the witchcraft of the place. This is something that had not been tried, and it brought excellent and lasting results. In recent years a number of preachers from Jinja have attended our campmeeting in Ashland.

At night, after the services were over, we drove up on the golf course beside the Nile. There we could see in the headlights of the car wild animals, mainly hippopotami, grazing beside the river. We even took our pictures with the animals nearby. I was always asked to back up closer to them, but I wasn't about to get between them and the river. They weighed thousands of pounds and could easily trample a person to death. Besides, I was backing up in the dark.

Harvest Glory

David Clark often took visitors on a big-game fishing trip. Nile Perch was the catch of the day.

From Jinja, we went to Kampala and preached in the church of Brother and Sister Arthur Dodzweit. God had used Brother Dodzweit, a missionary with the Elim Church in Lima, New York, after the great T.L. Osborn revival in Mombasa. There was such great fruit from that meeting that within the next year, Brother Dodzweit, with the help of a lot of other anointed people, had raised up more than one thousand churches in Uganda, as Brother Bud Sickler had raised up churches in Mombasa and throughout Kenya. ❋

38

"What Do You Girls Do?"

From Uganda, we flew back to Khartoum. When we arrived at the airport, we were notified that we were being placed under semi-house arrest, and we were transferred to the Grand Hotel. No one was willing to tell us why this was being done. The next day, when we caught our flight out of there for Chad, we learned that the Six-Day War was in progress in Israel. Because we were Americans, the Ugandans had chosen to restrict our movement inside their country.

We landed in Ft. Lamey (now known as N'Djamena), Chad. Since the Lord had spoken the name of Chad to me in my sleep, we knew that He had something important for us to do there. Ft. Lamey was hot, desertlike, and everything was, as a result, very expensive. Most everything had to be flown in from France. We also had noticed that things were always more expensive in places that had been former French colonies than in those that had belonged to the English.

It was late when we checked into a local hotel, and I was tired.

"What do you girls do?" the hotel manager asked.

"We're missionaries," I answered.

"Oh," he said, "there's a man you should meet while you're here. He has an orphanage. He's a very fine missionary." He mentioned the man's name, and we filed it in the back of our minds and went to bed.

The next morning, as we made a habit of doing, we went by the American Consulate to register. We found it to be a good idea, because if any type of emergency should arise, the embassy staff would make an effort to contact us and would make it their responsibility to concern themselves with our safety.

The consular official in charge of the registration asked us, "What do you girls do?"

We said, "We're missionaries."

"Oh," he said, "there's a man here in town you ought to meet. He has an orphanage here, and he's doing a very fine work."

We had been a little weary the night before when this same conversation took place and hadn't taken it very seriously, but now that we were hearing it for the second time, we knew that we had to meet this man — whoever he was.

"How could we find his telephone number?" I asked.

"I have it right here," he answered.

"May we use your telephone?"

"Sure," he said. "Help yourself."

We called the man and told him who we were, that we were just passing through Ft. Lamey, that we had heard about his good work there and that we would like to meet him. He invited us over for afternoon tea.

We arrived at the missionary's house at three-thirty or four, and as we sat down with him and his wife and began to discuss the miracles God had been doing for us as we traveled from place to place, they served us tea. We noticed that he seemed a little conservative and hesitant to respond to what we were saying and that his wife was even more hesitant, but we continued to share our experiences with them as if they were the most interested people in the world.

Afterward, they showed us the orphanage and the rest of the ministry. They were very nice people. Soon it came time for us to take our leave.

The wife said to her husband, "I'll take the ladies back to the hotel."

"No, honey. Don't you think of it," he said. "You just sit right here, and I will take them back."

We managed to get into his car, a little French model, and had driven only a little way when he suddenly pulled over to the side of the road. It became quickly obvious that he wanted to speak with us out of the hearing of his wife.

"I want to tell you," he began, "that I have an incurable disease. I've been in the country long enough that I speak Arabic fluently, and we have worked very hard to build up this mission station and to gain the respect of all the local people. But doctors have not been able to discover what it is that is causing the flesh to separate from my fingernails and toenails. It causes excruciating pain. When I was home the last time on furlough, I was examined by specialists from both Canada and Europe, but they couldn't diagnose my problem either. My mission board has finally decided that if I can't find some cure before I go home this time on furlough I won't be permitted to come back to the field.

"I have never really believed in divine healing, although I have heard people talk about Pentecostals and how they pray for the sick. Recently, I prayed, and I said, 'God, if You really heal the sick as these Pentecostals say You do, please send someone to help me, and quickly, before I go home on furlough.' "

We had arrived just ten days before his scheduled departure. We laid hands on him that day, and his pain instantly left. He was very excited, and we were very excited for him.

When he finally got us back to the hotel, we called the airport and arranged to fly out the next day. We felt that we had done what God had sent us there to do.

I have never been a good letter writer (as all my friends can attest), and we have not kept up, for the most part, with the many people we have met and

I Ask for Chad

ministered to over the years, so I cannot really say what happened to this man in the months that followed. All I know is that when we obeyed God, all his pain left, and he felt wonderful for the first time in many years. The rest we had to leave with God.

About a year later we were traveling in North Africa again. We flew down into a little place called Tamanrasset, far south in Algeria. When we got off the plane, we found a simple *caravansary*, an inn where the camel trains stopped while crossing the deserts. Another Western lady was staying there that night too. When we had a chance to speak, she asked, "What do you girls do?"

I said, "We're missionaries."

"Oh," she said, "it must be missionary week."

"What do you mean?" I asked.

She said, "A day or two ago, I met a man on his way to Ft. Lamey, Chad. He bought a Land Rover in Europe and was driving it back across Africa to his mission post."

I asked his name, and it was indeed the man we had met and for whom we had prayed. So God let us know that he had finished his year of furlough and was on his way back to his mission station. That meant that he was healed by the power of God.

I didn't have time to learn Arabic and to spend the rest of my life in Ft. Lamey, Chad, one of the most difficult postings in the world, but that man loved it and was saddened by the prospect of not being able to return. He had the respect of the local people and a great future ahead of him. He needed a miracle, and God sent us to help him receive his miracle. Those are the kind of "odd jobs" I have done all over the world for the Lord for many years. There is no other way to describe my work.

My life has not fit into any real pattern, other than the fact that anything anybody else could not do or would not do God would drop into my spirit, and I would do it. Sometimes God sent me to a pastor, sometimes to a king, sometimes to a church that was praying. But everywhere I went, it was by the revelation of the Holy Ghost. God did not give all the revelations to me directly, but I became good at listening to the revelations everyone else was receiving from God, and many times they were for my direction as well. ✳

≥ 39 ≤

"Don't You Know What's Happening Here?"

When we got to Lagos, Nigeria, a rather strange thing happened. We had just settled into the Baptist Guest House in Lagos one Sunday morning, left our luggage and gone to get some lunch. We sat down in a nice little restaurant and got ready to order. Then, without warning, we looked across the table at each other and, at the exact same moment, both said, "God just spoke to me that we should leave Lagos."

Since it was Sunday, we wondered if we would find any airline offices or travel agencies open. After we finished our lunch, we set out along the waterfront to see what we could find. We came to an office that didn't seem to be open for business, but someone was inside, so we ventured in to see if anyone could help us.

"Excuse me," I said, "could you help me? Are there any flights going out to America tonight?"

The lady looked at us rather strangely and said, "Don't you know what's happening here?"

"No," we answered, "we just arrived this morning. We've been traveling through Africa, and we haven't seen a newspaper yet today."

"Look out there," she said, pointing out to sea. "See that ship in the harbor? The rebels tried to blow that up yesterday. We're at war." This was the beginning of the Biafran War.

"The American government is flying in a special plane tonight to take all the Americans out, but it's already fully booked."

I asked what time that flight was scheduled, thanked her for her help, and we went back to the guest house to get our bags and get to the airport.

When we got to the airport, we found an atmosphere of chaos. We could feel the tension in the air, and many of those who had come hoping to get on the flight had passed through very dangerous areas and had experienced difficulties.

We went to the counter to check in and were told that there was absolutely no room on the plane. We might as well go back into town. "Would you mind putting our names down anyway?" we asked. "We'll wait because God has spoken to us to fly tonight."

124

I Ask for Nigeria

As we waited, we saw one very attractive lady arriving with her dog. She was visibly shaken, and we stepped up to help her check in. We were able to help others as well.

We eventually got on the plane, of course, and we were seated next to the woman we had helped in the airport. She began to relax and tell us her story.

She was from Texas, and she and her husband were working in the Nigerian oil fields. Rebels had killed people in her front yard. Being a nurse, she had tried to go to their aid, but the rebels had warned her that if she even tried to help the people who were falling in her yard, they would kill her as well. She was, of course, feeling very traumatized by the whole affair.

She loved her dog and told us that when she had first gone out, dressed in her high heels, to walk her dog, everyone had thought her a little strange. Before long, it had become very fashionable for people in that neighborhood to take their dogs out on the leash and walk them.

When she had left home and traveled across Nigeria to the Lagos Airport by car, rebels along the way had stolen everything she had. Even the rings on her fingers had been stolen.

We were happy to be safe and happy that God was leading us, keeping us from harm.

There were other stops on our journey I failed to mention: Brazzaville, Congo, Douala, Cameroon (where we stayed in the French Huguenout Guest House), Libreville, Gabon and Dakaar, Senegal, and from there we flew back to America. In each place God led us by His Spirit, making divine appointments, causing the soles of our feet to possess new territory, making sure that the Gospel of the Kingdom was preached in every nation for a witness before the end comes, using our voices as prophetic instruments to spark life into that which was dead. He was causing us to gather, by our prophetic voices, *Harvest Glory*.

✽

40

"By Faith, We Had Done the Route"

At the end of this six-month-long trip, when we figured up exactly what we had received (in order to fill out our income tax returns), everyone was amazed that we had existed on so little. We had been fine because God was faithful.

Ireland, England, France, Turkey, Syria, Israel, Egypt, the Sudan, Ethiopia, Uganda, Kenya, Chad, Liberia, Sierra Leone, Ghana, the Congo, Cameroon, Gabon, Senegal, Nigeria ... by faith we had done the route. It had taken us six months, and everywhere we had traveled, we were possessing the nations for the Kingdom of God and preparing ourselves for the greater things that lay ahead.

✶

⪻ 41 ⪼

"Make the Valley Full of Ditches"

That fall the Lord sent us back to Ethiopia to speak with Emperor Haile Selassie. As we were flying into Addis Ababa, the Lord spoke to me and said, "Make the valley full of ditches." I was familiar with the Old Testament passage where the armies of Israel dug ditches in the valley and, although there was no rain, the next day the ditches were miraculously full of water, giving water for the cattle and for the army so that they could win the war. What could the Lord now mean by this in connection with Ethiopia?

When we got to Addis, we checked into the Mennonite Guest House. I called the Palace and asked about a possible visit, but I was told that they were very sorry, but the Emperor was busy. He was meeting with Queen Juliana of Holland, then he had a meeting with Secretary General U Thant of the United Nations, and after that he had a whole series of other very important meetings. I gave my name and said that I would gladly wait.

While we waited, we learned that the Mattsons from Finland, missionaries in Addis Ababa whom we had met on the former trip, had moved from outside the city into town. They were sick, we were told, so we went to see them. Mrs. Mattson asked us what had brought us to Addis. "We've come to see the Emperor," I replied.

She said, "I'm glad you came. A year ago we rented this house to be near the University. We felt that God wanted us to work among the university students. I still believe that. From the very day we moved in here I have been sick in bed. Although we have been here a year already, we have not had a single meeting. Everything was ready for it, but my husband has had to wait on me hand and foot. I am so sick that he has to turn me in the bed. Please pray for me. We need to get on with what God has shown us to do."

We prayed for Sister Mattson, and the Lord raised her up. She was able to immediately get up and prepare a light meal for us. She was so happy.

"I've been praying for some help in this thing," she told us before we left. "Would you come and pray with us tomorrow?" We had nothing else on our schedule but wait for word from the Palace, so we agreed. The next day we all began to pray about eight in the morning, and we prayed until five in the afternoon, with only a short break for lunch. The Mattsons were quite elderly, and

127

as we prayed he would just nod his head in agreement and say, "Ja, Ja, Ja, Ja." Every once in a while, Sister Mattson would chime in with an "Amen" here or there or an occasional *"Kittos Jesus"* (praise the Lord), but not much more than that. At the end of the day, Sister Mattson said, "Oh, that was so wonderful! Would you come back tomorrow and pray again?"

"We'd be happy to," I answered. So the next day, we gathered again for prayer and prayed together through the day. At the end of the day, when we were about to leave, the same thing happened. She was so thrilled that she wanted us to come back the next day and pray again. And we did.

I don't remember how many days we prayed together like this, but I do remember that one day I suddenly noticed that the room in which we were praying was beginning to fill up with young Ethiopian university students. Somehow the word had gotten out that we were having prayer meetings. The room was filled with simple benches that had no backrest, but the students wanted to get involved — whether they could be comfortable or not.

When I saw more young people coming, I stood and preached a salvation message. Those who were not already saved were saved that day. Then I spoke a few minutes about the baptism of the Holy Spirit, and asked how many wanted to be baptized in the Spirit. All of the young people present raised their hands, and we began to go to them, one by one, and lay our hands on them and pray. About fifty students were baptized in the Holy Spirit that first day. From that day on, over a period of several weeks, more than five hundred university students were filled with the Holy Spirit, speaking in unknown tongues.

During this time of outpouring, leaders of many of the missions working in the city heard about what God was doing and came to be blessed as well. The principal leaders of all the missions in town were baptized in the Holy Spirit, and each of the local denominations began to experience revival. Wonderful miracles of healing took place in all these meetings.

This did not all happen without opposition, but God was gracious to reveal the opposition before it came to light. This encouraged the local people to believe that even the opposition had a purpose, and they were not overwhelmed by it.

One of those who was baptized in the Holy Spirit during this time was a lady doctor from England, Margaret Fitzherbert, who worked with the local leprosarium. She had been highly honored at home and abroad for her work. Queen Elizabeth presented her with the OBE, the Order of the British Empire, and she had also received a very special award from Emperor Haile Selassie. Now she began to experience wonderful miracles of healing from God upon her patients.

I Ask for Ethiopia

We were staying in the Mennonite Guest House, and one day we told Sarah Rush, who was in charge of the house, that we were determined not to leave town until she had also been baptized in the Spirit. We were not eating our meals at the Guest House, but she often kept something special for us and had it waiting when we came home at night. She was from Lancaster County, Pennsylvania and knew how to prepare the Pennsylvania Dutch treats. Her shoo-fly pie and her Lebanon bologna were exquisite. "You can feed us shoo-fly pie all you want," we joked, "as we've decided to stay until you're filled with the Spirit."

A few minutes after we went to our room that afternoon, we heard a knock on the door. It was Sarah. She had decided that if it were that important to us for her to be filled with the Spirit, she wanted to be filled right then. We laid hands on her, and she was baptized in the Spirit. The Mennonite Guest House became a place of ministering the Holy Spirit to the spiritually hungry. Missionaries and other guests were baptized in the Holy Spirit in every room of the house. They had come from the interior areas of Ethiopia for a rest, and God gave them power to return and do a greater work for Him.

We had not forgotten why we had come to Ethiopia, and one day I got a call from the Palace saying that the Emperor was ready to see me. I had said to Sarah Rush some days before the invitation came, "I would like for you to go with me to the Palace when the Emperor calls." She had seen him from a distance in many public appearances. It was His Imperial Majesty's habit to ride slowly in his car from the Jubilee Palace to the Grand Palace each day. Petitioners waited along the way. Sarah said she had never seen him in person.

"Let's go to the market," I said, "and buy some special fabric and have a special dress made for you. Then, when the Emperor calls, maybe you will get the opportunity to meet him too." She made herself a beautiful dress, and I had a new dress made too. Now, our time had come.

We were taken to the Palace, and I was escorted in to see the Emperor alone. His usual custom was to speak officially only in French or Amharic, but I had prayed that he would speak to me in English. The Lord was gracious to grant this request.

I told the Emperor about the revival and what God was doing for his people. I named many of those who were participating, and he knew some of them personally and told me he had already heard about some of the healing miracles. After we had talked for awhile, I said to him, "I have a word from the Lord for you. Would you like for me to deliver it now?"

He turned to the Palace minister and said something in Amharic. Then he turned back to me and said in English, "You may deliver the message of the Lord now."

I closed my eyes and began to prophesy as I had done many times before, but what came out was not what I was accustomed to. Usually I spoke with a steady flow of words and thoughts until the message was complete, but this time I spoke one short sentence, and then I paused. Then I spoke another sentence, and then I paused. It took a while to deliver the entire message. I was wondering just what the Holy Spirit was doing. This was different from any prophecy I had ever given before.

When I finally opened my eyes, I saw that the Palace minister was hurriedly writing down everything I was saying, word for word. I understood then what the Emperor had said to him and why the Lord had caused me to speak slowly and to pause between thoughts. The prophecy had been given at dictation speed.

When I thought about it later, I realized that if the Emperor had asked me to give the message at dictation speed, I might have gotten nervous. Even though I knew nothing about dictation, I did know the Holy Spirit, and He caused me to give the message so that it could be recorded.

When the Emperor opened his eyes, I remembered that Sarah was still sitting out in the reception area. I said to him, "There's a very lovely lady who's been here serving the Lord and your Imperial Majesty for twenty-six years." I explained that she had taught nursing to many of his people at the mission hospital. "She is now the hostess of the Mennonite Guest House where we have been staying," I told him. "Would you be so kind as to receive her?"

He sent the Palace minister out to the reception area to bring Sarah in. Later she told me that she had immediately sensed a great presence of the Lord in the audience chamber. She knew that His Imperial Majesty had bowed to a greater majesty.

I felt that it was very important for Sarah to go with me that day to honor her for her kindness to me. The believers in Addis knew that I had come to the city to see the Emperor. They all had agreed that it would be absolutely impossible. If I had gone alone, it is possible that some would not have believed what had transpired. Everybody in Addis Ababa knew Sarah and knew the veracity of every statement she made. She was thus able to attest to the wonderful door the Lord had opened for us.

Before we left the Palace that day, the Emperor gave me a beautiful autographed picture which I have kept until this day.

As I flew out of Addis Ababa, it was with great rejoicing. The Lord had told us to make the valley full of ditches, and we had done that through prayer. When the ditches were dug, He had filled the valley around the capital city with the life-giving flow of His river. Even to this day, many of those who were baptized in the Spirit during those months of revival are leaders in the Lord's work in many places.

One of them was Beta Mingistu, who is now considered by the Ethiopian church (which is scattered all over the world) to be the apostle of the church. The Ethiopian Christians hold conferences in such cities as Stockholm, Sweden, Rome, Italy, Sydney, Australia, Khartoum, Sudan, and Wheaton, Illinois — in the countries where there are large Ethiopian communities. He, along with others of those young people who were products of those meetings, lead the church forward.

Several years after we went to live in Jerusalem, Beta came to Jerusalem to see Menachem Begin. He and his wife came to our house. Remembering those early days, Beta said, "We were just young university students, and we hadn't married yet, but you prophesied over both of us separately that we would travel to the nations. We wondered how that would be possible because we didn't have enough money to get from one side of town to the other by bus and had to walk to the meetings. We were so poor. We have come to say thank you because every word you prophesied has been fulfilled."

He had graduated from Wheaton College, studied in Singapore at the Haggai Institute, and gone on to get his doctorate. He was the head of the Living Bible Committee for all of Africa and found himself dealing with world leaders often, whether it was in Africa or in some other part of the world. He credited the prophetic release that was imparted to him at that time for making it all possible.

He now has his headquarters in Nairobi and, from there, reaches out to many parts of Africa. His children, both natural and spiritual, are doing exploits in the Kingdom of God.   ✳

42

"Salu"

After visiting with Emperor Haile Selassie, we flew to New Delhi, India, where we ministered in and around the city. We were hoping that the door to Bhutan would open for us, but it didn't seem to be opening. My colleague had a vision in which she saw a great tome, and on the cover of the book was written the words, "What to do while patiently waiting." It was evident that the Lord had something else for us to do while we waited, so we prayed about what we should be doing next. The Lord told us to go back to America, and the door to Bhutan would open later.

While we were still in New Delhi, the Lord gave me the word *Salu*. It came to me several times. We felt that it must be a place, so we looked it up in the atlas and found that it was an island in the Salvation group, located just off the coast of French Guyana in South America. It was better known as Devil's Island. Apparently, the Lord had something for us to do there. As it turned out, a pastor on the island had been praying for someone to come help him with revival for his people.

After we returned to America and had been there for a while, the Lord told us it was time to go to Devil's Island. When we got there, we discovered that the island would soon be closed to all visitors. The French were making the island a missile launching site, and their future missile tests would be done from there.

We strongly believed the words of Jesus:

> *And this gospel of the kingdom shall be preached in all the world for a witness unto all nations; and then shall the end come.*   Matthew 24:14

The Lord had sent us to speak His words to the people on that island, for after that no outsiders, other than those involved with the missile tests, would be allowed on it. The timing of God is always perfect.   *

⚔ 43 ⚔

"With Greater Honor"

In August of that next year, I saw a small article in the newspaper stating that the King of Nepal would be coming to Washington as the guest of President and Mrs. Lyndon Johnson. The Nepalese Embassy was giving a special reception in his honor, and I received an invitation. It was to be the finest culinary display Washington had witnessed in many years.

The reception was held in the International Ballroom of the Washington Hilton Hotel. When I entered the large ballroom, I began to mingle among the guests, moving toward the opposite side of the room. When the arrival of President Johnson and His Majesty King Mahendra was announced, they were very far away, clear at the opposite end of the ballroom. *If only I had known where they would enter,* I thought, *I could have stayed closer to that doorway.* I was admonishing myself to learn how these affairs were conducted when I sensed God dropping faith into my heart. "Lord," I prayed, "if You want me to meet him, bring them here." In that moment, I watched President Johnson change course and head through the crowd in my direction. He came right in front of me and stopped to wait for the King who had been separated from him in the crowd.

When he stopped, I stepped forward and introduced myself. "Mr. President," I said, "I'm Ruth Heflin. I was in Nepal speaking to the Royal Family about the Lord." Just then the King caught up, and President Johnson introduced me to him. We were able to speak briefly. I think I was the only one that night who was personally introduced to the King by our President.

After the King had moved on to take his place, Betty Beale, social columnist for the Washington Post stepped up to me and introduced herself. "Who are you?" she asked. "You spoke to the King as if you knew him."

I realized that I probably could get a lot of publicity in the newspaper at that moment, but I knew that was not the best thing for the future of evangelism in Nepal. "I'm just a private citizen who went to Nepal to speak to the Royal Family about Jesus Christ," I told her.

A group of senators overheard what I said, and several of them, among them Mark Hatfield, came to me and said, "We heard what you said to Betty Beale.

133

We're also Christians. Tell us about your experiences." So, I had an opportunity to speak to a number of the congressmen and senators about my experiences in Nepal.

Later that night, I caught the eye of the Crown Prince and asked him if he would take me and introduce me to his mother. He did.

It all happened just as the Lord had said: I had met the King and Queen of Nepal "with greater honor." ✱

﹃ 44 ﹄

"Hello, Ruth"

God sent us on a trip through Europe, which included London, Munich, Vienna, East Berlin, Volgagrad, T'blisi, Moscow, Tashkent, Somerkand, Bukurah, back to Tashkent and on to New Delhi and Kathmandu.

When we got to London, I said, "Let's call the Nepalese Embassy, and just say hello to the Ambassador." I located the number of the Nepalese Embassy, called and said that I was a friend of His Royal Highness, Prince Bashundara, and that I was passing through London and just wanted to say hello.

"Just a moment," a Nepalese clerk said and left the phone for a minute.

I thought he had gone to get a pencil to write down my information, but a moment later, I heard a familiar voice saying, "Hello, Ruth." It was Prince Bashundara. He was so thrilled we were in London that he invited us to come to the Embassy that evening.

That night, while we were talking with the Prince and the Ambassador, the Prince sent an aide to bring his attaché case. When it was brought to him, he opened it and pulled out his New Testament. "I just want you to know," he said, to those who were present, "that I didn't know I would be seeing Ruth. I carry this with me wherever I go."

The Nepalese Ambassador looked at me and said, "My, you're a dangerous person. I won't be able to give you a visa to travel to Nepal in the future. You have influenced one of the members of the Royal Family." Thankfully, he was joking.

"Oh, Your Excellency," I laughed, "I guess I knew that, and that's why I got my visa in Washington, D.C., before I left America." Later, we all went out and had dinner together.

During the conversation at the restaurant, the Ambassador told me that he would like to have a Bible, too. I told him I would be glad to mail one to him and handed him my address book so that he could tell me where to send it. He wrote his name and address in my book, and after his name he added the words "a misguided soul who would like to be guided. Please help me." When I got to Germany, I bought a New Testament and mailed it back to him in London.

Harvest Glory

From Tashkent, we flew into New Delhi and on to Kathmandu. I had met the head of the Bible Society in New Delhi, and we ordered through him ten thousand Gospels to distribute in Nepal. They had sent them to Kathmandu for us, and they were waiting for us there.

When we arrived in Nepal, we were invited to an afternoon reception at the Indian Embassy, and there we met my friend Jagdish, the former Chief of Protocol. During our conversation, we spoke to him of mountain climbing, as we were planning to do some trekking on our own to distribute the Gospels. My friend said, "Ruth will climb better than me because she has longer legs."

With that, Jagdish told her a story about Big Jim Whittaker, the American climber who conquered Mt. Everest. After he placed the American flag on top of Mt. Everest, he collapsed. His little Sherpa guide had to pick him up, put him on his shoulders and carry him down the mountain. "It's not the height of the person, nor the length of his legs," Jagdish told us, "it's the strength of his soul that counts most when it comes to mountain climbing."

There were areas of Nepal we could reach by road, but we would leave those for later. First, we would try to reach the most inaccessible regions before bad weather set in.

We took a helicopter from Kathmandu to Lukla. Flying over that exquisite terrain was an amazing experience. From Lukla we started trekking up trails that were very narrow and very steep. We would trek into all the areas we could reach, then we would come back and get the helicopter again.

We started our trek at about nine thousand feet, and our goal was to get to Namche Bazaar by Saturday morning. We heard that villagers came from many miles around to an open-air bazaar that would be held that particular morning, and we wanted to give each of them a copy of the Gospel. About halfway up the last mountain, however, my traveling companion got very sick and actually fell over on the side of the mountain. I prayed for her, and she got up and went on. After only another twenty feet or so, she fell again and I had to pray for her again. This went on for about an hour. Then, just as suddenly as the sickness had come, it left, and we were able to make our way on up the mountain in time to give out the Bible portions.

Until that trip, we had known nothing about altitude sickness. Now we heard stories, for example, of those who had gone blind at nine thousand feet. They called it "pulmonary blindness." We learned that usually when a person is affected by altitude sickness, the thing to do is to take them down to a lower level as quickly as possible. We didn't know any better at the time, and from Namche Bazaar, we kept climbing higher.

We went all the way up to the last inhabited village before the famous base camp for Mt. Everest. Everest itself is nearly thirty thousand feet high. I'm not sure how close we came to that, but the air was awfully thin up there. My head was pounding from the lack of oxygen.

When we reached the last village, we found that some climbers had lost a yak, a cross between an ox and a cow, on the side of the trail, and they were cooking it. We ate yak that night (with lots of spices), slept there and started back down the next morning.

We had hired porters to carry our Gospel portions, and when we left Kathmandu, we made a conscious decision to go light on food so that we could take plenty of Gospels. Most climbers did just the opposite.

Before long we had nothing left but salt and pepper, some other spices, and a small package of Cadbury chocolates, less than a pound in weight. We had debated about whether we should take the chocolates or a few more Gospels. Later, when we were still high in the Himilayas and we had nothing left to eat, we were very happy that I had taken the chocolates.

While we were out on the trails, we walked as far as we could during daylight hours and then, as darkness began to come, we looked for the first available house where we could sleep. We were always warmly welcomed. We often slept just above the animals, and we could hear the mooing of the yaks and the movement of the other animals during the night, but at least we were safe and warm. Some of the houses were quite small, while others were much larger, but the food was always very simple. There would usually be a few vegetables available, and we would use our salt and pepper and other condiments to spice it up a bit. It was simple fare, but it kept us going.

Many times we arrived at a place in darkness and just put our sleeping bags on the floor, got in and went to sleep, without first being able to examine our surroundings. One night my traveling companion got up in the middle of the night and went outside. When she came back, she said to me, "Ruth, you'll never believe it. There are twenty naked Tibetan men sleeping in this room with us." It was true. She had been forced to tiptoe over the bodies on her way out and back in.

The Tibetan men were also travelers who had stopped at the same house for the night. They were so accustomed to the cold that they could sleep without clothes or blankets. I came to the conclusion that they probably did it because body lice were so prevalent, and it was more comfortable without the clothes.

Many of the houses had a room that was kept as a temple room. We asked if we could stay in that room. Some people would have been uncomfortable staying in a room full of idols, but we covered ourselves in prayer with the blood of Jesus, then stretched out and went to sleep. We never had a problem, and the next morning we were ready to go on with our journey. One night we slept in a monastery. The next morning I discovered that I had been sleeping all night over a huge rat hole.

We had many opportunities to pray for the people as we passed or as we stayed in their houses. One lady sensed what we were doing and motioned for us to place our hands on the spot where she was suffering. God performed many wonderful miracles for us as we traveled.

We were under the pressure of time. If we delayed too long and didn't get back to the airfield at Lukla, we were told, the rains might set in. If that happened, no helicopter could land, and we would have to walk all the way back to Kathmandu, another thirty days' trek.

As we started back down the mountain, retracing our steps, my associate became very ill, so ill, in fact, that I urged her to let one of the Sherpas carry her on his back. "Remember that story about Big Jim," I told her. I felt that the Lord had allowed us to hear that story so that we would know how to get her down the mountain. The trails were narrow and steep and dangerous, and there were many drop-offs of hundreds of feet. It would be tricky for one of the Sherpas to carry her, but she could not go on in her condition. We had no choice.

She finally agreed to be carried, but only after I promised not to take any pictures of her being carried in this way. As sick as she was, she refused to let me carry the camera and kept it with her at all times.

The Sherpa took a sheet and made a sling to hold her. After she was loaded on his back, he began walking in the most amazing rhythm. Then, he literally ran down the mountains. Going down is always more dangerous than going up, but the man who carried her never wavered nor missed in his rhythm as he carried her over the next two days down to Lukla.

We paid him one dollar a day to carry her back down the mountain. We arrived at this mutually agreeable price after much customary haggling before the journey began.

We arrived in Lukla in time for the scheduled helicopter flight to Kathmandu. Other travelers had preceded us and were waiting there too. Clouds suddenly rolled into the area, and the helicopter could not land. We sat on the airstrip every day for several days, spending the night at a house nearby.

Over the next few days, a great wedding celebration took place in the village. All the potatoes were used in making beer. We watched as the celebrants ate up all the food in the area, and there was suddenly nothing available to eat. A little rice was all that we could find. By now we had no more spices, so it was plain rice or nothing.

One day, we were sitting there daydreaming about good things to eat. "If I were in Paris," I said, "I would be eating [and I named a favorite food] at [and I named a favorite place]. If I were in Rome, I'd be eating [and I named something utterly wonderful]." We went on like this for awhile, daydreaming about our favorite places in the world and our favorite dishes. "What's your very favorite thing to eat?" I asked my associate.

Without hesitation, she answered, "Lobster."

I turned to one young Nepali believer who had accompanied us and who was waiting with us and asked, "Krishna, what is your favorite food?"

He said, "Rice."

We were dumbfounded, but he had never had much more than rice to eat, and he was happy to have it.

After a few days of waiting, the helicopter was able to land, and we were taken back to Kathmandu.

We reached some areas of Nepal by road, and during this time, Prince Bashundara was very gracious to us, loaning us a car to travel in and to transport our Gospels. The vehicle he loaned us was nothing elegant. It was a little red Volkswagon bug. We were unaware at first that it had special license plates that caused people along the way to recognize it as belonging to the Royal Family.

Many of the areas we were traveling in were up near the China border. China was still a very mysterious place and to be that near the border was very exciting. We saw Chinese laborers working on the road that China was building in Nepal. All along the road we passed out our Gospels to everyone we saw.

Mysteriously, as we neared any checkpoint, the guard on duty would automatically raise the barrier and then stand at attention and salute us as we went on our way. We didn't think too much of it. The excitement of moving ever closer to China took our attention.

On our way back, crowds of both Nepalese and Chinese workers stood and cheered as we passed. They waved their New Testaments to us as we went by. Later, we realized that they all thought we were somehow royalty because we were riding in a royal car.

We took Gospel portions to all the remote areas of Nepal and thus had the opportunity to reach out to Nepali people everywhere. Not a single region was untouched by that outreach. By car, by helicopter and on foot, we reached all the land.

In the succeeding years numerous teams, as well as individuals, from our church in Virginia trekked in Nepal, evangelizing remote regions with Charles Mendies and others. Phil Meager and Kenny Barr were imprisoned for several days for the Gospel. Jane Lowder visited Charles Mendies when he was imprisoned and spoke the prophetic release for him.

On another occasion one of my associates was giving out Gospels on the trail northwest of Pokhara. We learned that the King of Mustang, a closed kingdom north of Nepal, was returning to his kingdom on that same trail from Pokhara to Mustang that day. We had no way of informing our friend about this wonderful opportunity, but we prayed that she would be given the opportunity of presenting the Gospel to him. As she was trekking, suddenly an impressive animal train came by. She quickly began giving out Gospels to each person in the group. When a very impressive man appeared, she reached into the knapsack and pulled out the only full Bible she had and presented it to him. She later learned that he was indeed the King of Mustang. God had heard our prayer. ✳

With Rev. Samuel Doctorian, Zurich, Switzerland
in front of Excelsior Hotel owned by Bob
Guggenbuhl, 1962.

With Mother in Karimplave, Kerala,
India, 1961.

Mother and Daddy crossing the river to a
meeting in India, 1961.

Mother and Daddy with the people of
India, 1961.

With Mother and Daddy in front of the Pyramid and
Sphinx in Egypt, 1961.

With Daddy and Mother in front
of an Indian Airlines' plane, 1961.

With Daddy and some Indian brethren in front of the Pandal and Pastor P.J. Thomas's house, 1961.

Spiritual Fiesta, Quezon City, Phillipines, 1970.

With my brother and
Harold McDougal.

At Loyola College.

Hotel Royal, Katmandu, Nepal, 1965.

H.M. King Mahendra of Nepal (father of present king).

H.M. King Tribhuwan of Nepal (grandfather of present king).

With H.R.H. Prince Basundhara, Katmandu, 1965.

With H.M. Queen Hope of Sikkim.

With a palace guard, Gangtok, Sikkim.

With Brother Simeon Lepasana, my brother, the Nepalese Ambassador to the U.N., Harold and Diane McDougal, and Daddy.

Charles and Susan Mendies and family.

The Governor of Gondar, Professor Kassa, first cousin of the Emperor of Ethiopia.

H.I.M. Haile Selassie of Ethiopia.

Lady Rebecca Stevens, wife of Saika Stevens, President and Prime Minister of Sierra Leone 1984.

David Simbwa, brother of King Freddie of Uganda, Diplomat to Beijing.

At Petra, Jordan, 1970.

In front of St. Basil's
Cathedral, Moscow, 1968.

≈ 45 ≈

"Marbles, Our Royal Gift"

Early in my travels in India I was blessed to go to the lovely hill station town of Darjeeling in the northeast part of the country. There I saw for the first time people from Sikkim. Over the coming years I read about that isolated and quaint kingdom and about the King of Sikkim and his Queen, the American heiress Hope Cook. Later I learned that my associate had gone to school with Hope at Madeira, near Washington, D.C. We began to pray about making a visit to Sikkim. The Lord gave us favor. In response to some overtures from us, the Queen invited us to be her guests for a week in the Kingdom of Sikkim.

A friend, Alma Hagan, a Lutheran who with her husband Roy lived and served the Lord in Darjeeling, offered to drive us to Gangtok in her Jeep, accompanied by a Canadian friend. It was not an easy drive from Darjeeling to Kalimpong, along the river bed up to the border crossing to Sikkim and on to Gangtok, but it certainly was beautiful.

Sikkim was indeed an exotic spot. Orchids grew wild throughout the Kingdom, and the walls of the entranceway near the Palace were covered with exquisitely delicate yellow orchids.

When we arrived in Gangtok, we were made comfortable in the Royal Guest House and soon taken to the Palace for afternoon tea. I remember many details about the Palace, but one of the things that most stands out in my memory were the beautiful hand-painted tables that were placed around the drawing room. They were quite low, and each person was given an individual table. These were exquisite.

Before leaving America, we had been praying about what to take Prince Palden, Hope's son, as a gift. After all, what do you give a Prince that he doesn't already have? My associate had a vision of the boy playing with marbles. We went out and bought a bag of marbles, and that became our royal gift. We presented the bag of marbles that first day, and it was a sight to behold as we watched the Prince playing with them. He would throw the marbles all over the hillside, and the servants, in their beautiful Sikkimese gowns which reached all the way down to their ankles, had to go scampering over the mountainside to gather them up, only to see the Prince throw them again.

149

Harvest Glory

The Queen had a very soft voice. When she spoke, it was almost in whispers. Her husband was the Buddhist god-King, and he was head of the World Buddhist Association. The Lord told us that the Queen would not always be in Gangtok, and that we should speak freely to her of Jesus. So we did.

Queen Hope very graciously arranged for us to see other parts of Sikkim. Wherever we went, a Jeep was sent before us with someone instructed to prepare the local royal guest house for our use. A cook was also sent along, and a complete kitchen, so that wherever we went in the nation, we were looked after royally.

It was a wonderful week, one to be remembered.

Sikkim was a hereditary monarchy ruled by a *chogyal* (maharaja). The last such ruler was Palden Thondup Namgyal, who succeeded to the throne in 1963. Under a treaty with India in 1950, Sikkim received full internal autonomy, becoming a protectorate. Because of political unrest that started in the early seventies, the monarchy ended, and in 1975, Sikkim became an Indian state.　　※

≥ 46 ≤

"To Save A Nation"

In the fall of 1969 my associate came back from the Philippines very excited about what God was doing there. She had been sent to join the McDougals in some special ministers' meetings, and many others were drawn there at the same time. My brother, who was traveling in other countries at the time, had been compelled to drop part of his itinerary and hurry to the Philippines. The Chappells, Jack and Patti, members of our church in Virginia, had other plans, but God hastened them to the Philippines as well. The Robinsons, Bobby and Rita, had been traveling in Indonesia when the Lord told them to cut their trip short and return to Manila.

In the ministers' meetings God spoke in a number of ways and said that He was about to reveal His glory in the isles of the Philippines and that it would be sent out from there to many other nations. It was such an amazing word that on the way back to Manila from the conference, my associate turned to the others and asked, "What are we going to do about it? If we believe what God is saying, we have to do something." Over the next few days, they all prayed together and sat down and worked out a plan for some major crusades to be conducted the following January.

They would secure stadiums in four major cities: Quezon City (actually the capital of the country and part of what is now known as MetroManila), Iloilo City, Surigao City and Naga City. Plans were discussed about getting special stationery printed and about inviting all the politicians of the country as well as the people. One of the most important decisions that was made was to call the upcoming meetings "The Spiritual Fiesta." They couldn't have known the importance of this decision at the moment, but later it would prove to be very significant.

Both my father and my brother adjusted their schedules in order to participate in these meetings. It was suggested that I go early and help to prepare everything, and they would come closer to crusade time. As I prayed about this, the Lord told me that He was sending me to the Philippines as He had sent Joseph to Egypt, to save a nation. What this meant I would not fully know until much later.

We arrived in the Philippines in late November. I sensed that the spiritual preparations were as important as the physical preparations that had to be made. I asked God to show us what to do. He answered that prayer before we even got there. A terrible typhoon hit the Philippines and tore down the Bible school facilities the McDougals and their co-workers had in Tanay, Rizal. This forced them to bring all their students (about forty of them) and the teachers and their families into the capital city. They were all sleeping, for the moment, inside their church building on the floor.

Many of the neighbors were camped out with them. Their small houses were so pounded by the storm that they were forced to take shelter in the church until they could make the necessary repairs. When we arrived, the church was full of people and their loss had contributed to a spirit of prayer that was already in evidence.

Little by little the neighbors returned home, but God told the rest of us to suspend the normal Bible school activities and to spend our days and nights praising and worshiping Him and waiting upon Him for instruction for the days ahead.

We were not the only ones feeling a burden for the Filipino people in those days. In fact, we learned that two other major crusades were planned in the capital city area at the same time as ours. The names given to them represented the crisis of the hour. Things had suddenly turned difficult all over the country, and thousands of students had taken to the streets to protest against the government. A national transportation strike was threatening, a very serious thing in a country where the common people did not have their own vehicles and depended on the public transport to get them from place to place. The communist rebel forces in the countryside were growing stronger every day. The Philippines was in the throes of the greatest crisis of government since independence in 1946.

In response to all these problems, one of those other scheduled crusades was being called "Revival or Revolution," and the other one was being called "Christ or Crisis." While these reflected the reality of the moment, God had told us to use the term, "Spiritual Fiesta." The fiesta had been for centuries an integral part of the Filipino way of life, a celebration to which everyone was invited and for which no expense was spared. The fiesta was a time to forget problems and to rejoice and enjoy the good things of life. God had said that He wanted the Philippines to experience a "Spiritual Fiesta." To our knowledge it was the first time the term was ever used for a revival meeting, and the Filipino people loved it and responded warmly to it.

The government also liked the name of our crusade. They felt that "Revival or Revolution" and "Christ or Crisis" only emphasized the negative aspects of the current problems the country was facing. They were not ignoring the problems, but these were complicated problems that would require complicated solutions. What the country needed right then, they agreed, was a "Spiritual Fiesta."

From the early phases of planning and execution of the plan, the Philippine government put many government facilities and personnel at our disposal. Military bands would be present at every crusade to play the national anthem and do the official flag ceremony. Military planes would be used to drop our leaflets over major metropolitan areas. Water tank trucks and other similar equipment would be provided for the crusade grounds, and military officials would be assigned for our security.

This was only the beginning of a long and mutually-beneficial relationship. One of the men largely responsible for all this help was General Fidel Ramos. At that time he was the commander of the military base adjacent to the Church in Murphy, a barrio of Quezon City. Later, he became the President of the Republic of the Philippines during a very difficult time and was able to bring the country back to prosperity.   ✻

$\approx 47 \approx$

"I Will Heal Their Land"

As we worshiped in the little church in Murphy, God began to send people from other countries. Dr. Joshua Raj from India had already closed his clinic and dedicated himself to the ministry. God now sent him to the Philippines and told him to be part of what He was doing there. William Tooley, a male nurse from New Zealand, and his wife Joan and daughter Julie felt led to leave their homeland and to join what was about to happen. Jay Rawlings, who had been working as a hospital administrator in Canada and his wife Meridel joined the Philippine team. Irene Bredlow, a Canadian nurse, came by the Philippines to visit her friend Meridel in the days just before the Spiritual Fiesta began, and she was saved and joined the ministry. She later worked with us many years in Israel.

Those other crusades were backed by large organizations and ministries. They had full committees and plenty of money with which to work. We had no money at all, yet the Lord was telling us many things that should be done to get out the word of the revival. Our hours of praise and worship every day were resulting in concrete revelations about how to proceed and what preparations to make.

More than fifty huge billboards were erected around the capital city, each with the slogan of the crusade which God had given us:

> If my people, which are called by my name, shall humble themselves, and pray, and seek my face, and turn from their wicked ways; then will I hear from heaven, and will forgive their sin, and will heal their land.
>
> 2 Chronicles 7:14

Each billboard contained the place and dates of the upcoming crusade.

When Pope John Paul came to town to bring hope to the Filipino people, millions of them turned out to see him. As they passed every major intersection in the city, they saw the billboards and read the announcement of the upcoming activities. That slogan got down deep into the hearts of the Filipino people, and they realized that what the nation needed was a "Spiritual Fiesta."

Each step was one of faith, for we were working with a small and relatively-new mission, but what we lacked in money, we made up for in enthusiasm. Everyone gave themselves unreservedly, and the Lord was faithful in each step. When He spoke to us to put the crusades on television, we wondered how this would be possible.

My associate remembered her classmate in the American High School, Fred Elizalde, whose family owned a major newspaper, many radio stations, and a fairly new but competitive television channel that specialized in sports. He was now managing that station, Channel 11. She took us to see him, and he agreed to sell us an hour of live television each night of the ten-night crusade at competitive rates. I cannot forget the day we signed the television contract. We had to pass the hat among the team to get enough money to ride the local Jeepneys.

We felt that we needed to have something to place in the hands of the people who attended the crusade and made decisions for Christ, so we went to the Far East Broadcasting printing facility and ordered one hundred thousand copies of the Gospel of John in the simple Today's English Version.

As the revival broke further, we purchased from the Philippine Bible Society all their yellowing stock of every Filipino dialect and, from the Summer Institute of Linguistics, all their stock of available Gospel portions in the languages of the remote tribes. In order to get their missionary translators into the country, they had signed an agreement not to preach in the places they worked. They gave years of their lives to translate portions of the Bible into the languages of those remote tribes, yet, since they could not preach, many of those Gospel portions would just sit there in their storeroom once they were actually printed.

Each time a new language was produced, three copies were taken out. One went to the translator, one to the printer, and one into the permanent archives of the organization. Many times all the rest sat there undistributed. It seems to me that they had Gospel portions in more than one hundred languages.

The morning Brother McDougal and I went to sign the contract to buy them all, the lady asked us what we would do with them. When we told her that we would send teams into every tribe to preach and distribute them personally, she said to me, "If we had the kind of financial backing you have, we could give everything away too." We only smiled, knowing that we were living day to day and had only God's financial backing to count on. Before it was over, the Spiritual Fiesta teams would distribute 1,250,000 Gospels of John, and the history of the Philippines would be changed forever. ❋

⚝ 48 ⚝

"If You Can Produce Another Miracle Like That"

Several amazing things happened in connection with the actual crusade. We had secured the huge Quezon City Municipal Stadium with capacity for some fifty thousand people for the initial crusade in the capital city. We equipped more than fifty ushers with identification to seat the people and with special offering receptacles to receive their gifts to help cover the expenses of the meetings. Just as the crusade was to begin, however, the transportation strike finally became a reality, and people were powerless to get to the stadium. Being on the streets was even dangerous at night, and authorities were advising people not to be out if they could possibly avoid it. In that huge stadium we had a crowd of usually not more than a thousand people standing in the grass in front of the platform.

We had worried about how we would get our huge offerings safely out of the stadium and to the bank without incident and had decided on an oversize suitcase carried by several strong men. Our offerings were never more than $30.00 a night, and my father gave half of that amount. We had to believe God for greater miracles to meet all the financial needs.

The huge stash of Gospels we had under the platform at the stadium was barely touched by giving to those who attended the meetings, and was, during the following days of riot, distributed to seventy-five thousand marching students by military personnel.

The television proved to be the key to revival. We had hoped to bring fifty thousand people nightly into the stadium, but our captive audience now watching in their homes was estimated at half a million, and God gave them much to see.

The first thing that impacted the audience was the worship. Those students and missionaries had been praising God every day for more than a month, and they were on fire for Him. The Filipinos are excellent musicians and singers anyway, and the worship was captivating.

We feared that many of these young people, having come from poor barrios themselves, might be intimidated by the television lights. We encouraged them to get in the Spirit and to forget about the lights and cameras, and they did just that. If they felt nervous, they could just close their eyes and worship God.

I Ask for the Philippines

They were a wholesome and clean-cut looking group, with the joy of the Lord on their faces, and even their appearance impressed those who watched.

The thing that impressed the audience was the miracles God did. My brother spoke that first night from the theme verse. With the opening ceremonies, the prayers, the testimonies and the songs of worship, when he finished his sermon, the hour of live television time was nearly up before he got ready to pray for people.

He had challenged the people who had physical needs to come forward, telling them that God would perform a miracle for them. The first man he prayed for had been in a terrible accident and was crippled. After my brother prayed for him, he was able to straighten up for the first time in many months. Then my brother challenged the man to put down his crutches and walk, and he did — on live television — just as our paid hour of time was expiring.

It was at that point that God performed another great miracle. My associate was standing beside one of the cameramen, and he told her that Fred Elizalde had just called and said that if the preacher could produce more miracles like that, he would give us an extra half hour of time free. From that point on, God did great miracles in view of the people, and every night Fred called to offer free time. He was not disappointed by what God did.

These televised miracles proved to be the breakthrough for revival, for soon we were getting calls from Catholic schools and seminaries and other Catholic organizations saying that they had seen us on television and liked the way we worshiped God, as if we knew Him, and the way we talked to God and expected Him to answer. Could we come and teach them and pray for them to receive the same thing?

Prior to the Spiritual Fiesta, the relationship between the Protestants and Catholics in the islands was one of confrontation. The very next week, however, we found ourselves standing before a large group of the priests and nuns of Loyola College, telling them about what God was doing all over the world by His Spirit. In the coming months, Spiritual Fiesta teams would visit and pray for church leaders in every province of the Philippines, and *Time Magazine* would carry an article two years later about the revival, saying that already more than a thousand Catholic priests and nuns and more than ten thousand Catholic lay people had been baptized in the Spirit and were speaking in tongues. It was, according to the magazine article, the greatest thing happening in the Church anywhere in the world at that moment.

This is what the Lord had shown those who had gathered in the fall of 1969, and He was doing it. Before long, Filipino missionaries had taken the glory that struck their shores out to more than thirty other nations just as the Lord had said.

After the initial crusade in Quezon City, similar meetings were held in Iloilo,

Surigao and Naga City. In each of those places, God gave us wonderful miracles and wonderful open doors.

We were also on television in Naga City. The cameras were rolling when a lady with a large goiter came for prayer, and tens of thousands of people watched as that goiter went down and then disappeared under my brother's hand.

What people did not know was that, because we were traveling with such a large group of people (seventy-five of us including students, teachers and missionaries), life had to be extremely simple for us. We had been able to secure an old empty mansion to use for our team, mainly because everyone was sure it was haunted and, consequently, no one would rent it. The other reason we got it inexpensively was that it had no furnishings. So when people saw us on the platform under the television lights at night they could hardly imagine that we were sleeping on the floor at night and sharing the rice and vegetables we could afford to buy at the local market on dishes that we had carried with us for the journey.

It was during those days that we were first invited to speak to the Carmelites, a cloistered group of nuns who dedicate themselves to prayer. Hundreds of Carmelite nuns would receive the Spirit over the coming months and years and would move into an increasingly dynamic prayer life in the Spirit.

What a wonderful day it was when Brother McDougal, my brother and I were invited to participate in a Catholic service in the Cathedral! It was an historic moment. The scripture passage assigned to me to read that day was about Joseph going to Egypt to save a nation, exactly what God had shown me before I went. He was doing it before our very eyes. ✳

≈ 49 ≈

"To the Islands of the Sea"

When we got back to the capital, after a wonderful month of meetings throughout the country, the Lord spoke one night after the service and gave me a plan that would reach every island and every province of the nation. We had grown to love every place we had visited till then, but God had laid many other places on our hearts.

Very early in the Philippine revival, we had taken the tune of an old and familiar missionary refrain and replaced the cities and countries mentioned with Filipino localities God had placed in our hearts. We called it our Harvest Song, and it went like this:

> Marinduque, Tawi Tawi, o'er the islands of the sea,
> Cotabato, Iloilo, here am I, oh Lord, send me.
> Isabela or Manila, Bulacan or Surigao,
> Far away strand, or the homeland,
> Savior, lead the way.

Now the Lord showed us how to divide the large team into small groups, give them specific areas to cover and send them out to minister to religious, military, political and educational leaders and students all across the country.

The Ministry of Education facilitated this outreach by giving us letters of authority to enter every school in the country. Each team carried Bibles, Gospel portions and good books to place in the hands of key people. Each week they sent cables back home giving shipping instructions for more Gospels and other literature to be sent to the specific towns they would be visiting next. During the next two years, these teams would preach and pray with every school student in the country and with every governor, every mayor, every senator and with many other key people. The nation would never be the same.

It was all done by faith. The night I introduced the plan, Brother McDougal took me aside afterward and said to me, "I don't mean to sound negative, but we have been stretched to the limit to do what we have already done. Our budget this year has already surpassed everything we spent last year, and we are still in the early months of the year. If we do what you are saying ... I did some figuring. We will need $4,000 just to get started, $3,000 for literature and $1,000 for transportation." That was a lot of money for a small mission in 1970.

I knew I didn't have any money, but I told him that I knew God had given me the plan, and I was sure that God would provide the needed financing.

It couldn't have been more than five minutes later that Brother Chappell came out to join us. He had just received a call from his secretary in the United States to say that he had gotten a large refund on his taxes. Since he hadn't been expecting it, he decided to give it to God. "I want to give $4,000," he said, "$3,000 to help with the printing bill for the Gospels, and $1,000 to help with the transportation of the teams that are going out." He had not overheard our conversation. The Lord had performed the miracle and would continue to provide for this great outreach.

I left a few days later to travel to Hong Kong and on back to America, but Brother McDougal and his teams implemented that great plan. Today there are more than ten to fifteen million Charismatic Catholics in the Philippines as a result and a present-day Philippine revival that began with the Spiritual Fiesta.

The Filipino young people not only reached out all over their country, they reached out all over Asia and to many other parts of the world, as well. Filipinos were some of the first foreign Christians to minister in China (when China was still closed to foreigners) and became leaders in the great outreach of Brother Andrew's Open Doors. They went into many of the other places where it was difficult for Americans to travel as well. They have been influential in revival in Cambodia, Thailand, Vietnam, and many other places. We are continually hearing reports of their blessed work.

Among those who had a part in this harvest, Jack and Pattie Chappell deserve special mention. Their financial gifts were responsible for sending many to the islands and to the nations.

I often wished that I had recorded all the many wonderful miracles the Lord did during the Spiritual Fiesta. They were truly remarkable. One stands out in my memory. When I went back to the Philippines a few months later, a young brother came walking up to me and said, "Do you remember me?"

"I'm sorry, I don't," I had to respond.

"I was the young man in the wheelchair in the Quezon City Municipal Stadium," he reminded me, and then I remembered. When we had prayed for him, his legs were so thin that they seemed like bones covered over with a little skin. He had been so incapacitated by polio and so emaciated that few had given him hope. Yet here he was standing before me totally healed by the power of God. He had come to the Bible school to prepare himself for the ministry. What a great miracle that was!

The Spiritual Fiesta did not happen without great personal sacrifice on the part of many. All of the missionaries, the teachers, the students and many other local believers worked to make the meetings and their harvest possible. In the

I Ask for the Philippines

Manila area, for instance, many thousands of posters were printed to put up all over that great metropolitan area. Homemade paste was cooked in huge kettles by day, then by night, because of the terrible traffic jams in the capital area during the daytime, we all worked to put the posters up. The very people who were soon visible on television on the platform in the stadium had been out all night the night before putting up invitations for everyone to see. Although many sacrificed in this way, we always remember Diane McDougal's hard work because she was expecting her third child at the time.

We went right into the Congress building to give formal invitations to each congressman. Several of them sent us cables, declaring their support of our work and telling us that their prayers were with us.

Vice President Fernando Lopez was one of those Philippine officials who responded to the revival. I was able to pray with him and his whole family, as were other members of the team over time.

We are instructed of the Lord not to despise *"the day of small things"* (Zechariah 4:10). We must not always feel like we need great sums of money in order to do something for God. It's more fun to stand back and watch as God performs the miracles and meets every need. Just be willing to step out by faith and believe the word of the Lord. When God said that His glory would be revealed through all of Asia by means of the things He was about to do in Manila, we believed it, and He brought it to pass.

Later I began to understand what God meant when He said that He was sending me to the Philippines as He had sent Joseph to Egypt. What happened over the coming years not only spared the nation and returned it to stability but sent God's glory out from there all over the world.

The Philippines is the only Christian nation from the Far East to the Middle East. The Filipinos are such wonderful singers and such wonderful worshipers. We enjoyed immensely the island experience and the flow of God that comes forth from their lives. We were especially blessed with the young people from the tiny island of Hibuson in the Visayas and their anointed music. Some twenty missionaries were produced by that one island and their labors have blessed many nations.

Even today, God is using the Filipino people all over the world, dispersing them as great lights and testimonies. Besides those who have gone as full-time missionaries and pastors, millions more have gone as domestic help, contract workers for the oil fields, maritime workers, and doctors and nurses, and they have taken their faith with them wherever they have gone. Many times they have been able to go into countries where no Westerner can live. They have been God's salt, preserving the nations. They have been God's light, presenting a witness for Him in dark places. Anywhere you go in the world, you will find a Filipino who has been sent by God and who is thrilled to have had the pleasure. I thank God for the privilege of having a part in the great Philippine harvest.

Harvest Glory

One of the things that has blessed me about the revival in the Philippines is that the people have been so open to God, allowing Him to intrude on every part of their lives. Many Filipino shops and offices shut down at midday, and those who work there often grab a quick lunch and then gather to worship and study the Word of God. I preached at the office of the Philippine Petroleum Industry where meetings were held both at midday and in the evening when work was finished. The people who gathered were so eager and so excited about the Lord, and that blessed me.

Many Filipino theaters, discos and other public places are used on off-hours and weekends as worship centers. The Filipinos, totally unashamed to worship God wherever they are, have practically turned their nation into a place of worship, an example that many would be blessed to emulate. Certainly it is a pattern that will be used in nation after nation in the days to come.

Over the years, we had many wonderful experiences among the Filipino people. One night I went with Sister Henri Locsin to the home of Vice President Jose Laurel. It was his wife's birthday. Many important politicians were present that evening. Everyone was excited because of recent elections and were busily talking about the results.

I slipped out of the main dining room for a few moments to find a rest room and, on my way back, one of the vice president's daughters stopped me and asked if I would pray for her. I did, and she was so blessed that, one after another, she brought all the important officials to me in that side room, and I was able to pray with them. Many of them were filled with the Spirit that night. I was the last person to leave the party. Well after midnight I was still there praying for one leader after another.

The next night I was invited to an official reception for those who worked in the Palace. How surprised I was that many of the people I had prayed for only the night before were there as well.

Another night in a home Bible study in the Philippines I had a vision of a young man who was our host. I saw him in a military uniform. The Lord said to him, "I will do for you in the Spirit what was not possible in the natural." God told him that he would raise him up in great authority in the Kingdom of God and make him one of God's generals. I later learned that his father had been the Minister of Defense of the Philippines, a general who had been disappointed that his stepson had not followed in his footsteps, although he had trained in the military academy. Isn't it wonderful how God speaks so specifically to people? He does it with such ease by the Spirit. Thank God for the Holy Spirit's ecouragement.　　　　　　　　　　　　　　　　　　　　　　　　　✳

﹍ 50 ﹍

"Remember the Marketplace in Rangoon"

On the night of April 19, as we finished the Spiritual Fiesta activities, the Lord gave us His plan for reaching all of the Philippines. He also told me, "I'm going to deal with you in sevens and eights. Don't try to figure out what I'm saying, but I want you to fast seven days and eat on the eighth, and fast seven more days and eat on the eighth, and do it for seven weeks and eat on the eighth week."

The Lord showed me that He wanted us to take Jay and Meridel with us and return home going overland through the Indian subcontinent, the Middle East and Europe. Since they were Canadians and Meridel was due to deliver their baby any day, they flew to Hong Kong so that she could deliver the baby there. They already had one son, John David, and the very next day their second son, Christian, was born in the British Crown Colony. The same day in Manila, Diane McDougal gave birth to their second daughter, Dorie.

Although I loved Hong Kong so much, I felt an urgency to get to New Delhi, so we made only a brief stop in Hong Kong, asked the Rawlings to meet us in India, and we went on. We did stop over in Rangoon, Burma, where, in the marketplace, we met an Israeli man who became a good friend. Arieh Elan was the Israeli Ambassador to Burma (now known as Myanmar), and he invited us to dine with him that evening in the embassy. It was the first Israeli embassy I visited, and that evening was the beginning of a new thing that God was doing in my life. At that moment I had no idea that we would ever live in Israel, but God knew the future perfectly.

After we had been living in Israel for many years, I attended a lecture series at Beit Agron, the government press building. At one point the speaker said, "Everything I know I learned from my mentor when I was with him at the United Nations," and he mentioned Arieh's name. Then he said, "And we are very happy to have him here with us tonight." I looked around the room to see where Arieh might be sitting, only to discover that he was right beside me, blushing because of the acclamation he was receiving. I had slipped into the lecture at the last minute, took my seat and had not seen whom I was sitting beside.

I did not want to disrupt the lecture, so I took out my card and wrote on it,

163

"Remember the marketplace in Rangoon?" and I handed it to him. I could feel his excitement as he read it. At the end of the lecture, he threw his arms around me and said in his beautiful Oxford accent, "What are you doing here?" We were able to renew an old acquaintance we had first made during that stopover in Rangoon. We had a long-lasting friendship that began in Burma.   ✸

๙ 51 ๒

"Don't Delay Along the Way"

By the time we arrived at New Delhi, we were tired. We sat down to relax for a while. I absentmindedly picked up a local newspaper and started to scan it when I saw that the King of Bhutan was arriving in New Delhi that day as the guest of the government of Prime Minister Indira Ghandi. I was immediately energized and set about to find out at which airport he would be arriving.

When we knew, we quickly refreshed ourselves and put on some white gloves. My associate wrote on a calling card the message, "We would like to come to your country. We would like to visit Your Majesty," and she slipped the card inside her glove.

When we got to the airport, a private one, we could see Prime Minister Ghandi some distance away waiting beside the tent where, we assumed, the official welcoming ceremonies would take place. We asked a soldier to take one of our cards to her, saying that recently my associate had met the brother of the King of Bhutan at the marriage of the Crown Prince of Nepal and that we would like to be present for the welcoming ceremony. Prime Minister Indira Ghandi granted us permission, and we were seated on the second row of guests awaiting the King's arrival.

When the King's plane touched down on the tarmac, an officer came and asked us to move up to the front row. It was in this way that we became part of the official receiving line for the King.

There was the customary playing of the national anthems and welcoming speeches. As the ceremonies progressed and the King and Mrs. Ghandi walked toward us down the receiving line, we prayed that God would perform a miracle.

Just before the King reached us, he became visibly nervous and, perhaps because of it, he reached out his hand to shake hands with the gentleman in line just ahead of us, instead of placing his hands palm to palm in the customary *nameste* (greeting). This allowed my associate the opportunity to also extend her hand in a handshake. She did a very low, slow curtsey, and the television camera focused on the curtsey and not on her hand which was slipping the card into the hand of the King. When the King came to me, I also curtsied.

This was a very special moment that we had been waiting for and praying for

165

during the last several years. We also met the Crown Prince that day, the present King of Bhutan, and we also met Prime Minister Indira Ghandi. When the Lord had told us in Manila that night, "Go directly to New Delhi, and don't delay on the way," it had been because we had an appointment to meet the King of Bhutan. We were the only Westerners present to receive him that day. No diplomats were included in the ceremony, which had been a very intimate Indian affair.

The next day we were invited to the office of the President of India to meet the King's representative. We had brought two gifts for the King on a previous trip and had left them with a friend, Mrs. Ivy Nathaniel. I wasn't sure what future opportunity we might have, so I was determined to present the King with the gifts we had bought for him. They were recordings of the New Testament read in English and a beautifully bound Bible in both English and Tibetan. ✳

⚜ 52 ⚜

"By the Pile of Sunflower Seed Shells"

After a few days, Meridel and Jay joined us in New Delhi, and together we traveled overland on very limited resources. Fortunately I was fasting, but when the eighth day came and I wanted to eat, sometimes there was either little available to buy or little with which to buy what was available.

We crossed Pakistan by bus into Afghanistan, going through the Khyber Pass and across Afghanistan to Kabul. From there we went overland to Tehran. In Tehran, we found a direct bus bound for Munich, Germany. It was nicer than most buses, so we decided to send the Rawlings, with their two small children, on ahead. From Munich they caught a flight directly back to America, while we continued our trip overland. We crossed Iran, visiting Hamadan and Sushan (of Queen Esther fame) and Isfahan. Later, when we were living in Israel, we would meet many Jews who had emigrated from Hamadan. All along the way we were meeting interesting people and having exciting times as we spoke freely to those we met of our experiences in serving God.

We traveled on to Basra. In Basra, we took a bus that was so small and squatty that it looked more like a French bread truck. It only held a dozen or so passengers. This was our ride across the desert, and it was terribly hot that day. The driver placed a block of ice beside the gear shift and headed off into the desert. He was headed for Ur, birthplace of Father Abraham.

From Ur, we went to Babylon, where we saw the famous Hanging Gardens of Babel. From Babylon, we caught a ride to Baghdad with the British Ambassador who had also been touring Babel.

From Baghdad, we took one of the fine Iraqi service taxis to Amman. These are Mercedes vehicles that hold seven passengers, and we paid only for the two seats we occupied. Our driver insisted on leaving at night because it was too hot to travel during the daytime. To stay awake through the night, he ate sunflower seeds. He started off across the desert with a bag full of them, and as he ate them he threw the shells on the floor. We could tell how far we had traveled by the size of the pile of sunflower seed shells on the floor.

From Amman we traveled to Damascus and from there to Beirut.　　　　✳

⚞ 53 ⚟

"Look for a Ship"

Although it wasn't far to Jerusalem, we did not go to Jerusalem at this time. We had heard about an inexpensive airline that was flying out of Beirut to Europe, and we knew of another inexpensive flight we could get from Europe to America. We got to the Beirut airport just in time for the scheduled flight to Europe, only to learn that the budget airline we had hoped to travel on had gone out of business. We sat in the airport for a while praying. We didn't have enough money to travel overland the rest of the way to Europe. Anyway, it would have meant going all the way back up through Syria and Turkey and that was not a pleasant prospect at the moment.

While we were sitting there in the airport praying, the Lord told us to go to the port and look for an inexpensive ship going to Europe. We got to the port area and walked along the line of docks, shouting to the men we saw out on the decks of the ships in port at the moment, asking them where the ship was going. We eventually came to an Argentinian sheep boat that would be leaving in just a few hours for Bari, Italy. We got very excited, sure that this was the answer to our prayer. We had been away for several months in the Philippines and we had now spent another two months on the road returning overland, and the thought of a nice cabin and some good food was wonderful.

We found the captain of the ship, explained to him that we were looking for an inexpensive way to get to Europe, told him about our budget airline going out of business, and asked if he had room to take us onboard.

"I don't see any reason why I couldn't take you," he said, "but the owner of the ship is in Beirut today, so you need to talk to him. He is staying in the St. George Hotel."

We got a taxi and went to the St. George Hotel, where we saw Mr. Villanueva, the owner of the Argentinian ship. "I don't see why you couldn't go with us," he said, "but let me just check with the agent and see if our local consul has placed any limitations on us." He checked and found that it would be permissible for his ship to take us.

"How much will it cost us?" we asked.

I Ask for Lebanon

"I have my own cabin on the ship and I won't be using it this time," he said. "Please be my guests there. It won't cost you anything."

The whole process had taken a little over an hour. After we thanked Mr. Villanueva, we got a taxi back to the boat. The sun was just going down, ending the seven weeks of my fast. We had so little money left that we could not have purchased food for another week. That night, we ate the first of some wonderful meals aboard that Argentinian freighter. Several courses were served at each meal. In the evening, one course was always a pasta and another was always a wonderful Argentine steak of some sort. It would have been a wonderful treat for anyone, but much more so for me after so many weeks of fasting.   *

⚞ 54 ⚟

"You're Welcome to Stay Aboard"

It took us only two days to reach Bari, and we enjoyed every moment of those two days.

As we were approaching the port, the captain said to us, "We'll be loading grain here for the sheep. You're welcome to stay on the ship tonight. You may want to go off and do some sight-seeing, but come back and eat your meals with us on the ship. As long as we are in port, you're welcome to stay aboard."

We took him up on that offer, and when we got back to the ship that night we were told that the automated equipment for loading the grain was not working properly. The loading would normally have been done in a day, but because it would have to be done by hand, it would take many days. We were guests of the ship for nearly a week in the port of Bari. All during that eighth week, when the Lord had told me to eat, we were blessed to eat sumptuously as guests of the ship's captain.

From Bari, we took a train to Luxembourg, and from there flew to the Bahamas, Miami and back home to Virginia.

In later years, as I thought much about this whole experience, I realized that seven weeks (fifty days) before Pentecost is the Feast of Weeks. Although I could not understand what God was doing at the time, I came to recognize that He was working the sevens and eights into my spirit. Seven represents completion, and eight represents the new thing. It was almost as if I were living out that seven-week period even before God took us to Israel and began to do the new thing in us.

✺

55

"Your Feet Shall Stand on the Hill of Zion"

No sooner had we gotten home to Virginia after so many months of hard travel than my brother told us about a conference on Bible prophecy that was to be held the following week in Jerusalem. I didn't pay much attention to what he was saying. We had not yet gotten very involved with Jerusalem and, more importantly, I had not even unpacked yet. That night, however, while I was preaching in the church in Richmond, the Lord spoke to me in the middle of my sermon and told me to fly to Jerusalem the next day.

I had learned that when God says something He has a reason for saying it, so right in the middle of my sermon I turned to my associate (who was sitting on the front pew) and said, "Call and find out what time I can get a flight to Jerusalem tomorrow."

At the close of the service she told me what time my flight would be leaving the next day, and the believers gathered around to lay hands on me and pray, sending me on my trip to Jerusalem.

Mother, who often had an amazing word of prophecy at moments like this, began to prophesy: "Your feet shall stand on the hill of Zion." I didn't appreciate fully what the Lord had said until later. My thinking was that I was on my way to Jerusalem, so of course my feet would stand on Zion.

She also had a vision in which she saw an aide to Prime Minister Golda Meir. She described what he looked like and told me how old he was and said that I would speak with him.

As I set off for Jerusalem, I had few details about the conference that was to take place there and didn't even know who was sponsoring it. By this time my brother was taking tours to Jerusalem each year. He suggested that I call the owner of the travel agency he used there to see if he would perhaps arrange a complimentary room for me. I intended to do that, but on the way to Israel the Lord spoke to me to stay at the King David Hotel in Jerusalem.

Although I had been to Jerusalem several times, I did not know anything about the King David Hotel. We always stayed in the eastern part of the city, where most of the sights associated with the life of Christ are located. When I got to the airport in Tel Aviv, I asked about the King David Hotel, and a young Israeli girl told me, "There's a big conference in Jerusalem, and the hotels are fully booked.

I'm sure that the King David Hotel is full too." I asked if she would call and check, and she was surprised to find that they did have a room.

"How many nights do you want to stay?" she asked.

"Three," I answered.

She was amazed when the clerk told her they could accommodate me. I wasn't surprised. If the Lord had told me to stay at the King David Hotel, they would have room for me. What I didn't know was that the King David Hotel was the most expensive hotel in town. To this day heads of state and other important visitors to Jerusalem stay at the King David Hotel. This was my first time to be in such a Jewish atmosphere.

As soon as I arrived in Jerusalem, I went to the government conference center to register for the conference and learned that it was being sponsored by Dr. Carl Henry and his magazine *Christianity Today*. Next I called the Prime Minister's office and asked to speak to Mrs. Golda Meir. I was told that she was out of town, so I asked to speak to her aide. After several minutes, he came on the line and asked me who I was and what my business was with the Prime Minister.

I gave him my name and told him that I was from Virginia, that I had come to Jerusalem to attend the conference on Bible prophecy, and that I had a word from the Lord for him. He said that he was very sorry but his appointments were made five weeks in advance, just like Mrs. Meir's. He was about to hang up, when I repeated what I had said already. I didn't have any new information to give him. He must have heard the urgency in my voice because he said, "I'll tell you what: I'll see you tomorrow afternoon for five minutes."

In those days, I had no sense of humor, but I suddenly found myself saying, "You see me today for five minutes, and tomorrow afternoon you will call me."

The Jewish people are famous for their *chutzpah*, their boldness, and I suppose in that moment he felt that I had out-*chutzpah*ed everybody he knew. He laughed, and then he said, "All right, I'll see you this afternoon for five minutes." So that afternoon I made my way to the Office of the Prime Minister of Israel.

The man I was about to see was Eli Mizrachi. He was a fourth generation Jerusalemite. His mother was born in Rhodes, his great-grandfather in Aleppo, Syria.

Eli graduated from the Hebrew University in Jerusalem, where he majored in history, philosophy and political science.

From 1962 to 1967 he worked at the Israeli State Archives, part of the Prime Minister's Office, and served as Director of Research on the Arab-Israeli conflict and the question of Palestine during the British Mandate (1917-1947). During that time, he was assigned to work with Prime Minister David Ben Gurion. He stayed in the desert in Ben Gurion's kibbutz for six months, assisting the aging Prime Minister, founding father of Israel, in preparing his memoirs and diaries.

I Ask for Jerusalem

He was Director of the Office of the Director-General of the Prime Minister's Office, a post in which he served from 1967 to 1970, and he was much involved with the status quo of the holy places in Israel and in the sensitive negotiations with the Christian religious communities after the Six-Day War.

For ten years, from 1970 to 1980, he served in the Prime Minister's Bureau of the Prime Minister's Office in Jerusalem, first as Deputy Director of the Bureau, then as Director (equivalent to the American Chief of Staff of the White House) and as Political Advisor to Prime Ministers Meir, Rabin and Begin. He participated in the diplomatic negotiations related to the peace process in the Middle East, including ten official visits to the United States and meetings with King Hussein of Jordan, the Shah of Iran and President Sadat of Egypt.

He knew, aside from Hebrew and English, French, Italian, Spanish, Latin and Arabic. His writings included: *Guide to the Palestine Papers of Lord Samuel* and *Guide to the Papers of the Political Secretary of the Palestine Government, 1918-1925*. And these are only the things we are permitted to say.

I was seated in an outer office waiting for him for a little while. When he came out of his office toward me, I began to smile.

"What are you laughing about?" he asked.

"Two nights ago in Virginia," I answered, "my mother had a vision of you, and she described you perfectly. I can even tell you how old you are." I told him, and he was amazed. He had been to Buckingham Palace and to the White House and other important places on behalf of the Prime Minister and the Israeli government, but I was the first person whose mother had ever had a vision of him. It was a perfect icebreaker, and he immediately was interested in what I had to say.

I told him about Grandmother Ward's love for the Bible and the people of the Book and about my parents being such great people of the Word. I had been taught since childhood, I explained, that God had a great plan for the Jewish people. I told him how we had gathered around an old radio when I was a child, anxious to hear the results of the United Nations' vote for the establishment of the State of Israel. How excited we had all been when the vote was positive. We knew that the generation that saw Israel become a nation would also see the King coming in His power.

After we had talked for a while, I was suddenly conscious of the fact that we had gone beyond the allotted five minutes. It must have been more like half an hour. "I'm sorry," I said, "I didn't mean to take so much of your time."

He said, "You're not going to leave now. You're going to stay and tell me how God speaks to you."

It was some time later when he called for a chauffeured car to take me back to the hotel. Surprisingly, he got in the car with me and it headed off. I was not very familiar with the western part of the city, but I soon sensed that we were not heading toward the King David Hotel.

"This is not the way back to the King David Hotel, is it?" I asked.

"No," he said, "there's a view of the city that I'm sure you've never seen, and I want to show it to you."

I had come to attend the conference and to visit the Prime Minister's Office, and I had not reserved time for sight-seeing. I was very pleased that I was going to be seeing something that I had not seen before.

The car twisted and turned around the city and then stopped. We got out and walked onto a balcony overlooking a very old part of the city. "This is David's City," he began, and it soon became apparent that he was a walking historian and amateur archeologist. He was totally enthralled with all the things he was telling me. He clearly loved the city of Jerusalem.

After a while, I interrupted him to ask, "But where are we?"

"This is Mt. Zion," he said.

When he said that I felt the presence of God like electric bolts from the top of my head to the soles of my feet, and I remembered the words my mother had spoken just a couple of nights before in Virginia: "Your feet shall stand on the hill of Zion." I had thought the Lord was speaking of Zion in a general sense, meaning the entire Holy City. I hadn't understood how precise He was being. My feet would literally stand "on the hill of Zion."

The next day I attended the morning session of the conference, where I heard Professor Flusser and former Prime Minister David Ben Gurion and later met him. When I got back to my hotel, there was a little note in the pigeon box. It said, "Call the Prime Minister's Office."

When I reached Eli, he said, "You were right. I do want to see you again." He wanted to hear more about how God was leading me. For the next several hours we spoke of the places I had recently been and things I had done. The interesting thing was that every story I told was concerning a place where Eli himself had recently traveled on behalf of the Israeli government. I had just been with Emperor Haile Selassie of Ethiopia. He was deeply touched.

Eli invited me to come and live in Jerusalem. In response, I made what probably was the most foolish statement of my life. I said I was too busy to live in Jerusalem. In my own thinking, I was. Our family had always been busy in the work of God, and since I had begun traveling overseas, I was busier than ever before. I just didn't perceive what the Lord had in mind.

At the King David Hotel there was an art gallery on the mezzanine floor which was visible from the entrance lobby. As I looked at the painting of a Jewish rabbi teaching a young boy, I fell in love with the Jewish people. Through that painting I later met Dov Safri, the owner of the gallery, and later, Sarah Dromey, the artist, who grew up in Harbin, China, and immigrated to Israel at the age of nineteen. She was a Jewess of Russian immigrant parents. We were to become friends.

Eli Mizrachi also remains a good friend until this day.

The events of the conference culminated in a glorious reception given for the four thousand delegates at the Israeli Museum by the Mayor of Jerusalem, Teddy Kolleck. As I was the first guest to arrive, I had the privilege of meeting the mayor and being photographed with him. The picture of us together appeared on the album cover of a special convention record sent to all the delegates. I remain a personal friend of the mayor and his wife Tamara. ✳

56

"The Flutter of Their Wings"

It was a very quick trip to Jerusalem. I left Ashland, Virginia, on Monday night and got back on Saturday. That night when I got into my bed, I had an experience in which the Living Creatures from Ezekiel chapter 1 and Revelation chapter 4 flew into my bedroom. I cannot say for sure how long they were there, but their presence was glorious, and when they left, I knew that I would spend my life with the Jewish people.

The next morning as I was on the way to church, I could still feel the glory I had felt when they were in my room. It seemed that my arms were possessed of a great jet propulsion. I was trying to drive the car, but my hands would fly off the wheel and flutter as those of the Living Creatures. I would put my hands back on the wheel, and the surging power would hit them again. It was only the presence of angels that got us safely to church that morning.

On the way, I began singing the words to a new song God was giving me:

I can feel the flutter, flutter, flutter of their wings,
The Living Creatures in the wheel as they sing,
Holy! Holy! Holy to our God!
Which was, and is, and is to come.
I can feel the flutter, flutter, flutter of their wings.

I can feel the flutter, flutter, flutter of their wings,
That proclaims the soon coming of our King.
As the angels hover near,
Jesus Christ will soon appear.
I can feel the flutter, flutter, flutter of their wings.

I can feel the flutter, flutter, flutter of their wings.
As they cry Holy! Holy! Holy to our King!
So I fell on my face,
For the glory in this place,
Makes me feel the flutter, flutter, flutter of their wings.

I Ask for Jerusalem

The next day I told Mother that I would be living in Israel in the future. "But Ruth," she asked, "What about Bhutan? You've been praying about going there, and the door hasn't opened yet."

"Yes," I answered, "but I know that I'm going to Israel to live."

"What if something happens to you in Israel and you never get to Bhutan?" she asked.

"I don't know," I had to answer. "All I know is that I'm going to go and live in Israel."

We got most of our mail through a post office box in Richmond, and we usually passed by the post office on our way to church. I was riding that day with my father, and I said to him, "Daddy, stay here, and I'll go in and check the mailbox."

When I came out, I had an open letter in my hand, and I was crying. "What is it?" he asked.

"We're closer to the coming of the Lord than we realize," I said.

"What is it?" he asked again.

"It's an invitation from the King of Bhutan to be his guest in Bhutan."

The Lord was enabling me to tie up all the loose ends before entering a new phase of my ministry. ✻

≤ 57 ≥

"Give Emperor Haile Selassie a Message"

That summer, toward the end of campmeeting in Ashland, the Lord spoke to me and said, "I want you to be in Jerusalem for the new moon. And when it is the New Year for My people, it will also be a New Year for you. Oh, by the way, on the way to Jerusalem, I want you to stop by Ethiopia and give Emperor Haile Selassie a message."

I wasn't familiar with the significance of new moons, and I didn't know anything about the Jewish New Year, so I called the Jewish Community Center in Richmond and asked about it. The receptionist told me that the new moon would fall on the 17th in September.

"When is the new year?" I asked.

"September 17," she said.

It was already the first week of September, so to get down to Ethiopia and back up to Jerusalem in time, I would have to hurry. I checked with the airlines and found that there was only one connection that would enable me to do exactly what God had said. I would have to fly into Addis Ababa at about seven in the morning one day and fly out on the same flight the next day at just about the same time.

I called Addis and asked Sarah if she would meet me at the airport. She did.

"Why are you here now?" she asked.

"I've come to see the Emperor," I answered.

"Does he know you're coming?"

"No, not yet."

"Well, how do you think that you'll get to see him then? Remember, it took many weeks before you could see him the last time you were here."

"I know," I told her, "but this time I only have one day, and something that took time at first may not need so much time now. God has established our friendship. It will be easier this time."

"Well, maybe so," she said, "but I don't see how you can ever see the Emperor in just one day without a prior appointment. He's a busy man."

"Well," I answered, "let's just see what God does."

We went to her house, and I called the Palace and asked to speak with His

178

I Ask for Ethiopia

Excellency Teferawerk, the Palace Minister. When I told him why I had come, he said, "Ruth, I'm sorry, but the Emperor has a meeting with the Council of Ministers today," and he went on to give me a whole list of scheduled events.

"I'm only here overnight," I said. "I'm leaving tomorrow morning to go to Israel. This is the time God has given me, and I have a message for the Emperor."

I wasn't worried about it happening, and I gave him the telephone number where I could be reached at the Mennonite Guest House. Later that afternoon, the telephone rang, and I was informed that the Emperor wanted me to be at Jubilee Palace at four o'clock.

As I was arriving in the city that morning, the Lord had spoken to me and said, "I'm going to honor you more this time than I did the last time." I thought, *How could God honor me any more than He did the last time? That time was so wonderful. What could be a greater honor?* The first time I was received by the Emperor, the visit had taken place in the Grand Palace, in the audience chamber where the Emperor received heads of state, ambassadors and diplomats. This time, however, I was being invited to the Palace where he lived. This was his home, and I was honored to be received in such an intimate way.

Jubilee Palace was every bit as grand as the Grand Palace, but this time there was no pomp and circumstance. The Emperor and I sat face to face, much closer than before, and his little chihuahua, Lou Lou, sat near us as we talked of the things that God had put in my heart. God spoke to His Majesty concerning his future and let him know what he needed to do. I had not been aware of the fact that he was leaving the next day for China, but the Lord knew and had a sure word for him concerning that trip.

As I was leaving the Palace that day, the Emperor said to me, "Ruth, anytime God gives you a word for a head of state, don't hesitate to go and deliver it." I felt that was probably one of the greatest indications I received of how my visit had ministered to him. He was letting me know that I had come at the right time, and had been used of God to be a blessing to him. I was one of the last people that ministered to him before the troubles came. In the prophecy God forewarned him of what was about to happen and gave him an answer.

Later, when I was back at the guest house, the telephone rang again, and it was His Excellency Teferawerk calling to ask me to please come back to the Palace for a further time of questioning concerning the things that God had put in my heart. Although my time had been so limited, I was actually invited to the Palace twice in one evening. God was preparing the Emperor for the political events that would follow. ✻

~58~

"The Pleasure of the Sabbath"

After ministering prophetically to the Emperor, I took the flight the next morning for Jerusalem. I would have a couple of weeks there before going on to the appointment in Bhutan.

While I was there I noticed an ad in a newspaper for a twenty-day Hebrew *Ulpan* (language course) to be conducted during the high holy days — which included *Rosh Hashana,* New Years; *Yom Kippur,* the Day of Atonement; *Succot,* the Feast of Tabernacles; and *Simhat Torah,* the Day of the Rejoicing of the Law. We enrolled at Ulpan Akiva in Netanya where Shulamith Katznelson was the director.

On the first Friday evening we all had dinner together. The Jewish people, we learned, call the opening moments of the Sabbath *Oneg Shabbat* which means "the pleasure of the Sabbath." They welcomed the Sabbath as they would welcome a guest or a queen. With the welcoming of the Sabbath came dancing and singing and rejoicing.

After we had eaten the soup, there were Hebrew songs sung around the table. The people sang very exuberantly. I kept asking, "What does that mean? What are they saying?" I imagined it might be a popular song, the latest on the hit parade. I discovered that they were singing songs like, *"Therefore with joy shall we draw water from the well of salvation," "Israel, depend upon your God," "Rejoice with Jerusalem, all ye that love her. Be glad for her,"* and *"I have set watchmen upon thy walls, Oh Jerusalem, which shall not hold their peace day or night."* Between each course of food, more songs were sung.

At one point each person put his or her arm around the person next to him and sang, *"Behold, how good and how pleasant it is for brethren to dwell together in unity."* Everyone swayed back and forth together as they sang.

At the end of the meal, after we had been served dessert and coffee (European style), everyone got up and started dancing. Again I imagined that they might be dancing to some popular song, but they were singing the Scriptures and dancing to the music of the Scriptures. How they rejoiced!

They were also joining hands as they danced, and this was something new for me. I had finally gotten liberty in dancing before the Lord as an individual, and I cherished that liberty, but dancing together seemed like something altogether

180

different. I remembered hearing someone saying once, "Sometimes, when we dance in our church, we reach over and take somebody by the hand and dance with them," and I had thought that must be one of the greatest heresies I had ever heard. Imagine! How "fleshly"!

I couldn't help but be impressed with the joy with which the Jewish people danced and the sincerity of their praise to God. Before long, we found ourselves joining in with them and dancing just as exuberantly as they were.

When the twenty days had finished, I found that I had not learned as much Hebrew as I had hoped, but I had received quite an orientation to life among the people of God's great land. Shulamith Katznelson remained a friend. ✳

﹏ 59 ﹏

"One Thing I Asked of the Lord"

In December we went to Bhutan. To get into that Himalayan kingdom was a dream come true. So few outsiders had visited the tiny kingdom through the years that our visas were numbered thirty-six and thirty-seven. We were the guests of the King and stayed in the Royal Guest House for seventeen days.

One of the highlights of our visit was an invitation to a Royal Archery Contest. We were guests of the King and his family in their royal tent. The Bhutanese are world-renowned archers, and while we watched the contest, we were able to visit and speak with the members of the Royal Family. When we were asked what we wanted to do in the country, we said that we wanted to meet and speak with the leading lamas. It so happened that there were five of them, they were present that day, and we were introduced to them right then and there.

We were royally treated in every other way and were able to see many parts of that breathtakingly beautiful country. Within the valley, where roads existed, we were taken by government jeep, and into areas where there were no roads, we went on foot.

The museums of Bhutan, if I could call them museums, were their temples. They were adorned with paintings that were beautifully executed.

Bhutan was a Buddhist stronghold, and we were believing God that as we walked through the land He would open it to the Gospel of Christ. Today, Bhutan is a very different country, much more open to the Gospel. There is a strong Bhutanese church, and many people from all parts of the world go in and out of that country for the sake of the Gospel. The Lord used us to go in first and believe for the opening.

One of the close friends we made while in Bhutan was Princess Ashi Dikki, the sister of the King. One day we were scheduled to spend some time with her, and she had agreed to come by and get us in the guest house. She was late (as princesses often are) and while we were waiting for her, we began to worship the Lord, singing in tongues. Then the Lord gave us the interpretation of that song in English.

It was interesting because this was long before we had come into the fullness of the new song. We would sing a phrase in tongues and then receive that phrase in English, until we had a whole song:

I Ask for Bhutan

One thing I asked of the Lord,
And He gave me.
Two things I asked of the Lord,
And He gave me.
Whether great, whether small,
He answers my call.
He's my God, and I'm His child,
And He loves me!

Chorus:
Yes, He loves me,
Truly loves me.
His desire is ever toward me.
And I love Him,
Truly love Him.
My desire is ever toward Him.

One soul I sought of the Lord,
And He gave me.
Two souls I sought of the Lord,
And He gave me.
Whether rich, whether poor,
He is the open door.
He's my God, and I'm His child,
And He loves me.

One land I claimed for the Lord,
And He gave me.
Two lands I claimed for the Lord,
And He gave me.
Whether near, whether far,
He is their Morning Star.
He's my God, And I'm His child,
And He loves me.

By the time the Princess arrived, we were very excited about our new song and we said to her, "Listen to what the Lord has just given us," and we began to sing the song that the Lord had just birthed in our spirits. She loved it. Something that is newly-birthed has a freshness that speaks into the lives of people in a way that the old never can.

We later learned that a famous musicologist had come from the University of Liverpool in England and was traveling around the country recording the native music of the various tribal people of Bhutan. He was staying in the same government guest house, and because the partitions for the rooms did not go all the way to the ceiling and a large space was left for air to circulate from room to room, he had overheard the entire process of our receiving a spiritual song. Obviously the Holy Ghost wanted him to hear how a song is given in the Spirit.

Our days in Bhutan were delightful and much sowing was done for the Kingdom.

As we left, Princess Ashi Dikki gave us a beautiful dog as a gift, and we took him home with us. He was a Damshi Apso, the shorthaired variety of the Lhasa Apso. The Damshi Apso is the official royal dog of Bhutan and appears on the official stamp of the Kingdom. We named him Chung Ku.

While we were staying in the Royal Guest House, there was a birthday party for the Crown Prince's eighteenth birthday. He is now the King of Bhutan. ✳

⚛ 60 ⚛

"Flee for Your Life"

Once, when we were in New Delhi, we had a few spare days, so we took a bus to Dharmsala. Dharmsala is a town in Northern India given by the Indian government to the Dalai Lama as a refuge for himself and those accompanying him after he fled Tibet and made his way to North India. We were interested in Tibet and the whole Himalayan region and had a desire to meet the Dalai Lama.

After checking into a hotel, we went to the secretariat of the Dalai Lama and obtained an appointment to meet him the next morning at ten. We spent the rest of the afternoon walking about and enjoying Dharmsala. The very lovely and charming Indian hill town had now taken on a Tibetan ambiance.

Early the next morning, about four-thirty, I was awakened by the audible voice of the Lord saying, "Flee for your life or die by the sword. Flee for your life or die by the sword." I was suddenly wide awake and wakened my associate and told her what I had just experienced. I told her we must dress quickly and get the first bus out of Dharmsala.

She, too, had looked forward to meeting the Dalai Lama and was reluctant to miss this opportunity. She had not heard the urgency I had in the Lord's voice, so she was not as prepared as I was to leave. Nevertheless, we both quickly got dressed, went to the bus station and headed back to New Delhi.

When we arrived in New Delhi, we changed buses for a local ride across the city to Safdarjung Enclave, where we were staying with Sister Ivy Nathaniel. After getting on the bus, I happened to glance backward as the doors were beginning to close and was surprised to see a Tibetan Lama, a Buddhist monk, attempting to board the same bus, only to be prevented from doing so by the closing door. I recognized him from photos we had taken at Namche Bazaar in Nepal a few years earlier. I had seen him in the midst of the crowd. He obviously had followed us that day from Dharmsala, intent on doing us harm. He would have known about our Scripture distribution among the Himalayas and would have seen it as a threat to the Dalai Lama.

When I saw him I said to my associate, "Look! Quick!" When she saw who was following us, she suddenly understood why the Lord had spoken to us to leave.

✳

185

≋ 61 ≋

"From the Sands of Zanzibar,
to the Coral of Bora Bora"

The following spring, God sent four of us ladies on a trip down the Amazon River from Iquitos, Peru, to Manaus, Brazil. We traveled aboard a simple river boat with small cabins and fasted and prayed our way much of the length of that great river. When the boat stopped along the way, we were also able to minister to people living along the river.

One of the ladies slept on the bunk above me, and one night during the night I heard her saying, "From the sands of Zanzibar to the coral of Bora Bora, from Khabarovsk to Novasibirsk, from the islands to the captives, My people have caught the vision." My first thought was that she must be reciting some sort of British nursery rhyme or something from a fairy tale she had learned while growing up in England. As I got a little more awake, however, I realized that what she was saying was no nursery rhyme but an important word from the Holy Spirit.

I fumbled for a pen and piece of paper and said, "What did you say?"

Amazingly, she repeated the same thing word for word, and I wrote furiously in the dark to get it all down: "From the sands of Zanzibar to the coral of Bora Bora, from Khabarovsk to Novasibirsk, from the islands to the captives, My people have caught the vision."

That little rhyme went over and over in our spirits, and as the days passed lazily drifting down the Amazon, I was very anxious to get to a place that had an atlas so that I could look up the places she had mentioned and see how a trip could be planned that would include them. I was convinced that God was mapping out for us an important journey.

When we reached Manaus, we were able to locate an atlas and look at it closely. Zanzibar is off the coast of Tanzania on the east side of Africa. Bora Bora is part of the Tahitian group of islands in the South Pacific. Khabarovsk is in the farthermost part of Siberia and Novasibirsk is in the central part of the former Soviet Union, where Siberia begins. What did this all mean?

Since I had traveled enough already that I felt I was an expert at arranging airline tickets and getting the most out of the allowable mileage, I began to plan how we could get all four of the places into one ticket. It could be done, but not the way the Lord had said it, and I knew somehow that how He said it was important. Traveling to the four places in the order the Lord listed them would mean the equivalent of going around the world twice (some fifty-five thousand miles), a very expensive and tiring trip, to say the least.

When we had completed the work the Lord had given us to do on the Amazon, we caught a plane to Miami. There we transferred to Nassau, Bahamas, to join my father and his team in a crusade he was conducting and, after several weeks of ministry in those islands, we returned to Virginia. ✶

⚖ 62 ⚖

"Take That Trip Immediately"

The trip the Spirit had laid out for us was never out of our thinking; it occupied an important place in our spirits; but it didn't seem practical or possible at the moment, so we did nothing further on it.

By this time, it was toward the end of May, and it would soon be time for our summer campmeetings to begin. Such a trip would surely take a very long time to complete and a lot more money than we had at the moment. In 1972, each of our tickets would cost more than five thousand dollars.

Then, one night the Lord spoke to us and said, "I want you to take that trip immediately." We hastily arranged the trip, God supernaturally provided the great sum of money we needed, and we started off on our fifty-five-thousand-mile journey. Over the next month, every several days, we moved on to another city or country, eventually changing time zones many times. It was an intense experience.

At the beginning, we had no idea exactly what God was sending us to do. We had this wonderful rhyming phrase that guided us, but what were we to do when we got to Zanzibar or Bora Bora or Khabarovsk or Novasibirsk? We didn't yet know. We had to be very sensitive to the Holy Spirit in order to learn it.

We flew into Tanzania and got a plane to Zanzibar. When we stepped onto the soil of Zanzibar, the first person we greeted was a Jewish man, someone who had lived in the Arab environment with his family for many years. From then until we landed in Russia, several weeks later, we stopped on one island after another and met one Jewish person after another. After Zanzibar, we visited Reunion, Mauritius, Australia, New Zealand, Bora Bora (of South Pacific fame), Hawaii and Japan.

Something about Zanzibar amazed us. We never knew that the place is famous for having some of the most beautiful white sand beaches in the world, but the Lord knew that in advance when He spoke to us about "the sands of Zanzibar."

Something about Bora Bora amazed us. The airport was built on a coral atoll, and from there we were taken by boat to the main part of the island. The Lord had known that when He spoke to us of "the coral of Bora Bora."

As our boat approached the jetty in Bora Bora, we saw that only one person waited there, a man who owned a small hotel on the island and was there trying to drum up some business. He handed us a card and invited us to stay in his hotel.

We said to him, "You're Jewish, aren't you?"

"How did you know?" he asked.

We knew because the first person we had met in every place had been Jewish, and by this time we realized that God was taking us to see the dispersion of the Jewish people. He was causing us to see that His people were scattered to the most remote islands of the world, and He wanted us to believe in the years ahead for the ingathering of the exiles back to their homeland. "From the islands, to the captives," the Lord had said, and until that moment, we had visited all islands.

From Tokyo we flew to Khabarovsk, and when we finally reached that place and took a tour around the city, we noticed Jewish emblems — stars of David, menorahs and others — on buildings that were no longer used for their original Jewish purpose. When we toured Novasibirsk, God allowed us to find Jewish synagogues, schools and other institutions that had been closed. We had to see all that in order to believe for the release of His people and their ingathering.

We took many pictures on our trip, and later were able to deliver copies of those photos to the Jewish Agency in New York City. They were of sites they had not formerly known existed.

We would naturally have liked to spend much more time in each place, but the purposes of the Lord did not require it. He was calling us and equipping us for a specific task, and only He understood it well. In thirty days we traveled fifty-five thousand miles and received an education in the dispersion of the Jewish people.

To get back to Virginia for campmeeting, we had to make the long flight from Moscow to New York then go right on to Richmond. We would be tired, but it would be worth it to get into some good meetings with people from many other places.   ✸

◄ 63 ►

"I Will Say to the North, 'Give Up!' "

Normally I would have been more rushed to get back to Virginia because it had been my privilege over the years to preach the opening week of campmeeting. This particular year, however, my father had invited someone else to speak that week, so I could have the pleasure of listening to another preacher, and I was looking forward to it.

When we arrived in Virginia, my father met us with the news that the lady he had invited to speak the first week of camp had canceled at the last minute and that I would be speaking that evening and every evening for the next ten days. I was so glad in that moment that the Holy Ghost is the Preacher.

As the service progressed that evening, a lady who had never traveled out of America stood and began to prophesy the words of Isaiah:

> *I will say to the north, Give up; and to the south, Keep not back: bring my sons from far, and my daughters from the ends of the earth; Even every one that is called by my name: for I have created him for my glory, I have formed him; yea, I have made him.*   Isaiah 43:6-7

They were the same verses God had given me to speak from that night. I had not yet had time to tell the people where I had been or what I had seen and experienced, yet God was laying out before us His plan. It was the beginning of something that would forever change our lives. For the next ten nights, I spoke by revelation of the Holy Spirit, night after night, about the Jewish people and God's purposes for bringing them home, God's purposes for Zion, His purposes for Jerusalem, His purposes for Israel.

Tape recording was not as commonly done in those days, but I often wished that I had been able to preserve those ten nights of preaching. The revelation of the Holy Spirit was glorious. By the time the ten nights were over, God had shown us that a team of twenty-five young people must prepare to go live in Israel. Each of the twenty-five had been individually called for that purpose and had accepted God's call. My brother reserved a great government conference auditorium in Jerusalem for a meeting to be held in early November of that year. Just that quickly the Lord had set our eyes in a new direction.

I Ask for Israel

This was the beginning of our call to Jerusalem, and in preparation for it, the Lord had dropped the Jewish people into our hearts, not only from the major nations of the world, but also from the remote and seemingly insignificant places of the Earth. It all began on that small river boat on the Amazon when God dropped a word into my associate's mouth during the night. He had said, "From the sands of Zanzibar to the coral of Bora Bora, from Khabarovsk to Novasibirsk, from the islands to the captives, My people have caught the vision." Very soon, God's people all over the world would begin to catch the vision that it was time for them to return to Zion, and we would have a part in their catching that vision. ✿

➹ 64 ➻

"St. Peter-en-Gallicantu"

As soon as campmeeting ended, two of my associates flew to Jerusalem to look for a place for us all to live and worship. Because God had been speaking to us about Mt. Zion, I urged them to find a place right there on Mt. Zion. I didn't know just how difficult that would be. There are just not many places available.

I had stayed several nights in 1971 with the Rose family in their beautiful house on Mt. Zion, but when the two sisters searched in that area for suitable housing for us, they hit a dead end. Someone directed them to inquire at the Catholic church on Mt. Zion, known as St. Peter-en-Gallicantu. At one time there had been a small hotel halfway down Mt. Zion called the Silver Hotel, and those who had known it thought it might still be in existence. The building that housed it, however, had been purchased by the church, and it now housed a monastery.

My associates met with the Dutch priest, Father Theodore, and as they told him of how God was speaking to us and of our desire to find housing for our group, he was moved. "Those are the same scriptures that brought me to Jerusalem," he said. "I wish we could help you with housing, but we can't. We might be able to help you with a place of worship. We would be very happy for you to use our church during hours that it is not occupied."

They were sure that the Father had not understood who we were. "Father," one of them said respectfully, "we wouldn't be able to worship here because we're Pentecostal."

"That doesn't matter," he said. "You love our Lord."

"But we're the noisy kind," she said.

"That doesn't matter," he insisted.

To every objection she raised, his answer was the same. It didn't matter.

She tried to think of everything that conceivably could happen in our meetings (as if it would happen in every meeting), and his answer didn't change.

Having nearly exhausted all her ideas of why we might not be acceptable, she finally thought of the major objection that might be raised, and she broached the subject: "If we were in our own church, we would take communion at least once a month."

"Consider it your own church," he said. "I'll take full responsibility for your activities here."

192

I Ask for Jerusalem

In this way the Lord wonderfully opened the doors of St. Peter-en-Gallicantu to us. We worshiped there regularly for the next nine years, and we still have a wonderful association with the Assumptionist Fathers there.

When it became apparent that finding housing on Mt. Zion was impossible, the ladies were led to Rehavia where they rented three small apartments: one for the young men, one for the young women, and a third for the three of us. Ours was a block away from the others. It was in this way that Ernie Meyer of *The Jerusalem Post* became our landlord.

The famous Benyanei Haooma Government Conference Center had been rented, and the arrangements were in place for our Conference on Bible Prophecy. More than a hundred people from America had expressed a desire to attend. The McDougals would be bringing a group from the Philippines as well.

Because my brother's tour was going to Russia, it soon became apparent that we needed a second tour from America. The young people who would be living in Jerusalem needed a cheaper fare and a more direct route. Several other people who were having difficulty getting enough time off from their work to go on the Russian tour told my brother that this would also suit them better. So a few others were added to the smaller group.

When my father overheard my brother saying that he needed to find someone to lead the second tour group directly to the Land, he said, "I'll do it. God has spoken to me to take the young people into Israel." Those who knew my father understood what a great miracle this was because he had never been interested in leading any tour groups at all, anywhere.

Being accompanied by my father was a wonderful experience for the young people, and I knew that they would be blessed by the stories of faith that he constantly shared, but his willingness to lead the group had far more significance for me. We were entering into a whole new phase of our ministry, and to have my father leading us into this new phase was comforting.

I also came to believe that this was the fulfillment of something God had been saying to Daddy over a period of many years. Through the years when people prophesied over my father, they often said, "As God was with Moses, so He will be with you." Daddy was always a little uncomfortable with this comparison. He had always been very humble, and he found the thought of being compared to Moses to be rather embarrassing. As Moses led the people of Israel to the Promised Land, Daddy would lead our young people into Jerusalem to begin a new ministry. The fullness of what God was saying, however, was only perceived much later. ✻

193

≤ 65 ≥

"I Came for the Gift You Have for Me"

I decided to accompany my brother's group going to Russia. When we stopped over in Helsinki, Finland, on the way, a brother there asked us if we would like to carry some Bibles into Russia. We knew how dangerous that could be at the time, as we were still in the Cold War, so we presented the idea to the whole group and let it be known that there was no pressure on anyone to do it. Those who wanted to could, and those who did not want to did not have to. It was an individual decision.

A few members of the group said they would rather not risk it, but most of the group found it to be a very challenging prospect, so the brother gave us more than a hundred Russian Bibles, and we dispersed them among the group.

Some of the ladies hid Bibles in large hats. Some hid them in their under garments. Our mother, who has always been so holy, was one of those who did this. Some, in anticipation of the opportunity to take Bibles, had actually sewn large pockets into the lining of their coats to accommodate the Bibles. If we could get the Bibles through Russian customs and immigration in this daring way, we told everyone, I would then gather all the Bibles once we were inside the hotel in Leningrad and would take charge of transporting them and delivering them inside the country. If anyone should get caught bringing in Bibles, I wanted to be the one.

Things went well for us in the Leningrad Airport. Well ... pretty well. We had made the mistake of carrying with us the special commemorative song sheets we had printed especially for the conference in Jerusalem, and the customs agents objected to the Star of David and the references to Israel they contained. In the end, they confiscated them and told us they would hold them until we left the country. We could reclaim them on our way out.

We knew that all the hotel rooms were bugged in Russia, so after we had all gotten settled in our rooms, I took a flight bag and went from room to room, saying to our people, "I came for the gift you have for me." Finally, I got all the Bibles into my room.

My brother and I had carried identical large suitcases (for the first time in our lives), and I emptied mine to put the Bibles into it. They overflowed that giant suitcase, so I had one suitcase and one flight bag full.

194

I Ask for Russia

After supper that night, I went back to my room and started getting ready for bed. Then the Lord spoke to me to go down to the lobby. I went down as quickly as I could, and just as I was entering the lobby, I saw my brother entering from the opposite direction. "Why did you come?" I asked him.

"God told me to come," he said.

We looked at each other, knowing that something demanded our attention, and that we were both there for a reason.

Just then we saw one of our young tour members being led into the hotel by two KGB agents. We asked him what was wrong, and he told us that he had just been arrested.

"For what?" we asked.

"For passing out three small pieces of paper with John 3:16 written on them in Russian," he said.

Before he left home, he had hand copied the verse from a Russian Bible onto several small pieces of paper. After supper he had gone out and begun to give them out. He had given out just three of them when he was arrested. Russian officials had been observing the group because they expected large Christian groups to try something like that. We had warned our people to be very careful, but this brother, in his zeal for the Gospel, had not taken the necessary precautions.

We accompanied the brother to the interrogation room, and while we were waiting for other officials to arrive, we talked with his accusers. We told them that he was just a very young man and that he hadn't realized the severity of what he had done because back home he could hand out literature freely. As the leaders of the tour group, we were ready to take full responsibility for him and to be sure that he didn't repeat this same mistake again — if they would release him into our custody. After many hours of questioning, they agreed, but only with the condition that my brother and I come the next day to KGB headquarters.

We were off to a good beginning in Russia.

The next day we were taken down a long, dark hallway to meet the man in charge of the KGB in the city. After another period of discussion, he warned us that if there were any further problems with our group, they would permanently confiscate the materials we had left in the airport and we would not be permitted to retrieve them when we left.

We had a wonderful time touring Leningrad, but we decided not to try to deliver the Bibles there. Instead, we took them on with us to Moscow. We were being watched much too closely at the moment.

One night, while we were in Moscow, the Lord spoke to me and said, "A portion for Judah, a portion for Levi, a portion for Issachar ..." and He listed the various tribes of the children of Israel. I knew in that moment that we had brought the Bibles into Russia for the Jewish community. After discussing this with my brother, we developed a plan to get them to the local synagogue.

I had to have help because the suitcase full of Bibles was very heavy, so I asked one young man if he would help me. On a certain day, at a prearranged time, some of our people jumped off the bus and went in one direction, some jumped off and went in another direction, and the young man and I quickly went in a third direction. We got in a taxi and had the driver take us directly to the Moscow synagogue. There we were able to present the Bibles we had brought. We had also taken some Hebrew language tapes and some other material with which we knew the Jewish people would be thrilled, as they had not been available in Moscow for many years.

At the same time we were doing this, one of our group was visiting Communist Party Headquarters to deliver a letter I had written to the Secretary General of the Soviet Union, Leonid Brezhnev, in which I was asking his favor in allowing the Russian Jews who wished to return to their own land to do so. We had gone to Red Square and joined in prayer for the release of God's people, prophesying, "Let My people go." Just a few days later, we saw in an English language newspaper that Russia had decided to release twenty-five thousand Jews. It was the beginning of their *aliyah.*

When we got to Israel, I immediately called my friend Eli Mizrachi at the Prime Minister's Office and told him what we had done. He had heard me speak in the past of my love for the Jewish people, but now he said, "Your actions speak louder than your words." ✵

⚞ 66 ⚟

"Eight Israeli Flags"

The Conference on Bible Prophecy was glorious. It had been a great step of faith to organize it, and God had helped us at every turn.

When we got there, for instance, we noticed that the platform was rather bare. We had not thought to bring anything from America to decorate it, and we were now faced with a last-minute decision to do something.

I spoke to some of the staff in the hall and asked them if they had any Israeli flags. They found eight flags that we could use. We placed seven of them on the huge wall behind the speaker and we used the eighth flag to drape the podium. It was beautiful, and God was again speaking to us of the sevens and eights. He was fulfilling His purposes for Israel, and this was a time of new beginnings.

Sometimes we do things under the anointing of the Spirit not realizing just how significant they are.

On the opening night of the meeting a crew from Israeli television arrived to interview us. Under a great anointing I began to prophesy that it was time for the events of Ezekiel 39 to come to pass, that God would now breathe His life into His people and that they would stand up in the authority of the Holy Spirit and be brought from the north, the south, the east and the west to this land to fulfill His purposes.

When it came time to open the conference, I stepped to the microphone and encouraged everyone present to join me in shouting the name of Jesus three times. That name had never been shouted in that particular building before, but suddenly the power of it began to go through the atmosphere. The declaring of His name in Jerusalem opened up a whole new era for what God was about to do in the land.

My father preached in one of the afternoon services, and many people said that it was his finest hour. When he began to lay hands on the people, they were slain in the Spirit, and from one side of the auditorium to the other, people were on the floor under the power of God. Nothing like this had been seen in Jerusalem in modern times.   ✹

﹋ 67 ﹌

"Through His Seed, Both Natural and Spiritual"

After the conference, I decided to travel with the tour group to the northern areas of Israel. My brother's groups came often and, since I had seen most of the holy sights they would be touring, I did not often accompany them. This time, however, both of my parents were along, as well as some of my sister's children, so it seemed right for me to be with them. We would be together as a family in the land.

While we were all on top of Mt. Tabor, my father preached to us all concerning the glory of the transfiguration, and the glory filled the Church of the Transfiguration. When we were leaving the church after having this glorious experience, I was stopped just outside of the church and given a prophecy concerning the fact that the Lord was going to take my father home and that his ministry would continue "through his seed, both natural and spiritual." My brother would bring people to the land, and I would be there when they came.

The rest of the group had moved down a pathway to an area where the taxis were to pick us up. Because of the hairpin curves on the road going up to the top of the mountain, tour buses park halfway up the hill, and the passengers are transferred to taxis and taken the rest of the way to the top. When I walked back to the area where the taxis were loading, my brother was there. He said, "Ruth, you should have been here a few minutes ago."

Thinking that he was distressed because I had been delayed, I said, "Oh, I'm sorry, but the Lord was speaking to us just outside the church."

"No," he said, "that's not what I meant. Brother Hollis [one of the ministers on the tour] prophesied that God was going to take Dad home, that he would not live to see the fulfillment of his vision in the natural, but that it would be fulfilled in his seed, both natural and spiritual."

At two points on the same mountain, God was speaking about our father.

The year before this, our whole tour group had spent the night in the guest house operated there on Mt. Tabor by a group of Italian nuns. Early the next morning we had heard my father praying on the side of the mountain. He had gone out onto a balcony overlooking the Plain of Jezreel, raised his hands and was praying over Israel. Someone took a picture of him there interceding for the nation and the people with his hands up toward Heaven.

I Ask for the Nations

When he came to breakfast that morning, someone said to him, "It's dangerous for an old man like you to be as lost in prayer as you were on the mountain this morning."

Tears came to my father's eyes, and he told us that while he had been praying his feet had actually lifted up off the ground, as he felt himself being lifted from the mountain earlier that morning. He immediately thought of the work that was left undone, and, in that moment, he came back down to Earth. As he stood in the glory of that experience, he had to wonder if he had made the right choice. Now he was here in the exact same spot a year later, and the Lord said that He was soon going to take him home.

The next morning, we were touring the ruins of the ancient city of Capernaum. After we listened to the description offered by our tour guide, my father took Brother Hollis by the arm and brought him over to where we were all standing. He said, "Brother Hollis, I want my family to hear directly from you what God is saying to me," and Brother Hollis repeated what God had shown him on Mt. Tabor.

I had said good-bye to my father dozens of times through the years, but when I saw him off at the airport a few days later, it was totally different. I knew this was the last time I would see him alive, and he knew it too. About five weeks later, I received a phone call saying that my father had gone to be with the Lord, and I flew home for his funeral.

He had brought in the new generation. He had seen the land. Now, like Moses, he could retire and go to his reward. ✳

﹏ 68 ﹏

"Don't Worry About Not Knowing Anything"

When we began our ministry in Jerusalem, the Lord spoke to us: "Don't worry about not knowing anything about ministry to the Jews. I'm going to teach you by My Spirit." During the daytime, we were studying Hebrew (in five-hour sessions) and four nights a week we were worshiping on Mt. Zion.

One night a visiting American minister, who had been working in Nigeria, spoke to us. He looked over our group of young people, saw that they were all vigorous, and decided that they should be out passing out tracts. With his past experience he could visualize how we could reach the whole city of Jerusalem in a short time and was calculating how many thousands of tracts could be distributed. "You must be out sowing the seed," he said.

Everything the brother said was biblically true. We believed in sowing the Word and had done great Bible and Gospel distribution programs in other countries. We had even rented helicopters in Nepal to lift us into remote areas with our Gospels. We had crossed barriers, with the help of the Royal Family, to distribute them. In Jerusalem, however, there were certain restrictions.

What the brother said just wasn't God's answer for Jerusalem at that time. In every country God has a plan. There is not necessarily one single answer that works everywhere or one practical solution that fits every situation.

As the brother was speaking, I could sense that our young people were being challenged. That night I prayed, "Lord, give me Your answer for Jerusalem."

In the middle of the night the Lord spoke to me and said, "You sow to the heavens, and I will sow to the earth." That was the way our ministry of praise on Mt. Zion was born.

I didn't have a precise scripture verse at hand to back up what God was saying to me, and I didn't understand yet all that He meant by "You sow heavenward, and I will sow earthward," but I was determined to learn.

Night after night we gathered to praise the Lord. He spoke to us and said, "You are only beginning to praise Me. I will teach you by My Spirit how to praise Me." We learned a lot in the coming weeks.

When New Year's Eve came, we had been praising on Mt. Zion for about six weeks, constantly urged on by the Lord to more and higher praise. We were not only praising Him with our lips, we were praising Him with the clapping and the uplifting of our hands and with dancing, all wonderful and biblical forms of praise.

On New Year's Eve the Lord spoke to us and said, "Even now, while you are praising Me, I am pouring out My Spirit in another part of the city." We got very excited. We could hardly wait until the next day to see what God had done in some other part of the city.

The next day we learned that a group of twenty-five Arab Baptist young people had gathered for a social evening when suddenly the Holy Spirit had been poured out upon them, and they began to speak in other tongues. Twenty-five at that time in Jerusalem was like two thousand, five hundred in the United States. How thrilled we were! God had promised to teach us, and He was doing it.

We began coming to the services with greater anticipation and praising the Lord with greater fervor. Several weeks later the Lord spoke one night and said, "While you are praising Me, I am pouring out My Spirit in Gaza." We began to hear reports of the outpouring of the Holy Ghost in Gaza.

A few weeks passed. God spoke to us of an outpouring of His Spirit in the Galilee. Subsequently we heard of the outpouring of the Spirit in the Galilee.

A little more time passed and the Lord spoke to us and said, "I will come to My people, the Jews, and will reveal Myself to them where they are — in the *kibbutzim*, in the fields, in the factories." Jewish people began coming to our place of worship, telling us that they had received a personal revelation of Jesus.

We learned that we could praise the Lord in Jerusalem, sowing to the heavens, and that God would take our praise and sow it back on the Earth — in Jerusalem, Gaza, and Galilee — all over Israel. Later we were enlarged to see that praise would likewise reap a harvest to the ends of the Earth, and we entered joyously into what would prove to be years of praise ministry that would change nations for God.

Because of our previous experience among the Catholics of the Philippines and other countries and because of the openness of the Assumptionist Fathers to us in Jerusalem, we spent a great part of the coming months reaching out to all the Catholic communities in Israel. Every holiday was especially spent in this way. Many Sisters and Fathers began to speak in other tongues. It was a glorious time that none of us would ever forget.

The Lord had told us that we would be in Jerusalem for six months, and at the end of that time, He led us to take our group and leave.

As we were leaving Jerusalem for home, we split into groups and took different routes so that we could stop in various European cities and speak with the Jews about returning to the land. This was the beginning of what would become a vast outreach to Jews in more than eighty countries of the world. God had called us to become "the fishers" who would go find God's people and urge them to come home to Zion. Leaving Jerusalem for the time being was not to be the end of this ministry, but a stepping-stone to greater things.　　　　　　❋

﹏ 69 ﹏

"Of Course, in the Chapel of the Holy Spirit"

That summer God spoke to us during campmeeting to take a group of people to England for ministry in August. Thirty-four people responded.

My associate flew over ahead of the rest of the group and found a house where we could all stay. It had no furniture in it, but we all took sleeping bags and slept on the floor. We were wall to wall people. We took two large pots with us in which to prepare our evening meals.

We were able to secure, through Canon Collins of St. Paul's Cathedral, the use of St. Nicholas Cole Abby, a beautiful Wren church. We had meetings in the church in the evening, and we had street meetings in Trafalger Square, where we stood and preached on the Plinth.

We also borrowed a Methodist church near where we were staying for morning prayer. We all have great memories of the glory that descended upon us daily and of the beginning of new songs coming forth from our souls.

Each morning we split into small groups, giving each team member a bus ticket for the day and a packed lunch. We thus traveled throughout London and other parts of England reaching out primarily to the Jews and the Chinese (China had not yet opened). In the church at night, people danced before the Lord and worshiped Him, believing for revival in England and all Europe.

A well-known Christian leader in London who was deaf in one ear came and was healed as he sat in those meetings. We had not known who he was. Afterward this brother told us about a Charismatic conference being conducted at the University of Surrey at Guilford. It was the first joint Catholic/Protestant Charismatic meeting in England, and we decided to attend.

We found that those who were attending the conference were talking about the Holy Spirit, but no one was laying hands on the people and praying for them to be filled with the Spirit. As we sat with some of the people during mealtime, we asked them if they wanted the experience they were talking about. One of those who responded favorably was the Dean of the Cathedral in Paris. Yes, he wanted this experience and wanted us to pray for him.

"Would there be somewhere we could pray for you?" we asked.

"Of course, in the Chapel of the Holy Spirit."

We walked with him to the Guilford Cathedral, where we went together into the Chapel of the Holy Spirit. There we laid hands on him as he knelt in prayer, and he was instantly baptized in the Holy Spirit and began speaking in other tongues.

There were nuns from Belgium in the conference, and we not only prayed for them to receive this charism, but also we taught them how to pray for others to receive it. They began to lay hands on others, and they spoke in tongues as well. Before going to England, we had received a prophetic word that we would pray for people who would be used of God to bring revival to France and Belgium, and God had brought it to pass. After the conference, we went back to our meetings in London.

Years later, when I was invited to speak in Southampton, I met Lady Bronwen Astor and discovered that she had been one of the sponsors of that first charismatic meeting. A man who later became a good friend, Canon Francis Collins, had been the Catholic chaplain at the University of Surrey at the time those meetings were conducted. Others I later met who were involved with the Catholic Charismatic renewal in England had also been at that first conference. Even though I was not aware of it then, God was putting things together for a future day.

We spent a fruitful month in London before flying back to Virginia.   ✳

"Alemán"

In the early seventies, the McDougals were operating the camp outside Quito, Ecuador, and I felt led to visit them for a few days. Just prior to my leaving, I was sitting on the platform of the church in Richmond when the Lord spoke to me the word "Alemán." I recognized this as the Spanish word for German, but surely there had to be some other meaning to it. After all, I was on my way south. When God drops something into my spirit that I don't understand, I just tuck it away for future reference. That's what I did now, knowing that the meaning of this word and God's purposes concerning it would be made plain soon enough.

The McDougals met me at the airport with a group of their lovely people. We had no sooner greeted each other outside the Quito International arrivals' terminal, however, than someone from the crowd stepped up to greet Brother McDougal and speak with him. As they talked in Spanish, I wasn't paying particular attention, but I overheard the word "Alemán." When we were on our way out of the city, headed for the camp, I turned to Brother McDougal and asked him why that word had been used.

"Oh," he said, "the very well-known Latin American minister, Luis Palau, is coming to Quito for a great crusade. To prepare for that meeting many cooperating pastors will be gathering at the camp this week. They are coming to learn what is expected of them and how they can best prepare themselves and their people for the crusade. The man who is doing all the arranging is Rev. Alemán from Argentina." I was very interested in this Rev. Alemán.

When Rev. Alemán arrived at the camp, he had a lot to do, but he agreed to see me the following morning. Before I went to meet with him, I asked one of the sisters in the camp to pray with me for a while. As we prayed, she saw a beautiful sheep. It was fat and the wool on it was absolutely beautiful. The sheep seemed to be perfect in every respect, but the two front feet had a barbell attached to them, and the two rear feet had another barbell attached to them. The sheep was so weighed down that it could not move about freely. I knew that this was the message Brother Alemán needed to hear.

When I met with him, I first told him how God had given me his name while

I was praying in Virginia, and then I told him the vision the sister had. He said, "Sister Ruth, you couldn't ask for a better description of my life right now. God has blessed me and used me so wonderfully, but there are some present circumstances in my life that have absolutely weighed me down so much that I'm not free to move." I prayed with him, and ministered to him prophetically, and God released him from the weight that was holding him back so that he could have the freedom to move about in God. I have not heard from him since that time, but I know that he continues to be a great blessing in the Kingdom of God.

That was such a simple little thing that I could have missed it so easily. Sometimes we think that God's messages have to be complicated, but they're not.

From Ecuador, I went on to Bolivia to deliver a message to a young man God was using mightily in revival there. ✳

⚜ 71 ⚜

"Nice Is Nice"

During campmeeting in the summer of 1974 the Lord spoke to me the words, "Nice is nice." He had always spoken to me very simply, and this was about as simple as it could get. "Nice is nice," such simple words, yet they became life-changing for us and for thousands of people whom we would reach from Nice, France over the coming months.

The Lord told us to establish a center in Nice. It would be, first of all, a place of prayer to believe for revival in France and all of Europe, and it would also be a place from which we could travel throughout Europe, reaching out to the Jewish people and encouraging them to return to Zion. Nearly thirty people responded to this call during campmeeting and made a commitment to accompany us on this venture.

As soon as camp was over, two of my associates left for France to look for suitable housing. Just outside of Nice, along the Var River, they found a lovely little medieval village called Carros, and there they rented three houses close to one another for our use. They bought a French bread truck that had been turned into a small camper.

The Lord performed many miracles to get us all to Europe. In the end, we took a cheap flight to Luxembourg and were met at the airport with the camper. We were all so excited as we stood in the parking lot of the airport that we began to sing Merv and Merla Watson's great song:

Awake O Israel, put off thy slumber,
And the truth shall set you free.
For out of Zion comes thy Deliv'rer
In the Year of Jubilee.

Chorus:
O Hallelujah, O Hallelujah,
Hallelujah, Praise the Lord. (2x)

For in the furnace of much affliction
I have chosen thee, behold!

207

Harvest Glory

And for iron, I'll give thee silver,
And for brass, I'll give thee gold.

Thou art My chosen, for I have sought thee,
Thou art graven on My hand.
And I will gather all those that gather.
They shall come back to their land.

In the exuberance of the moment, we all danced the *hora* in the parking lot of the airport. It was a glorious moment!

Soon after arriving in Nice, I went on a forty-day fast, believing God for the breakthrough in France, and for His further purposes for all of us. We immediately started morning prayer meetings from eight to twelve every day, and it was amazing how quickly word of these meetings spread around the country. Before very long, we had priests coming from long distances to join us. It became a common occurrence for priests to load up their cars with parishioners on Friday after the work week had finished, drive all night, arriving at our doorstep on Saturday morning. They would stay and pray with us all day Saturday and Sunday and then leave Sunday night to make the long drive back to Paris just in time for their parishioners to get back to work on Monday morning. It seems hard to believe, but the hunger of the French people was just that great.

People were coming from as far away as Barcelona, Spain, a two-day trip by car, and they came from a variety of other countries as well. They were coming because the glory of God was in that house.

We prayed together every morning, and then everyone went out to the University of Nice in the afternoon to learn French. We needed to know enough of the language to be able to function inside the country.

Another memorable part of that early period was the richness of revelation that the Lord began to give us. For one thing, He gave us wonderful choruses. Nearly every day there was a new one, and they were beautiful and inspiring. Many of them had to do with the Jewish people and the ingathering back to Zion. Then there were visions and prophecies that were also enriching our souls in a very special way and preparing us for the tasks that were ahead.

After a while, the Lord began to speak to us to send out small groups to the various parts of Europe to speak to Jews about returning to Zion. Each group traveled, led by the Spirit, to some part of Europe and were led to specific people God had prepared to receive them. One group, for instance, made trips along the Danube, visiting all the towns along the way, ministering to literally thousands of people.

One group traveled in the truck, while the others used any means of public transportation available, and daily we believed God together for our financial needs to be supplied. Every day was a miracle in so many ways.

One group made an important trip to Vienna, Austria. Vienna was being used as a halfway house for Jews coming out of Russia. They very rarely went directly to Israel. From Vienna, a decision had to be made about their final destination, and many of them were choosing to go to America rather than to Israel.

Julie Tooley, a beautiful young girl from New Zealand who has since gone to be with the Lord, was one of those who traveled to Vienna. After arriving in the city, she went to visit several Jewish organizations she was able to locate and asked them where the Russian Jews were staying. They, of course, had their orders to protect the Jews and, not knowing for sure exactly who she was, they would not tell her. Julie was a praying person, and as she prayed, the Lord told her that if they would go out by faith, He would guide them. They followed the Lord from street to street and block to block until they came to the very building where the Russian Jews were housed. They were able to go from floor to floor and from apartment to apartment speaking to the exiles about choosing to go to Israel rather than to America.

It was in Nice that we learned a very important lesson about the need to openly show affection, something for which our upbringing did not always prepare us. The French are very affectionate, and they kiss each other on both cheeks in greeting. When a priest arrived one day, I noticed that one of our sisters presented him with a stiff arm and hand for shaking, as if to hold him at a distance. I felt that I must take her aside and speak with her about this.

"These men are hungry for God," I told her. "Let's not do anything that would alienate them. I understand your reluctance. I have the same problem myself, but we must let God change us. The French people are accustomed to warm greetings."

She said, "Ruth, my family was German; I grew up in a hard-working immigrant family; and we just didn't kiss anybody."

"I know," I said, "but we've been fasting and praying for revival, and we must let God use us to warm the hearts of His people."

She fasted and prayed that week and let God change her, and when the group arrived the following weekend, she was a different person. Since then she has been able to very affectionately greet others.

I understood just what she was experiencing. As we were growing up, the custom of kissing was not yet common in the church. There was one lady in our church who kissed everyone, and as children, when we saw her coming, we would run to the other side of the church to avoid being kissed. Now we were learning how very important it was to allow God to demonstrate His love for others through us.

Harvest Glory

That forty-day fast was not an easy one for me. It was cold in Nice in October and November, and the houses we had rented were on a hillside where they got plenty of wind. In the final days of my fast, I remember taking every possible opportunity to climb into bed just to get warm.

Toward the end of the fast, the Lord spoke to me that we should leave others in charge so that we could go on to Israel to learn more Hebrew. We left three of the ladies in charge of the outreach in France. It was their first time to have such full responsibility and to have to believe God for the whole group, and it was good for them. The Lord used that time to develop them so that He could use them in other places in the future.

Those who were privileged to take part in this outreach from France look back on the period with fond memories. I came away from it convinced that God had taken us to France, not only for the blessing that France would derive from our stay, but to instill in the consciousness of our people the reality of the dispersion of the Jewish people throughout Europe and to give them an awareness of European culture. Later, when we were all living in Jerusalem, we would meet Jewish people from all the European nations, and we were at ease with them because we understood their cultural background.

In Israel, we often bumped into people to whom we had actually spoken on those trips from Nice and had encouraged to go to Israel. They had been moved by our words and it had helped them reach the right decision, to choose God's will above economic considerations.

Our group lived outside of Nice for a year. Later we had a house in St. Paul de Vence, a very lovely tourist area also not far from Nice, and they, too, were successful in reaching out to the people of that area. In more recent years, my own ministry has taken me into other parts of France, but I cannot forget that very special time. What an amazing year that was for all of us! The Lord was right, Nice is nice.

Later, I ministered several times in the Pyranees, in Panasac, in Pont de Tois near Paris, in Lyon and in Belfort.

Bill and Debbie Kendrick and their year-old daughter Ruthie went to France with us in 1975 when we lived in the Medieval village of Carros. Later they would go to Israel with us for several years, living in Jerusalem and Tiberias. After returning to America, they stayed at the campground in Ashland. In 1983 Debbie traveled with me to England for the meeting at the Royal Albert Hall. While there the Lord spoke to her to prepare her family, which now numbered five children ranging in age from a year and a half to nine, and return to England. They invited Sherry Rule, an eighteen-year-old girl who had come to our camp from Joliet, Illinois, to go with them. After a year in England, they returned to the south of France and lived in Menton, about twelve miles from Nice.

I Ask for France

When the Kendricks returned to America in 1986, Sherry stayed in France, working among the French people. Within a year, she met Peter Madan and they subsequently married. Peter is a gifted musician and frequently plays the cello with the Lyon Symphony. Together they pastor a church in Cannes, the famous city on the French Riviera.

In 1996 I spent a lovely afternoon entertaining an English couple at tea in my living room in Jerusalem. When I asked them where they lived, I was amazed when they said, "Carros, France." They were Michael and Dorothy Madan, Sherry's in-laws. They have lived in Carros since 1985. Their other son and his wife pastor a church in Nice.

Interestingly enough, the year-old Ruthie who accompanied us to Nice is now Ruth Kendrick, the photographer whose photo adorns the jacket of this book.

✹

≋ 72 ≋

"This Is Your Inheritance"

We were planning to attend the Holy Spirit Conference in Jerusalem, sponsored by *Logos* Magazine and Al and Dan Malachuk. My associate, who had been traveling in the Gulf States, got there first. On her way up to the Holy City from Tel Aviv, she decided to stop by the Garden Tomb and say hello to Jan Willem Vander Hoven, the Keeper of the Garden Tomb. When she got there, she found that he was very excited because there had been a lot happening in the city that week.

He told her about two men who had come from America. Back home, they had fasted forty days, and God had told them to bring a banner of the name of Jesus in Hebrew and to stand at each of the city gates with the banner unfurled for one day. The banner they made was not very big, perhaps four feet long by three feet high. It was made of a simple white fabric and it had red felt lettering that said, "Yeshua."

When the men got to Jerusalem with their banner and some of the elders of the city heard about their plan, they warned them that they must not stand at the gates with the banner unfurled. If they did, it was sure to cause political unrest. They could stand in the gates, and they could have the banner in their arms, but it must not be unfurled.

The men obeyed and had stood for a day in each of the gates with their banner without unfurling it. This was their last day, and had been standing all day in the final gate with their banner of the name of Jesus in Hebrew.

My associate was introduced to the two men. They told her that the Lord had instructed them to bury the banner in front of the Golden Gate once they had completed the act of standing in each of the gates with it. They were planning to do this the next day, they told her.

"How are you planning to bury it?" she asked them.

"We hadn't thought of that," they said.

She said, "If you want to avoid trouble, you must not dig in the ground in front of the Golden Gate. That's a cemetery, you know. But let me tell you how you should bury it. Do it the way they did in the Bible. Build up a memorial with stones over it."

212

I Ask for Jerusalem

They were grateful for the advice, and she left them and went and checked into a little hospice, the Casa Nova, for the night. I was expecting to join her the next day.

That night God awakened her and told her that she must go and get the banner. "That banner is for Ruth," He told her. "It is her inheritance from the Lord."

She realized that she had no idea what time the men would bury their banner, so she said to the Lord, "If you want me to go do that, you will have to wake me up at the right time."

When she was awakened later, she dressed and went out to the cemetery in front of the Golden Gate. She arrived about ten minutes after the banner had been buried. Looking around, she saw a small heap of stones. Removing stone after stone, she found a small red child's lunch box. She opened it, and there was the banner, folded up inside the lunch box. When she took it out, the Lord said to her, "Walk where you will, and claim what you want." She began to walk over the area of Mt. Zion where we had held our church services before, and, as she walked, she was possessing in the name of the Lord. Later that day, I arrived from America.

Before I left home, Mother had been trying to make some decisions about my father's estate. The Lord had spoken to me and told me not to accept my father's natural inheritance, only to accept his spiritual inheritance. He told me to go to Jerusalem and get my inheritance from the Lord. I had not told anyone about this. All anyone knew was that I was attending the Holy Spirit Conference in Jersualem.

My associate met me at the airport in Tel Aviv and, as we were on our way up to Jerusalem, she was telling me the story of the men who had come to Jerusalem and prayed at each of the gates of the city, holding their banner with the name of the Lord on it. That was as far as she went with the story.

When we got to the hospice and we went to our room, I leaned back on the bed and we were talking. She went over to her suitcase, whipped out the banner and draped it over my legs. As she did this, she said, "This is your inheritance from the Lord."

She knew nothing of what the Lord had been saying to me in America concerning my father's estate, but, through her, the Lord had told me that He had given me this inheritance. It would be my privilege to openly declare the name of Jesus in Jerusalem.

When we went back to Jerusalem to live the following year and to reopen the ministry, we decided to process from Zion Gate down to St. Peter-en-Gallicantu with those who would be coming to our service that night.

Among that group were two women who knew all about the banner and its history. They had arrived on the scene of its burial about twenty minutes after it had been buried (and some ten minutes after my associate had picked it up). They had discovered that the box was empty, but they had not realized what had happened. As we processed from Zion Gate, we then told the story of my inheritance from the Lord.

The banner (there is a photo of it in the book) hung draped over our pulpit at St. Peter-en-Gallicantu for many years. We took it out and used it when we processed through the streets of Jerusalem on Palm Sunday. Today it hangs in our house in Jerusalem. The Lord wanted that banner of His name, not to be at the gates of the city rolled up, but unfurled so that all could be blessed by it.

❋

Palm Sunday Procession with the Custos of the Holy Land, Father Mancinni. Holding the banner, Ricardo Bonet and Michael Nelson, Jerusalem, 1976.

In front of the Golden Gate, Jerusalem, 1975.

My brother and I kneeling at the star of the Nativity, Bethlehem, 1974.

Conference in Jerusalem: I'm at the piano and Daddy is preaching in the Binyanei Haooma Government Conference Center, 1972.

Daddy praying on the balcony at Mt. Tabor overlooking the Plain of Jezreel and the Valley of Meggido, 1971.

With brother, Daddy and Mother at the Garden Tomb, Jerusalem, 1970.

My brother praying beneath an ancient olive tree in the Garden of Gethsemane, Jerusalem, 1972.

Leading songs on the bank of the Jordan while my brother baptized.

An Armenian Father at Bethlehem presenting me the key to the church, 1980.

St. Peter-en-Gallicantu, dedicating baby Nathaniel and praying for parents Bill and Debbie Kendrick, 1976.

With the Faithful Four: Irene Bredlow, Alice Ford, Susan Woodaman and Janet Saunders.

With Asher Kaufamn, overlooking Jerusalem from the Mt. of Olives, 1992.

With assumptionist Fathers, Father Frances, Father Patrick, Father Amiran.

With Mayor Teddy Kolleck and his wife Tamara at the Citadel, Succot Reception, Jerusalem, 1992.

With Mayor Ehud Olmert, Jerusalem, 1996.

Halcyon House, our house in Jerusalem.

Halcyon House entrance: with Joe and Henri McClees, Bennie Daniels and Senator and Mrs. Bob Carpenter.

With with Jashil Choi in a procession through the streets of Jerusalem, 1980s.

⚞ 73 ⚟

"Push the Second-Floor Button"

We arrived early at the big conference center where the Holy Spirit Conference would be held, and the doorman recognized us. We had rented that same hall a few years before, and I had ministered there, so the staff called me "Miss Hallelujah."

"Go directly back to the elevator," the doorman said, "and, when you get in, push the second-floor button." We assumed that everyone had gone up there to have a prayer meeting before the actual event was to begin, so we did exactly as the doorman had instructed.

When the doors of the elevator opened on the second floor, we quickly realized that we were in the wrong place. We were in the middle of an official reception. On one side, we spotted General Haynes, and on the other side, we saw one of the special guest speakers from America, Kathryn Kuhlman. We could see Teddy Kolleck, the mayor of Jerusalem and many of his committee. We saw Archbishop Raya, from the Orthodox church and other representatives from the Christian community in Jerusalem. There was no lobby between us and them. We were right in the middle of everything.

What we immediately noticed was that all the guests were standing back in their own places. There was no mingling. The local committee had not yet been introduced to the foreign speakers, and the government officials present seemed to be totally isolated.

We were so embarrassed that we had crashed such an important reception to which we had not been invited that we, at first, thought of doing whatever was necessary to quickly get ourselves extricated from the situation. But something in us also wanted to help with this awkward situation we saw in front of us.

I took the liberty of stepping over to speak with Miss Kuhlman. We had something in common. I had just flown in from South America, where I had met and talked with her spiritual son, Julio Caesar Ruibal, in La Paz, Bolivia. He had such an amazing story. He had been outside a Kathryn Kuhlman meeting, unable to get in, but still God had done a great miracle for him. He started praying for the sick who were outside the hall, and God healed them. This is the way his dynamic healing ministry was launched. He had gone back to Bolivia and was

Harvest Glory

drawing crowds of twenty-five to fifty thousand people wherever he went. He was martyred for the Gospel in Colombia in 1997, I understand, but at the time I saw Kathryn Kuhlman in Jerusalem, he was at the height of his ministry success.

It was a pleasure to bring her greetings from her son in the faith, and we talked a little about him and about his ministry in Bolivia. Then I took her and began to introduce her to some of the important people who were present at the reception, especially to my friend, Mayor Teddy Kolleck.

While I was speaking with Kathryn Kuhlman, my associate stepped over and began speaking with General Haynes. Since her father had been a military officer, she was comfortable addressing the general. After she had spoken with him for a few moments, she took him and began to introduce him to the others present.

We had opportunity to speak with Mayor Kolleck and to Archbishop Raya, head of one of the aspects of the Greek church. As soon as we saw that everyone was mingling, we realized that our presence was no longer needed, and we slipped out unnoticed, headed for the open elevator and quickly descended to the lower level, where the auditorium was located and the meetings would soon begin.

In the meeting that night Miss Kuhlman came off the stage, laying her hands quickly on all those she could reach as she moved down the aisle. She came directly back to the second section where I was sitting on the front row and laid her hands on me as well.

One of our friends, an Arab businessman whose family shop is just inside Jaffa Gate, received a great miracle of healing in that service. Through the years, again and again, he has told me and countless others the story of his miraculous healing. Without the touch of God, he would have remained a helpless cripple, but now he is made whole. He is a member of the Greek Orthodox Church.

Miss Kuhlman returned to Israel a second time, and I had the privilege of being in her meetings in both Jerusalem and Tel Aviv.   ✴

⚝ 74 ⚝

"The Patriarch Tour"

One year David DuPlessis came to Jerusalem as the Honorary Chairman of the Holy Spirit Conference. I went to his hotel to see him the night before the meetings were to begin. I had a great respect for him since we had met in Hong Kong many years before. He was Mr. Pentecost and had been used to build bridges with brothers of many other churches.

"How are you feeling?" I inquired.

"Ruth," he said, "I'm not feeling too well."

"What's the matter?" I asked him.

"You know how I always love to meet believers at the churches," he began.

"Are you not going to do it here too?" I asked.

"I want to do it here," he replied, "but I wrote to the brothers, and they said they couldn't arrange it."

"Are you still interested?" I asked.

"Oh," he said, "Am I? Of course I'm interested."

"Give me an hour," I told him, "and let me see what we can arrange."

On our very first stay in the country, we had reached out to all the different Catholic communities. Later, when we saw that a Catholic Charismatic meeting was being held once a week at Ecce Homo on the Via de la Rosa and there were other charismatic happenings among the Catholics, we turned our attention to the Orthodox communities. Jerusalem has many different groups of Orthodox Christians — the Egyptian, the Greek, the Russian, the Ethiopian, the Syrian, the Armenian and others.

Every Sunday morning we had our young people split up and go to different Orthodox churches. They did nothing offensive there. They stood with the people, prayed in the Spirit, and reached out in friendship. It took about a year before the Orthodox leaders opened up to us, but this ministry did bear fruit.

Now I called the house and asked Alice Ford and Janet Saunders to see if they could arrange a meeting for Brother DuPlessis with the Orthodox patriarchs. When they called back a little later, it was to say that it was all arranged. Over the next several days, I took Brother David DuPlessis on what I called "the Patriarch Tour."

Brother DuPlessis' books were on sale at the conference and I bought several and put them in my purse. As we met the various Patriarchs — the Greek Orthodox Patriarch, the Syrian Patriarch, the Catholic Patriarch and the Armenian Patriarch — I would reach into my purse, pull out one of his books, and have him autograph it and present it to the Patriarch. He was surprised, but pleased that I had thought to bring the books along.

The Patriarch was pleased and immediately sent one of his aides to bring one of his own books, and he, in turn, autographed it and presented it to Brother DuPlessis. At the end of the several days, he had met all the most important leaders in the city.

David DuPlessis, as the Honorary Chairman of the Holy Spirit Conference, stood on the last night of the meetings and said, "You brethren know that I always like to go to the local churches. I wrote to the brethren in Jerusalem, and they were unable to arrange anything. The first night I was here, however, I saw my old friend Ruth Heflin, and she said she would be very happy to take me to meet the patriarchs. Since I have no problems with women's ministries, I took her up on the offer." Then he began to tell of his experiences of the last couple of days and of the wonderful way in which we had been received by the other Christian groups. It was a high moment in his life and something that thrilled us all. ✴

⚚ 75 ⚚

"It Was Located In Sheikh Jarrah"

That next fall we returned to Jerusalem in strength and resumed the ministry on Mt. Zion. The Lord enabled us to open several houses in various parts of Israel and people began to come from all over the world to be with us on Mt. Zion, some just to attend the worship services and others to stay for longer periods of time. It was not unusual to have people from more than a hundred nations in the course of a year.

At first we rented the same former apartment in Rehavia and, soon afterward, a house at 4 Oved Street in Abu Tor, for a ministry house. We grew rapidly, and it soon became apparent that something more was needed.

Most everything available was quite small. We looked at place after place, but nothing seemed to be right for us. One day my friend Ahed Abu Haj, owner of the National Hotel, called to say that he had found the house I was looking for. It was located in Sheikh Jarrah in an old diplomatic area of Jerusalem, and its neighbors were embassies. The house was situated on the largest piece of private property in the city.

We went to look at the house, and it was exactly what we needed. God gave us favor with the landlady, and we continue to rent from her twenty-three years later.

The house was unfurnished. God gave us the friendship of Victor Hallak, a neighbor who sold antique furniture from his house and our house was quickly furnished.   ❋

☙ 76 ☙

"Sing A New Song"

Besides the powerful ministry of prayer and intercession that God had already led us into, He now began to teach us another new aspect of ministry. As we worshiped on Mt. Zion, He began to give us a new song, a spontaneous song birthed in that very instant by the Spirit in us.

When He first spoke to us about the new song, we were not sure exactly what He meant by that. Did He mean that we should sing with a different beat? Did He mean that we should sing a different melody? Did He mean that we should sing in a different style? None of us were particularly talented musically, but we earnestly wanted to praise God in a way that would be pleasing to Him.

One day, as we were praising, we began to sing a little song that we had never heard, never learned, never been taught, and never memorized. We just sang out of our spirits spontaneously. We found that God was pouring into our spirits and all we had to do was release it.

As usual, when God is leading us into something new, we were unsure of ourselves and went slowly at the first. We would put our toes in to test the water and then bring them back out again. But we were so blessed when we sang spontaneously that we were soon doing it more and more.

At first we only sang the new song in our prayer meetings in Bethlehem. When we were in the church on Mt. Zion, we conducted the services as we were accustomed, with songs and choruses we already knew. Then the Lord said to us, "Can't you trust Me? If you can sing spontaneously in the prayer meeting, why can't you sing spontaneously on Mt. Zion?"

"But, Lord," I said, "people come thousands of miles to be in our services. We don't want to make mistakes in front of them. What if it doesn't work?" He insisted that we trust Him and prodded us until we started singing spontaneously in the regular services as well.

From then on, we never looked back. We sing spontaneously in every service. After all, if David could sing until he had accumulated the wealth of material we now call the Book of Psalms, we could too.

Outside the Greek chapel in Bethlehem, where we prayed on Friday and Saturday mornings for several years, we had a big sign: PENTECOSTAL PRAYER MEETING 8 to 12 NOON. After a while that sign embarrassed me. I thought,

I Ask for Israel

We're not really praying anymore. We were raised on travail and intercession, and now we were spending most of our time singing and dancing and rejoicing. Despite my misgivings, it was during this time that the Lord gave me the song, *I Ask for the Nations.* It was given to me spontaneously in the prayer meeting, and we spent the whole morning asking for different nations. We were no longer doing it in the formal way we had been taught, but what we were doing was moving the heavens.

As we worshiped, God was speaking to us about nations and their problems, and as we declared victory for them, prophesying it into being, and rejoicing to see it come to pass, He was working. We were no longer agonizing, weeping and supplicating as before. We didn't quite know what to think about this new thing.

I was sure that the teaching we had received in years gone by was good, but I was also sure that God was showing us new and better ways of accomplishing His purposes.

After the Lord showed me that I no longer needed to travail, someone that I greatly respect came to visit us in Jerusalem and ministered the old teaching on travail. That teaching is not wrong. God is just showing us easier ways.

When I heard this person speak of travail in the traditional sense, "... we get down and pray until we feel in the spirit the birth pangs, feel the burden for people, as a woman giving birth, and bring forth individuals into salvation, bring forth even nations ..." etc., I said to the Lord, "I really want to know if I understood you correctly. Give me a little further indication concerning this new thing."

The wife of one of our couples was expecting a baby. She didn't know what I had asked the Lord. She told me later, "That next day the Lord woke me up with this verse: *'Before Zion travailed, she brought forth.'*"

"What does that mean, Lord?" she asked.

That day she and her husband were busy and suddenly she felt a twinge of discomfort. She mentioned it to him, and he suggested stopping by the maternity house since they were nearby.

"I know the baby isn't coming yet," she protested. "These are not labor pains."

"It won't hurt to stop," he insisted. "We're nearby."

So they stopped. The doctor was in. He put her on the examining table and began to check her over.

"The baby is coming," he said, surprisedly.

"It couldn't be," she said. "I haven't done what I am supposed to do yet." (She and her husband had taken some lessons on just what to do to give birth.)

"I can't help that," the doctor said, "the baby is here."

When she told me that, I said, "Thank you, Jesus! Thank you, Jesus!"

Then I noticed an article in an Australian women's magazine entitled: "SING

Harvest Glory

YOUR WAY TO A PAINLESS CHILDBIRTH." The article, written by a famous French obstetrician, said that it was referring not just to the singing that comes from the mouth, but the singing in which the total woman is involved. When she is caught away in song, the author insisted, she could have a childbirth without pain.

After that when any of our ladies were about to give birth in Jerusalem, her husband stood on one side of her and I stood on the other side, and we all sang in the Spirit. The Moslem doctor came to expect it. We got lost singing in the Spirit, and in a few moments the baby came.

Jerusalem is a place of revelation. For some time a diplomat from the Australian Embassy in Tel Aviv came up to Jerusalem every weekend to attend our services. This was just at the time when China was beginning to open and when there was much activity in the Middle East. He had access to diplomatic pouches, to intelligence information from the Mossad (the Israeli intelligence agency), from the CIA, from British Intelligence, from Australia, and from other Western countries. It was his job to send back to the foreign office in Canberra telexes concerning new information and new movements. He told us that the information coming forth in the Spirit in our prayer meetings concerning China was six months ahead of the diplomatic pouches.

One day, while we were in prayer, God showed us that Syria would enter the war in Lebanon. Until that time she was not actively involved and had kept to herself in her own territory.

This man was very excited about what the Lord was showing us and wanted to act on it. He couldn't send a telex, however, saying, "I was in a prayer meeting on Mt. Zion and God showed us a vision and we know that Syria is going to enter the war." He needed something more concrete. He searched the local newspapers carefully for any substantiation of this.

Within a day or two Prime Minister Menachem Begin made a comment that Syria would be entering the war soon. Armed with that new information, the diplomat went to his ambassador saying, "I think we ought to send this information to Canberra."

"That was just an offhand statement," the ambassador answered him. "We can't build something on a passing statement." (Of course, I knew that Menachem Begin never made an offhand statement.)

When our friend tried to press the issue, the ambassador replied, "Listen, I'm having dinner tonight with several of the ambassadors. Let me put out some feelers first. We can always send your message tomorrow."

When he came into the office the next morning, he said, "Send it!"

Within a few days Syria entered the war.

230

I Ask for Israel

Numerous times there were similar situations in which the Holy Ghost was so very faithful. God wants our praise and worship to bring us into glory and the realm of revelation, so that we can be effective in prayer.

Another important issue the Lord began to deal with us about was the importance of every member of His Body. He showed us that we had much to learn about unity, that true glory only comes as we can unite in the Spirit, and that when the glory comes, it brings with it a greater unity.

During the time we were worshiping in the Catholic church on Mt. Zion, some Pentecostal people in the city wouldn't think of coming to that church. Our own ministry had gradually reached out to Arabs, Jews, Protestants, Catholics, Armenians, Syrians, Orthodox and Greeks alike. It was not uncommon to have people from many faiths together in our services, prayer meetings and in fellowship in our house.

My background did not prepare me in any way for this ministry to all people. When I went out to Hong Kong to serve the Lord in 1958, I had never attended any church other than a Pentecostal one (except for a funeral). My father was very ecumenical and attended the local ministerial meeting, but I had never been to an interfaith meeting, had never heard of a united prayer meeting and had never been in an interdenominational church meeting. The change in my own life came about through a divine working of the Holy Ghost within me. God can do it and *will* do it for each of us, if we have a desire for it and an appreciation for the whole Body of Christ.

Before going overseas, the only hymnal I knew anything about was our Pentecostal hymnal. God was beginning to move among the historic churches, however, and I embraced that move. Since then, my life has been enriched with Episcopalian hymns, Presbyterian hymns, Baptist hymns and many others. I love to sing some of the Orthodox songs and the Catholic Charismatic songs. Thank God for the privilege of sharing with brothers and sisters of many other groups. All of God's children are wonderful.

When we first went to Jerusalem and people would ask us where we were from, we would always say that we were from Virginia. Originally, many of us were from Virginia, and others had come to the camp from neighboring states. As time went on and the Lord began to add to us, I found that I could no longer answer in that same way. We now had people from France, Australia, Japan, the Scandanavian countries, England and other countries, and the Virginians were now in the minority.

Our group also changed in another way. When we first went to Jerusalem and people asked us what denomination we were, we would say Pentecostal, because we were all from the Pentecostal campground in Virginia. As time went on, I would have to say, "We are all Pentecostal except this lady, and she's Lutheran." Then I had to include a Catholic in the exceptions and then a Baptist, a Methodist, a Presbyterian and many others. Before long, the exceptions outnumbered the Pentecostals. God had changed the nature of our group and made it international and totally interdenominational. Later we never asked the denominational background of any person. ✵

✎ 77 ✎

"A Soul Is a Soul"

When we first went to Jerusalem and started having meetings in St. Peter-en-Gallicantu, the Lord spoke to us that a soul is a soul. Thus we never differentiated between a Jew or an Arab or any other people. We were one of the first places in Jerusalem where both Arabs and Jews worshiped together. Today there are a number of places where this happens, but it was not so at that time.

Once, when I returned to Jerusalem from America, the Lord gave me a word of knowledge for one of the Arab pastors. The Lord said that on a certain day in August he was going to give him a miracle in regards to America. I didn't know that his son wanted to go to America to study. Brother Najeeb took his son to the American Consulate on the very day that God had spoken of, expecting a miracle. For years now, it has been very difficult for foreigners to get a visa to come to America. Knowing this, Najeeb stood outside the Consulate on Nablus Road and prayed while his son Musa went inside to apply.

When Musa's turn had come to be interviewed and he sat before the consular officer, the man looked over Musa's application and other documents. After a few moment's, he banged his fist on the desk and said, "I am *not* going to give you a visa to go to America." But something else was happening too.

At that very moment, the official began to nod. Musa watched as the man's head descended until it rested on his chest, as if he were fast asleep. A moment later the official jerked his head, as if he were waking from a deep sleep and declared emphatically, pounding his fist again for emphasis, "I *am* going to give you a visa to go to America." It was an amazing miracle, and Musa knew it.

Musa had been rather cool in his relationship to Jesus recently, but he walked out of the American Consulate a changed young man. He had his visa in his hand and his heart was aflame with a renewed love for the Lord. He was sure that he had witnessed a miracle.

One day I was rushing through the Old City with one of my associates on the way to the Church of the Holy Sepulchre to attend a meeting promoting unity among the churches in the city. I was looking straight ahead because I did not want to be distracted by the shopkeepers trying to sell me their wares as I passed through the narrow streets of the city. Suddenly my eye was drawn to a beautiful antique table. It was inlaid with mother of pearl and was clearly from Damascus. The owner of the shop, who was standing near the door, beckoned me to come inside and look at the table more closely.

"I know this table," I said to him.

"No, you don't know this table," he replied.

"I was having morning coffee with my neighbor, Victor Hallak, at his house yesterday, when a salesman tried to sell him this very table."

"You do know this table," the shopkeeper had to admit.

Later I assisted the merchant in writing a book on *Traditional Palestinian Embroidery and Jewelry.* This experience opened many other doors for me in Jerusalem, as well. ✳

≥ 78 ≤

"Because of His Mother's Prayers"

Just before we went to the church in Jerusalem one night, we heard on the news that there had been a terrible crash on Tenirife in the Canary Islands. Two jumbo jets had collided on the runway. I mentioned this tragic news that night in church and asked everyone to pray. The Lord gave me a prophetic word that out of that apparent tragedy He would raise up one who had been reluctant and that he would preach and bless many people of the world. It would happen, the Lord said, "because of his mother's prayers."

Several months later a couple from our ministry was in California preaching and heard a pastor announce that Norman Williams, a survivor of the 747 crash in the Canary Islands, would be speaking the next Sunday. They were very excited to hear this, and they told the pastor of the prophetic word that had been spoken in Jerusalem the night of the crash.

The following week, when Norman came to preach in the church, he was told the story of the prophecy in Jerusalem, and it was a great encouragement to him. He had gone to an Assembly of God Bible school and prepared himself for the ministry, but when he got out he lasted only one year as a preacher. Because he was not doing very well financially, he decided to quit and go into business.

He did well in business and eventually opened his own business management school. His spiritual life did not do nearly as well as his business. Although he was a good man, by the time of the crash, he had lost the active working of the Holy Spirit in his life and was no longer speaking in other tongues.

When the crash occurred, many were killed. In all, five hundred and eighty-three died from the crash. Norman, however, was supernaturally lifted out of the plane and placed on the wing. Although it was a long way to the ground, he jumped, and when he landed, he was not only quoting scriptures, he was speaking in other tongues.

When he examined himself, he found that he was splattered from head to foot with blood from other people's wounds, but aside from a broken ankle suffered from the jump (and that healed very quickly), he was doing amazingly well. In fact, he was the only person to survive the crash without becoming either emotionally or physically crippled by it.

Instantly he became a celebrity and a spokesperson. Because he had survived the crash, doors opened for him to give his testimony through every type of news media. Over the next several months he was busy, speaking again and again.

By August of that year, he had grown tired of traveling and speaking and was seriously thinking of abandoning the mantle he had taken up and going back to full-time business. It was then that he heard of the prophecy in Jerusalem, and this spurred him to continue.

Sometime later, Norman was invited to accompany George Otis on his tour to Israel. He intended to contact the two people the pastor in California had told him about, the couple who told of the prophecy, but by then he had forgotten their names and had no idea how he could find them.

That couple, not knowing that Norman was in Jerusalem or that he would be preaching that very night, told us that they were planning to stop by the YMCA and attend the meetings of George Otis. George Otis, not knowing that they were coming or what time they would arrive, delayed introducing Norman Williams until much later than he had anticipated. Just as the couple was coming in the door, he introduced his speaker of the night, and they were pleased to see who it was.

After the meeting that night, our couple rushed up to Norman and introduced themselves. It was a divine appointment. The next night Norman came to our church. He was accompanied by his mother and a film crew making a film about his life. He wanted to know about the prophecy spoken over his life in Jerusalem, a prophecy that would change his life forever.

"Ruth," he told me later, "They took me to a Catholic hospital, and there, on the wall, of my room was a crucifix. I had hated the Catholics for many years, and I hated the Crucifix. During those days I spent in that Catholic hospital, however, God changed my heart, and now, for the first time in my life, I love Catholics."

I said, "Norman, that's wonderful! If the accident had not happened, you probably would not have come to speak for us (since we were worshiping in a Catholic church on Mt. Zion at the time). Even if you had come, you might have felt uncomfortable in this building. Now, you are right at home."

Later, Norman returned to the Canary Islands and preached to thousands of people there.
                                                                                    ✸

≈ 79 ≈

"God Spoke to Me to Go" — Anwar Sadat

Part of our ministry in Jerusalem was to bless the city and the people, to pray for the peace of Jerusalem. One night in the service on Mt. Zion the Lord spoke to my associate to go to Benin in Nigeria. As I was praying for her, the Lord said that on the way to Nigeria she should stop in Cairo, Egypt and pray, and the Lord would break the power of Pharaoh. There was an inexpensive family hotel in Cairo where we often stayed, but this time I found myself encouraging her to go and pray at Mena House, a lovely and rather expensive historic hotel.

While praying at Mena House, she felt impressed to get up early and climb to the top of the pyramids. She did it — carefully and prayerfully. When she got to the top, the Spirit of prophecy came over her, and she began to prophesy to Egypt, thus breaking the power of Pharaoh. The only thing that concerned her was that President Sadat was not in Cairo at the time. She wondered why the Lord had sent her to Cairo at that time when the President was not in the land.

President Sadat was in Romania, where he announced to the world that he was going to Jerusalem to make peace. Reporters asked him, "Did President Jimmy Carter tell you to go to Jerusalem?" He said that he had not.

"Did the President of France tell you to go to Jerusalem?" they asked. He said that he had not.

When they persisted, asking if other world leaders had told him to go to Jerusalem, he replied that they had not. "Well, then, who did tell you to go to Jerusalem?" they asked.

"If you must know," Sadat replied, "God spoke to me to go to Jerusalem."

In the days leading up to his proposed visit, people everywhere were making bets as to whether or not he would actually go through with the trip. Until the last minute, many believed that he would not dare do it, for no Egyptian had visited Jerusalem in modern times.

In both Cairo and Jerusalem, the proposed visit of Sadat was the hottest topic of conversation. Few could imagine that he would actually carry through with it. If he did, it would be a most bold and daring decision.

When Anwar Sadat landed in Tel Aviv, we were glued to the television in Jerusalem, witnessing this momentous event. As he stepped off the airplane onto

Israeli soil, in a moment it seemed as if there was suddenly a lightness to the atmosphere over Jerusalem I had never felt before. The city seemed twenty years younger. Later, we learned that in Cairo reporters had questioned the populace concerning their feelings and impressions of their president's trip. One man said, "When Sadat put his feet on Israeli soil, it felt as if God had come down to man."

That night we were praying all night at our house, and in the middle of the night suddenly I felt that we should go to the Western Wall to pray. I invited those in my house who wanted to accompany us, and quite a few responded.

Security was tight because President Sadat would pray at dawn at the Mosque, and we were unable to drive all the way to the Dung Gate. We parked and walked the rest of the way.

When we got to the Wall, it was deserted. It was the one and only time I had seen the Wall without many people praying in front of it. Our brothers went to the men's side of the Wall, and we sisters went to the women's side. Then we all joined hands at the back of the prayer area and danced slowly all the way up to the Wall. We danced back, and then repeated this several times.

I did a quick count of our people and realized that we were eleven. *How wonderful it would be*, I was thinking, *if there could be twelve.* Just at that moment, another sister joined us. She had been praying there all night for many nights, and I had forgotten that she would be there. She had gone into a side room to warm herself, as it was November and the night air was cool, and she was praying inside there. She had not heard us with her natural ears, but had been drawn by the Spirit to come out and join us. Now twelve, we danced back and forth in a glory that I had never experienced before at the Wall.

The Sadat visit to Jerusalem was historic. God had indeed spoken to him to come, and it was the beginning of the peace process. ✷

☙ 80 ☙

"Pray for the Soul of the Shah of Iran"

After relations between Egypt and Israel had been normalized, many people wanted to travel to Cairo from Israel, but they found that the visa took longer to obtain than they had considered. During this time, God spoke to me to go to Cairo for a few days. I called a travel agent and booked a flight from Tel Aviv to Cairo. When I asked how I could obtain a visa, they told me I could get it at the airport upon arrival. I left the next day for Cairo, not knowing why I was going.

In the meantime, I played. I went to the Cairo Museum and saw the great Tutankhamen Exhibit. I rode out to Mena House and had coffee overlooking the Pyramids and the Sphinx and enjoyed the ambiance of that lovely old historic hotel. I went to the Abdeen Palace and visited with Dr. Zechariah Azmy, personal assistant to President Sadat. I had dinner at the lovely restaurant beside the Nile. In this way I passed two days.

Then Saturday night, in the middle of the night, I was suddenly awakened and told to pray and intercede for the soul of the Shah of Iran. I prayed until I felt the assurance that God had heard my prayers and all was well with his soul. Then I fell asleep again.

The next morning, I got a taxi back to the airport, boarded the plane, and flew back to Tel Aviv. I got in a taxi at the airport headed for Jerusalem. The driver turned on his radio to get some news. The Shah of Iran had died in the night in Cairo, Egypt. ✳

≤ 81 ≥

"I Want to Finance These People"

Jerusalem became a launching pad for many of us to reach out to other areas of the world. When two sisters from Sierra Leone, Princess James and her sister, the wife of Pastor Ade Jones of Freetown, came and spent a few days with us, we fell in love with them. They were enthralled with what God was doing in our midst and invited us to come to Sierra Leone.

They were such lovely people. Brother and Sister Jones had been in the diplomatic corp of their country for many years and served in many other countries. After they found the Lord, they entered the ministry and were, at the time we met them, pastoring a lovely church in Freetown, Bethel Temple.

God used those two ladies to draw our focus again to Africa, and He spoke to us during the days they were there that He wanted to use us to take the whole continent. We were willing, and we had the personnel, but we had no money.

A lady who was attending our meetings in Jerusalem had just received an inheritance from her mother. She came to me and said, "I want to finance these people going to Africa," and she did. Thirteen teams of two went out to all parts of Africa.

We bought the least expensive tickets available and gave each team enough money to get started, but they would all have to trust the Lord for the rest of their needs. Each team was gone from thirty to forty-five days, and we thus preached in every nation of Africa, declaring the outpouring of the Spirit.

Most of those who worked with us in those days were young people, and this was a great launching pad for their ministry. Many of them went on to do great things for God.

Later, when I was traveling in various parts of Africa, I would meet people who had been blessed by this outreach. For instance, I went to Namibia in response to an invitation from some Namibians who came to Jerusalem and saw our ministry there. When our Namibian friends met me at the airport, they had a pastor and his wife with them. In the course of the conversation, they told me that a group had come from Jerusalem about ten years before and had been a great blessing to them. I was able to say, "I was the one who sent them." They were so thrilled that they opened wide the doors of their church to my ministry. This was repeated over and over again.   ❋

"The Holy Hush of God's Presence"

One day, when I had just returned to Jerusalem from an overseas trip, I walked into our fellowship in Jerusalem, and I felt the glory of God in a way I had never felt it before. There was an awesome sense of His presence in that place.

Many have experienced what we call the "holy hush." After great praising and rejoicing and much worship, it seems as if a conductor has brought an orchestra to a quiet moment after the crescendo and everybody stands in total quietness, feeling the majestic presence of God's glory. That day in Jerusalem I felt it as never before.

I suddenly knew how easy it is to raise the dead and to heal all manner of sickness and disease. How easy it is in that realm of glory! How easy to see people leaping out of wheelchairs and off of stretchers! How easy to see blind eyes opened and deaf ears unstopped! In the glory realm nothing is impossible.

That glory must have stayed with us two or three hours. God was giving us a foretaste, as He often does, of a greater day, so that we could encourage ourselves and others to move into the glory realm.

God showed me that day that if there is no death working in me, if there is no bitterness, no strife, no criticism — nothing of death — I can command death. If death is working in me, I have no authority over death. If only life is flowing through me, I have an authority over death, and I can command it in the name of the Lord. As we moved deeper into the resurrection power of God and learned to live in the glory realm, I knew that we would see the miraculous as the world had never seen it before. It was a beginning of greater things for all of us. ✷

≈§ 83 ≥.

"Someone Important"

If we ever thought that we were going to Jerusalem to settle down, it didn't take long for us to learn differently. One year I remember taking a major trip every month. We were blessing the nations from Jerusalem.

Some of our trips were for traditional meetings, such as conventions and church revivals, but more and more we did very unusual trips for the Lord. One of those trips involved a visit to the Soviet Union.

One day the Lord spoke to me and said, "If you go to Moscow for the weekend, I'll have you meet somebody important." These were still Cold War days, and I didn't know how to arrange a trip to Russia from Jerusalem. I had gone several times to the Soviet Union, but always from America, and I only knew how to apply for permission in Washington, D.C. There was a specific travel agent there who could help you with such arrangements.

Everything about a trip to the Soviet Union had to be prearranged. The total itinerary had to be laid out in advance. All hotel rooms and other daily provisions had to be detailed on the application before a visa could be granted. The validity of the visa was totally dependent upon sticking with the prearranged travel plans. I had traveled to Russia like that several times in the past, but never from Jerusalem. Since there were no diplomatic relations between Russia and Israel at that time, how did one go about arranging these things?

As I was meditating on how to make these arrangements, the Lord spoke to me and impressed me to call the telephone operator in Cyprus and ask her if there were any local travel agents dealing with travel to Russia. I had never called Cyprus before, but on Monday I called and asked the operator if she could help me find someone doing business with Russia. Without hesitation she put me through to just such a travel agent.

I said to the agent, "I would like to go to Russia for the weekend." I knew that it took weeks to arrange something like this, even from America, but the Lord had placed faith in my heart for a miracle.

"I don't think I can arrange something that quickly," the agent answered.

"Let me give you my number," I said. "I only want to stay the weekend and come back. Please call me if you find a way to do it."

242

I Ask for Russia

At that moment another thought came to me. "How would it be if I went ahead and sent my passport over to you?" I asked him. "That could save some time. You could get my visa there."

"Good," he answered. He looked up the next flight from Tel Aviv. A Cyprus Airways flight would be leaving Tel Aviv that night. He would meet the plane, he told me, if I could get someone to take my passport to him. He would be standing in the airport with a sign to identify himself. I sent my passport as pre-arranged.

He called back within a day or so and said that he had my visa and that I could catch a Cyprus Airways flight to Cyprus on Thursday afternoon, spend the night in Cyprus, get my flight out to Moscow on Friday and be back to Tel Aviv on Monday. I never knew how he arranged all that, but he did it.

I told the agent to book me into the National Hotel, just across from Red Square. It was my favorite in Moscow. It had always been difficult to get a room there, but I had managed it on several occasions.

By the time I reached Moscow, it was late in the evening, so I decided to look around a little and then go to bed and get some rest. When I woke up the next morning, there were several things I wanted to do. I wanted to go to a service in the Moscow Synagogue and pray, I wanted to walk along the boulevard in front of communist party headquarters and pray, and I wanted to walk all the way around the Kremlin and pray.

On other occasions, when I had been in Moscow, it was so cold that it was nearly unbearable to walk from the door of the hotel to the taxi. It was a much warmer day than usual at this time of year in Moscow, and I was able to do all the walking I wanted. The synagogue was absolutely gorgeous, and as I sat there marveling in its beauty, I was believing God for His people.

When I finally got back to the hotel, it was late Friday afternoon. When anyone comes in from the cold into a warm room, if you're not careful, you get very sleepy. It happened to me that day, and since it was already dark, I decided that I would just go to bed early. I wasn't very hungry anyway.

I had been in bed for no more than ten minutes when the Lord said very plainly to me that I should get up, get dressed up and go down to the restaurant for dinner.

When I went into the hotel restaurant, the *maitre d'hotel* told me that it was full. I said that I would wait, and I sat down. In just a few minutes, he was back to say that if I did not mind sitting at a table where someone else was sitting, he had a place for me. I told him I did not mind at all.

He ushered me into the dining hall and gave me a seat opposite a man and a woman. Now I did feel bad. The two of them had chosen this very exclusive restaurant to spend an evening together, and they surely would have appreciated

243

a little privacy. Yet, here I was sitting across the table from them. I turned my head from them and looked toward a small stage where a group of musicians were performing. I especially enjoyed the balalika music. I kept turned in that direction as much as possible.

Suddenly it seemed that the hand of the Lord fell on my head and with it came this reminder, "I told you if you would come to Moscow for the weekend, I would have you meet somebody important. This is the man. Look." So instead of looking away, I looked straight ahead.

I decided that the man was probably French. He was speaking in very polished French, at least. He seemed to be some sort of diplomat.

Just at that moment, the waiter came and began to speak to me. I answered in English, and this let the couple seated across from me know that I was an English-speaking person. As soon as the waiter left, the gentleman asked me, "Would you care for some wine?"

I said, "No, thank you," but this opened the opportunity for conversation. I asked him if he was in diplomacy or in business. He said, "Diplomacy." As it turned out, the man was Russian. When this was revealed, I suddenly knew that I must say to him everything that I wanted to say to Secretary General Leonid Brezhnev.

The Russians were very careful in those days not to let their citizens mingle with foreigners. When a foreigner came with a group, they placed the flag of his country on the table, and this let everybody know who was who. When they started allowing the entrance of individuals, they still did the same with the flag. They were not yet ready to allow their citizens to be "contaminated" by foreign ideas. The Lord knew what He was doing and allowed me to be seated at the same table as this Russian.

I spoke to him about Jerusalem and about the ingathering of the exiles from all over the world. This required, I told him, the release of the Jewish people in every place.

Prime Minister Menachem Begin of Israel was, at that moment, in London and we talked about that fact. In the course of the conversation, I told him several stories about being sent by the Lord on special assignments. We talked for what must have been several hours.

Before we parted, he said to me, "Since you go to important places to pray at important times, then I'm sure you'll be coming to Geneva. Let me give you my card." When I looked at the card later, I learned that he was the Secretary General in charge of personnel for the United Nations and was at that time over a staff of several thousand diplomats in Geneva.

How I rejoiced in the wonderful opportunity God had given me to speak with him!

I Ask for Russia

The next day was Sunday. In addition to attending a service in a Russian Orthodox church, I went to the Tetrakov Museum, one of my favorites in Moscow. There they have the famous Rublov icons.

On Monday I flew back to Cyprus and on to Jerusalem. I had met "someone important," just as the Lord had said.　　　　　　　　　　　　❋

≈ 84 ≈

"Much More Dangerous Than the First"

We were not always able to take every trip ourselves, but we were blessed to have many faithful companions who could respond when we could not. One day, for instance, we got a call in Jerusalem from Eleanor Shifrin, a friend who, with her husband, lived in another part of Israel. She told us that she was very concerned about her parents. The Potonikos had both been surgeons with the Russian Army, but when they applied for permission to immigrate to Israel, they had lost their positions. (These were still Cold War days.) They protested the loss of their jobs and the denial of their visas by locking themselves into their apartment with another daughter, and they had all been locked up like that for the past five years.

They had survived this ordeal with the help of sympathetic neighbors. The family would periodically drop a basket attached to a rope from a window, and neighbors would place food or other necessary items into it. When their money ran out, they paid for these items through barter.

During the years of their protest, they had become symbols of resistance among the dissidents, and their case had been widely publicized. Senators Scoop Jackson and Ted Kennedy had actively tried to help secure their release, but nothing seemed to be working. Eleanor was asking if we had someone we could send to Russia to check on the welfare of her parents because she had not heard from them in more than six months.

We had gone into Russia on special missions many times, and the Lord had recently been laying Russia on our hearts again, but something we had heard recently gave us reason for pause. Just a few days before this a Russian Orthodox priest had said something to Janet Saunders, who had developed a wonderful rapport with the Russian Orthodox community in Jerusalem, that let her know that his colleagues were aware of our trips into Russia. "We understand that the big one (referring to me) was recently in Moscow, and the little one (referring to my associate) was recently traveling in Estonia and some of the other Baltic states."

When Janet told us about this, we sensed that it would not be wise for either of us to go back to the Soviet Union right then. We were too fresh on people's

246

I Ask for Siberia

minds. I told Eleanor that we could probably not go ourselves, but I would pray and see if somebody else could do it.

When we prayed, the Lord spoke to us to send Alice Ford. Because it would be a dangerous trip, I asked the Lord to speak to her directly as well, and He did. After He had already laid Russia on Alice's heart, I asked her if she would be willing to undertake that specific mission. She prayed about it and decided that she would.

Instead of sending her directly to Moscow (it was impossible to fly directly from Tel Aviv to Moscow in those days), we sent her to Copenhagen, and there she was able to get a tourist visa for Russia.

Eleanor had told her how to connect to Novosibirsk which was at the beginning of Siberia, what bus to take, where to get off and where she would find her parents' home. She also instructed her about what to say to her parents once she found them and gave her some codes that would identify her as a friend and not a foe. The two ladies had a picture taken together, and Alice carried it with her to show the parents. We gave Alice Bibles and other items to deliver to believers in Russia, to take advantage of her trip.

Alice knew no Russian, so she could not read the street signs. What was worse, some of the bus routes had been changed and things did not work out exactly as she had been told to expect. The only thing that saved her was knowing the Holy Spirit and being able to hear the voice of the Lord. As she was riding along on one bus, the Lord told her that she was going the wrong way. She got off and got another bus going the opposite direction. Step by step, the Lord led her to the house she was looking for.

Eleanor's parents had taught themselves a little English from reading the book *Exodus* by Leon Uris and a little Hebrew from the Hebrew Bible, so Alice was able to converse with them in their few words of English and Hebrew. She was very moved by their plight. They had been reduced to living in a very tiny house. Her spirit rose up within her, and she began to prophesy their release. The couple was so excited by her prophetic word that they got out some beet juice they had hidden away and they all toasted their imminent release. Alice had taken some gifts for them, but when she saw how little food they had, she wished that she had taken more food. Otherwise, it had been a marvelous trip.

Soon after Alice made this daring visit to Siberia, the Russian government suddenly decided to grant the couple their requested exit visas and ordered them to come to a government office to process them. They had been living in such fear for the past five years, however, that they were sure this must be a trick of some kind, so they refused to go.

After several months, Eleanor called to ask if Alice would be willing to go to Siberia again. I was sure that a second visit would be much more dangerous than the first, but I would leave it to the Lord to decide. When I prayed about it, the Lord not only told me to send Alice but to send her directly this time. He assured me that the Russians knew that she was coming and why she was coming and that they would help her. This time, I sent Alice to Cyprus where she got a direct flight to Moscow.

While Alice was waiting for her flight in Cyprus, we got another phone call from Eleanor. She said she had just received a call from her father in Novosibirsk. He said that the Russian authorities had contacted them that morning and said that Alice was coming, that she was coming to help them and that if she needed any assistance while she was there, they would be glad to provide it. On the day of Alice's visit, the government office that issued exit visas was scheduled to be closed. It would open, however, so that she could take the couple there and help them secure their exit visas for immigration to Israel.

The family was still not sure that what they were hearing could be true. They decided that the husband would risk it first. If he got to Israel and found that it was safe, he would send a coded message to his wife and daughter to follow. Alice went with Mr. Potoniko to get his exit visa.

When he arrived in Israel the first place he wanted to go was to our house in Jerusalem, to thank us for our efforts on behalf of the family, and to give thanks to the Lord.

Because he had suffered the loss of his military rank for his desire to immigrate to Israel, Prime Minister Menachem Begin conferred upon him an honorary rank in the Israeli Army. We were invited to a special ceremony at the Department of Defense in Tel Aviv the day the award was given.

By the time he arrived in Israel, he had not practiced his specialty (eye surgery) for more than five years, and his skills were rusty. He had, however, invented eleven different instruments for use in this highly technical field. He went to work with the Research Institute in Israel and was able to invent other instruments for eye surgery. He lived many useful years in Israel before his death, at which time the Israeli government named a street after him in the city of Netanya. Alice was written up in Israeli magazines and became known as "The Angel Sent to Novosibirsk." ✳

≈ 85 ≈

"Every Word You Ever Prophesied Has Come to Pass"

I made many trips over the years from Jerusalem to Australia. I had begun ministering there in the early seventies, my brother went many times, and many of our church co-workers have gone there over and over again. God used us to birth revival there.

When we first started going to Australia, most of the Pentecostal churches were quite small, of one hundred members or less. Only a few exceeded that number. We declared that they would increase. We prophesied God's blessing over individual people as well.

At the beginning many Australian pastors thought we were speaking out of ourselves, that what we were saying could not be of God. The pastor of a large church in Brisbane later told my brother, "When you first began to prophesy these things into my life, I sincerely thought it was all fairy tales. I couldn't believe that any of those things would ever happen to me. Yet every word that you ever prophesied over me has now come to pass."

The Lord had spoken to that particular man that he would not only be used in Australia, but in the neighboring islands, in southeast Asia and in other parts of the world. It seemed impossible at the time, but every word came to pass.

When we started going to Australia, the main mission focus was New Guinea. The Australians had only one missionary in Africa in those early days. Since then the Australian church has become a great missionary church and has reached out and blessed the world. Much of that vision for the nations was imparted through our ministry.

Every time I went to Australia, God had something new to reveal to the people there. For instance, on one of the trips I made, everywhere I went there were angelic visitations. It happened in Perth, then in Adelaide, and by the time I got to Canberra and was telling the pastor about the visitations in Adelaide, his phone rang and someone from Adelaide was calling to tell him the very same thing.

God's glory was revealed in our meetings there. One night, for instance, in Newcastle, New South Wales, I was ministering at Sister Pat Cochran's church. I had been there for several nights already and had ministered to many people.

249

Harvest Glory

This particular night a young boy came forward and said to me, "I want you to pray for me because I feel a pressure on my head." Normally I would have just stretched out my hand and prayed for the pressure he felt to be lifted, but I felt a check in my spirit.

"How long have you had this pressure?" I asked the boy.

He said, "Since the other night when you prayed for me."

"I don't want to pray for that pressure to be lifted," I told him, "because that is the weight of glory resting on your head." I had been experiencing the same thing in Jerusalem, and I knew that it was not something bad, but something good.

Through our ministry, many groups in Australia which were not formerly Spirit-filled became Spirit-filled. When I was invited to go to Hobart, Tasmania, for example, I had never met the pastor of the church, but I was looking forward to being with him. I was to be with him for one evening prayer meeting and one evening service in the church.

We arrived just in time for the meeting and had just a few minutes to freshen up, so there wasn't much opportunity to get to know him or his people before we began. I knew that he was Charismatic and that the church was a Church of Christ congregation.

After we had sung a few songs, he introduced me, and I decided to ask the people to worship with me in the Spirit. My feeling was that I would take their spiritual temperature. "Let's all sing a few hallelujahs," I said, and I began to sing myself. After a few hallelujahs, I began speaking in tongues and, sure enough, everyone joined me, singing in tongues. *This must be a good Charismatic group*, I thought, as I ministered to them with abandonment.

After the service we were all invited for tea and biscuits and I was able to speak with some of the people about their experience. "How long have you been Charismatic?" I asked one sister.

"Not until tonight," she answered.

When I got this same answer from several people in the congregation, I realized what God had done. Only the pastor and a few of the members had been Spirit-filled. At the moment we began singing "Hallelujah" and singing in the Spirit, at that moment they, all with one accord, had become Spirit-filled and had spoken in tongues. This same scene was repeated over and over again in different parts of Australia through the years.   ✸

⚞ 86 ⚟

"Bridges to Australia"

Many of the trips I made were a result of something that God was showing us in Jerusalem. One year God sent me to Canberra, the capital of Australia because a man I knew had been elevated to head of the China desk in the Ministry of Foreign Affairs, and I wanted to share with him some of the things God was showing us in Jerusalem.

Because of the Islamic Revolution in Iran and the Russian intervention in Afghanistan, and because of the new consciousness of the importance of the emerging nations of the Pacific Rim, Australia had suddenly taken on a stature among the nations that it had never before enjoyed. God had been showing us new bridges going up between the United States and Australia, between Israel and Australia and between China and Australia. I felt that my friend would want to know the details of what God was revealing to us. Several years later it was stated in a political magazine that Australia had been the bridge between China and Israel.

I preached in just one Australian church, in Elizabeth, before going on to Canberra. After we had worshiped the Lord together for a while that night, I asked if anyone had seen a vision they wanted to share with the rest of us. One man spoke up and said, "Sister Ruth, I want to tell you about the building I've just seen. I don't know what it might be, but it is shaped like a round canopy. All around the sides of the canopy are arches," and he described them.

I had to say, "Brother, I don't know what that building is either, but when God gives us a vision like this we must tuck it away in our hearts and draw it out at a later time, when the Lord somehow reminds us of it."

The next day I flew to Canberra, saw my friend at the China desk and told him the things that God was showing us in Jerusalem. As a seasoned diplomat, he listened courteously, but made little comment. The next morning, however, everything that I had shared with him in private had suddenly become headlines in the Australian newspapers, and the importance of Australia on the international scene was confirmed.

The Lord had shown one of our people a peacock. I wasn't sure what a pea-

251

cock could have to do with what God was saying about the new importance of Australia on the international stage, but the day after I had related the vision to my friend, I opened the Australian papers to read that Mr. Andrew Peacock, the new Australian Foreign Minister, was traveling in Asia, cementing agreements for the new realities in the Pacific Rim.

As I was preparing to leave my hotel that day, I passed a window and noticed what a beautiful view I had of the city from that high floor. Since the city was new to me, I took time to look it over. One of the buildings that stood out to me was immediately recognizable as the same building the brother had seen in his vision two nights before in Elizabeth.

I ran down to the lobby of the hotel to see if I could find a postcard with a picture of that building and saw that it was the National Academy of Science. I found a taxi and asked the driver to take me there.

"I'm sorry," he said, "but that's the only building in Australia you cannot go into."

"What do you mean?" I asked.

"It's top security," he replied.

"Why?" I persisted. "If it's a science building, what's so top-secret about that?"

"It's not just any science," he said. "It is nuclear science. They are developing the bomb. That's the most important building in this nation."

That very week China was forging a military alliance with Australia. The strategic implications of the alliance were being played down, but the Holy Ghost had focused in on that building as a place of strategic importance.   ✳

87

"Anoint Bob Hawke"

The special anointing God had given me early in my ministry for kings and ambassadors and other people of position continued to work during our time of ministry from Zion.

One day in our prayer meeting in Jerusalem, I had a vision, and the Lord told me to go to Australia and anoint Bob Hawke to be the next Prime Minister of that country. I knew almost nothing about politics in Australia and, although I may have seen his name at some time in a newspaper article, I did not really know very much about him. I got the next possible flight to Australia, and when I arrived, I flew into Sydney and called friends of mine, Dr. and Mrs. Richmond Ricard-Bell.

"Ruth, what brings you to Australia this time?" Joanie asked me. I am known for being carried away by the winds of the Spirit to do unusual things, and the question was a legitimate one.

"I have come to anoint Bob Hawke to be the next Prime Minister of Australia," I answered her.

She didn't seem to think that was so unusual. "It just so happens," she said, "that Bob Hawke's best friend is in the hospital here in Sydney, and he is flying in here every other day to visit him." As it turned out, her daughter was the best friend of the wife of Bob Hawke's best friend. "We'll see what we can do to get you an invitation to speak with him," she told me. Well, God seemed to be taking care of things, and I was excited to see how He was going to arrange for me to meet Bob Hawke.

Nothing happened over the next couple of days, and I had to fly to Melbourne. One day, while I was in Melbourne, staying with Pastor and Mrs. David Reekie of the Assembly of God Church in Blackburn, I was called to the telephone, and a deep, man's voice said, "This is Bob Hawke. I don't know about visions, but I hope you're right." We began to make plans to get together. I was going to Elizabeth, near Adelaide, to attend the wedding of Anita and Don Ridge, who had been very good to us in sending us to the nations. I would be back over the weekend. He told me to call his secretary when I got back, and she would set up an appointment. It was a lovely wedding, and when I got back into town and called the secretary, the arrangements were made, and Pastor and Mrs. Reekie drove me in their car to the headquarters of the ACTU (the Australian Council of Trade Unions).

In the period leading up to our meeting, I had learned a lot about Bob Hawke. He had been the leader of the Union movement in Australia for some years, but he had just recently resigned that post to run for Parliament. That was an important step, for in the Australian system of government, one must be a member of Parliament to be considered for the post of head of the government.

I had learned that he was a great friend of Israel. He had made the statement that if he had ever had a spiritual experience in his life, it was in regards to Israel. Surely that was why God was about to elevate him, I felt.

Not everything I learned about Bob Hawke was positive. In fact, everyone had a strong opinion, either pro or con, about Bob Hawke. God had sent me to anoint him to be Prime Minister, and that was what I intended to do.

When I was ushered into his office, I was given a seat about six feet away from his desk. "Would it be all right if I moved my chair up a little closer?" I asked him.

"Fine," he said

I moved closer, and we began to talk about a couple friends we had in common in Israel. Before long, I told him about how I had been praying in Jerusalem and what God had told me. "Is it all right for me to lay my hands on your head and pray for you?" I asked. He was very gracious and said I may.

As I started around that big desk, it suddenly seemed huge, but God was with me. I stood beside him and began to prophesy, and then I anointed him prophetically to be the next Prime Minister of Australia.

After I finished, he thanked me, we spoke a few pleasantries, and I left.

When I finished praying for Bob Hawke, Pastor and Mrs. Reekie were waiting outside the ACTU Building to take me to the airport. I had been planning to fly directly from Melbourne to Israel. As I came out to their car, however, the Lord spoke to me that I should go to Sydney to the hospital to pray for Bob Hawke's best friend, George Rocky. I got a plane from Melbourne to Sydney, took a taxi and went to the hospital where he was a patient.

He was, of course, surprised to see me, and surprised again when I told him that God had spoken to me to come and pray for him. He said that Bob had just called and told him about my having anointed him to be the Prime Minister.

George Rocky was totally different than I expected. I had heard that he was considered to be the king-maker, one of the important and influential politicians in Australia, and I am not sure what I was expecting. As it turned out, he

I Ask for Australia

was a member of Hungarian royalty and a beautiful, gentle man.

I talked with George for some time. He wanted to hear the entire story of how God had spoken to me in Jerusalem, how I had arranged the trip and what had transpired along the way. He was a very gracious man.

I told George that I wanted to have prayer with him, and as I prayed I asked God to heal his sickness, and I asked God to let the spirit of revelation work in his life. After we had finished praying, I said good-bye, went to the airport in Sydney and took the first plane to Hong Kong and, from there, back to Jerusalem.

As I had time to think about what had transpired and why I had been led to fly to Sydney, I felt that the Lord wanted George Rocky, the man who had mentored Bob Hawke, to meet me and make a judgment as to whether or not I was a valid person so that he could influence and encourage Bob Hawke concerning my prophecy. God also wanted him to know that the dreams he had dared dream for Bob Hawke, and which had caused him to give Bob Hawke so much time and attention, would indeed come to pass.

I heard that Bob Hawke had won his seat in Wills Can area of Australia and would take his place in the Australian Parliament. Each time I went to Australia to preach I asked how he was doing, but I was resting on God's word. God had sent me to anoint various people for the ministry and for government, and once I had obeyed Him, it was out of my hands. I was busy helping to believe God for the revival to come into every part of Australia and was occasionally traveling and speaking there.

A couple of years went by, and one day in 1983, as I was praying in Jerusalem, the Lord told me to fly again to Australia. He didn't give me any details about why I was going, but we don't always need to know. Sometimes He tells us on the way; sometimes He tells us when we get to where we are going; sometimes we don't know until after we leave a place; and sometimes it is years later when we perceive the real reason we went. I got ready and left for Australia again.

I again arrived at the home of Dr. and Mrs. Richmond Ricard-Bell and, again, Joanie asked me, "Ruth, what's up this time?"

"I'm not sure," I told her. "What's happening with Bob Hawke?"

"He's not being too active," she replied, "even in this Franklin Dam question, he's just being very low-key." This was unusual. Bob Hawke had always been at the forefront on current issues. It was not like him to be "low-key."

When she said this, suddenly the anointing of the Holy Ghost came on me, and the Lord said, "I have brought you here so that My word may be hastened concerning Bob Hawke." Right there in that lovely dining room in Bay Sands I began to declare that the word of the Lord would be hastened and that God would quickly bring to pass His word concerning Bob Hawke being the next Prime Minister of Australia. In the next several minutes we released our faith and believed God for His purposes to be hastened.

It was either that day or the next that Prime Minister Malcolm Fraser announced surprise elections. It was not time for regular elections in Australia, but he had taken a calculated risk that if he announced surprise elections his party would have the advantage.

Tom Haden was the head of the opposition party, but there was suddenly an outcry for the candidacy of Bob Hawke. "I will not step aside for Bob Hawke," Haden announced. "Over my dead body. There will be a bloodbath before I will step aside for him." The very next day, however, Tom Haden quietly stepped aside, and Bob Hawke assumed the leadership of the opposition party in Australia. None of this surprised me. I knew what God was doing.

I had prior commitments in New Zealand for the next couple of weeks for ministry, but I would then be coming back to Australia, and it was arranged for me to meet Bob Hawke and his wife when I did. We met in the Southern Cross Hotel in Melbourne. I got there on Wednesday night, and we met the next morning. The campaigns were finished. Wednesday night was the last night the candidates were able to advertise on television. From then through Saturday, election day, there would be an advertising blackout so that voters would not be unduly influenced by last-minute media blitzes.

When we met, there were several current events in the morning papers that we spoke of, and then I asked him, "Did you ever think that you would become head of the Labor Party so easily?"

"No," he admitted. "I never dreamed it would be so easy."

"God is going to give you the election just that easily on Saturday," I continued. "You will win by the largest percentage of votes in Australian election history."

Before we had met that day, many people had given me advice about just what to say. Everyone seemed to know just what Bob Hawke needed to hear, and everyone, of course, wanted me to pray with him to be saved. Each time I got this advice, I just smiled politely and thanked the individual, but I was going to do exactly what God wanted because He does things so differently than we do. I now heard myself saying, "On Saturday morning, I want you to come aside and let God know that you recognize that it is not because of your talents or abilities that you have been chosen to head the country, but that it is God who is putting you into office." He said that he would do that.

After I had finished speaking with him, I went into the next room and spoke with his wife, Hazel. She was busy packing because they were getting ready to fly off to Tasmania for a few days rest. I told her how happy I was that she had recently spoken to the media and let it be known that she and Bob had a faith. "Sometimes we are not aware how important these things are," I said, "but it's very important that the people who vote for you know that you have a faith, even if it's not a formal faith that includes attending church every Sunday."

After we finished our meetings that day, I went to the airport and caught my scheduled flight to Hong Kong. I would have to rush on, as I was due to meet Margaret Thatcher in the British House of Commons a few days later.

I got into Hong Kong on Friday. The next day, I woke up totally carefree. I went out to do some shopping, and all day long a little song went over and over in my spirit. I was singing the words of the Psalm:

> Some trust in chariots, and some in horses: but we will remember the name of the LORD our God.　　　　　　　　　　　　　　　Psalm 20:7

I had not said a prayer all day long concerning Bob Hawke's election, but I knew that it was an accomplished fact and that God had placed this song in my heart as an indicator of that assurance.

That night the reports began to come in from the elections in Australia, and we learned that Bob Hawke was winning by the largest percentage of votes in Australian election history. I looked up that verse in the Psalms, added the next verse, and sent it in a telegram to the Prime Minister-elect. It said:

> Some trust in chariots, and some in horses: but we will remember the name of the LORD our God. They are brought down and fallen: but we are risen, and stand upright.　　　　　　　　　　　　　　　Psalm 20:7-8

That's the way the Lord fulfills His promises.

I believe that Bob Hawke was in power longer than any other Australian Prime Minister. He became the first Labor Prime Minister to win a fourth term in office. Not everyone was happy about that fact. Sometimes when I preached in Australia, pastors hoped I would not mention their Prime Minister by name. One night in Brisbane a pastor invited all the board members of his church over to meet me. When he introduced me to them, he said, "She's a great woman of God, with the exception of her prophesying over Bob Hawke."

"Promise me you won't mention anything about Bob Hawke," some pastors said to me before I ministered. Each time this happened, I let people know that I had no vested interest in Bob Hawke's being in power. I was being obedient to God.

Some of the Australian pastors were upset that God had not used an Australian believer to prophesy over him. "You are all so prejudiced against him," I told them, "that God had to bring me all the way from Jerusalem to do it."

After I had first prophesied over Bob Hawke, I learned that his father was a congregational pastor and that even before he was born God had spoken to his mother that she would have a boy and had told her, "The government shall be upon his shoulders." It is easy for us to make judgments about a particular individual, but we often don't understand God's dealings with that person. Perhaps God blessed Bob Hawke simply to keep His promises to his parents. Who are we to judge?

During his stay in power, I often received letters from Australian Christians asking me to pray that he be put out of office. I never prayed one way or the other until one day the Lord said to me, "I'm not yet finished with Bob Hawke." I knew then that Prime Minister Hawke would win yet another election and stay in power even longer.

I never met Bob Hawke again after that, but sometimes when Australian believers would meet him in the walkabouts when he was campaigning, they would ask him if he remembered me. He would say, "Of course." Sometimes they had tapes from my meetings and would offer them to him. He always received them very graciously. Whenever God has brought him to my mind, I have prayed for him, just as I have done for many others.

It is the Lord who raises people into authority, and when He joins us to those purposes, and we have opportunity to declare it, it is glorious.

In later years, when I was leaving Brisbane for Hong Kong on another trip, I found that the international boarding lounge was very crowded. The flight should be leaving, but it was apparently delayed for some reason.

I noticed three Chinese men dressed in very finely tailored Mao suits, typical of important Chinese government officials of that time, and I went over to speak with them. Two of the men only spoke Chinese and, since my conversational Mandarin still left a lot to be desired, I quickly discovered that the third man spoke excellent English. He was an official of China's Department of Foreign Affairs, and it was a privilege to speak with him.

As we talked, I discovered that he and the other two men made up an official delegation en route to speak with Prime Minister Bob Hawke. We talked for at least an hour before it was announced that our plane, at last, would be departing.

We boarded the plane; the three Chinese gentlemen went upstairs to first class; and I went to my tourist-class seat. After we got seated, someone said to me, "Wasn't that terrible? That strike?"

I Ask for Australia

"What strike?" I asked.

This person answered, "That's why we were in the airport waiting so long. There was a strike by the ground staff, otherwise we would have boarded the plane an hour ago." It was only then that I realized what the Lord had done. He had allowed the ground staff to strike just at that moment in order to give me the opportunity of meeting those Chinese officials.

As I pondered this, I realized that if these men were going to meet with Bob Hawke, they would be able to deliver a message to him for me. I took a calling card and wrote a short note on the back of it to the Prime Minister. Then, I went to the front of the plane and asked the stewardess if I could go upstairs and speak with the three Chinese gentlemen. She gave me permission to do so.

When I asked my newfound friend if he would mind delivering the message, he told me that he would be seeing Bob Hawke in just a few hours and wouldn't mind delivering my note. I went back to my seat.

When we arrived in Sydney, I saw the Prime Minister's plane parked, waiting to take the Chinese dignitaries to Canberra. The red carpet was unrolled, and a band and honor guard were in place. Only then did I realize what a great miracle God had given me. If I had not met the men in Brisbane, when they were waiting for a delayed plane, I would never have had the opportunity.

The English-speaking Chinese man became a very good friend, and we had the opportunity to see him several times in Beijing. His children went swimming with Deng Xiao Ping each summer when they were on holiday together. God is so gracious to give us such friendships.

I have seen the Lord make these divine appointments again and again, and every time there is a new excitement in my spirit for the way He does it and the eternal purposes that are being accomplished.

✻

⚔ 88 ⚔

"Command Time for Cory Aquino"

Again, I was praying one day in Jerusalem, and the Lord showed me a vision of myself with my hands uplifted like Moses when he interceded on the mountain for the people of Israel. As long as his hands remained lifted, the battle went well for the people of God, but when he got tired and his hands began to fall, the battle went against them. The Lord told me to go to the Philippines and to stand in that intercessory prayer position for President Cory Aquino.

The vision changed, and I saw Joshua with the next generation of Israelites. He was led to do something much more radical, something that had never been done before, to enable the people to win a battle against their enemies. God dropped faith into his heart to command time to stand still.

He had seen that the people had everything they needed to win. They had the necessary personnel and armament. The only thing in short supply was time.

The sun was about to go down, and if the enemy was allowed to regroup to fight another day, there was no guarantee of victory. Joshua pointed at the sun and the moon and commanded them to stand still in their place until the battle could be won, and God honored his faith. The Lord said to me, "Go to the Philippines and command time for Cory Aquino."

I had never met the President and had no connection to her administration or family. Because of our involvement with the Philippine revival, we had many contacts in the previous government, that of President Ferdinand Marcos and Vice-President Fernando Lopez, but this government had replaced them in the famous People's Revolution. How would I get in to meet the new President? I knew that God could give me the connection I needed, since this was His command, not mine.

I had other friends in the Philippines, and I began trying to make contact with anyone connected to the President or her administration. I also began telling everyone I met about the two visions God had given me and asking them to believe with me for the purposes of God to be fulfilled.

I had known the Go family since my days in Hong Kong. They had owned the Fukien Times in Manila for many years. Since Betty (Go) Belmonte was a friend of President Aquino's, I asked her to make any contact she could for me, and did the same with anyone else I could think of. Still, the days passed by, and no positive response came from any of these contacts.

I knew that God was working when, the week after I arrived in the Philippines, the issue of *Time* magazine that week had a picture of President Cory Aquino with the caption: PRAYING FOR TIME.

In the meantime, I kept busy preaching and ministering to those I met. One night I was visiting the Elizaldes when I learned that their daughter had become ill and was being rushed to a children's hospital in Pennsylvania for treatment. I had a brief moment to speak with Mrs. Elizalde. She asked my forgiveness for rushing off, but she had to catch the flight that would take her daughter to the United States. She told me to feel at home and to stay as long as I wanted.

As I sat there for a few moments praying, wondering what I should do next, I noticed an elderly lady being taken out in a wheel chair. I asked one of the servants who she was and was told that it was the mother of Mr. Elizalde. When, a few moments later, they brought her back in, I asked if I could have permission to go upstairs and pray for her, and they graciously agreed.

I had no idea what Mrs. Elizalde's condition was, but I knew that God could heal her. After I prayed, I encouraged her to raise her hands with me and to praise the Lord, and she did. I told her nurse to get her to do that every day, that praising the Lord was powerful and that it would bring complete healing to her and would keep her well. She promised me that she would do it.

As I came back down the stairs, a servant brought me some mango juice and, while I sat and drank it, the telephone rang. One of the servants said to me, "The telephone is for you." I was surprised. I wasn't expecting a call, and didn't think that anyone even knew I was there.

When I got to the phone, I found that it was Mrs. Elizalde's daughter who lived across town. "I understand you just prayed for my mother," she said.

"Yes," I replied, "I did, and you would be pleased. She was praising the Lord."

"Yes, I understand she is doing things she couldn't do before," the daughter said.

"Really?" I asked, "What couldn't she do before?"

"She has not spoken in many months," she said, "and I understand that she is talking."

"Oh, yes, she was talking well," I said, "I didn't know she hadn't been talking. What else is she doing that she couldn't do before?"

"Well," she answered, "I understand that she was raising her hands and moving her arms."

"Couldn't she do that?"

Her reply excited me: "No, she hasn't been moving her hands or arms for some time now."

Harvest Glory

God had performed a wonderful miracle and the news of it spread quickly. A few days later I got a call from Doña Aurora Aquino, mother-in-law of the President. She asked me to come pray for a son-in-law who was hospitalized because of a sudden heart attack. At the hospital we gathered around the bed of her son-in-law and prayed for him. Then I encouraged everyone in the room to praise the Lord. Within a few moments, they were all speaking in tongues. This included her daughter and the granddaughter, wife and daughter of the sick man.

When I got back to the place I was staying, the telephone rang, and it was a secretary from President Cory Aquino's office. "Could you come right away to Malacañang Palace to meet the President?" she asked.

I didn't hesitate. "Yes, of course. I can be ready to go right away."

Before she hung up, she said, "You really are a Ruth."

I didn't understand exactly what she meant, so I said, "Pardon?"

She repeated it again, "You really are a Ruth."

Again I didn't fully understand and said, "Pardon?"

"It was the mother-in-law who arranged for you to come to meet the President," she said in way of explanation. Doña Aurora Aquino had called her daughter-in-law to tell her the miracle God had done.

I was staying in a very lovely Filipino home where they had several fine cars with their respective chauffeurs, but at that particular moment not a single vehicle was available to take me to the Palace. We called for a taxi, and the one that responded seemed to be the worst one in the country. I was determined, however, that nothing would spoil this moment. I was on my way to the palace to meet President Cory Aquino.

As we made our way through the traffic of MetroManila, some of the things fellow believers had asked me to say to the President on their behalf tried to come to mind. Everyone seemed to have a message to deliver. What I did in those moments, however, was to clear my mind entirely so that when I met the President, God could use me to say what He wanted to say. I walked into Malacañang Palace with an empty head.

When I was ushered into the President's office and I sat there before her, I began to have a vision. I saw exactly what the Lord wanted to say to her, and I reached across the table, took her hand in mine and began to prophesy that which the Lord had shown me. She had been a housewife, but had agreed, very reluctantly, to run for the presidency against the entrenched Marcos' regime. To everyone's surprise, she had won, but what did she know about governing seventy million people? Her martyred husband had been the politician in the family. She had much to learn and God wanted to help her, but the Filipino people had quickly lost patience with her young administration, and she was in danger of being ousted by a military coup.

I Ask for the Phillipines

That night, after I got back to the house where I was staying, I got a call from Doña Aurora. "I was just with the President," she said. "Her granddaughter came rushing up to her and said, 'Grandmother, I met her.' The President said, 'Yes, I can still feel what I felt when she took my hand to pray for me.' "

Thank God for that touch of the Spirit that gave Cory Aquino more time and allowed her to finish out her administration. She laid the groundwork for the man who would succeed her and bring the Philippines back to financial stability.

Several years later I was back in the Philippines and was the guest of Doña Aurora Aquino in her lovely home. ✳

≈ 89 ≈

"You Are Georgian"

One day in Jerusalem the Lord gave me a vision of fires of war burning in the nation of Georgia, and I saw that the Lord was allowing the fires to burn for the release of the Jews from the Caucasus and their return to Zion. I saw the fires moving east from Georgia to the next country and the next, until every country in the Caucasus was on fire. The Lord told me to go and speak with President Eduard Shevardnadze in T'bilisi, the capital of Georgia, concerning this vision and the need for him to let God's people go.

I had been in T'bilisi years before, during the Cold War, and had prayed for God's purposes to be fulfilled in that nation, but I had no idea how many Jews were living in Georgia. I decided to take two of our fellow ministers, David and Marilyn Govendor, and go to Georgia.

There was plane service between Tel Aviv and T'bilisi, but there were no diplomatic relations between Israel and Georgia, so we could not secure a visa before going. We were permitted to board only after we had signed a waiver, releasing the airline from responsibility in case we were not permitted to enter Georgia and had to turn around and come back on the next available flight. We had no problem signing the waiver, because we knew God was going to give us favor.

Our seats were in the tourist section. As we were settling in, we noticed a delegation of very important-looking men who had boarded the plane and were seated in first class. Later, one of those men came back to our cabin, and we were able to speak with him. He was part of a Georgian delegation that had been attending an agricultural conference in Israel. The group was made up of parliamentarians and other important officials.

We told him that we were on our way to T'bilisi but that we had not been able to secure a visa beforehand. "Don't worry about it," he said, "as soon as we get there, we will arrange for your visa at the airport." And that was exactly what happened.

We got a hotel for the night and the next day we went looking for a church. God opened a wonderful door for us with a group of believers who were meeting in a hall, and we ministered to them every day we were there. They were in a modern part of T'bilisi, a little removed from the downtown, and their gatherings were very wonderful. They were very gracious to us all during our stay, could not cook enough for us, and their hospitality was amazing in other ways as well.

That first day we also went to find the office of Eduard Shevardnadze. When we got to his office, who should we bump into but one of the men we had met the day before on the plane. He was very excited to see us. Since his English was limited, he found someone to interpret for us, and we were soon led into the President's office. There we met his appointment secretary and were promised a meeting with the President the next day.

The next day, as we were waiting in the lounge for our meeting with President Shevardnadze, several ambassadors went in ahead of us. When they came out, they spoke with the appointment secretary concerning the fact that a journalist had been allowed to go in and see the President earlier. The appointment secretary should not be allowing journalists to take up the President's time, they told him. After all, he was the President. "You cannot just allow anybody to impose upon the President's time."

Overhearing this conversation, I became aware of the fact that the enemy was trying to hinder our opportunity to see the President. A few minutes later, the appointment secretary came over to us and said, "I'm sorry, but it will not be possible for you to see the President today."

The three of us had been sitting on a sofa in the reception area, and he told us this before we had a chance to stand up. In that moment, however, we stood up, and when we did, an unusual thing happened.

I am already tall, but it seemed that the Lord made me two feet taller, and the man had to look up at me. The Lord also gave me authority. I heard myself saying, "Your Excellency, you must not allow these foreigners to influence you in this way. After all, you are Georgian, and you Georgians are known for your unique hospitality. I am expecting you to deal with us in the same wonderful spirit of Georgian hospitality that I have always experienced."

Suddenly, God had changed his spirit. "Oh yes!" he said. "Yes, you can see the President. Come back tomorrow at this same time, and I will arrange for you to see President Shevardnadze."

That next day the three of us arrived and were taken in to see President Shevardnadze. He was very gracious to us.

We told him that we had come from Jerusalem, sent by God. We explained the vision God had given me showing the fires of war, and I told him what God had said — that the fires of war had been permitted so that the Jews of Georgia would return to Israel.

"For two thousand years," he said, "we have maintained a wonderful relationship with the Jewish people among us. They have become part of our community, part of our life. We would hate to lose them. We would hate to see them go."

Harvest Glory

"Yes, Mr. President," I answered, "but when you know that this is what God wants, that it is His time to gather the Jews back to their homeland, then you become willing. If God desires it, we must be willing to let them go." He told us that he would consider the matter more fully.

The young man who was translating for us took us into the Parliament Building and allowed us to be present for the proceedings that day. We discovered that he was Jewish. He had never considered the possibility of returning to Zion.

When our week was ended and we went to the airport to return to Tel Aviv, we noticed that the people who were boarding had their belongings in boxes. They had no suitcases. When I was living in Asia, it was not uncommon for the people to take boxes with them when they flew, but it was always the latest television or the latest mechanical toy. These people were just poor.

After we checked in, we went into a lounge. There were no chairs, so we were all standing around waiting. After we had been waiting for quite a while, it was announced that our flight would be delayed. Later, a further delay was announced. We spoke with an airline representative and learned that there was no jet fuel available for our plane, so we would have to wait for other planes to arrive. Some fuel would be siphoned from each of the arriving flights so that our plane could have enough fuel to get us to Tel Aviv.

When we realized that we would be there waiting for an extended time, we began to look around the room more seriously, to see who was traveling with us. The people were immigrating to Israel, and they were traveling in clans, many generations traveling together. We could see the great-grandmother, the mother, the child, the grandchild, and the great-grandchild.

When we were finally able to board the plane, eight or ten or twelve hours later, we saw something we had never seen before or since. The cargo bays were filled, and the ground crew had piled boxes of the passengers' belongings in the aisles of the plane. It was a good thing we did not need to go to the rest room on that flight because we could never have gotten through the aisle.

The overhead racks could not be closed because they were stuffed with large boxes. If everything had shifted during flight, some of us might have been injured.

The dangers aside, traveling to Jerusalem with a plane-load of Jewish immigrants and their meager personal belongings was one of the most moving experiences of my life. I never forgot it. ✳

266

⚞ 90 ⚟

"The Red Carpet Treatment"

My trips did not always involve ministry to people. Sometimes they were for the purpose of declaration and prophetic release, as in the case of a trip I made to Brazil.

One day in the spring of 1984, shortly after I returned home to Jerusalem from ministry in Australia, God gave a powerful vision in our prayer meeting. Maria Deane, a sister from Poona, India, saw a line going from Jerusalem to the middle of the Northwest Coast of Africa, continuing on to the middle of the East Coast of South America and then proceeding up the East Coast of the United States to Ashland, Virginia.

As she was giving the vision aloud, I began to follow it in vision also. I saw Sierra Leone in West Africa, Sugar Loaf Mountain, where the beautiful statue of Christ overlooks Rio de Janeiro, and Virginia, where campmeeting would soon be beginning.

Although I had not intended to leave Jerusalem so soon, I knew God had just mapped out an itinerary for me. I telephoned Rev. and Mrs. Ade Jones in Freetown, Sierra Leone, and asked them if they could use my ministry there for a week. They had invited me more than once, and I had never gotten there yet.

My plane connected to Freetown through Lagos, Nigeria, and when I was checking in, it was discovered that I was lacking some required vaccination. I would have to take a taxi, go into town and get the required vaccination.

A lady had given me $100 before I left Jerusalem, but after I paid the taxi, the vaccinations and the return taxi to the airport, there wasn't much of it left. As I sat there waiting on my flight, I was talking to the Lord and wondering how we could have the wonderful meetings I was sensing in my spirit when I had no money. The Lord was about to show me that He could do it all without me spending a single cent.

I arrived in Freetown in the middle of the night to the "red carpet treatment" — literally. A red carpet was rolled out to the airplane for me to walk on. Bouquets were presented. Dignitaries were there to welcome me. And the people of the Bethel congregation were there singing songs of welcome. How exciting!

When I called them I had made no stipulations. I only wanted to be a blessing and was willing to minister in whatever capacity they desired. I was surprised to learn they had rented the Town Hall. Night after night it was packed. The Mayor and his wife attended, as did the President's wife and family. I had rarely seen such a response to the Lord by people anywhere. They told me that there had never been a meeting in Freetown in which people had been so touched by the power of God.

On Monday I flew from Freetown to Lagos, Nigeria. I was scheduled to transfer there to a flight to Rio de Janeiro, Brazil. As I waited on my flight, an announcement was made that it would be delayed. This concerned me because, despite the fact that God had done such great things in Freetown, I still had very little money. The people of Sierra Leone had given me a piece of beautiful African fabric and some other gifts, but I had said to the Lord, "You know I'm going to need some money, and I don't have any." A local lady came up and handed me a one-hundred-dollar bill. It was quite something, not only that she would have that amount of money, but also that she would have it in U.S. currency. One hundred dollars is not much, however, when you are traveling. When the announcement was made that our flight was delayed, I sensed that God was meeting my need.

The airline, for having delayed the flight, took care of my hotel bill in Rio de Janeiro and also provided limousine service to and from the airport. I still had my $100, and I would need it to do what God had laid upon my heart.

When I arrived in Rio, the airlines put me in a hotel on the beachfront at Copacabana and I had a wonderful night's rest. I had seen a vision of Sugar Loaf Mountain and the statue of Jesus that overlooks the city of Rio, so the next day when I got up I went to the top of Sugar Loaf. First, I praised and worshiped the Lord for a time, and then, with my hands uplifted, I prophesied to Rio and to all of Brazil. I was conscious that God was changing the atmosphere over the city and over the nation.

Later that day, I returned to the airport and boarded a plane for Miami. From there, I flew on home to Virginia.

That Thursday I called my friend, Pastor John Lucas in Calgary, Canada and told him what I had just done. He said he knew why I had done it. Rev. Morris Cerullo was having a huge evangelistic thrust in Brazil. It was billed as the fourth largest media event in the Americas that year. He was having a closed-circuit satellite hookup to ten stadiums in Brazil and sixty or seventy auditoriums in the United States and Canada.

He initially wanted to conduct the meeting in Sao Paulo because the spiritual atmosphere in that city was considered to be better than Rio, but for technical reasons he had to have the meeting in Rio. I had been at the top of the mountain on Tuesday and this great meeting was to begin on Saturday. God had sent me to take care of the spiritual atmosphere over Rio.

I heard reports from a pastor's wife in the Detroit area that the power of God was so evident as she watched the Cerullo crusade that she found herself prostrate on the floor by the power of the Holy Spirit. I was so glad that God had given me a small part in that great harvest of souls. ✳

"In All His Regalia"

It had been such a blessing to have Princess James and Sister Jones come to Jerusalem several times through the years and for me to visit them in Freetown that when we received word of Sister Jones' homegoing, I felt moved by the Spirit to fly to Sierra Leone for her funeral. She had done such wonderful things for God that I felt it important to show honor to her before her people.

Sister Jones and the wife of the President had made it a practice to pray all night on many nights for the wellbeing of Sierra Leone. I have always believed that it was her prayers that preserved the nation. This seemed to be confirmed when, after God took her home, Sierra Leone plunged into political chaos and an extremely destructive civil war. There are those whom God seeds into a nation, and they become His gift for that nation. Sister Jones was just such a person.

It was quite a wonderful funeral with many dignitaries present. Among them were members of the President's family and the Mayor's family and representatives from both the legislature and the courts. With all those dignitaries present, however, I was given the privilege of preaching the funeral. I spoke of Sister Jones' life, of her faithfulness to God and her faithfulness to the nation, and of how she had come up to Jerusalem again and again to stand before God in the Holy City on behalf of the people of Sierra Leone.

Because I honored Sister Jones, God honored me. The next day I was taken to meet the President. I had met his wife some years before, but I had never met him. He was celebrating his eightieth birthday, and I was among the invited.

This was a wonderful opportunity because Sierra Leone had relations with some of the countries with which the United States did not have relations. That night the ambassadors of many of the nations I had been praying for were present, and I was able to speak with them. They included the ambassadors from North Korea, North Vietnam and Cuba. Since I had been invited by the President, I was given a special escort who took me around and introduced me to everyone. What a wonderful opportunity!

President Siaka Stevens had decided that he would retire on his eightieth birthday, so plans were being made for the next elections. The man he had hand-

I Ask for Sierra Leone

picked to succeed him, General Moma, was a Methodist. It was arranged that I would meet him and pray for him the next day.

When I arrived at the house of General Moma, he was not home yet, but I had a lovely time with his wife. Before long, General Moma, who was at the time Chief of Staff of the military in Sierra Leone, arrived in all of his regalia, with his many insignias and stripes. After I talked with him for a while, I began to prophesy over him concerning his future.

I was amazed when the first words out of my mouth were: "Fear not!" Who would have ever imagined that the man had any fear at all in his heart? If he would put God first, he was told, God would bless him. He was the President of Sierra Leone for seven years. ✱

≈ 92 ≈

"It Will Be To You As A Fast"

Before I left for Hong Kong the very first time as a teenager, Mother extracted two promises from me. She made me promise that I would not be moved by the plight of the Chinese children and adopt a baby. She had known a number of single missionaries who had adopted children and this complicated their lives. She also made me promise that I would never try to cross over into mainland China, even if someone there asked for my help. She didn't realize just how impossible it was at the moment to go there.

During the time that China was so closed, most people didn't believe that it would ever open again, and we would have been thrilled just to place our feet across the border, be there five minutes and prophesy; but God had something much greater in mind. I recall the morning in the campmeeting in Virginia when the Lord suddenly dropped a knowing into my spirit that China would open again and that we would have the privilege of going there. For many years, I had such a deep desire to go to the mainland that I had actually prayed that my plane would be hijacked and diverted there. Every time I got on a plane, I thought about it. I knew that if I could just put my feet on Chinese soil, I could believe for a release for the land to open.

In Jerusalem every year, just prior to the ten days before Pentecost, we held an around-the-clock prayer time. We broke the prayer into watches of four hours each and assigned someone to be responsible to pray during those hours, but we all tried to be in the prayer room as often and as long as possible.

One particular night, I went to my bedroom quite late to rest for an hour or two, but before long I was drawn back to the prayer room. As I entered the room, I found that one of our young men was there alone. He was totally lost in the Spirit and was singing: "We're gathering the pearls and flinging them to the gates of glory." Over and over again, he sang this beautiful song. As I came in the door, he was flinging some of those pearls and hit me in the mouth. I was unhurt, and I knew instantly that the pearls we were to gather were Chinese people and that God was going to soon open the door to that land. I had no idea how He would

272

open that seemingly impenetrable door, but I sat down in my favorite big, red velvet chair and began to believe Him for it.

Before long, my associate was also drawn back into the prayer meeting and, when she came in, she heard Michael singing that same song. He was lost in the Spirit and was repeating over and over that one phrase: "We're gathering the pearls and flinging them to the gates of glory." She, too, understood immediately what God was saying.

After about an hour, Michiel stopped singing and, when he did, my associate came over to me, laid her hand on my head and began to prophesy. The Lord told me to drop everything I was doing in Jerusalem and to leave on the first flight I could catch to Hong Kong. There I was to study Mandarin for two weeks, eight hours a day. If I would do that, He would open the door to China for us.

The dialect I had learned as a young girl in Hong Kong was Cantonese, but Mandarin is the dialect spoken by most people on the Mainland. If I was willing to study Mandarin intensively, the Lord told me, it would be unto me "as a fast."

I quickly rearranged everything in Jerusalem, and I was off for Hong Kong the next day. I didn't know what God was going to do or how He was going to do it, but I knew that He would lead me step by step.

When I got to Hong Kong, I felt to call the Yale Institute of Language. I located the number in the telephone directory and asked to speak with the director. I asked him if he knew of anyone who could tutor me eight hours a day for the next two weeks. It must have seemed like a very strange request to him, but he was very kind. "Would you get back to me a little later?" he said. "I think I know somebody who can do it."

That somebody turned out to be his own wife. She was well-known for teaching Mandarin on Hong Kong television and in some of the local colleges. That very day she had just finished her winter teaching session and had exactly two weeks free before she would start teaching the summer session. She told me later that normally she wouldn't have wanted to give up her two weeks of vacation, but she agreed to do it for my sake. I went to their home the next day to begin my lessons. Of course she was getting paid very well.

Studying eight hours a day and being the only person the teacher had to concentrate on was very intense. All the questions were for me, and I was expected to have all the correct responses. When lunch time came, I welcomed the break.

I didn't want my teacher to feel obligated to invite me for lunch, so I told her I needed to do a few things on the street and that I would come back in an hour. I got something to drink and looked around the neighborhood a bit before returning to continue the lessons.

When I returned, she said to me, "I'm so sorry. I should have invited you for lunch with me and my mother. I wasn't thinking. Maybe you could stay for lunch tomorrow. My niece will be joining us as well." She didn't say who the niece was, but I accepted the invitation.

When my lesson was over that day and every day during the next two weeks, I was so exhausted that I didn't feel like enjoying the wonderful restaurants and other exciting activities of Hong Kong. I went back to my room and fell into bed, to rest so that I would be ready for my studies the next morning. That first night I had no idea the surprise the Lord had in store for me at lunch the following day.

As we ate our lunch, I told my instructor and her family of my love for China, how very much I wanted to go there, and how I had often prayed that my plane would be hijacked so that I could experience China at last. "I understand," I said, "that the only way an American can get in now is to be invited by a resident diplomat."

With this, the niece spoke up and said, "Well, my husband and I would be very happy to invite you to come to China."

"Pardon?" I said.

"My husband is with the Australian Embassy in Peking," she explained. "We can invite you."

I had no way of knowing that her husband was an Australian diplomat living in Beijing and that she had come to Hong Kong to shop a little bit before going back to the Chinese capital. You can imagine how excited I was. It was only my second day in Hong Kong, and already I had an invitation that would enable me to get into China, an invitation for which I had been waiting many years.

God was doing what He said He would do, and it was the beginning of flinging the pearls toward the gates of glory. This had all come about because of the flow of the Spirit in our midst in Jerusalem. ✹

﹊ 93 ﹉

"The Australian Heavens Were Open"

Before I left Jerusalem the Lord had given me that very interesting word, that my intense study of Mandarin would be unto me "as a fast." I did not yet understand what He meant by that.

When I left Hong Kong, I flew to Jakarta, Indonesia, and on into Perth, Australia. I was to have a week of ministry in Australia on my way to America. When I got to Perth, some friends I had made on previous ministry visits met me. I would be flying out that same evening to Adelaide, but they wanted me to go with them to their home and minister prophetically to some friends and associates who had gathered. I gladly agreed.

Later, I was taken back to the airport to get my flight to Adelaide. From there I would go to Melbourne, from there to Canberra, from there to Sydney and from Sydney to Brisbane. Each time I got on the plane, I began to have a very unusual experience. At first I thought I was just falling asleep and dreaming. Whatever was happening, I would be conscious of prophesying. I thought that I was prophesying so much on the ground and in every service that when I got on the plane and fell asleep, I was dreaming about prophesying in my sleep. Before long, however, I was not so sure.

I began to be conscious of the fact that I was remembering only the first line of each prophecy and the last line. I could never remember anything in between. In the end I realized that I had not been sleeping at all, but had been carried away in the Spirit. I was conscious of the first line, as my spirit was being carried away, and of the last line, as my spirit came back into my body.

Later, when I got back to Jerusalem, there was a postcard there that I had sent back telling everyone about those amazing days and that I must have been carried away in the Spirit at least a hundred times during that short period. I came to the conclusion that it was all connected with what God had told me about Hong Kong: because I had obeyed God in the "fast," He had rewarded me in the same way He always does after a long fast, by taking me into realms of the Spirit I have never known before.

The one thing that continued to elude me was why this had all happened over

275

Australia. Why not on the ground? When I asked the Lord about this, He told me: "I want you to let the Christians of Australia know that the heavens above Australia are open." So many of them had felt that the reason Australia was not having revival was that the country had too many bad spirits, the lingering effects of aboriginal experience, hanging over it in the air and preventing the revival from breaking. The Lord was showing us all that this simply was not true, and from that day forward I began to declare that some of my greatest experiences in the Spirit had taken place in the airspace over Australia, and that I knew that the Australian heavens were open. This experience was the beginning of many exciting events in connection with China.　　　　　　　　　　　❋

"Like A Happy Face"

That summer during campmeeting, my brother was very excited about the opening door to China. The first night of camp he said, "Ruth has a wonderful opportunity to visit China. Let's all pray for China and for this open door." We all prayed together.

After the service that night Jane Lowder, a sister from North Carolina, came to me and told me about a vision she had seen. She had been saved only about a year and a half and had recently felt a burden for the camp and came to Virginia early to help get the grounds ready for the summer activities. She never left, and is today still a part of our ministry. At that time, however, having a vision was a relatively new experience for her.

"When we all prayed for China," she said, "I had a vision. I saw a man who was unusually short for a Chinese man. He had a round face like a happy face. I saw you standing with him in China. Although I don't know what it meant, I also saw a banner that had just one word on it. It said AGAIN! And God told me that I should give you a bolt of material. I don't understand why, but that's what God told me to do."

I wasn't sure why I needed a bolt of material. I probably needed some new clothes, but I didn't think I needed a whole bolt of the same color. I encouraged her, however, to obey the Lord. Whether I understood what He was saying or not was irrelevant.

We all were busy and Jane was not able to act on what God had told her. Then, about twelve days later in the service one night, my brother felt the anointing for China again and told everyone how God had opened the door to that country for us and used the diplomat to get us the needed invitation. "I want us all to pray for China," he challenged.

After the service, Sister Jane came to me, as before, and told me that she had seen the exact same vision again. "This time," she said, "the banner that was over his head was rolled out in welcome to the Bible. I haven't bought that bolt of material yet, but I don't want to go to bed tonight without giving you the money to buy it."

Harvest Glory

We hadn't known for sure how many yards of cloth were in a bolt, so we had called a local fabric store and asked. "It depends on the weight of the fabric," we were told. "Some bolts have fifteen yards, some twenty and some thirty or more." Sister Jane felt led to give us enough money to buy a large bolt of material.

The next morning, I asked my nephew David to go to the local 7-Eleven and buy me a Washington Post. Prime Minister Menachem Begin of Israel was in Washington for the first time since winning that country's elections, and I wanted to see what news there might be of his visit.

My Israeli friend, Eli Mizrachi, Director of the Prime Minister's Bureau, was traveling with the Prime Minister. He had asked me to call him at Blair House when I got a chance. I was anxious to know what had transpired the evening before during their state dinner at the White House, so I called him now.

While we were talking, David brought in the newspaper and laid it down in front of me. I began to leaf through it absentmindedly as I talked. Suddenly my eye was drawn to a photo with the caption: LAST NIGHT, A BANNER, 40 YARDS LONG, WENT UP IN TIENAMEN SQUARE STATING THAT DENG XIAO PING HAD MADE A POLITICAL COME-BACK.

I looked for some other article with more details, but there was none. I knew immediately that this was the banner Sister Jane had seen in her two visions. God was about to do something wonderful in China, and He had revealed it to us. You can imagine my excitement!

The China experts in our State Department, officially known as Sinologists, were stunned by the return to power of Deng Xiao Ping, the man who would hold the reins of power in China for the next twenty years. In fact, experts from many nations, some of whom were perched on the borders of China, watching every political nuance, were stunned by this turn of events, but God knew it and revealed it to us by His Spirit.

The following day a few more details about Deng Xiao Ping and his amazing return to power emerged. They included the facts that he was unusually short for a Chinese man and that he had a round face that looked to many "like a happy face." That face would soon become known to the whole world.

A few weeks later, when my associate and I made our first trip into China, we took with us a bolt of material (forty yards long) and the clipping from the *Washington Post.*　　　　　　　　　　　　　　　　　　　　　　　　✤

278

≤ 95 ≥

"You'll See ... Just Wait!"

As it turned out, I didn't actually use the invitation from the Australian diplomat. I was in Argentina when I noticed an ad in the newspaper for a tour into
China. Tours had not been accepting Americans, as we did not have diplomatic
relations with China, but I called when I got to Australia and asked if they would
make an exception, and they agreed. They had two spots available on their tour.
I made a reservation for my associate and myself, and that's how we first went
into China. We were about to make a very exciting trip and to carry many Bibles
into China for the believers there.

Being in China was such a privilege for us that we could find nothing wrong
with the country. Everything was delightful in our eyes. We spent a couple of
days in several different cities of the south of China before moving on to the
capital.

When we got to Beijing, it was pouring down rain, but we didn't care. We
toured the Forbidden City in the pouring rain and loved every minute of it. It
was the dream of a lifetime fulfilled, and we took ten full rolls of pictures in spite
of the inclement weather.

As soon as we got to the capital, I sat down and wrote a short note to the Premier and sent it to him with the clipping from the *Post* and the bolt of cloth
through the foreign ministry. In the note I explained to him that God had shown
us his return to power twelve days before it was announced to the world press
and again the night before his return to power, and how excited we were about
it because we knew that God would use him to give the Bible the opportunity of
reentering the land. I spoke of China's great destiny.

Since we had received no answer to the note, I realized that our window of
opportunity to meet and speak with the Premier was getting increasingly narrow, because our tour was in Beijing only a few days. From Beijing we would travel
north by train to Ulan Bator in Mongolia. After a couple of days there, we would
make the return trip to Beijing. Our schedule, however, was to arrive in the city
at five in the evening and then leave early the following morning by plane for
Tokyo. We would not be in the city during normal office hours.

Before we left for Ulan Bator I wrote another note to the Premier. I told him that we were leaving early the next morning, but that we would be coming back a few days later and would like the opportunity to meet with him. We would be arriving at the train station at five o'clock in the afternoon and that would be our only opportunity. I apologized for having such a limited time but said that I hoped he would extend us the privilege of meeting him. My associate chuckled a little at my boldness, but I felt that God was going to do it.

It was a twenty-four-hour trip to Ulan Bator, Mongolia, and our coaches were pulled by a coal-fired locomotive, so by the time we arrived in the Mongolian capital, our faces were black, and our clothes were unbelievably dingy. When it came time for the return trip, I said, "I believe someone will be there to meet us when we get back to Beijing. Let's keep a good dress out of the suitcase. When we get near the capital, we can clean up and put on fresh clothes and be ready." She laughed at this, but I noticed that she kept a dress out anyway.

About an hour before we arrived at Beijing, we washed up as the train swayed (while holding on for dear life with the other hand) and put on our fresh dresses. With a little extra spray of perfume, we were ready.

As the train pulled into the Beijing station, I began looking expectantly out the window, to see the person I knew would be there waiting for us.

My associate said, "Nobody is going to be there. Who in the world would come out at five o'clock in the afternoon? Your best friend wouldn't even meet you at this time of the afternoon. Why should some government official be here?"

"You'll see," I said. "Just wait."

And suddenly I saw him. "Look," I said excitedly. "That's the man. He's here to meet us."

"Oh, stop it!" she said. "Nobody's coming to meet us."

A few minutes later, however, our tour host came into our compartment to announce, "There is someone here to meet Miss Ruth Heflin." I was so excited at that moment! I hadn't known how God was going to do it, but I knew that He would.

We got off the train and were introduced to Mr. Du Chung Ying. Exactly who he was we didn't know yet, but he ushered us toward a beautiful reception lounge, and we followed. Much later, we learned that he was a "best friend" of Premier Deng Xiao Ping.

We knew exactly what we wanted to say to Deng Xiao Ping and sensed that this was our opportunity to say it. If he trusted this man enough to send him to meet us, we had to trust God to use him to get the message to the Premier, so we didn't hesitate.

We repeated to Mr. Du Chung Ying the same things we had told the Premier in our note, what God had shown in the visions, that Deng Xiao Ping would be used of God to bring back the Bible and freedom for Christian expression in China.

I Ask for China

It was amazing what happened next. The Chinese are very poetic. When you look at a Chinese painting, the words written under it may be more a work of art than the painting itself. My associate was now swept up in the Spirit and began to speak by vision and prophesy in beautiful poetic form.

She saw the sun rising over China and its rays warming the people of the nation. Within three years, God said, China would become "the darling of the Western world," for God would enable her to take her place among the nations.

Mr. Du Chung Ying was surprised at this. "Oh, we're very far behind the other nations," he insisted. "Because of the excesses of the Cultural Revolution, it will be at least twenty-five years before we can be expected to take our place among the other nations."

What God was saying did seem difficult. The Cold War was still on, and people everywhere still had strong memories and strong feelings against Communists and Communism everywhere. It was difficult to see how things would turn around so quickly.

God knew what He was talking about. Three years later, almost to the day, Deng Xiao Ping was traveling across America. He was entertained by our government, welcomed by our people, and lauded by the world press. In a few short years people had almost forgotten that he had ever been a Communist, and he was being treated like a hero. He had become, just as God said, "the darling of the Western world." To be invited to a reception where Deng Xiao Ping would be was the most sought-after invitation of the day. People wanted to meet him more than they wanted to meet the Queen of England.

Later, we were in Geneva, Switzerland, and decided to make a courtesy call at the Chinese Embassy. When we mentioned that we knew Mr. Du Chung Ying, we were told that he was head of Chinese operations for all of Europe and was in town for a United Nations gathering. We had dinner with him and his wife at the Chinese Embassy. It was a fabulous Chinese feast.

We left China totally elated, knowing that God was working. Within just a few months, the United States and China had normalized relations, and the door was opened for thousands of other Americans to travel to the Middle Kingdom, as the Chinese call their country.

Not long after we took that first tour into China, we went back to Virginia and told Mother about it because I felt that she should go. We had gone with a group, but she could go alone. "I could get the Australian diplomat to invite you," I told her.

"We're so busy right now," she told me. "If you could stay here in my house and look after the church, I'll go." So that's what we did. She stayed in the Beijing Hotel and was looked after and assisted by our diplomatic friends.

She couldn't speak any Chinese, but she prepared little cards on which she had phrases in Chinese printed. Everywhere she went in China she would pull out a little card to communicate whatever she needed to communicate. One card asked for a taxi, for instance.

Whereas we had been blessed to go in on one of the first organized American tours into China, Mother had the privilege of being one of the first individual Americans to travel alone in the land. What a wonderful time she had! ✴

≈ 96 ≈

"That's My Son"

When that first tour into China came to an end, the group flew from Beijing to Tokyo to spend several days in Japan. After that, the rest of the tour group would return to America, and we were on our own. Since we were so close to Korea and had been hearing such wonderful things about Dr. David Yonggi Cho and his church in Seoul, South Korea, we decided to take advantage of the opportunity to visit him. When the organized tour ended, we flew from Tokyo to Seoul.

Friends of ours in Australia were on the board of Dr. Cho's ministry and were part of his church growth program. They had said to us, "If you ever get to Korea, feel free to use our names." We took them up on that offer, and we were able to stay in the missionary guest house adjoining the church. Dr. Cho was very gracious to us, although he is an extremely busy man and has important people to meet all the time. He told us how much his mother-in-law loved Israel, and said that he hoped we would get an opportunity to meet her.

We wanted to be sure to visit Prayer Mountain, so we went there the next day. It took us about an hour and a half to get there. After a young Korean brother had shown us around Prayer Mountain, he asked, "Do you want to see where Pastor lives?" And he pointed to the top of the mountain. It was a very hot day, and I really didn't want to climb to the top of the mountain to see where Pastor lived. Before I could say no, however, he was already scampering up the hill, and we were obliged to follow him.

When we got to the top of the hill and entered a house, we were introduced to a very small Korean woman, whom we discovered to be the associate pastor of Dr. Cho, his mother-in-law, Sister Jashil Choi. She didn't speak any English, but there was a Japanese man there at the time, and Sister Choi, because of the Japanese occupation of the Korean Peninsula during the Second World War, spoke Japanese well. She spoke to him in Japanese, and he translated her greetings into English for us.

Our visit with Sister Choi would have been polite and very brief. Just at that moment, however, I remembered that a few nights before, when I was in Beijing, I had been awakened to pray for a Korean person by name. I asked Sister Choi, "Does this name mean anything to you?" And I told her the name.

"That's my son," she said.

"Well, the Lord awakened me one night in Beijing to pray for him," I told her. She was instantly my friend for life.

Much later I learned that the son in question had been living in America and was not planning to come back to Korea. Although the Seoul church was doing well, with more than one hundred thousand in membership, Sister Choi was burdened to pray more for her son than for others. The fact that the Lord had awakened me to pray for him and gave me his name as well deeply impressed her. That son, Kim Sung Kwang, returned to Korea and pastored Prayer Mountain. Later he started a church. The last time I heard, he was pastoring a congregation of nearly ten thousand members.

We laid hands on Sister Choi and prophesied. She was thrilled with the prophecy. What I remember of it was very simple. The Lord told her three things: Forget your age; accept all your invitations to the nations; and don't worry about the language. We could tell that she was thrilled, but she didn't tell us the full story until some time later. She asked us to write down the words of the prophecy, and my associate wrote them on an envelope and gave it to her.

We returned to the guest house. At ten that night we decided to attend the weekly all-night prayer meeting. When we arrived at the church, ushers seated us in a special section of the balcony where they had headphones for simultaneous translation of the service into many languages. We had been seated only a few minutes when I saw Sister Choi move back from the microphone and pick up a telephone. I knew instantly she was calling an usher to come and bring us down to the platform. A few minutes later, an usher arrived to invite us to the platform, and we had the opportunity of preaching and ministering to the all-night prayer meeting crowd of about ten thousand.

The next morning, they were having a meeting for their cell group leaders. We slipped into the back of the chapel and sat down. At some point, Sister Choi turned and saw us sitting there. She motioned for us to come forward and sit beside her. As we watched, she pulled the envelope with the prophecy written on it out of her pocket and then she kissed it and patted us to show how much it meant to her. We were sitting on either side of her and she did this first to one of us and then to the other. There was no missing her meaning. Needless to say, we became fast friends.

We stayed for the Sunday services, and then we flew back to Jerusalem. About a year later, we got a telegram saying that she was arriving. Since this was the first we had heard of it, we assumed that she would be having meetings with someone else in town. We would visit her and pay our respects.

I Ask for Korea

When she arrived, however, we were surprised to find that she had come all the way to Jerusalem just to thank us. The Koreans believe in saying thank you with an offering, and she had brought a substantial offering for us as well. She now told us the rest of the story.

Sister Jashil Choi had prayed all night long every night for ten years, taking small catnaps in the daytime, and had seen her son-in-law's work grow from five people to more than a hundred thousand. When the church reached that number, she felt that her work was finished and that she could retire. She had lived a very sacrificial life, but now she went out and bought a special bed for herself, one that cost a thousand dollars, a staggering sum in the Korea of that day. While there is nothing wrong with having an expensive bed, the purchase was a symbol of her plans for retirement.

No sooner had Sister Choi decided to retire than a large growth appeared in her body. She had not considered that there was further ministry for her, as Koreans in general consider themselves to be "elderly" before Americans do. She was challenged by the prophecy that the end was not yet.

The prophecy had seemed, to us, to be rather simple and general, and some might have wondered why such simple words were even spoken, but to her it was specific and exactly what she needed to hear. She was not to worry about her age, she was to accept every invitation and she was not to hold back because of her lack of English. Those words released her, and she immediately made plans to travel. The tumor disappeared. In that next year, she established sixteen churches in sixteen nations. She was coming all the way to Jerusalem to say thank you. We were all elated and had a wonderful time rejoicing together.

We had such a good time together, in fact, that we decided to conduct a prayer and fasting conference together in Jerusalem. I would organize it in Jerusalem and she would work to bring people from other nations, especially Koreans. I would lead the worship, and she would preach. We were very excited about the prospect.   ✷

✑ 97 ✑

"Believe Me and Declare It"

That trip to China was to be the first of many for us as well. Every time we could pray in the money, we made another trip. Periodically, we would call from Jerusalem to the China Travel Service in Hong Kong and ask if there were any upcoming tours that we could join because at that time all travel within China was handled only through the China Travel Service. Each tour group was different and had different interests in going to China, and by going in with different groups, we got a different perspective on the country each time we went.

One time we went in with bankers who were exploring banking possibilities on the mainland. Representatives from banks that had done business in China before the coming of Communism were looking for ways to renew their business there. One time we were with a group of specialists in Chinese food who were interested in learning more about Chinese cuisine. Once we went in with representatives of British Airways sent from London to investigate the future potential for air transport in China. We enjoyed the business and commercial perspective on what was happening in China.

Each of those early trips was scheduled for about ten days, visiting five cities. Because everyone wanted to see Beijing, Shanghai and Guangzhou (the former Canton), those three cities were nearly always included in these trips along with two other cities. Because of this, it took us many trips before we were able to say that we had been in twenty-two major cities of China. The opening of China was one of the greatest miracles any of us had ever witnessed. We wanted to put our feet in as many cities of China as possible.

The Lord had said to us, "If you will go to China and stand on the Great Wall and prophesy the opening of the churches, I will open them." On our next trip to the country, we did what He told us.

The only open church in the capital was a little one on Rice Market Street. Some African diplomats attended the services along with a few Chinese. The services, for the most part, consisted of singing a few hymns and praying a prayer. No preaching was permitted, and there was no special music.

Still, I was thrilled the first time we went. The Bible reading that day was

286

concerning Jerusalem and Zion. We were living in Jerusalem at the time, and God was giving us the privilege to possess our inheritance among the Chinese people from the Holy City. I sat through the entire service with tears streaming down my face. I was so blessed to be singing and praying together with the Chinese people in their church on Rice Market Street.

Within a very short time, many churches had opened. The first day the church in Shanghai opened, there were two thousand in attendance. Many of the old-timers were still afraid that this new openness was a trick of some kind and were biding their time to see what would happen before they committed to the newly-opened churches. Those who were attending were new people, young people for the most part, and God was working in their lives. They were not afraid to be seen going to church to worship the Lord.

We attended many of the newly-opened official churches throughout China and discovered that the Chinese church is the only church in the world where when the person in charge says, "Let us pray," everybody in the building prays. You could see the spirit of prayer on them. How beautiful to see an entire congregation, with nobody looking around, nobody daydreaming or making any plans. They prayed. They were lost in prayer.

Unlike in the West, the only division in the churches in China was between Protestant and Catholic. There are no denominations within the Protestant church, and both Protestant and Catholic churches were reopening. When we passed any church that had not yet reopened, we reached out our hands to it and declared its opening.

There was a little church on Shamian Island in Guangzhou that was one of our favorites. We loved it very much, and we prayed for it to be opened. The next time we returned to China that church was open and functioning. When we had prayed for its opening, we hadn't thought about whether it was a Protestant church or a Catholic church. As it turned out, it was Catholic.

Because the Catholic Charismatic movement had not yet started when I was living and working in Hong Kong, I was not aware of the fact that there is a distinct vocabulary difference between Protestants and Catholics in Chinese. For instance, the word church is different. The Protestants say the equivalent of "worship hall," while the Catholics say "holy hall." When I began conversing in Chinese with the priest in that newly-opened church, he immediately recognized that I was a Protestant. I wondered how he knew. I had been trying to sound so ecumenical. This, however, did not dim our enthusiasm in the least, nor his. We were overjoyed for the opening of the church.

Then one day the Lord said to us, "If you will believe Me and declare it, I will begin to open the seminaries." Because we believed what the Lord was saying,

287

we bought a slide projector and slides from the Holy Land and sent them with a diplomat from the Finnish Embassy in Beijing, so that when the first seminary opened, they could study Israel and the Holy Land.

Over a period of time we bought many books that we knew would be appreciated as textbooks for those soon-to-open seminaries, books on the Holy Land, its history and its archeology.

The official church headquarters in China was in Nanjing, and the first seminary that opened was in that city. A man with whom we became good friends was chosen President of that newly-opened seminary.

Although the church in China was now nonsectarian, it had not always been so. When my associate first met this man, she had introduced herself as a Pentecostal and asked him if he had ever known any Pentecostals.

"Oh, yes," he said with a smile.

She asked, "What denomination were you?"

He said, "I was a Methodist."

As it turned out, when he had been a student for the Methodist ministry, he had often visited a certain hospital. There was a Pentecostal mission across the street from the hospital and, as he went by, the Pentecostals would spit on him.

She said to him, "Oh, I'm sorry! We're spitting less these days."

He smiled, all was forgiven, and they became instant friends.

In May of that year, *Time* magazine wrote an article about the resurgence of Christianity in China. It spoke of the opening of the Nanjing Theological Seminary. A photo was included of a classroom full of eager students in the seminary. On the blackboard in front of them was written, in both Chinese and English, the subject of the class they were studying. It said, "The History of Israel." That blessed us because we remembered how, in faith, we had bought the materials and gotten them into China — even before the seminary had reopened.

From then on, we began to believe for one seminary after another to open, both Catholic seminaries and Protestant. We watched as God did it. Before long there were nearly a dozen seminaries open throughout China.

Each time a new seminary would open, we would arrive from Jerusalem with the materials God had told us to buy that would be useful in their studies. After that, we began to send a book of some kind each month for the libraries of the Chinese seminaries. We were even led to present books to the head librarian at the Potella in Lhasa, Tibet.

Something else that was greatly appreciated by the Chinese churches and seminarians was the panoramic view of Jerusalem we presented to many. Later, when we went back to these places, we found the panoramic view framed and displayed in a place of prominence.

I Ask for China

There is a lovely church in Beijing located down a very narrow lane in an area not too far from the train station. It was always packed when I went there, and I had many wonderful experiences in that place.

One morning one of the sisters who speaks English there came up to greet me after the service and asked me where I lived. I said, "I live in Jerusalem." She was very excited when I mentioned Jerusalem, as we found most of the Chinese believers to be. Hers was an excitement with a difference. "Do you know my friend Wu Bai He?" she asked. "She is in Jerusalem, and she comes here often."

I could see her face light up with wonderful memories. She obviously was touched that a person from Jerusalem would be so moved by China that they would often visit the Chinese church there.

"Yes," I was happy to say, "I do know your friend in Jerusalem. She is my friend as well."

It was very exciting to watch the unfolding of God's great plan for China.

After a few years of permitting tourists to come into China only on tightly-controlled and restricted tours, China opened further the door. Most of the restrictions were removed, and tourists were allowed to travel however and wherever they wished. We and many of our people took advantage of the lifting of these restrictions. One summer my associate did nothing but travel around China by train. By the end of that summer she had logged fifty-five thousand miles and, as she later recounted, "had eaten fifty-five thousand miles of noodles."

Aside from the life of the high-dollar-paying tourist, life was still pretty simple in China in those early days. There was not a great variety of food available, and we slept, for the most part, in the cheap dormitories where local people also stayed. In this way, God gave us the opportunity to go into every part of China.

My brother was challenged very early to take ministry tours into China, and this proved to be so blessed that he began to do it twice a year. He would have a whole busload of people praying and believing for the complete opening of China. There was not a single area of the Middle Kingdom that he, my mother, and many others from our ministry did not cover.

I went with him on one of the last trips he took to China. We were together in Kunming. It was interesting because my associate and I were in Kunming with one of the first churches in the early eighties and now my brother and I were in the same city fifteen years later. When we went into the local church there, we were invited to come forward and sing. We were able to sing several songs and to testify, before and afterward, what the Lord meant to us.

Among the songs we sang was my song *I Ask for the Nations,* in which we corporately asked for Kunming and for China. As we were leaving the service, all the believers pressed in to our group, believing for healing and miracles. My brother prayed for a lady who had been deaf since birth and God healed her. Then he prayed for a woman in a wheelchair, and she was healed and began walking.

My brother sat in the wheelchair and encouraged her to push him, and she did. Then he encouraged her husband to sit in the wheelchair and allow his wife to push him home. This caused no small stir among the five or six hundred believers, who followed us to the bus, and my brother encouraged the tour members to get on the bus quickly.

As many Christian groups from around the world did, on our first trips into China we took many Bibles. Then, as God began to open the door for Bibles to be printed right there in China, we bought our Bibles there, from the Bible Society in Guangzhou, Shanghai and Beijing, and distributed them.

God gave us the privilege of being involved in many different aspects of the ministry in China, as well as with the diplomatic community in Beijing. On one trip that my associate made into China, the Lord told her that He would open Africa while she was there. She responded, "But, Lord, I'm going to China, not Africa."

One Sunday she attended the Rice Market Church in Beijing. After the service, a nice young African teenager greeted her. When he said that he was from Uganda, she replied, "Oh, we have been in Uganda." In the course of the conversation, she mentioned that we had even visited the Queen of Uganda and prayed for her.

Later that afternoon, at the hotel where she was staying, she received a telephone call from the boy's father, inviting her to their home. He questioned her in a little more detail concerning Uganda and then revealed to her that he was David Simbwa, King Freddie's brother, the uncle of the present-day *Kabaka,* the tribal King, in Uganda. This opened a wonderful door to African diplomats.

David's son, Peter, lived in our home with Alice in Hong Kong and went to school there. Later he lived with us for a season in America and in Jerusalem, and today, when I am in Beijing, he shows me the latest "people's" restaurants.

So many of the African diplomatic children had grown up with only the benefit of the Rice Market Church, so when Bishop Tutu from South Africa arrived in Beijing for a visit, my associate arranged a special private diplomatic service in which the Bishop could dedicate these children to God.

One would be amazed at the spirituality of the African diplomatic wives. Many are praying women who spend their days visiting the sick and looking after the needs of the diplomatic people, not only among the African communities, but among all the nations. My associate attended many receptions and luncheons and they opened doors of friendship for us to diplomats of many nations. In the diplomatic community of Beijing, David Simbwa of Uganda has the most senior-

I Ask for China

ity, and he's a great tennis player, as well. Often the African wives line up their ambassador husbands and children for prayer with the laying on of hands. One of the African ambassador's wives used one of the great reception areas in the Embassy for a weekly Saturday night service and kept that room reserved only for services every week. I was impressed with their love of God and the lengths to which they went, to maintain their spirituality in foreign lands. There is today an international church for the diplomatic community.

My Australian friends, Don and Anita Ridge, later lived in Beijing. When they sowed into China in the late seventies and early eighties, they had no idea that they would be living in China, reaping the benefit of what they had sown many years earlier. Don had no idea that his business would take him to Beijing and that he would be on the Board of the International Church in Beijing. The ways of the Lord are past finding out. In addition to the Internationational Church, many of the diplomats still attend many Chinese churches, both Catholic and Protestant, in Beijing.

On many of our early trips into China we stayed in the Beijing Hotel. It had three different sections. The oldest section had originally been known as the Grand Hotel Peking. Later, another section was added. The newest section was built in Communist times. At one time or another we stayed in each of those sections, and loved every one of them. In the oldest section, especially, we had the opportunity to enjoy a bit of Chinese history.

When we went to China on that first trip, we were free to contact our Australian diplomatic friends. They invited us to dine with them near a lovely park. In those early days, there was only one store to which tourists were taken. Because it was exclusively for foreigners, it was called The Friendship Store. "Where do you buy, and what do you buy?" we asked our friends that day.

"There's a little shop called The Theater Shop that has some of the old silver serving pieces from the Grand Hotel Peking," we were told. "They're in terrible condition, but they're beautiful silver pieces, and you can have them restored in Hong Kong." The pieces in question, we discovered, were by Cristoffle, the famous French silver company. We bought several pieces, took them to Hong Kong and had them re-silvered, and we use them in our house in Jerusalem.

On subsequent trips, we found a small antique shop in one of the parks in Beijing. It was a little hole-in-the-wall, but it had great antique porcelain. One had to look beyond the dust and dirt to find it. My brother saw our blue and white vases and wanted to know where we had purchased them. I carefully told him where the little antique shop was. I told him that the shop was so small he should not attempt to take his whole tour there. When he returned to America, I excitedly asked him what he had found at our little shop. He answered, "Nothing! I didn't want any of that junk."

Harvest Glory

I love to attend church services in China. There are many other things I enjoy about the country: seeing the Great Wall, shopping, visiting the museums and partaking of the delicious Chinese food. There is something special, however, about going to church in China. The more Sundays I can be in China, the happier I am.

The reason I enjoy the Chinese services so much is that no church in the world is a better example of what the Lord wants to do in His people. The Chinese believers are being made perfect in one, for people of many denominations attend the same services and worship together. This came about primarily because of the many years of persecution the Chinese believers suffered during the infamous Cultural Revolution and through the various Communist regimes that followed it. God has ways of uniting us.

To my way of thinking, the two greatest miracles the church world has witnessed in our generation are the establishment of the State of Israel and the reopening of the nation of China for the Gospel of Jesus Christ.

When China first opened, many American churches were not interested in going there because they could not build a church building with their name on it in China. God sent into that land those who were willing to work toward the building of His Kingdom. It was such a joy to speak with the people, pray with them and lead them to salvation in the Lord Jesus and the baptism of the Holy Ghost.

For nearly thirty-five years the church leaders in China were closed off from the rest of the world. Now they could be encouraged by hearing what God was doing everywhere.

The laying on of hands as we practice it today did not come into prominence until the revival of the fifties, and when that revival took place, China was closed and the Chinese leaders knew nothing of it. When my associate laid hands on one of the most important Chinese leaders and prayed for him to be healed, he wept and told her that it was the first time anyone had ever laid hands on him and prayed. It was our joy to lay hands on many Christian leaders in China and see them filled with the Holy Ghost.

China is very special to God. One reason is that one-fourth of the world's population are Chinese. That seems hard to believe, but it's true. It was a wonderful day when we had our first Chinese pilgrim coming to Jerusalem. He was from Shanghai and attended our Congress at the Feast of Pentecost. Pentecost represents firstfruits, and we wept with joy that this was the firstfruits of what was to come.

The Chinese people have many wonderful characteristics. They are very gentle and hospitable people. They are very simple and grateful for anyone who helps them. When I met one pastor, he said to me, "I remember the day I met your associate." He proceeded to tell me the month, the day, and the year.

I Ask for China

When he left the room I said to her, "Why does he remember that day like it was Christmas?"

She said, "Because that was the day he was baptized in the Holy Ghost."

Men who had loved God and served God all their lives had just never heard that He was baptizing people with the Holy Ghost and causing them to speak in tongues, as the disciples did at Pentecost.

Many times, when we were in China, we sat under the pastors of the Three-Self Church, the officially sanctioned church. I had heard many criticisms of this movement. I listened and understood their Chinese and knew that there was enough Gospel in their sermons for their people to be born again.

We went again and again and made contact with these pastors. We sat by the hour and told them about what God was doing all over the world. They were starved for news of the Church universal.

In Hangzhou I was talking with the principal of the seminary. He mentioned that a well-known American evangelist was coming to China and was going to speak to the Chinese church. I knew that Billy Graham was coming, but the Principal had not mentioned a name. I asked him if he had ever heard of Billy Graham. He said he had not. It was an indication of how totally isolated the Chinese pastors had been from what God was doing worldwide.

Each time we attended the Rice Market Church in Beijing, there was a little more liberty. When we first went, they only read the Scriptures, sang hymns and had a prayer. Then they introduced sermons. Then they began to have special musical numbers. Later I remember their Christmas program. This seemed to the Chinese Christians the height of liberty, to be permitted to have a Christmas program and sing Christmas carols. To them it represented total normalcy. How thrilled they were!

We met many pastors who had suffered. Even before we went to China, my associate one day had a vision of an area in the west of China. She saw a man in prison garments, and the Lord made her know to pray for him. She did.

We didn't have a very good atlas with us at the time, but she looked the place up and found that it was a lake area known as Lake Kokonor, the Tibetan name for Ching Hai Lake. Years later we discovered that most of the pastors who were imprisoned under the Chinese Communist system had been kept in that particular area.

She was sorry that she hadn't perceived all that God was saying. It was more than just a particular pastor who needed prayer. It was an untold number of pastors imprisoned for the sake of the Gospel. We had the privilege of meeting many of those men and of letting them know how faithful the Lord was in causing her to see their suffering, so that we could all pray and believe God for the suffering church in China.   ✤

_ℳ 98 ℒ_

"How Faithful the Holy Spirit Had Been"

I was invited to a lovely lunch in Georgetown given by Pat Sims. Among the guests was Mrs. Robert McFarland, the Indian Ambassador's wife and others. In the course of the conversation, as we were talking about China, Mrs. McFarland mentioned having had lunch with Nien Chieng, the author of *Life and Death in Shanghai*. I was instantly excited. I had read Nien Chieng's book and was anxious to meet her. I mentioned this desire, hoping that she would offer to introduce me, but no such offer was forthcoming. We had a lovely time, speaking of other nations as well.

When I got back to Ashland that evening, I was sitting in my mother's kitchen. Suddenly the thought came to me that I should call the Washington operator and get Nien Chieng's telephone number. I had not considered that it would even be listed, but I immediately responded to the promptings of the Holy Spirit. The operator instantly gave me her number, and before I realized it, I had Nien Chieng on the line.

It all happened so fast that I suddenly realized I had not even thought about how I would approach her. I found myself saying that I had lived in Hong Kong as a young girl and that I loved the Chinese people.

She said, "I, too, was in Hong Kong in 1963. When were you there?"

I said, "I was there from 1958 to 1962."

I knew that she and her husband had been with the Shell Oil Company, so I asked her if she had met my friend, S.K. Sung. She said, "Oh, when my husband was Consul in Australia, his sister Esther Sung, was our good friend. So when I was in Hong Kong, I did meet him. How are they?"

I was glad to have up-to-date news concerning S.K. and his family.

Within minutes I was invited on the telephone to come and meet her in Washington, after she returned from a speaking tour at several universities.

My time spent with Nien Chieng was wonderful. She had not heard any up-to-date news of her church in Shanghai. I had just returned from China, had attended her church a Sunday or two before, not knowing that it was her church. I told her how the balconies even overflowed and spoke to her of the pastors I had met after the service and the great spirituality we had experienced throughout the entire service. She was thrilled to have news of her church, as she still felt reluctant to write freely in her letters to China.

I had enjoyed reading Nien Chieng's book so much because she was still imprisoned in the early eighties when I was visiting China. Many of her observations were things that we had come to know by the Holy Spirit and her comments, coming from such an experienced Shanghai resident, let us know how faithful the Holy Spirit had been to reveal these things to us. *

⚝ 99 ⚝

"China Before the End of the Year"

One night in Jerusalem, there was a very wonderful sense of the presence of God in our services. Nothing was actually said in the meeting that night concerning China, but personally I had a deep feeling during the service about China.

After the meeting, I discussed with my companions my feelings, and one of my associates had felt some of these things concerning China, too. I said to her, "One of us should make an effort to get to China before the end of the year." Then we went to bed.

About two in the morning the telephone rang. It was our friend S.K. Sung, the husband of Nora Lam. He was calling from San Jose, California, to say that Nora had been scheduled to host a tour into China for Jim Irwin, the astronaut, but, because of what was currently happening in China, she felt it was not a good time for her to go. Could I help them, he asked, by co-hosting the tour in her place? They would pay all my expenses if I could do it. I asked him to give me until the next day to decide and promised to call him back in the morning.

When I hung up the phone, my associate asked, "Who was that calling?" I told her what it was all about.

"Oh, I can tell you're getting old!" she teased.

"What do you mean?" I asked.

She said, "Any other time you would have said, 'Of course I'll go.' You wouldn't have needed even a few hours to think it over."

We had just been praying about China a few hours before, and so quickly God had opened the door. Why hadn't I jumped at it?

"It wasn't because I'm getting old," I laughed. "It was because I was half asleep."

I immediately called Brother Sung back and told him that I would be very happy to co-host the tour.

I was introduced to Astronaut Jim Irwin at the San Francisco Airport as the tour lined up at the counter to check in for our flight. The Chinese government was thrilled about the visit of a U.S. astronaut, and they were planning to roll out the red carpet for him. We would benefit from his celebrity.

Jim was given the privilege to speak at many places in China — especially in aeronautical institutes and other institutions involved in preparing China's youth

296

I Ask for China

for the space program — and everywhere he went he gave his testimony. As a boy, he had many desires in life, and one of those desires was to go to the moon. Another of those desires was to go to China. Because China was so closed to Westerners, going to the moon had almost been easier than going to China. In the end, it was his going to the moon that had opened the door for him to go to China.

When Jim Irwin went to the moon, the thing that amazed him was that the Earth appeared to be the size of a gold ball. It was so life-changing for him. He determined that if God could love this small planet so much that He was willing to send His Son, then he would go back to Earth and dedicate his life to the ministry. He took a ball the size of the Earth as seen from the moon, about the size of a golf ball and carried it with him wherever he went as a reminder of that perspective.

In Hong Kong we stayed in the Hilton Hotel. Before breakfast Jim ran all the away to the top of Hong Kong Peak, duly impressing all of us. As we traveled on throughout China, he always got up early to run. I especially remember him running to the top of the Great Wall and back down. His health consciousness convicted a number of us who joined his table, which was only served vegetarian food the whole time we were in China. Of course, he did supplement his meals with a large bag of Quaker Oats, which he ate by the handful, as one would eat potato chips.

He had a wonderful film he showed of his lift-off into space, but he was never hesitant to tell what the Lord meant to him personally. Every time he shared that film and his testimony, I caught a dramatic sense of the Rapture of the Church. It was as if the Lord had allowed these explorations to be done by the scientific world to emphasis the catching away of God's people in the future.

Later, I hosted Jim Irwin's visit to Jerusalem. I borrowed St. Andrew's Church, the beautiful Scottish Presbyterian Church, which sits up the hill from Sultan's Pool. The church was packed as Jim gave his testimony again in the same clear tones that I had heard him speak in China. When God took him home, I happened to be in America and had the privilege of being at Arlington Cemetery for his funeral service. I met his wife and rekindled my friendship with his mother and son, who had both been with him in China and Jerusalem.   ✸

🖎 100 🖎

"Kabuki"

As I was leaving China on one of these occasions, I intended to fly directly to Jerusalem, but the Lord spoke to me and said, "I want you to go to Japan. You don't have time to minister there, but I am going to send you to someone who will be speaking in many conventions. I want you to tell him what he should speak on."

"Who are You sending me to?" I asked the Lord.

He reminded me that two years before when we had first gone to Prayer Mountain in Korea and met Sister Choi, she had used a Japanese brother that day as her interpreter. The only thing I could remember was him telling us that he had just built a church between Narita Airport and Tokyo. That's like saying that he had just built a church between Los Angeles and San Diego and, now, when the Lord was telling me to go see this man, I wondered how I would find him.

I flew into Tokyo, went directly to one of the airport hotels, got the telephone, and began calling churches in the area. I first called the Baptists. I told them who I was, that I was from Jerusalem, that I had met a Japanese man in Korea who had built a church within the past several years that was probably Pentecostal or Charismatic and was located somewhere between Narita Airport and Tokyo. They couldn't help me, but they gave me the number of the Assembly of God Church.

I called the Assembly of God Church. They also didn't know the brother I was looking for or anything about his church, but they did know a brother who, they said, was moving in Charismatic circles, and they gave me his telephone number.

I called that brother and went through the same introduction a third time.

"Sister Ruth," he answered, "I have never met you, but some of our people went to Jerusalem and attended your Bible school. I know the brother you're talking about. Let me give you his telephone number."

When our conversation ended, I called the number he gave me. "Brother," I said, "you probably don't remember me. Two of us, sisters from Jerusalem, met you at Sister Choi's place at Prayer Mountain several years ago."

I Ask for Japan

"Oh yes, I remember you two sisters from Jerusalem," he answered. "I have often prayed for you. Where are you now?"

"Well, I'm at the airport," I told him. "I have a message from the Lord for you. I came to Japan just to see you."

"Oh Sister, I am so sorry," he said, "I am just getting ready to leave for a conference."

"I know," I told him.

"You know?" he seemed surprised. "Well, I'm packing now, and I will leave later today. Could you come quickly?" He gave me instructions for the train.

When I was still on the plane from Hong Kong, I had asked the Lord, "What is the message that this man should preach to the conference?" He reminded me that just before I left Jerusalem I was praying and He had said to me, *"Kabuki."*

Kabuki, I knew, was a Japanese art form, a traditional play, but when God said *kabuki* to me, I didn't think He was talking about plays. What could He mean by that?

We had a Japanese brother in our Jerusalem fellowship at that time and I thought, *When I have time, I must remember to ask the brother what* kabuki *means,* but I had forgotten to do it.

Now on the plane from Hong Kong to Tokyo, when I asked the Lord what the message was, He said to me again, *"Kabuki."*

I called the Japanese flight attendant over and asked her, "What does the word *kabuki* mean?"

"It's a classical Japanese play," she said.

"Yes," I said, "I know it's a classical Japanese play, but what does the word *kabuki* mean?"

She thought a moment, then replied, "*Ka* means 'song,' *bu* means 'dance,' and *ki* means 'art.' "

I understood immediately that God was speaking about the song/dance art of praising Him.

When I arrived at the train station the brother met me and took me back to the church where he and his wife lived in some adjoining rooms. We made small talk about my trip to China and about Israel as we drank Japanese green tea together.

When we finished drinking the tea, he was ready to get down to business. He asked, "Sister, why have you come?"

"I have come," I told him, "to give you the message you are to speak at the conferences."

He seemed surprised when I said "conferences."

"This is the first conference I have ever been invited to speak at," he told me, "but it is true that I have already been invited to others. What is this message?"

"The answer for revival in Japan," I told him, "can be found in one Japanese word — *kabuki.*"

He looked at me strangely, possibly thinking of the Japanese play.

I repeated the word syllable by syllable: "*Ka - bu - ki* — the song/dance art of praising the Lord." Tears filled his eyes.

"I have been praying for the message for the conference," he said. "Each time I prayed God told me to speak on singing and dancing. I told the Lord that I knew singing would play a very important part in the revival in Japan, but not that ungodly dancing. Each time I prayed I got the same answer, and each time I rejected it."

God had taken me all the way from Jerusalem and through China to confirm to this tenderhearted man that revival in Japan would indeed come through worship, through singing and dancing before the Lord.

After I ministered to him and his wife prophetically, he took me back to the train station. I went back to the airport hotel, got my bags, and boarded the next flight for Jerusalem. My mission for that day was accomplished.   ✳

At the Great Wall, Badaling, China, 1979.

With Mr. Chun Lun Kaai, Ministry of Foreign Affairs, China 1980s.

Looking out from the Great Wall.

Jim Irwin, the astronaut, center front, with our group at the Aeronautical Institute in China. I am on the second row, second from the left.

With Nien Chieng author of *Life and Death in Shanghai.*

Our group in Seoul, Korea, waiting to go into China, 1980s.

Rice Market Street Church, Beijing, China, 1980.

On a Bactrian camel, Gobi Desert, Mongolia, 1979.

The Potala, Lhasa, Tibet, 1980.

With Bruce Fisher and Mother.

Rabbi Shlomo Carlebach, Jerusalem.

With Don and Anita Ridge in their home, Elizabeth, Australia.

With Norman Williams, in my living room,
Jerusalem.

With Sarah Rush, Jerusalem.

With Lady Bronwen Astor in front of Royal Albert Hall, London, England, 1983.

With Victor Hallak, Christmas Reception at
Halcyon House, Jerusalem.

With Lance Lambert and Abed Abu Omar (peeking over
his shoulder).

Our church, Calvary Pentecostal Tabernacle, 2701 Hull Street, Richmond, Virginia.

With my parents on the platform in the Richmond church.

Mother dancing.

My brother's tent.

My brother on the platform of the Richmond church.

My brother speaking in a synagagoue, Kabul, Afghanistan, 1978.

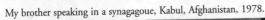

My brother praying for Jaco Noteboom in our chapel in Jerusalem,

The tabernacle of our campground, Ashland, Virginia.

My brother praying for a child.

Michael, Pat, Anne and Katie Heflin

Daddy with the camp cooks, Sister Owen, Sister Hicks, Sister Clark, Sister Brown and Sister Ganzert.

⚜ 101 ⚜

"Feel the Great Rhythms"

One night in Jerusalem we received a message that there was a Japanese group coming to visit us. It was not a church night, and often, when special groups came on nights that we didn't have services, we would invite some of our people who lived in other houses to come over for a time of fellowship. The living room, dining room and sun porch area were large enough that we could gather a large group and still have room for singing, dancing and rejoicing. We always wanted to let visiting tour groups feel the atmosphere of rejoicing in Jerusalem. Many of our people had already gathered on this particular evening, and we awaited the arrival of the Japanese group.

When they were delayed more and more in arriving, we decided that rather than just sit and wait, we would begin to rejoice in the Lord. When the Japanese arrived, we were in the midst of an Israeli line dance in which the person behind puts his hands on the shoulder of the person in front and the line continues around the room.

We had formed a long line and were worshiping the Lord in this way when they came in, and the line was passing by the door where they would enter. As each person came in, someone pulled them into the line and went on, until all the Japanese believers were dancing, interspersed among us. They loved it.

After we had danced for a while and were all standing and worshiping the Lord, I started to give a prophetic word. I gave the first sentence and expected the Japanese interpreter to interpret that sentence before I went on to the next sentence. When he didn't, I gave the same sentence again, then I waited for the interpretation. When there still was no interpretation, I opened my eyes to make sure that the interpreter understood that I was waiting for him to repeat the message in Japanese so that his people could also understand. I was astonished to see that he was indeed interpreting the message, but in sign language. No one had told me that the group was made up almost completely of people who were both hearing and speech impaired.

What surprised me was that I had distinctly heard many of those Japanese believers speaking in tongues. I discovered that while they were dancing and rejoicing in God, many of them had been baptized in the Holy Spirit. If we had

309

known that they could neither hear nor speak, we might have felt self-conscious and not known how to get the activities of the evening started. When we started rejoicing before they got there, the Spirit took care of our lack.

By being included in the dance, they began to feel the great rhythms and anointings of the Spirit, and it had not been difficult for them to receive the Spirit and speak in other tongues. Many of them said that they had never experienced such a thing. It was the most wonderful night of their lives and a great night for us as well. ✳

⚓ 102 ⚓

"The Beefeater"

During the time in which the door to China was opening bit by bit, a wonderful thing happened to me in Jerusalem. Every afternoon we had several hours of Bible school on our back terrace, which is now the area of our chapel. I had been teaching on several special subjects, and each time I had been tested on what I had taught. This particular day, when I taught on seeing in the realm of the Spirit, I said to the people, "Let's not leave until we allow the Lord to show us something." We began to praise the Lord, and after a while I said to those present, "Do any of you have something to share that God is showing you?"

One sister raised her hand and said, "I just saw the Beefeater, and a Chinese man was standing beside him."

Instantly I knew the direction her vision was flowing. The Beefeater is a type of guard who stands at the Tower of London, and I had learned that Chairman Hua Gua Fong had gone to London for a state visit. The lady who saw the vision didn't know that.

The next person who spoke said, "I just saw a great hall. Every twenty feet or so there was a tall and beautiful statue."

A third person said, "I just saw a room with many seats, and they were covered with green material."

A fourth person spoke up and said, "My vision doesn't seem to go along with anybody else's, but I see western winds blowing on a country. These western winds are very destructive, but I see God raising up a covert, or a protection, so that only the best parts of the western winds are being filtered into the country, while the rest are being filtered out so that the country is not destroyed."

All of this took only minutes to say, but when it had been said, I knew that I had to be on a flight to London the next day. It was already nearing five in the afternoon, and I remembered that our travel agent closed about that time, so I quickly left the class and rushed to the phone.

I called our travel agent and asked him to come by and leave a ticket for me to fly to London the next day with a return flight in two or three days via Paris. He did.

When I got to the airport in Tel Aviv the next day, I checked my luggage and went to buy a newspaper to read while I was waiting for the flight to board. I went to pay for the newspaper, only to discover that I didn't have my change purse with all my money where I usually kept it.

I called back to the house in Jerusalem to see if I had left it there and had someone look on the bedside table and on the dresser. Had it fallen on the floor? I asked, and they looked, but couldn't find it anywhere.

At that moment, I had to decide whether I was going ahead to London with no money and no credit cards, or if I would miss my flight and go another day. I had just taught the day before on faith, and now I was being tested.

At the time, I didn't know anybody in London that I could call on for help. Later, I would have many friends that I could ask to come and pick me up, but that time I was on my own.

Somehow I knew that the timing of my going was important. If I was to see the fulfillment of the word the Lord had miraculously spoken, I had to get on that plane. So I did.

I refused to worry on the plane from Tel Aviv to London. God would take care of me. Of that I was sure. When I got there, He would show me what to do.

When I arrived in London and went to pick up my bag from the carousel, the Lord spoke to me to open it. When I did, I discovered that I had done something I never did before or since. In my haste to pack I had put my money in a little cosmetic bag where I keep my toothbrush and other toiletries. When the Lord told me to open my bag, I quickly found it.

I checked into a hotel and called the Chinese embassy to make sure that Chairman Hua Gua Fong was still in town.

"Yes, he is," I was told.

"Is there some event in his schedule tomorrow that I could attend?"

The embassy worker checked the schedule and then replied, "There is a reception tomorrow afternoon in the House of Commons."

I called the House of Commons and arranged for one of the parliamentary secretaries to give me a tour the next day. When I walked into the House of Parliament that next afternoon, however, I knew that I was seeing the same great hall that the young girl had seen in her vision. About every twenty feet there was a tall statue.

The tour took me into the House of Lords where I saw beautiful benches, but they had red leather upholstery, so I knew they were not the ones she had seen. As we walked into the House of Commons, I was thrilled to see that the seats were upholstered in green. I was seeing the vision unfold before my eyes.

There had been several English people in my class in Jerusalem that afternoon, but none of them had been excited about what the Holy Spirit had said. They had not discerned that the visions concerned their own Parliament.

I Ask for China

But surely the rest of the vision must be the important part. What did it all mean, the Beefeater with the Chinese man? This was during the time that the Chinese people had erected the democracy wall and were placing on that wall all sorts of messages. Democracy was coming in very fast, much too fast to suit those in government who were responsible for the welfare of the people. They were afraid that it would bring chaos with it.

The message, I now realized, that I was to deliver to the Chinese Chairman, was that he need not fear the western winds that were blowing upon his country. God was raising up a covert to protect China from the worst aspects of democracy, while permitting her to share in the best aspects. In this way, the country could remain open to the Gospel. And it did. ✸

⚜ 103 ⚜

"I Thought You Were Either
Bible Smugglers or Gunrunners"

As soon as was possible, we began to include Tibet in our China itinerary, and we were able to go there several times. The first time was in the fall of 1980, and there were no hotels yet in all of Tibet. What seemed like former military compounds were being used to house the tour groups, which were limited to no more than twenty per group. It was very exclusive.

Later we got to know our tour leader, an American who lived in Hong Kong. He laughed and said, "I thought you girls were either Bible smugglers or gunrunners. I never felt such heavy suitcases in my life, and I noticed that when we came out, they were awfully light!" Along with placing our feet on the land and prophesying to the winds over Tibet, we had delivered some eternal treasures.

On that very first visit, we also carried a very special message from the government of Israel for the Chinese officials.

One Saturday evening, as I was visiting Prime Minister Menachem Begin at the Prime Minister's residence in Jerusalem, I asked him if I could have the privilege of making a contact between Israel and China.

He said, "Don't you think it's too early?"

I said, "Well, before Russia moved into Afghanistan, it would have been too early, but now all the emphasis has shifted to that part of the world. I don't believe it's too early for Israel to begin making contacts with China."

He agreed for me to try, so on this, our next trip into China, we sent a letter requesting further contact with Chinese authorities regarding future relationship between China and the State of Israel. It was quite an exciting trip in many ways, and we were doing things that we had never done before anyway, but this proved to be the highlight of the trip.

We arrived in Guangzhou and were nearing the end of the trip when the answer came. Our tour guide got on the bus, and, thinking that this was all some sort of joke, laughingly said, "Did somebody from this tour bus make a contact with Premier Deng Xiao Ping?" We raised our hands rather sheepishly, and the guide was amazed that we had been able to make such a contact.

I Ask for Tibet

We were taken off the tour bus and introduced to a government official who proceeded to give us a message in regards to our overtures, a message to deliver to Jerusalem. In this way, the Lord actually gave us the privilege of being the first persons to officially contact China on behalf of Israel.

On my very first trip to China, I sent a postcard back to my friend Eli Mizrachi, then Director of the Prime Minister's Bureau, and he has told many people that the first communication Israel ever had from China was that postcard I sent.

On our third trip into Tibet, we met the Panchen Lama. He is the most powerful Tibetan Lama in China today and represents Tibet in the government in Beijing. We were traveling in the very remote eastern areas of the country, areas in which nobody from the west had traveled before. We got permission from Chendu and then we hitchhiked on gasoline trucks. They would drive all night through the mountain passes, and they let us sit up front in the cab. When we got closer to the cities, we found buses.

When we got back to Chendu, the man in charge of the Tibetan areas said that the some of the area we had been traveling in was totally closed to foreigners. It was too late. We had already done it.

In one very remote area of Tibet, we could not travel without special permission from the mayor, so we went to see him. When he asked how old I was, my associate told him a year older than I really was (the Chinese count age from birth, not from the first birthday). He was delighted because he was the same age as I, and he was suddenly willing to help us. She always teased me that if I had been humble more often, we would have had more help.

Getting to Tibet was the realization of many years of dreams and prayers. It came about because of fasting and prayer and the release of our faith.

The thing that had first sparked my interest in the Himalayan region was the Spirit's message to me through my mother, but the further interest in the whole area — Nepal, Sikkim, Bhutan and Tibet — came because of the challenge of God's Word that *"And this gospel of the kingdom shall be preached in all the world for a witness unto all nations; and then shall the end come"* (Matthew 24:14). We were very conscious that some of these places had not ever been open to the Gospel, and we were believing God for the opening.

Every time we met someone who had any type of connection at all to any of these remote areas, a great excitement was kindled in my spirit. It was like finding a great treasure, like finding the missing piece of the puzzle.

When we finally got there, I was fully aware that it was by God's grace and we cherished every moment of our stay.

When we get to Heaven and see all those who have chosen to join us there, we will come to realize that many are there because of seeds we have sown. And there will be great rejoicing. There will be Tibetans there, and some of them will be from the most remote corners of that nation. What a great inheritance!

I could go on and on about the beauty of Tibet itself. Suffice it to say that at fifteen thousand feet, in that rarified atmosphere, things look different. The water looks different, as clear as eternity. The ground looks different. The sky looks different. Everything looks different. It seems like you can see forever. Someday, when we stand on the mount of God, everything will look different as well. We will see with very different eyes. ✺

≈ 104 ≈

"Da! Da!"

One year, while I was ministering in Australia, the Lord brought to my mind something he had said to me in America. He showed me that I should travel across both China and Russia, fasting and praying as I went, believing for the release of the land and its people. I knew that it was time to fulfill that call. The Lord told me that I would have seven major stops inside Russia.

I obtained a visa for China in Hong Kong and boarded the train going to Beijing. At every stop, I prayed and believed God for spiritual revival in the land.

I spent a couple of days in Beijing, got my visa for Russia, and then boarded a train going to Moscow. There are two routes, one through Harbin and the other one more direct. I chose the long route, and it would take me some eleven days to reach Moscow from Beijing. From there, I would fly back to Israel.

The same train took us across China and Mongolia and then on into Moscow. It just changed kitchens along the way. We started off with a Chinese kitchen; it was changed for a Mongolian kitchen while we traveled through Mongolia; and that one was traded for a Russian kitchen when we got into Russian territory. All of this was just interesting to me because I wasn't eating anyway.

There were, just as the Lord had said, seven stops in Russian territory. Sometimes we came to a stop during the night and sometimes during the day. If it was at night, I would set an alarm so that I would be wide awake when we reached a scheduled stop. At each stop, I would step out on the platform and pray and prophesy. The words the Lord gave me, different for each place, were declaring the release of the Jewish people and the spiritual release God wanted to bring to the country as a whole.

I made some good friends during those long days of travel. There were some Chinese diplomats who preferred taking the Siberian Express rather than flying. More than anything else, my days and nights were spent in prayer.

While I was still in Australia, someone had a vision in which they saw something happening to me at the next to the last stop on this journey I was about to begin. I always think positively, and I was looking forward to the good thing that would happen to me at that stop. When I arrived at that place, the melting snow had reformed into ice, and I didn't realize it until it was too late. I had just finished prophesying when I found myself sprawled on the platform.

Harvest Glory

A couple of Chinese diplomats saw what had happened and got off the train to help me up. I found that I was unable to put any weight on my right foot, and the men had to help me back onto the train.

I was in a lot of pain as we moved toward Moscow, but I sat there praying. In my pain, I had a vision of the airport in Zurich, and I wondered what that might mean.

When we reached the final stop, I could not walk on my own, so someone called a baggage carrier to help me. He brought a luggage cart, put my suitcase on top of it and me on top of the suitcase, and he pushed me out to get a taxi.

He wanted to call an ambulance right then to take me to a hospital, but I insisted that I wanted to go to the National Hotel. Normally tourists were not given the privilege of choosing their own hotel, but I was sure that in this situation they would make an exception for me, and they did.

When we arrived at the National Hotel, the doorman was kind enough to help me hobble up to the desk. No sooner had I checked in than I noticed that it was nearly five in the afternoon and the travel bureau would soon be closing. Remembering the vision I had in the train, I said to the lady at the desk, "Could you please call the travel bureau for me and see if there's a flight tomorrow morning going to Zurich, Switzerland." There was one, and I asked her to book me a seat on it. I needed to get back home to Israel. If I could get home and our people could pray for me, I was sure that I could recover from this injury. For now, however, how was I going to get to my room?

Two employees of the hotel brought a luggage carrier, put a chair on it, and sat me on the chair. In this way they wheeled me into the elevator and up to my room. Once at the room, they helped me into bed. About a half hour later a doctor arrived at my room. She spoke no English. She took hold of my foot and moved it a little, she said, "Da! Da!" I knew that Russian word, and I knew that she was saying that my foot was broken. Within a few minutes an ambulance had arrived to take me to the hospital.

Because of the severe hardship brought upon the Communist countries through their economic system, electricity was always in short supply. The thing many Westerners remember about Communist countries is how dark it was there at night. The hospital where I was taken in Moscow was a good example. There was a single bulb far at the end of a long hall for illumination. I was being wheeled into a strange room on the flat of my back in otherwise total darkness. I had never been a patient in any hospital before, and now I was coming under these circumstances.

None of the staff present spoke English, and people were sent running to find someone who could. When a doctor who spoke English could be located, he came, took X-rays of my foot and handcrafted a cast for me.

I Ask for China, Mongolia and Russia

This same man rode with me in the ambulance back to the hotel. On the way, I told him that my only concern was that I would not be able to see my favorite places in Moscow. I loved the city, but I would not be able to do any sight-seeing. He and the ambulance driver talked among themselves for a moment and then announced that they were going to take me on a private tour of the city. It was already after midnight, but we toured the Kremlin and Red Square and drove around several of my other favorite places in that ambulance. The streets were practically empty as they took me past the Bolshoi Theatre and then back to the National Hotel.

Early the next morning we went though the same process with the luggage carrier and the chair, and the hotel staff managed to get me down to the taxi. At the airport they put me in a wheelchair.

When the Russians learned that my final destination was Israel, everything changed and all acts of kindness ceased. Rather than being wheeled through the jetway to the plane, I was taken in the wheelchair onto the tarmac in front of the long flight of steps going up to the front door, and the man who got me that far did not make a motion to help me go farther. Sitting there in front of that long flight of steps, I was sure that I could never make it up on my own. I had no crutches to help me.

When the engines of the plane were suddenly started, I realized that I had to do something. I remembered that some European planes have a shorter set of steps at the back of the plane, and I motioned the man to take me to the back. "You'll have to help me, Lord," I prayed. "You'll have to show me what to do." Then it came to me. I had the man take me as close as possible to the steps, and then I sat down on the second step. From there I pushed myself up backwards to the next step with my hands and kept doing this one step at a time until I reached the top. I crawled down the aisle far enough to get into the last seat.

The Swiss Air staff members, usually very helpful and friendly, had to stand there helplessly and watch all this. The Russians had warned them not to help me. It was a very awkward moment for them. The Cold War was a terrible time for everyone concerned.

When I finally got into my seat, I was startled to realize that I was the only passenger on the plane. I could have eaten sumptuously on that flight, but I refused to break my fast. I allowed the flight attendants to serve me a beverage, but nothing else.

When the plane arrived in Zurich, it was quite a different matter. They used a catering lift to lower me in a wheelchair, and from then on, I was well cared for. I called Jerusalem and asked for someone to meet me with a wheelchair because I was coming home with a broken ankle. As the trip ended, I told the

Lord He owed me one in connection with Russia, and we have gone back many times and had wonderful successes there.

God wonderfully answered our prayer. The Iron Curtain fell, the Cold War ended, thousands of Jews were released to return to Zion, and a great door of ministry was opened in all the former Soviet states. Since that time, our family has had many wonderful auditorium and church meetings in Russia, and many churches were planted as a result. When my brother made his first trip to Russia after the Cold War, I met him at the Washington National Airport. He was helping his people with their luggage. As he worked, I asked him, "How was Russia?"

Tears came into his eyes, as he replied, "If I wasn't born for any other reason, I was born for these past two weeks in Russia." They had been the greatest weeks of his life. In one service alone fifty-six hearing- and speech-impaired Russians had received their healing, and thousands had been saved and filled with the Spirit.

One night I saw the New Jerusalem coming down over Moscow. There will be a great revival in that city. The Lord said that as we have gone to Russia to be a blessing to the Russian people, in the future we will receive blessing from them. I believe it.   ✳

⚔ 105 ⚔

"Buy A Car"

We had been desperately needing a car in Jerusalem for a while, and a European friend told us that we could buy a reasonable Mercedes in England, one with a left-hand drive. The British pound was very weak at the time, and one American dollar was nearly equal to a pound. It was a wonderful opportunity, and I was believing God for a miracle of finances while I was in America for summer campmeeting to make it possible for us to buy a car.

The offerings from the services the first week of camp were not very large, however, and the matter of a car seemed out of the question ... until Friday night of the second week. Uncle Bill got up that night and said, "God just spoke to me to take an offering to buy a car for Sister Ruth for Jerusalem." I was due to leave on Monday and I had not said anything to anyone about my desire to buy a car in England. God had indeed told him to do it.

The offering that night was not very large, and I was wondering why the Lord would have told him to take the offering that night and not a lot sooner. If he had done it the week before, for example, it could have been accumulating.

Still, when I got to my room that night I was led to call London and see what was available. I knew that the owner of the dealership was Jewish, so I was not sure if they would be open. It was already Saturday morning in London. They were not only open, they had a secondhand Mercedes, exactly like I wanted, and I could buy it for about $8,000. During the next several services, my brother was able to raise the balance of the money needed. I decided that I would fly into London, take possession of the car and drive it across Europe.

I flew into London and the owner of the dealership met me at the airport with the car. Because the car was for export only, I was not allowed to drive it inside England, so he drove me to Dover where I would get the boat to Calais. We put the car on the boat in daylight, and it was night when I reached France. (I remember because it took me a while to figure out how to turn on the lights.)

I had planned to find a room in Calais for the night and go on to Paris the next day, but Paris is so wonderful at night that I decided to go directly there instead. I got on the road right away. Before I had left home Mother had made me promise that I would not pick up any hitchhikers. I wondered why she had said it, but at my first petrol stop as I was crossing France, at about two in the morning in France, there was a group of hitchhikers wanting a ride. I had to tell them I was very sorry, but I had promised my mother that I would not take any hitchhikers.

I got into Paris about four in the morning and went and sat at the Champs-Élysées and had a cup of coffee under the lights. There was a little hotel in Paris that I had stayed in a time or two called the Baltimore, and I thought I might spend the night there. When I got to the Baltimore, however, I found that the prices had risen considerably. It was no longer the reasonable place to stay it had been before. Since I was only planning to be there three or four hours, it seemed ridiculous to pay those prices.

I used the hotel facilities, then I went out and stretched out in the back seat of the car and slept for several hours. When I woke up, I went back into the Baltimore and freshened up again before going across the street to get a cup of coffee, and then I got on the road.

I drove until about ten that night, and reached Menton on the Côte d'Azure, where our good friends Bill and Debbie Kendrick and their family were living. I arrived there just in time for Debbie's birthday. Debbie and I had a lot of catching up to do, and we talked until two in the morning.

When I woke up the next morning, we bought one of the wonderful fruit flans that France is famous for, and we celebrated Debbie's birthday. Then I got in the car, about four in the afternoon, and started driving again. I reached Vienna at about eleven that night. All of the gondola taxis were still plying the waters. The atmosphere was festive as it can be on a late summer's night in Vienna.

When I had planned this trip, I had not thought of sleeping in the car alone, but since it had worked so well the first night, I decided to try it again. I found a petrol station near the highway. It had a big light, so I pulled into their lot, climbed into the back seat and fell into a deep sleep.

I continued crossing Europe in this way, driving along the Dalmatian Coast, passing Split and Dubrovnik in Yugoslavia.   ✻

⊰ 106 ⊱

"I'm Seeing You Again"

As I was making my way through Europe, I noticed on the map that it was possible for me to get to the border of Albania. It was one of the closed nations, had been closed for many years, and was showing no signs of opening any time soon. I had prayed many years for it to open. *If I can just drive the car across the bridge,* I was thinking, *even if they won't let me in, I'll at least be on Albanian soil and I'll be able to pray.*

I drove across the bridge into Albania. A guard stopped me at a checkpoint and wanted to inspect my documents. He immediately got on a walkie-talkie and began to consult with a superior.

When he came back to the window he advised me that it was impossible for me to go into Albania. That was not unexpected, but all the time he was checking my documents and talking to his superior, I had been praying and believing God for Albania, declaring that it would soon be open to the Gospel. It was enough for the moment.

When Albania did open, many of my friends were blessed to go in and participate in the Lord's work there. Among them was a ministry team from the Catholic Bible School in Nutbourne, Chichester, West Sussex, England. I am a patron of the school where Joan and Michael Le Morvan are the founders and directors.

After my foray into Albania, I turned north and went into Belgrade. From there I drove to Piraeus, Greece, arriving just in time to take the ferry boat that takes cars across the Mediterranean Sea. We went to Rhodes, Cyprus and on to Haifa. I arrived in Jerusalem on Sunday morning.

It was a wonderful trip and, aside from a lot of mosquito bites I got while sleeping in the car on the Dalmatian coast, I was no worse for the wear. It was one of those trips I would gladly take again, especially if I had a nice car to do it in.

Last January, I was on my way home from France and Switzerland. At Dulles Airport in Washington, D.C., I boarded the mobile lounge that would take us from the plane to the terminal. It was crowded, and I had to stand. Standing next to me were several men holding passports of a different color than I had seen before. "You have an interesting looking passport," I said to the gentleman nearest to me. "What nationality is that?"

"It's Albanian," he said. Then, thinking that I probably knew nothing of Albania, he asked, "Have you ever heard of Albania?"

"Oh, yes," I answered, "I prayed for many years that Albania would open again to the west, because I wanted your people to have the opportunity to receive the Gospel of Christ."

At that moment, we arrived at the terminal, and I noticed that there was someone very official-looking waiting there to receive this Albanian party. A few days later I was attending the Presidential Prayer Breakfast at the Hilton Hotel in Washington. After the opening prayer, I walked past several tables to present my new book, *River Glory*, to President and Mrs. Clinton and to speak with them briefly.

As I was returning to my seat, I passed Secretary of State Madeleine Albright and was about to greet her, when a gentleman sitting next to her spoke up and said, "Oh, I'm seeing you again, how are you?" It was the man with whom I had spoken on the Dulles shuttle. He was so warm and friendly that Madeleine Albright thought I must be meeting an old friend. I hadn't known until that moment that this man was the Prime Minister of Albania. What a privilege it was to meet him! And what a privilege it was to stand before the Father on behalf of the people of Albania! ✸

↯ 107 ↯

"The Chapel Would Have Marble"

When we left St. Peter-en-Gallicantu in the early eighties, we began conducting our worship services in our house. By using the living room, the dining room and the sun porch area, we could accommodate many people. It was crowded though and, after a time, we began believing God to give us more space.

There was a terrace at the back of the house, and we decided to enclose it and make a chapel. We would do it very simply, and we didn't plan to spend a lot, but it would serve us well.

We had just started to work on the chapel when the Intifada, the Arab uprising that lasted about nine years, broke out. In the confusion that followed, the project sat there unfinished. About this time we met Bob Tilton from Dallas, Texas. His former pastor and his current missions' director, Marvin Crowe, was the pastor of Dr. Elizabeth Vaughan and Geri Morgan. Pastor Crowe brought Bob Tilton and several of his staff to our house for dinner.

On their next trip, they invited us to the Hyatt Hotel for dinner. Brother Tilton told us that he was interested in buying land on the Mt. of Olives to build a prayer chapel. Most of those who owned land on the Mt. of Olives were unwilling to sell it at any price. We mentioned to him that we had begun a chapel ourselves and had not been able to finish it. We already had a daily prayer ministry that had been faithful for many years, and we were willing to pray for his ministry and partners.

He decided to go with us and see what we were planning. He liked it and said that he would help us finish it. Over the next few months, the chapel was built.

Our simple plans were now changed. Instead of a concrete floor, the chapel would have marble, and the windows would be done in Jerusalem style. That fall he came with his television crew and did a live telecast from the chapel and the adjoining garden. While he prayed for the needs of his partners from outside, we joined him in prayer inside. Thousands of prayer requests were faxed to us. We prayed for them in those great anointings that fell in our prayer meetings. Miracles followed.

People from all over the world have been blessed in our chapel, and we are grateful to God and Brother Tilton.   ✹

"The Front Door"

When China first began to open, we were going back and forth from Jerusalem so much that we eventually decided to do something more permanent in Hong Kong. This was not to be just for the sake of the work in China, but for the benefit of the church in Hong Kong as well.

I knew many people in Hong Kong, and I was concerned with the lack of spiritual growth in the churches there. There were a lot of believers, but not many of them had been filled with the Spirit. Although the local believers were faithful to their churches, the basic message of the churches was salvation, and it did not lift the believers into higher experiences in the Lord. If we could send someone to Hong Kong who could pray for revival among the Chinese, host our trips in and out of China, and pray for local believers to be filled with the Spirit, it would mean a lot to the spiritual life of the Chinese people in Hong Kong.

Hong Kong was important to me personally for another very special reason. It was there, in the early days of my missionary experience, that a love for China had been birthed in my spirit. Although China was closed while I was living there, and I had not been able to go into the mainland, I was blessed because many of the missionaries who had lived all over China, and who had been driven out by the coming of the Communists, came to live in Hong Kong. I was privileged to get to know many of those missionaries. When I moved into that building at the corner of Argyle and Kadoorie Avenue in Hong Kong, there were missionaries living upstairs who had served in China. Beatrice Lawler, for example, had grown up in Shanghai. Her mother was a great missionary there. When the Communists first came to power they began to close churches. Congregations from sixteen churches worshiped in the Lawler church. It was big enough to contain them all. Mother told me that Beatrice Lawler had stayed in their house in Washington, D.C., when both she and mother were children.

Many of my secular friends in Hong Kong were refugees from the mainland as well. Professor Wedikent, for instance, who taught me a little language in Hong Kong, had been a professor in Shanghai. He spoke ten or eleven languages. I personally knew people who had lived in Chongqing and in Kunming,

I Ask for Hong Kong

in North China, South China and Central China. I never tired of sitting and listening to their wonderful stories.

Yes, Hong Kong was special, and God had something special for us to do there.

We rented a house in the New Territories, and God showed us to lay hands on Alice Ford (who had served so faithfully with us in Jerusalem from the beginning days) and anoint her for the work in Hong Kong. The night we prayed in the service in Jerusalem and God spoke to her in prophecy was a difficult one for all of us. Halfway through the prophecy, I realized that I was sending her away for a very long time. I began to cry and she began to cry as we suddenly discerned God's purposes.

After Alice arrived in Hong Kong, many doors opened to her there. She was able to lift many churches and ministries into a new dimension in God. She kept the mission house open for travelers going into China and she prayed for hundreds of Chinese to be filled with the Spirit. She was a great blessing there.

Alice traveled and ministered in China as well. She began going in as the country was opening to the Gospel, and she continued to make trips afterward.

Having a coordinator between Hong Kong and China proved to be very important, especially when God opened the doors more fully and some of us were able to actually live inside China.

The ministry in Hong Kong proved to be so important that the Lord showed us that we should buy a piece of property there. A nearby house was for sale and He told us to buy it. He performed a great financial miracle to make that purchase possible and it was accomplished.

One of the reasons we wanted to buy instead of rent was that the time was fast approaching when Hong Kong would be returned to Chinese government control. If we could be property owners when the Chinese returned, we would be considered a China inland mission.

The agreement reached between the British (who had leased Hong Kong from the Chinese for ninety-nine years) and the Chinese declared that the Status Quo would be respected for fifty years. We understood the concept of Status Quo because the Government of Israel has operated on the same basis.

The British controlled Palestine until 1948, and when the Israelis took over the portion that now makes up Israel, they allowed all existing churches to continue to operate as before. If, for instance, the Church of England had fifty visas reserved for their church staff before the Israeli period, they have fifty visas until now. Another church that may have had only one congregation and four visas at the time of partition, still has one congregation and four visas at the dawning of the twenty-first century. Other churches wanting to establish congregations in Israel have not been permitted to do so, and no permanent visas have been accorded them.

Harvest Glory

When we left St. Peter-en-Gallicantu, we were called in to the Ministry of the Interior and given four special visas for religious leaders, thus showing that we were recognized as a church — a privilege that very few have been granted. We still have those special visas to the present day.

While many missionary societies were packing up and leaving Hong Kong in fear of what would happen when the Chinese took control, we were doing just the opposite. When we asked the opinion of a government official in Beijing in this matter and told him that we hoped in this way to get "in the back door," he said, "Oh, in that day, Hong Kong will be the front door, not the back door." So God knew what He was doing when He gave us that open door.

One year, my associate rented the big Cultural Center in Hong Kong for a meeting to coincide with Chinese New Year. That building, one of the most beautiful auditoriums in the world, is located right on the waterfront across from the Peninsula Hotel. Because Hong Kong is such a sophisticated place, I went out and bought a few new dresses for the occasion, but when I arrived in Hong Kong for this event, I found that the airlines had lost my suitcase.

That didn't seem like a very big problem because the Chinese are such good tailors, and you can get a dress made there within twenty-four hours, but not on Chinese New Year, it turned out. Not a single shop was open.

We had three meetings a day — morning, afternoon and evening — and I had only the dress I had worn on the plane. It was not one of my favorite dresses, but each night we washed it out and each morning I put it on again for the meetings of that day.

One day, as I was sitting at the little keyboard that was our total musical accompaniment for the meeting, I began whistling in the Spirit (something I do with increasing regularity) and I whistled into the microphone. When I did, it caused an immediate stir among those who had come. They had never heard anyone whistle in the glory and they brought people from every direction over the coming days to hear. Their lives were changed as a result. Those people didn't even notice what I was wearing. They were too busy moving into the glory and experiencing the treasures of the soul.

How blessed we are to have a part in the harvest of Hong Kong! ✳

≋ 109 ≋

"Walk On Water"

Because we did not know how long the doors to China would remain open, we wanted not only to take trips there but also to have some of our people living right there inside the country. We were praying about this in Jerusalem the day we got the telegram from Sister Choi saying that she was coming for a visit. She brought with her a spiritual son as her translator. He was Brother Harvard Jee, and he was to play a great role in our lives in the next several years.

When we heard Brother Jee say that he was doing business inside China, she asked him if he could help us get more permanent visas. He said that he was setting up a factory in Wuhan to produce small solar-powered calculators and that he would be very happy to take our missionaries on as quality control experts and supervisors with his company. This, he was sure, would facilitate the visas.

When Brother Jee was ready to open his factory, we sent some of our people to Korea to be trained in quality control. While they were there, they had the privilege of being entertained by Sister Choi and of attending Dr. Cho's church in Seoul.

Several months passed, however, and the needed visas still had not arrived. Our folks grew weary of waiting, some returned to Los Angeles to be with Brother Jee, and others went on to Hong Kong to wait there.

A couple of weeks before Thanksgiving that year I was praying in Jerusalem one day about this situation. Should we continue to wait? How long should we wait? Or did we need to do something to get things moving? Suddenly, the Lord said to me, "On Thanksgiving Day, you will have something to be thankful for."

The Friday before Thanksgiving week I was in our regular service in the Church at St. Peter-en-Gallicantu, and after the service two ladies came up to greet me. They looked so familiar that I said to them, "I know you." They didn't think so because they had never been in the church before, but I was sure that I had seen them somewhere, so sure that I asked them to give me a minute to think about it. As I thought about it, I remembered where I had seen them. "I do know you," I said after a while. "About a year ago, I saw a video of a Phil

329

Donahue Show, and you were on that show. You are an eye doctor," I gestured to the one lady, "and you were on his show with Brother R.W. Schambach to verify the miraculous healing of Ronald Coleman's eye."

"Well," she smiled, "I guess you do know me." She was Dr. Elizabeth Vaughan and her associate was Geri Morgan. They were from Dallas, Texas. I was very happy to meet this well-known eye surgeon, and I invited her to speak in our service the following day.

I was rather distracted in those days. I sensed that I needed to urgently make some decisions related to the China question. If I needed to be in Hong Kong for Thanksgiving Day, I would have to move fast to arrange it. Things move more slowly in Jerusalem than in the West. "Lord," I prayed, "please give me some insight today of Your will in this matter."

When Dr. Vaughan got up to speak, she said, "Today, I will be speaking on the subject, 'Walk on the Water.' " I knew immediately that God was telling me that we had to take a step of faith concerning China. I would have to fly to Hong Kong and believe Him for a miracle on the way. And that's exactly what I did.

It was Saturday, and I realized that the travel agency would be closing by noon or one at the latest. If I was to travel to Hong Kong, I would have to slip out of the service, missing the rest of the sermon, and go see the agent now. I did that and was able to secure a ticket that day that would take me nonstop from Tel Aviv to Los Angeles and from Los Angeles on to Hong Kong. I left on Monday and got into Los Angeles on Tuesday.

Nobody was expecting me, so they all asked, "Why are you here?" I explained to them what had happened when I was praying concerning the delay in the visas and how the Lord had told me to "walk on water" and His hand would be moved. I asked Brother Jee to check with his people in Japan to see if there was any word. Later that night, we got word back that the long-awaited visas had finally come through. How excited I was! We had taken a step of faith and God had responded. We left the next day for Hong Kong.

Our team members who were in the colony met us at the airport, and we went directly to the China Travel Office, arriving just before closing time. The officers there were able to process our papers and issue us our entry permits. We got back to the house just in time to share together a wonderful Thanksgiving dinner that Alice had prepared. The Lord had said, "On Thanksgiving Day, you will have something to be thankful for," and it was indeed true.

There was more to the "walk on the water" than I might have imagined. Brother Jee had originally agreed to financially support our team in China. After all, they were his "quality-control experts," all eleven of them. I was going in on the first trip to help set things up. He had me listed as a "project director." Just before we left Los Angeles, however, he called me aside to tell me that he had

I Ask for China

suffered some business reverses and that he would, therefore, not be able to keep his commitment to support our people in China. I had to take a deep breath and decide to go forward anyway. We had come this far by faith and our faith would carry us on.

The reason his decision seemed like such a blow at the time was that it was very early in the opening of China to the West, and all foreigners were still expected to stay in hotels. In that moment, I could imagine how very expensive it was going to be to keep a team of young people in China. The Lord had said, "Walk on the water," and He meant what He said. Just existing every day during the coming months would be a walk on water. I can't really tell you how the Lord did the miracles. I can only say that our faith was stretched to the limit over and over again in the months ahead.

We were led to put one team of our people in the Peking Hotel, one of the finest hotels in China. Most of those who were living there were prosperous business people. Those who had a limited budget didn't stay in the Peking. Yet, that was where the Lord kept our people. At meal times, someone would go out on the street and buy noodles for everyone. Placed in thermoses, the noodles would keep until they were consumed.

Many exciting things happened during this time that our people were living in Wuhan, China, including the fact that one of our sisters gave birth while living there.

It was exciting to be the first Americans who had the privilege of living in China for the Gospel on a day-to-day basis. Although many others would follow, we were privileged to be pioneers.

Very recently, I was told by Mike Coleman, the CEO of Integrity, Hosanna! Music Company that a Chinese brother was opening a school of worship in Wuhan. God had told us that if we would cast our bread on the water, we would receive His results. Now people from all over China are being taught in that place how to worship the Lord. ✺

"He Has An Appointment with Me"

One of my favorite countries in the world has been South Africa. Many South Africans came to Jerusalem to visit and they attended our meetings at St. Peter-en-Gallicantu. Some of them invited me to come to South Africa, and my brother was invited to minister there as well. Our relationship to the believers in South Africa, however, seemed to get off to a shaky start.

One day we received a phone call from a lady saying that a Catholic father who had been involved in the Charismatic Renewal in Johannesburg was coming to Jerusalem for a visit. Would it be possible for him to stay with us? she wanted to know. I was very honored that he had even considered staying in our house and there was no hesitation on our part at all. I even moved out of my bedroom and let him have it so that he could be as comfortable as possible during his stay.

When Father Paschal arrived at our door and I went to greet him, the Lord said to me, "He has an appointment with Me in Jerusalem." I thought, *That's wonderful. The brother is going to have a great time in the city.* But I sensed that what I was feeling went much deeper. God was going to meet him in a very special way.

I noticed that Father Paschal seemed to be very tired during the days he stayed with us in Jerusalem, but I supposed it was because of his journey and the time change. It affects some people more than others. He had not come directly to Jerusalem, but had stopped in Malawi to visit friends and to minister.

Our sisters took meals to Father Paschal's room the first few days he was with us, and, without my knowing it, one of them had asked him if he would like for her to pray for him so that he could stop smoking. He said he would, so the young sister prayed, and he was instantly delivered from his cigarettes.

After several days of rest, Father Paschal was feeling better, and began going out. Each day he would celebrate communion in one of the churches of the city, and he would do a little touring, but always when he came back he would need to rest.

When I got word that Mother was coming to visit us, I asked Father Paschal if he would mind transferring to another of our houses located in another part of the city. Our house was always quite crowded, and there would be more room for him in the other house. He would be comfortable and well-attended there. He was happy to make the move.

A few days later, we received a phone call from Sister Ida Wade who was staying at that other house. She said that she had heard Father Paschal fall and had gone into his room to see what had happened, only to find him on the floor. He had fallen off the bed. He was taken to a local hospital to be examined to make sure that he was all right, and she suggested that I might want to visit him there.

When I got to the hospital, I met a doctor specializing in tropical diseases. He had examined Father Paschal and quickly came to the conclusion that the father had black water fever, a very deadly disease spread through mosquito bites. The doctor suggested that he had obviously gotten it while he was in Malawi, and the miracle was, the doctor said, that he had lived as long as he had. After just a day or two in the hospital, Father Paschal died.

When I got word of his passing, I immediately remembered what God had said to me that first day I met the father. "He has an appointment with Me in Jerusalem." Who would have believed how literal that message turned out to be?

Father Paschal had been a Passionist priest, and we contacted the Passionist Fathers and explained to them what had happened, and they arranged to conduct his funeral in their beautiful monastery on the Mount of Olives. Mother and I and all our staff attended. He had been a missionary all his life, yet none of us who were present had known him much more than a week. Such a beautiful man ... Why?

I was feeling terrible about the whole thing. We pray for the sick and experience miracles of healing. Why had this precious man died on our watch?

I also felt terrible because I was scheduled to make my first trip to South Africa in just a week or so. How would the believers there feel about my coming when Father Paschal has just died in one of our houses? I had no reason to be concerned.

What we later learned was that Father Paschal had been the first Catholic father in South Africa to befriend the Charismatic Renewal. It was just beginning among the Catholics, and the Bishop had been very negative toward it.

When word of Father Paschal's death reached the Bishop, he was sure that he must have died in the house of the Passionists.

"No," he was told by the sister who was reporting the details, "he died in a Charismatic house in Jerusalem. That's where he wanted to be."

When the Bishop heard that the father had died in a Charismatic house, it moved him deeply. If this great man had been willing to die in a Charismatic house, there must be something more to this experience. Soon afterward he sent a letter to all the Catholic churches and orders throughout South Africa. From then on, he told them, whether or not to participate in Charismatic Renewal would be an individual decision for each one to make. In this way, God allowed Father Paschal to accomplish in death what he had not been able to accomplish in life, and because of his sacrifice, the Charismatic Renewal came to all the Catholics in South Africa who were hungry for God.

When I arrived in South Africa, I was very well-received by the nuns and the priests.

Later that same year, we received a knock at the door of our house in Jerusalem one afternoon, and there stood two lovely Irishmen. They were the brothers of Father Paschal, and they were on a tour of the Holy Land. One of them was a priest, and the other was not. This is the story they told:

They had an aunt who decided that if her nephew had thought the Charismatic Renewal was that important, she would visit some of their meetings in Ireland. As a result, she too, received the Holy Spirit and the gift, the charism, of speaking in other tongues.

Then, because she felt that she was too elderly to go to Jerusalem herself, she decided to pay the way for her other two nephews to go and visit the Holy Land where her favorite nephew had gone to be with the Lord. "We wanted you to know," the brothers told me, "that his desire all of his life was to die in Jerusalem."

They had told us when they arrived that their time was very limited between tours. They had only planned to stay thirty minutes, just enough time to deliver their message, but I was able to say to them, "The finest gift you could give your brother is to allow me to pray for you to receive this experience as well." They began to praise the Lord with us, and before long they were speaking in other tongues through the Holy Spirit.

After we waved good-bye to them that day, we had no further contact with them, but I know that they are part of what God is doing in Ireland. ✳

≈ 111 ≈

"The Cloud of Glory Was Coming In"

Of my many other stories from South Africa, one of my favorites is from more recent years. Just a few years ago I traveled with Amada Vander Walt throughout a number of areas of South Africa, ministering. I was scheduled to preach three nights in Pretoria: one night on praise, one night on worship and one night on glory. Usually, on the glory night, I invite people to come forward, and they stand in the glory and begin seeing visions of Heaven. It is normally a very sedate experience.

This particular night, however, after everyone had come to the front (all twelve or thirteen hundred of them), I looked over to the right and saw a cloud of glory beginning to come into the hall. I called Pastor Nevil Nordon, whom I had just met two nights before, and told him to come up on the platform so he could see what I was seeing. He was standing at the bottom of the steps in front of the platform, but he quickly got onto the platform, and I pointed out to him the cloud of glory that was coming in.

Just at that moment about fifty of the people over to our extreme right, where I had seen the cloud, fell out under the power of God. Then the cloud began to move, and as it moved, people were slain in the Spirit in its path.

The cloud did not move in a direct line across the front. It moved in a circuitous route, much as a river would move, but as it passed, people fell in groups.

It took only a minute or so for the cloud to complete its route across the front of the auditorium, and by the time it had passed, two-thirds of the people present were on the floor under the power of God.

Then everyone began to laugh. This was in a time when laughter was just beginning to break out among people around the world, and it had struck South Africa. Before it was over, people were getting drunk in the Spirit all over the place. It was several hours before the most of the people were up off the floor.

There was a very sophisticated woman there that night, very tall and thin. She was the chief intercessor for a particular church. When I met her for lunch the next day, she described to me what had happened to her that night. When she tried to get up, she found that she had no strength. After she regained enough strength, she crawled on her hands and knees to a pole where she could pull herself upright. I had to laugh because she was such a proper lady.

335

What God did in that place was the beginning of what He would do in every city we visited on that trip. In one town, where we ministered at a ladies' meeting, I looked over at Amanda, who was playing the piano for me. I had noticed that she had stopped playing, and I wanted to tell her to continue. What I saw, however, was that she was in no condition to play. She was slumped over the piano, totally intoxicated in the Spirit. Her hand was still moving as if she were playing, but it was not touching the keyboard, and no sound was coming out. This same thing happened everywhere we went.

In a suburb of Johannesburg called Rand, we were in another ladies' meeting. The place was small, but it was crowded. Just before they turned the service over to me, a lady spoke up and said, "I would like to read a verse of scripture," and she read from Isaiah about God doing a new thing. Another lady said, "Oh, I've got a verse too," and she read from the next chapter about God doing a new thing.

When I got up to speak, I said, since two verses have been read about doing the new thing, I cannot do the old, and began to speak about the new things God was doing in South Africa.

At the end of the service, a lady came forward, the Holy Spirit came on her, and she began to spin around and around. Every lady she touched fell out under the power. If her shoulder touched them, or her hand touched them, or any part of her body touched them, they fell out under the power of God.

Sometime later, she fell out under the power herself, and when she got up, she said, "I must repent! I must repent!" I was waiting to see what it was she felt she had to repent of, and she said, "I must call my sister and repent. My sister lives in London, and she told me about meetings where people were laughing, and I told her that she mustn't go to any of those meetings, that they were not of God. I must repent because now I know that it is God."

About a year later, I was back in that same area and was invited to a church in Johannesburg. When I walked in, I discovered that it was the church this woman attended. The pastor said, "We have heard of you because this lady has attended our church for years. It was that meeting that morning that took her from being a back-row person to a front-row person. Before she had never gotten involved in the activities of the church, but now she has become one of our most active participants. She is involved in everything God is doing."

When I got to Utenhaag, right across the river from Port Elizabeth, I saw an article on the front page of the South African newspaper about the wife of a pastor in Port Elizabeth and the unusual revival that was taking place at their church. I arranged to have lunch with her so that I could learn what they were experiencing. She told me that her husband and a group of the elders from the church had flown to Singapore to attend a seminar on church growth. While they were away, the One who knows more about church growth than anyone else in the world visited the church, and those who were present experienced a sovereign work of the Holy Spirit. It was so startling that she called her husband and asked what they should do. "Don't let it stop," he said. "Keep doing whatever you're doing until we get back."

The woman was very short and, because the Lord instructed her to lay hands on the heads of all the people who were attending and pray for them, she had to have a chair that she moved along with her, standing up on it in order to reach the heads of the people. This didn't prevent them from falling under the power or of receiving the deep joy that God was pouring out upon the people of South Africa.

I spoke that night in a rather conservative Pentecostal church. My hostess, a member of the Dutch Reformed congregation, accompanied me. The South African people are very social, and my hostess was always beautifully and meticulously dressed. Her purse and shoes always matched her outfit, which she changed several times a day.

After the message and a time of waiting in the glory, I invited those who had received some vision or revelation to come forward and share it with the others. After sharing her revelation, this sister fell under the power of God right on the platform, and this was fine — until she tried to get up. Every part of her body was able to get up except her chin, which stuck to the platform. She was a very delicate and graceful person, and she now moved herself this way and that, trying to get her chin unstuck. What a funny sight she was! And we all laughed and laughed together as she struggled to free herself. We were laughing with the joy of the Lord.

That sister was so drunk with joy that we had to carry her home after the meeting, and all through the night I could hear her laughing. The next morning she looked twenty years younger, as if she had received a total face lift. I saw her last year in a conference in Jerusalem, and she told me that her experience that night had been life-changing. She has never been the same. As she told it, joy and laughter broke out in our midst and many others experienced being "stuck."

This experience, the supernatural move of the Spirit, happened in place after place throughout South Africa where God sent us.   ❋

﹅ 112 ﹆

"Do It!"

Sister Choi (Dr. Cho's mother-in-law) and I quickly developed a very unique relationship. After her initial visit to Jerusalem, she called me often. Our telephone conversations were very limited by her lack of English and my lack of Korean. She would say, "Glory!" and I would answer, "Glory!" She would say, "Hallelujah!" or "Jesus!" and then more "Glory!" and I would respond accordingly. Before the conversation was over, she would always say, "I love you." I would always answer her, "I love you, too." Sometimes we conversed more fully through an interpreter.

I had the opportunity to visit Sister Choi in Korea, and this deep love she felt for me was demonstrated. She would take her delicate chopsticks (the Korean chopsticks are as fine as crotchet needles, much finer than those of the Chinese or Japanese) and she would lovingly and tirelessly feed me morsel after morsel of Korean delicacies, in addition to the ever-present *kimchi*. Her close associates had never seen her ever feed anyone, but she never seemed to be embarrassed by it.

When she came to Jerusalem that first time to thank us, we enjoyed her and her ministry so much that it was decided that we would do conferences together in the Holy City each year. For several years after that, we did Prayer and Fasting Conferences at the government conference center, and people came from many nations to attend. We were particularly blessed with the attendance of some of the Korean ministers who have been used so mightily by God as missionaries to other parts of the world.

During the daytime we formed a procession and marched through the streets of the Holy City, singing and praising God. The Koreans marched through the streets in their beautiful long and flowing national costumes, waving flags and banners. One of the banners declared: WE PRAY FOR THE PEACE OF JERUSALEM. Local florists came out of their shops and presented a rose to each of the marchers.

This was one of the earlier of such groups that came to the city to show their love for Jerusalem and her people, before other Christian groups marched through the streets demonstrating their love. The presence of such sweet and loving people made the city glad.

In the prayer conference services, I always led the preliminaries and Sister Choi did the preaching and ministering to the people. Her son, Pastor Kim, came from Los Angeles to be her interpreter.

Her strong point was fasting. She had fasted with such dedication all her life that she spoke of it with great authority. It was one of her points of spirituality. I don't know of anybody who was more powerful on the subject than she was.

One night in the great government conference center, she told of a Japanese chicken farmer who was losing all his chickens to sickness. She told him to have the chickens fast for two or three days, and when the chickens fasted, they were all healed. A baby was dying in the hospital, and she told the parents to persuade the doctor to let the baby fast for twenty-four hours. When the baby fasted, it was healed and lived.

She told many stories like that, one after the other. She had more amazing stories concerning the power of fasting than anyone else I have known. In her stories, it was always the sick person who fasted, not the well who fasted for the sick. It was the chickens fasting for their own healing and the baby fasting for itself. And the result was always the same. God always brought healing.

At the end of the service this particular night, she had a long line of people coming to the altar for her prayers. Some of these people had known the Lord for many years, and some were new believers, prominent and successful business people. She did something that night that I have never seen before or since. As the people passed in front of her, she would point her finger at them and call out a certain number of days they should fast.

"Thirty!" she would say to one person with great authority and without a moment's hesitation.

"Twenty!" she said to others.

To some it was even "Forty!"

I think I was the only person she didn't point to that night and give a number of days to fast.

I began to understand why the Korean businessmen have been so blessed over several decades. Those who had only known the Lord a short time could grow quickly as they developed a lifestyle of prayer and fasting.

In another of her powerful messages, she gave people four things they needed to do to be spiritual. They were (1) Much speaking in tongues, (2) Much fasting, (3) All nights spent in prayer and (4) Do it. I loved them all, but I found her point number four to be particularly powerful. "DO IT!" That was good advice for all of us.

What a marvelous woman she was! We were so blessed to know her! We called her "Hallelujah Mama." Sister Jashil Choi has now gone on to be with the Lord, but it is safe to say that the last years of her life were the most productive for the Kingdom of God.

Sister Choi instituted all-night prayer meetings to be held every Friday night in Jerusalem, and we continued that tradition for many years afterward.   ✷

~ 113 ~

"Offer Them More"

In 1981 I was invited to England to speak at a Charismatic Catholic layleaders' conference at La Salle College in Southampton. Many Protestants attended. The conference convener, Ron Nichols, had attended a large Catholic Charismatic conference in Rome where he met David DuPlessis. At the close of the conference he asked David to recommend a speaker to speak on "Vibrant Praise," and David recommended me. Ron went back and spoke with his committee, which included Joan and Michael Le Morvan. They agreed to invite me. I spoke at that conference several years in succession and later, Joan and Michael invited me for a conference, which led to the founding of their Catholic Bible School in Nutbourne.

When the first invitatation came, we had been praying for Great Britain, in both Jerusalem and in the Ashland camp, and God had given us a vision of trouble springing up there. The very next day we began to get news reports of riots in various English cities. Before the rioting ended, eighteen cities were affected, and the unrest came to be called The Brixton Riots.

As we prayed and believed God for the rioting to stop, God said to me, "If you are really concerned about Great Britain, call your friends there and offer them more than just a weekend." That seemed a little presumptuous since the brothers had invited me just to do a weekend meeting, but I did what God said. "Could you use me the whole month of August?" I asked.

"August is a terrible month for Britain," Ron replied. "Everybody's on holiday, but if you don't mind speaking to small groups, we'll be happy to set it up for you."

I said, "I'll speak to anyone who comes."

Every day during the month of August I traveled to a different city in England, and every night I spoke to a different group of people. Most of the meetings were small. Sometimes only fifty to seventy people gathered, and sometimes, when the meetings were held in someone's home, the crowd was only twenty to thirty. Still, hundreds of British people were filled with the Holy Ghost that month, and by the time the conference time rolled around, it was glorious. It was during the days of that conference that the Lord first spoke to me about writing a book on the glory.

I was invited back the next year and the next to speak in that same conference in Southampton. One year when we were in prayer concerning the upcoming conference, God gave us a number of visions. One of them concerned Prime Minister Margaret Thatcher. I saw her with the flag of Israel being draped around her, followed by the Union Jack. The word of the Lord came to me that if she would embrace Israel a little more than she was doing, God would give her a second term in office. The Lord commissioned me to get that message to her.

When I arrived that year in London in July, I called a friend who is a Lord in the British House of Lords, thinking that maybe he could help me. He was away in France at the time. I went on to the conference in Southampton, and when I got there, I spoke to the conference leader concerning what God had said about Mrs. Thatcher and about Great Britain.

He said, "Lady Astor is here. Maybe she will be willing to help you get in contact with Mrs. Thatcher." In that way, my friendship with Lady Bronwen Astor was born.

When Lady Astor witnessed the vibrant praise and majestic worship at the conference, she thought that there should be a larger venue for such praise and worship meetings and offered to make it possible. After looking for a suitable sight, she decided on the beautiful Royal Albert Hall. We went into the hall together and looked around. I stood on the platform and tried out a few hallelujahs to test the acoustics. Nearby the London Philharmonic Orchestra was practicing for a special concert, and the cameras of the BBC were being focused on them. I liked the feel of the place, and it was booked for that August. It was decided to call the scheduled event the International Praise Gathering, and we determined to invite people from many other nations to attend in support of the British people.

I hadn't given up on the desire to see the British Prime Minister, but while I waited for an opening, I flew to France for meetings. When I got back to London, Lady Astor met me and took me to the country estate of one of the former members of Mrs. Thatcher's cabinet. She wanted me to express to him my desire to speak with the Prime Minister. During our conversation, I told him what God was doing in many parts of the world. Later, as he showed me around his house, I knelt with him in his private chapel, we prayed together, and he began to speak in other tongues.

Just before I left his house, I was signing the guest book, and he asked me if he would still be able to speak in tongues after I left. I assured him that he would and suggested that he try it again right then and there. He immediately began to sing in a beautiful language of the Spirit.

I Ask for Great Britain

It was arranged that I would meet Mrs. Thatcher, but when I returned from Australia for my appointment, Mrs. Thatcher had just flown off to the Falkland Islands. Lady Astor and I were able to speak with Mr. Ian Gow, Mrs. Thatcher's Chief Parliamentary Aide. He took us into her office at the House of Commons. As my feet trod on the area where the Prime Minister conducted her daily business, I believed God for an anointing for her to accomplish the great things purposed for her and all of Great Britain.

I later saw Mr. Ian Gow again and told him that I believed the English would have elections by June.

"Oh, no," he answered, "we're not planning on them until October of next year."

A surprise election was held in Great Britain that June and Margaret Thatcher was reelected by a powerful majority. One of the reasons was that she began to reach out to embrace Israel more.

In a vision, one of our people saw the Royal Albert Hall and its silver dome as a great covered silver meat platter. A hand came down and lifted up the lid, and a great feast became visible, enough for all. I was believing that God would bring it to pass.

The Royal Albert Hall, with its ornate opera boxes, was a place worthy of an international praise gathering to honor our Lord Jesus. Lady Astor invited all her social friends. I was believing for the meeting to be much more than a praise gathering. I was believing that God would use it to change the spiritual atmosphere in the country and bring forth a great spiritual liberty for the British people. Great Britain needed to take its rightful place once again and begin blessing all of Europe and the world.

We invited an Israeli friend, Shlomo Carlebach, an Hassidic rabbi, to come and sing for the event. When he began to sing about Jerusalem, a love for the Holy City and its people was dropped into the hearts of those who heard him. We were believing that the Christians of Great Britain would be awakened to God's purposes for Jerusalem and for Israel in the last days.

After Lady Astor had rented the Royal Albert Hall, I realized that I would need to travel throughout England to raise up praisers for the event. It was one thing to call an international praise gathering, but we also needed those who could fill the auditorium and could lift their voices in praise to the Lord. There was little vibrant praise in the churches of England at that time.

As I was praying about what I should do, I had a dream about our late President John F. Kennedy and the English town of Runnymead. I was not aware at the time that Runnymead was just outside of London and that it was the place of the Magna Carta. When I learned this the next day, I made a trip out to

Harvest Glory

Runnymead, and once there I also discovered that it was also the site of a Kennedy memorial. Across the facade of that memorial was written one huge word: FREEDOM. In another part, I read a quote from President Kennedy's inaugural speech. He said:

> *Let every nation know, whether it wishes us well or ill, that we shall pay any price, bear any burden, meet any hardship, support any friend, oppose any foe, to assure the survival and the success of liberty. This much we pledge — and more.*

I read the words out loud and as I did, I sensed that God was calling on me to make the same pledge for Britain. I was ready to "pay any price," to "bear any burden," to "meet any hardship," to "support any friend," to "oppose any foe." Our cause was just and right. We would "assure the survival and the success of [spiritual] liberty [for Great Britain]." I was ready to do whatever was necessary to see God release spiritual freedom upon the whole nation.

For the next three months I traveled throughout England, Ireland, Scotland and Wales, boarding the train each day for another place, praying for the people in every town to be saved and filled with the Spirit, raising up praisers for the great event to come. I ministered each evening and on many mornings as well. Often our meetings would last until late into the evening, for the people were hungry and wanted prayer. Afterward, I would often sit up and speak with my host and hostess, answering their questions far into the night.

One of the places to which I traveled was called Seven Kings. After I spoke there one afternoon, there were four or five hundred people who spoke in tongues for the first time. Among them was a ninety-year-old priest and an eighty-year-old nun. She later told me that she had waited ten years for someone to pray for her to be filled with the Spirit and speak in tongues.

I stretched so far to lay hands on all the people who wanted prayer that during the night I suffered severe pains in my chest. My first thought was that I was having heart pain. *I'm going to die in this house,* I was thinking, *and these people don't even know where I'm from.* (I had just met my host and hostess that afternoon.) As it turned out, I was just suffering the consequences of using muscles I hadn't used in a very long time.

Little by little, day by day, we were gaining support across the British Isles to believe God for the great outpouring of the Spirit He wanted to bring to the country. I fell in love with the Isles and their people during those days and thoroughly enjoyed myself in every place.

We asked people in other countries to take Britain on their hearts during the weeks leading up to the gathering, and many from America, Hong Kong, South Africa, other parts of Europe and the world made plans to join us there. In this

I Ask for Great Britain

way, believers from many lands joined their faith with ours for the outpouring of the Holy Ghost upon the British Isles.

Lady Astor, being a very social person, had chosen the dates for the gathering to come just before the popular proms. It is a season known for the beautiful orchestra music played every night in the Royal Albert Hall. She was very bold when she was interviewed concerning the event and told reporters frankly that there would be singing and dancing, speaking in tongues and prophecy. "We're just going to have a spiritual party, a spiritual celebration," she would say. Thank God for such a woman.

I had asked her, "What do you want us to do?"

She had answered, "Anything that you want to do, I want you to do. I only ask that once or twice you have a moment of silence so that people can hear God speak." So I had total liberty to minister in those meetings as I usually did.

We took a portion of my song "I Ask for the Nations," and adapted it as "I Ask for Great Britain," and it was printed as a program for that special meeting. On the back of the program we wrote a little concerning our vision for the nation, what God had told us He would do, and our desire for the land and its people. God said that the people of Britain had everything they needed to experience a move of His Spirit and that He would now give them the gift of liberty to demonstrate their spiritual abilities.

On a previous trip I had learned that a friend of mine was a close friend of Mrs. Thatcher's daughter Carol, a journalist and radio reporter. My friend gave Carol the tapes of some interviews we had done, and she said that when I next came to Britain she wanted to interview me and to introduce me to her mother. She interviewed me for the Royal Albert Hall meeting, as did the BBC.

The enemy, foreseeing what an impact the upcoming meeting would have on all of Great Britain, tried to keep it from occurring. When I had finished the three months of traveling around the Isles and returned to London, Lady Astor met me at the airport and told me that some people had risen up in opposition to the meeting. She asked if I would be willing to meet with them and discuss it. I told her that I usually found such meetings to be unprofitable, but when she seemed to want it very badly, I consented.

The meeting was much as I imagined it would be. Those who had risen in opposition were very angry about my success in England. They were determined to convince Lady Astor to cancel the meeting.

Aside from Lady Astor, I felt that I was very much alone in that meeting. She sat very quietly next to me listening to everything they had to say, but she was not moved by it and eventually excused herself, saying that she had another appointment.

As I was climbing the steps of the plane that would take me back to Jerusalem that day, I suddenly felt very weary. I had poured out my strength and energy to Great Britain day after day for three months. Just then the words of a little chorus began to come to me. The chorus speaks of the resurrection of our Lord, but the Holy Spirit was using the words to speak to me. He was saying, "I will raise you up. I will raise you up." I knew that God was going to give us a wonderful meeting no matter what opposition came, and that is exactly what He did.

When the day arrived, we were moved by the response of the people of Great Britain and the world. It was a very hot August, and the British are not accustomed to the heat. Although there was no air-conditioning in the Royal Albert Hall, the people responded wonderfully.

During the service, we prayerfully and humbly offered our song to Her Majesty, Queen Elizabeth, to Mrs. Thatcher, the Prime Minister of Her Majesty's Government, and also to the people of Great Britain. God had told us that as we believed many would catch the vision for Great Britain, and we would see miracles, signs and wonders performed.

The Jewish people of the London area had been invited to attend the gathering on Friday evening and we used as our theme song, "Let There be Love Shed Among Us."

In the Hall itself, there was a large circular area left open for promenading at the proms, and we also left it without chairs so that we could have room to pray for people. During times of worship, Lady Astor would step out and motion for the people in the balcony to come down and use that area to dance before the Lord. They did.

About a thousand people came forward for prayer. I had told the ushers to leave about five feet between the rows so that there would be room for people to rest in the Spirit, falling out under the power of God. I touched the first person in a row, and about twenty-five people went down. I had to move fast to catch up with the glory cloud that was moving all down the line of people. I would sometimes touch the tenth person or the twenty-fifth person, and the rest of the people in that line would go down under the power of God without hands ever being laid on them. They were falling like dominoes. Eventually, everyone was on the floor. Many wonderful healings and miracles took place. It was the greatest demonstration of God's power that England had seen for many years.

On Saturday afternoon, I wanted to pray especially for people to be filled with the Spirit, so I took extra time laying hands on their heads individually. About four hundred spoke in tongues that night, and again great miracles were performed.

We spoke a spiritual release for Great Britain, spiritual liberty for men and women throughout the Isles to know Jesus as their Savior, that they should be transformed by the mighty power of God, and the impact was powerful. ✶

⚜ 114 ⚜

"We Have Decided to Invite You Home for Lunch"

We received an invitation from Dr. Colton Wickremenayake to send a delegate for the Impact Conference he was conducting in Columbo, Ceylon (now called Sri Lanka). He was bringing together some twelve hundred ministers, mostly from the developing nations and was taking responsibility for their food and lodging and, in many cases, their airplane tickets. It was a remarkable step of faith.

Several years earlier, we were invited to the same conference, and, because we were busy, we sent one of our couples to attend. I was thinking to do the same thing this time, but the Lord spoke to me to go myself.

I arrived in Colombo a little early, checked into the Mt. Lavinia, a beautiful hotel where I had stayed with my parents in 1961, and prepared to go to the official hotel where registration was taking place. When I arrived at the hotel, I met Brother Johan Lukoff, head of the Christian Embassy in Jerusalem. He had come to attend the conference too. We had a nice visit together in the hotel that evening.

The next morning, as we all arrived at the large conference center in Colombo and proceeded up the very long walkway leading to the entrance, I could see the various delegates from all the developing nations, and they were all beautifully attired in their native dress.

I was feeling a little dull and drab in my normal clothes, when I noticed an elderly gentleman walking alone with a cane. I went over to him, gently took him by the arm, and we walked slowly together into the conference center. We found a good seat, and I helped him be seated in the hall.

Before long, I noticed that everyone, those from Sri Lanka and those from other countries as well, were coming by to shake hands with this stately-looking gentlemen. He was Rev. W.J. Beiling, an old Pentecostal pioneer who had been in meetings with Smith Wigglesworth, was known by everyone and considered to be one of the most important people in the conference. As people came by to shake hands with him, he introduced them to me.

After an enjoyable morning session, there was a break for refreshments. We went out to the lobby and looked around at some of the booths where books and other items related to the conference were being offered. As I was walking

347

around, looking at everything, two ladies came up to me and said, "We've looked everybody over, and we have decided to invite you home for lunch."

"Well, thank you so much," I answered. "It would be quite an honor to be in a Sri Lankan home. My stay here will be very brief this time. I'm only here for the conference. If it were not for the fact that you are inviting me, I probably wouldn't have the opportunity to be in a Sri Lankan home." I was excited about the prospect.

"We'll be back to pick you up after the morning session," they said, and we parted.

I later discovered that they had gone to the phone immediately, called home and told the cook what to prepare for lunch. They called several of their relatives and invited them to join us too. By the time I got to the house, a wonderful luncheon was waiting.

The two ladies were sisters. One of them was the widow of the nephew of Mrs. Sirimaro Bandaranaike. Her daughter, Chandrika Bandaranaike Kunaraturgu, leads the country as President and today serves as Prime Minister under the Republic. She served in that post for some seventeen years or more. When her husband had been living, he had been the favorite nephew of Mrs. Felix Bandaranaike, and through the years of her tenure as Prime Minister, he had served in many different government positions. He had been the Minister of Finance and the Minister of Justice. She had traveled to all the important places around the world with her husband.

They were an Episcopalian family, but they enjoyed attending Pentecostal meetings. During lunch they began to tell me about sickness in the family and other needs they were believing God to meet. I began speaking to them concerning the need of being baptized in the Holy Spirit. At the end of the luncheon, I prayed for every one of them, they were all baptized in the Holy Ghost, and the Lord gave them some wonderful healings.

The family was very kind to me and took me sight-seeing around Columbo. If I had come to the conference just for that luncheon, it would have been worth it, but I had also met many other important delegates from all over Asia and Africa. It was there that I came to know Pastor Kriangsak from the Hope of Bangkok Church in Bangkok, Thailand. It was exciting to see how God is raising up men and women of authority throughout the third-world nations.

A few days later, I was in Beijing. While visiting the home of one of the Sung sisters that had recently been turned into a museum and opened to the public, I saw a photo containing the very lady I had recently visited in Columbo. Also in the photo were Mao Tse Tung and other Chinese leaders. The Lord had sovereignly given me the opportunity to bless that important family in Colombo, Sri Lanka, in such a special way.

I Ask for Sri Lanka

Recently two Sri Lankan families visited our weekend revival meetings. The father, Dr. Mendes, is a professor in Colombo. Someone gave his wife a copy of *Glory*. She began to move into worship dancing and has led her people into it as well. The second night they were here their daughter had oil flowing from her hands. Before the evening was over, others had oil in their hands and gold dust appeared on their arms, faces and necks, coming through their pores. It was a beautiful sight. Since they returned to Colombo, these signs have begun to appear in their meetings there.　　　　　　　　　　＊

≈ 115 ≈

"The Berlin Wall Will Come Down"

A group came to Jerusalem from Germany, and we had special meetings in our house for them. I told them how Debbie Kendrick had prophesied seven years before that the Berlin Wall would come down shortly. Some time after this one of our brothers called in the middle of the night. He was very excited.

"Sister Ruth," he said, "I'm very sorry to awaken you, but ..."

"What is it?" I asked.

"The Berlin Wall is being breached," he continued. "People are crossing over from the east to the west. Some haven't even taken time to get dressed. They are crossing in their underclothing or pajamas. It's cold, but many have rushed out of their houses without putting warm clothes on. It is a most exciting thing, and I knew you would want to know. I apologize for waking you up."

By that time I was wide awake with the news and just as excited as he was. What a wonderful day it was for the whole world!

I have preached in East Berlin several times and had East German tour groups in our meetings in Jerusalem. I have also been blessed to have known Brother and Sister Bauer from Germany. Andreas is from West Germany, and Adelheide is from East Germany — a prophetic marriage. The two parts of the country were destined to meet.

I have a small piece of the Berlin Wall. Some painted a cross on it as a re-minder of the miracle God did to unite those two long-divided countries. ✳

⚹ 116 ⚺

"The New Will Come Forth From Spain"

One day in Jerusalem we heard that Margaret Thatcher's leadership had come into question and that the following day there would be a vote concerning her future leadership. I was a big Margaret Thatcher fan and came into the prayer meeting that day ready to pray that God would keep her in power.

After about ten minutes of praise and worship, the glory of God came, revelation knowledge began to flow, and Nancy Bergen began to prophesy about England. God said that England had been a great shipbuilding nation and that ships had gone out from her to distant ports all over the world.

I was wondering why the Lord was reminding us of England's great seagoing history, when suddenly there was a shift in the flow of the message, and I heard these words. "But when the ships went out to the New World, they did not go out from England." We all knew our history and were aware of the fact that the ships that discovered the New World had gone out from Spain. In that moment I knew that the new focus of political activity in Europe would shift to Spain and the rest of the continent. I also knew that the next day Margaret Thatcher would lose her leadership vote. She was trying to hold back the tide for the European Union, but God was letting us know that the new would come out of Spain and out of Europe and that we should not resist it. The next day Mrs. Thatcher was no longer Prime Minister of Great Britain.

When it was announced that the Israeli peace talks would take place in Madrid, Spain, I told our staff that we must be the slowest people in Jerusalem. We should have been the first to know that the peace talks would be held in Madrid because the Lord had told us that the new would come out of Spain. Sometimes, when the Lord tells us something in regards to a person or event, we relate it only to that person or event and do not allow it to flow over into those things which are to follow. This is what happened to us when we prayed about Mrs. Thatcher's leadership, and it can happen to us in any situation if we fail to follow on to understand completely what the Lord has said.

From that moment I knew that the peace process would be successful (not necessarily the peace, but the process), and I knew not to fight against it. I also knew that Bibi Netanyahu would become Prime Minister of Israel. I saw the anointing fall on him for leadership, as Prime Minister Shamir rested his hand upon him in the famous photo taken in Madrid.   ⚹

ॐ 117 ॐ

"Anoint the Heads of the People By Faith"

One day in 1992 in our prayer meeting in Jerusalem, God gave us a simple song. It didn't seem particularly dynamic at the moment. The words were: "Anoint the heads of the people of Israel by faith," and we started singing it together.

As we sang this song, I had a vision of Yitzhak Rabin, who had been Prime Minister from 1974 to 1977, before Menachem Begin had come to power, and I also saw his assistant. I said, "Yes, Lord, I will anoint the heads of the people of Israel by faith," and I picked up a large urn of oil in the Spirit and began to pour it over their heads.

Until that moment, Shimon Peres had been the leader of the opposition party, and little was heard of Yitzhak Rabin. The very next day, however, news spread that there had been a dramatic shift in popularity and that Yitzhak Rabin would surely become the next Prime Minister of Israel. It happened within a matter of weeks. By June of that year Israel had a new Prime Minister ... and the rest is history.

On November 4, 1995, after our Saturday evening service in Jerusalem, we turned on the television to catch the news. There was a great political rally taking place in Tel Aviv, and Prime Minister Yitzhak Rabin was finishing a speech. As he moved among the cheering crowd, a shockwave suddenly went through the people, as everyone became aware that the Prime Minister had been shot. We remained in prayer for some time until the news came that he was dead. On Sunday afternoon we were among the thousands who passed by his bier, as his body lay in state in front of the Knesset, the Israeli Parliament building, to pay their last respects.

The next morning, thinking it was Tuesday, I quickly got up and dressed and took Nancy and two others with me to attend the weekly Christian media prayer meeting at the King David Hotel. As I walked through the revolving door of the King David, I came face to face with Mayor Teddy Kolleck. We were both happy to see one another. He embraced me warmly and kissed me on both cheeks. We exchanged words of comfort. Then I turned and watched as he exited through the revolving door I had just entered.

I Ask for Israel

Security was very tight that day, and the head of security had just witnessed this meeting or we might never have gotten in. After seeing our warm encounter with Mayor Kolleck, he waved us on through.

The four of us went into the dining room, were seated and began to eat, while we waited on the others to arrive for the prayer meeting. After awhile I suddenly realized that it was not Tuesday at all, and the prayer meeting would not be held on Monday. We had a lovely breakfast together anyway.

After we had finished our breakfast, we went back out through the lobby toward the exit, only to discover that television cameras were set up, aimed at the revolving doors of the hotel and news crews were obviously waiting for someone important to come at any minute. We found a spot close to one of the columns, where we could be out of the way and yet still see the revolving door. Before long Prince Charles came through the door. He walked within two feet of me, and I was able to greet him.

The dramatic entrance of Prince Charles proved to be only the beginning of a long line of royalty, prime ministers, presidents, and other heads of state, ambassadors, senators, congressmen, diplomats and other dignitaries who passed within feet of us that day. Periodically, I whispered to some of the foreign newsmen the names of individuals they did not recognize.

We stood there for more than an hour, quietly praying and observing the parade of nations. The prophet Isaiah had foretold that the kings and queens of the Earth would bring their glory and honor to Jerusalem, and in Prime Minister Rabin's death, this scripture had been fulfilled. Eighty-five world leaders had come, bringing with them the glory and honor of their nations, and we had an opportunity to bless them all. ✳

☙ 118 ☜

"Young and Old, Rich and Poor"

Through the years, we had many wonderful visitors in Jerusalem — young and old, rich and poor, noble and common. From every nation people came to give thanks to God and to seek His face in the Holy City. What a day of rejoicing it was when we had our first visitors from China and our first visitors from East Germany. For many of these visitors, regardless of their country of origin, coming to Jerusalem was a life-changing experience. Pastors who visited Jerusalem, for example, suddenly had a vision for the world.

For example, a lovely pastor and his wife came from Nagaland, a state located in the northeast part of India, adjoining the border of China. This man sold his motor scooter in order to be able to make the trip to the Holy City. China was just opening, and we were praying extensively for China and the Chinese. While he was in Jerusalem, he was touched in the Spirit for China. Although his town bordered China, and he could actually see over into China, the border was closed for political reasons, and he had not been able to go there.

When he returned home from the conference, he was determined to bless China. He fasted and prayed until the necessary finances came in. Then, he and his wife went to Calcutta and got a plane for Hong Kong. In Hong Kong they secured a visa for China and traveled into the western part of China, just across the border from Nagaland (also not far from Lhasa, Tibet.) While they were there, they ministered to the people.

Can you comprehend the tenacity and vision of such people? That pastor had more than fifteen hundred churches back home and could have remained in the comfort of his own home. God had brought him to Jerusalem to show him the possibility of doing even greater things in ministry, and he had responded. Later, he and his wife became missionaries to China, living, along with other members of his family, in Hong Kong and going in and out of China.

Our own group was made up of five faithful sisters — myself, Susan Woodaman, Irene Bredlow, Janet Saunders and Alice Ford — and anyone else who cared to join us at the moment. Four of us were from Virginia, Irene was from Canada, and the others were always from a wide variety of nations. Living in Jerusalem changed us all forever. ❋

◢ 119 ◣

"He Is Our President"

After concentrating my efforts overseas for so many years, my focus was suddenly drawn to Washington and America. I came home to attend the Second Inauguration of President Ronald Reagan. During his First Inauguration four years earlier, I went with friends in political circles to some of the breakfasts held around the capital on the morning of the inauguration. During each inauguration, many such breakfasts are held, some by the party that has won the election, and others by various Washington power brokers. People who are considered to be of importance in the nation are invited to attend. This is all fine, but where were all the praying people at a time like this?

I found that because Washington is very crowded on Inauguration Day, many people who have ministries there go out of the city for the day to avoid the hustle and bustle. *Wouldn't it be wonderful,* I thought, *if someone would organize a prayer meeting for inauguration morning that ordinary people could attend? Should we not give special attention to this, the most important day on our nation's calendar?*

These thoughts were strong in my spirit again as I walked through the corridor of the Sheraton Hotel the morning of President George Bush's Inaugural. I was concerned that there was not a single prayer meeting we were aware of that we could attend on that very important day for America and the world. When I mentioned this to my friend, Connie Snapp DeBord, who was Director of Media in the Pat Robertson Campaign and later had been a party unifier in the Bush Campaign Headquarters, God spoke to me and told me to organize such a prayer gathering. I told Connie what the Lord had said, and she answered, "You can do it, but you would have to make the arrangements at least a year in advance." I began planning right then for the next presidential inauguration.

When God spoke to me to host the Presidential Inaugural Prayer Breakfast four years later, we didn't know who would be the President-elect or which party would win the election. We didn't even know who the candidates would be. When Bill Clinton won the election, many Christians made it a point to boycott the Inauguration that year and, instead, met in Philadelphia for prayer.

The well-known syndicated columnist and commentator Cal Thomas wrote an article which he was kind enough to fax to me before it appeared in the newspaper. In that article he said, "He asked for bread, and they gave him a stone." Bill Clinton had spoken in his Baptist church in Little Rock, Arkansas, before leaving for Washington, and had asked Christians everywhere to pray for him. Instead, everyone was ready to stone him.

Whether or not we agree with his every point of view, he is our President, and we were called to support him with our prayers. It was a wonderful gathering of pastors, layleaders and believers from many different Christian groups, congressmen, senators, ambassadors and diplomats. The embassies of many foreign countries sent their representatives to attend.

We worshiped the Lord together and then believed God for a great outpouring of His Spirit upon America in the days ahead.   ✳

≤ 120 ≥

"May Your Glory Fill These Chambers"

One Friday in Jerusalem I was watching the news on CNN when I saw a group of U.S. Congressmen. I was drawn to pray for one of them. Throughout the day that day, every time that same segment would be replayed, I would feel that same concern to pray for the same man, and I prayed for him all day long. The television noted that he was Congressman Tom Lantos from California.

Connie and Bill Wilson were living with us in Jerusalem at the time. Bill was helping us with our work, and Connie was volunteering at Ulpan Akiva during the week. When she came home that night and the same segment was repeated again on the news, I told her about the burden I had felt all day long for that Congressman.

That next week Shulamith Katznelson, the director of Ulpan Akiva, told Connie that an American congressional delegation would be visiting the Ulpan the following week. It would be headed by Congressman Tom Lantos, and Connie was given the responsibility of taking flowers to Mrs. Lantos at the hotel in Jerusalem. She told her the story how I had been impressed to pray for her husband the week before. Annette wanted to meet me, and Connie brought her by the house.

In 1995, Congressman and Mrs. Lantos arranged for me to be the guest chaplain for the day in the U.S. Congress, and on February 14, 1995, I stood before the representatives of the various states and led them in prayer.

After I was introduced by the Speaker of the House, Newt Gingrich of Georgia, I prayed:

> *Holy are You, oh Lord, just and righteous in all Your ways. You are awakening and healing our nation by Your presence in this crucial hour, in this strategic day, for Your presence heals, creates and effects change, not only in our nation, but in all the nations of the world. We declare the hastening and fulfillment of Your plans and purposes for our great nation through these yielded men and women who have been given authority by You and the people of this country. Be unto us wisdom, knowledge and understanding, and*

*establish peace, justice and righteousness in all our dealings. Let Your love
be shared among us.*
*Thine is the kingdom and the power and the glory, and may Your glory fill
these chambers. Hallelujah!*

In Your name I pray,
Amen!

As I declared that the glory of the Lord would fill the Chamber and fill our
nation, I did not yet realize that I would be given the privilege of coming back
to America to help to bring this to pass.

As I came down from the podium, the first person I was introduced to by Chaplain Ford was Congressman Bill Richardson from New Mexico. He was to become
our Ambassador to the United Nations in the second Clinton administration and
later Secretary of Energy, but as Congressman he was already troubleshooting
for the President and had just come back from North Korea. When he learned
that I was interested in going there, he told me he would help me.

When we left the Chamber of the House of Representatives that day, we were
invited to the cafeteria of the Sam Rayburn Building for lunch. Many congressmen sat at tables all around us. I saw Mrs. Madeleine Albright, then our
Ambassador to the United Nations and soon to be our first woman Secretary of
State in the second Clinton administration. I hurried over to her and introduced
myself, and we spoke for a few minutes. When God gets into the picture, He
knows how to put us in the right places with the right people to get the assigned
task accomplished. I have had further contact with her since then.

Exactly a year later, in February of 1996, I had the privilege of being the Guest
Chaplain in the Pennsylvania State Senate for two days. After saying the opening prayer, I was permitted to remain in the Chamber all day. I sat and prayed
for the state and the nation. It was very meaningful to me to be able to return
to the very womb of America and intercede for revival.

In April of that same year, my brother was given the opportunity of being the
Guest Chaplain of the Pennsylvania State Senate, as well.

God had something wonderful in mind and was elevating us for the sake of
revival in America.   ✽

ᗰ 121 ᗺ

"A Delegation of Ten"

When I spoke with Congressman Richardson about my desire to visit North Korea, it was not a light matter. I had, by then, been in nearly every country of the world — even those that purported to be "closed" at the time. During the two years before this, I had had the privilege of going to Hanoi in the former North Vietnam, to Phnom Penh in Cambodia and other such places that had for a long time been inaccessible. Only two countries remained for me to visit — Cuba and North Korea. I felt that it was time to visit these countries as well.

After the fall of the Berlin Wall and the collapse of world communism, most of the former communist countries had opened their doors to the West and to tourism and also to the Gospel. The Church was thriving in all the former Soviet states, in Vietnam and in China. Cuba and North Korea, however, were still stubbornly holding to their determination to be different, and travel to both of those countries was still very restricted.

Cuba first began to open its doors, just a crack, and in 1995, the Lord allowed me to go there for the first time. It was a short visit, but I knew that God had arranged it. Fidel Castro was out of the country at the time attending a conference in Colombia, but I was able to communicate with the director of his office. How thrilled I was when I saw the picture of Castro taken in civilian clothes rather than his usual military garb. I knew that it was a sign of the opening of Cuba to the Gospel.

Later I hosted the head of the superintendent for the Assemblies of God in Cuba at our home in Jerusalem, and several of our brethren and friends have had the privilege of ministering extensively in Cuba.

In 1996, just a few weeks before my brother's death, the Lord gave me the privilege of going to North Korea. It was now the last of the closed and inaccessible countries I was believing God to open.

There was another, very different reason for my long-standing interest in North Korea. Sister Choi had been born there, and through my association with her, something had been birthed in my spirit. When she knew that we were going into China, she would ask us to go to the northeastern part of the country, along the border with North Korea and take Korean Bibles to the North Koreans who lived there. She often prayed publicly for North Korea to open again. She not only wanted to go back and see the place she had been born and raised, but she also longed to bring the Gospel to those who were left behind.

I had been praying for North Korea for a very long time, but my desire had recently intensified and I had been trying through various channels to get an invitation. Bill Richardson made some gestures on my behalf, but the political climate had changed, and he himself was no longer traveling there. In the end it was Pennsylvania State Senator Stewart Greenleaf who invited me to join him and a delegation of ten to North Korea as his assistant.

The Senator's group was welcomed because he took in humanitarian supplies — medicines, food, gifts and toys for orphans. He was also interested in making contacts on behalf of some of the still-missing American POWs.

It was early in December, and it was snowing in Pyongyang when we arrived. We were taken to a private dinner that night with a North Korean official from their Foreign Office (he is currently the Ambassador from North Korea to the United Nations).

While we were in North Korea, we were able to tour flood-damaged areas of the country, to assess the damage and see how the United States could respond.

We visited a church and met the pastor and the Bible woman assigned there. After presenting gifts (I had been given some beautifully bound Korean Bibles to take), we had time for singing and, later, a private prayer with the pastor.

As had become our custom over the years, we claimed the land for God and prophesied the release of the people and the opening of the land for the Gospel.

Before leaving, the delegation made arrangements for future shipments of food and medicines that would be forthcoming.

Another place was difficult to reach for another reason. There is a little island in the Pacific where I wanted to go for many years. It is called Rarotonga. The problem was that the island was only accessible from New Zealand by ship, and the round trip took an entire month to make. How happy and excited I was when the first commercial flights started operating there!

There was already a lovely Pentecostal church full of island people on fire for God when we arrived. The pastor had been saved and filled with the Spirit years before, just about the time we started praying for Rarotonga. He later started the church at the prompting of the Holy Spirit and he was pastoring it. We ministered in the church and were so blessed. Island people are wonderful. They are so hospitable to strangers and so open to God.

I have been blessed by my visits to the nations. In some of them I was able to stay only short periods, while in others my stay was quite lengthy. A few I visited only once, but others I visited over and over again. North Korea was the very last country I had been believing God to send me to, and the fact that He took me there signaled to me that He had something new for my life. I was to learn about it much more quickly than I could have anticipated.   ✳

122

North Korean Reception

One morning during a service at campmeeting I received a FAX inviting me to a North Korean reception at the United Nations headquarters in New York that same evening at 6:30. Since I had recently been to North Korea with a delegation of ten Americans, I was tempted to forget it. We were busy, and I wouldn't have much time to arrange the trip.

I realized, however, that just a year before I would have given anything for such an invitation, and I simply could not treat the miracle God had given me lightly. So I sent someone out of the service to find out what shuttle flights were available to me from Washington to New York.

When I had been in North Korea I had been told that Ruth Graham, the wife of Rev. Billy Graham, had been trying for years to go back there. She grew up there as a child, but now she was denied entrance. Realizing the exceptional privilege I had been given to go to North Korea, I simply had to go to New York to show my gratitude to God.

Our service ran late that day, and I had little time to get to Washington, park the car, catch the shuttle and make it to the reception. I missed the 4:00 p.m. shuttle, but made it in time for the next one at 5:00 p.m.

I arrived in New York a little past six and stood in line to get a taxi to the hotel where the reception was being held. When I got to the Knickerbocker Room, I saw some of the others who had been part of our delegation. One of the men, a Catholic lawyer, said, "I read your book two times. Then I gave it to my twenty-year-old daughter to read." We had gone to church together in Beijing, first I went with them to the Catholic church, and later they went with me to the Protestant church.

The Catholic church service that morning was wonderful. A young Chinese deacon was the speaker. He had lived for two years in Switzerland in a Catholic Charismatic community and wanted to tell about the outpouring of the Spirit there. Here we were in the Catholic Cathedral in Beijing, and they were talking about the outpouring of the Spirit. I sat and cried through the entire service.

We were remembering now what God had done. I had good fellowship with others of the group who had accompanied me. I spoke with the North Korean Ambassador and many other dignitaries who were present that evening.

Then, suddenly, I realized that it was already 8:00, and if I didn't hurry, my carriage would turn into a pumpkin. The last shuttle leaves New York at 9:00, and I had almost forgotten that fact. So I took my leave of everyone and hastened for the exit.

When I went out the front door of the hotel, I found a long line of people waiting in line for taxis. The doorman was down the road waving down any taxis he could find and sending them our way. Twenty minutes passed, and I was still standing there waiting.

When I finally got a taxi, I discovered that my driver was an Indian from the city of Chandigarh. I told him I had preached there many times, and he was amazed. He said I was the first person he had ever picked up in New York who had been to his home town. He drove fast and got me to the airport in time for the 9:00 shuttle.

When we approached Washington, it had begun to snow, and the plane made several passes without being able to land. The pilot reversed directions and tried an approach from a different direction. For some reason, he still could not land, and we accelerated and went back up.

After several attempts, we were able to land safely. Everyone on board was very grateful. I had seen some businessmen doing some serious praying. I don't know if they were praying at any other time in their lives, but they certainly were praying that night.

I had left the camp car I drove in a short-term parking lot, and now I made my way back to it. When I saw it, I realized that I was totally unprepared and unaccustomed to clearing snow from the vehicle and wondered if I even had a scraper. The only thing I found was a coffee mug from 7-Eleven. It was stiff enough to use as a scraper, and I used it to clear all the windows. It took me awhile, but it did the job very nicely.

That night I had to drive back home to Ashland very slowly and cautiously. Finally, after I had passed Fredericksburg, the snow turned to rain, and I was able to get on home.

What a wonderful day I had spent! I was sorry to have missed the night's meeting at camp, but God had given me a very wonderful open door and I felt I had done the right thing in obeying His urges on impulse.

I was only at the reception for a little more than an hour, but the whole time I was there I was declaring the purposes of God and speaking them into the lives of those people. I was happy to hear the next day that the American government had agreed to intervene in the food shortage in North Korea. Until then, America had been slow to respond because of the complicated politics of the region. God had given us a miracle.   ✴

⚜ 123 ⚜

"Daughter, Come Home"

When I got back to Virginia, I had one last service with my brother before flying out to Jerusalem. He had very recently done great crusades in the Philippines and Brazil, but my last memory of him is through a miracle.

It was a Sunday morning, and there was a great healing flow in the service. I was moved to say to the people, "Those who are in need of a miracle, come forward, and we'll pray now." The musicians continued to play anointed music as we prayed.

One of the people who came forward that day was a friend of Debbie Kendrick's, a journalist. She is Russian Orthodox and part Jewish, and she and her husband had tried for a long time to have a baby, but nothing happened, although they had gone to many specialists.

As my brother was praying for her, I had an unusual vision. I saw the creche in her stomach. I told her about it: "I've had an unusual vision. I saw the creche in your stomach. Either you're going to conceive on Christmas Day, or your baby is going to be born on Christmas Day."

In January she was reporting for a newspaper in Washington, D.C., covering the Inauguration, and she didn't feel well. She thought she had the flu. When she got back home to Virginia and went to consult with her doctor, he told her, "You don't have the flu; you're going to have a baby."

"Can you tell me when I conceived?" she asked.

He said, "It looks like Christmas Day."

The baby boy, Daniel, was born and is the delight of his parents.

I flew back to Israel for Christmas, but after Christmas I left again, this time for meetings in Ouagadougou, Burkina Faso. I was in my hotel room in Ouagadougou when I received a call from Virginia saying that my brother had passed away. It would be many hours before I could get a flight back to America, and while I waited alone in my hotel room, one verse of scripture repeatedly went through my spirit: *"upon whom the ends of the world are come"* (1 Corinthians 10:11). I knew that my brother's homegoing signified that the coming of the Lord was at hand. I felt God's time clock accelerating and knew that God would use my brother's passing to stir many people not only to be ready for His coming but to get on with the work of the harvest because of the shortness of time.

The next several days proved this to be true, as large numbers of ministers, both American and foreign, passed by the casket to pay their respects to a man who had blessed their lives. I could see that they were greatly stirred by his passing. From words that many expressed about my brother in those days, we formulated the following tribute:

Rev. Wallace H. Heflin, Jr., born August 24, 1932, passed from this life Friday, December 27, 1996. He was a prophet to the nations.

Brother Heflin was born-again on July 5, 1962 and began immediately serving the Lord with zeal. He first traveled with his father, doing tent meetings throughout Virginia and North Carolina and pastoring the Calvary Pentecostal Tabernacle in Callao, Virginia. Then he began traveling the nations of the world, training men and women who today move in similar prophetic anointing throughout the Earth. Although he ministered to more than one hundred and fifty nations, he had a special burden for Israel, China and Russia and ministered with teams in those countries at least once a year. He was a dynamic evangelist with an outstanding healing and miracle ministry. Many knew him simply as "The Miracle Man."

Upon his father's death in 1972 he became co-pastor (with his mother) of the Calvary Pentecostal Tabernacle in Richmond, Virginia, co-director of the Calvary Pentecostal Campground in Ashland and the overseer of existing satellite churches. Under his leadership and guidance, the ministry his parents established in 1937 has greatly multiplied in size and outreach and has touched every nation of the world.

Brother Heflin's life and ministry has reached hundreds of thousands of people around the world. He was an apostle and father in the faith who encouraged hundreds of men and women to enter the ministry and to step out into a deeper life of faith. He was uniquely generous and encouraged many others to give their way out of poverty. He had a beautiful prophetic gift and was tireless in ministry, giving all his strength to the Lord and to the people – until the end. He leaves behind a prophetic example in this unique time in which we live. He has already laid his hat at Jesus' feet and is even now in the war room of Heaven, looking over the plans for Triumphal Reentry and his rightful place as general in God's army.

Later, the Lord would impress upon me the positive aspects of the verse, *"upon whom the ends of the world are come,"* and He caused me to sense the great responsibility we had on our shoulders to bring in the last-day revival in all its glory and magnificence. I knew that we had the God-given ability to bring in that final harvest.
❋

≈ 124 ≈

"Uniquely Prepared for Revival"

I felt uniquely prepared for revival. I had been born in revival, had grown up in revival and had been privileged to pioneer revival in many parts of the world. I had witnessed the outpouring of the Spirit through many decades and had a very great consciousness of what revival glory is. I could not remember a time that I was not blessed by a measure of revival and a measure of the glory. Now, God was taking us all into greater glory, and He was calling me to participate in this revival.

Even before my brother passed away, God had spoken to me that I would be spending more time in America in 1997. I knew that I was coming to help with the breaking revival in America, but didn't realize that the Lord was already preparing us for what was to come in our own family and ministry.

I had been out of America in ministry for the better part of thirty-nine years and had only returned at campmeeting times. Not many people knew me around America. In a CBN Revivalfest meeting at the Founder's Inn in Virginia Beach in September of 1996, Cindy Jacobs, not knowing who I was, had called me out and spoke a word of prophecy, "Daughter, come home. You are needed in America." I had pioneered revival in other parts of the world, and I was ready to pioneer again, this time in my homeland.

When I got word of my brother's sudden death, I flew back to make funeral arrangements. Right after the funeral, I flew back to Israel. We had been invited by the Prime Minister, the Speaker of the Knesset and the Mayor of Jerusalem to be present at the Knesset for the last event in connection with the Three-Thousand-Year anniversary of King David. I had planned that a long time before. After that event, I immediately flew back to the States to be here in time for our annual worker's convention.

At our workers' meeting, the Lord said, "I will give you the pattern of what to do." I suddenly saw both of God's hands on a gossamer fabric which He was dropping down from Heaven. On it was an outline of the United States. Lights began to come on all across America on the banner until there was not a city, town or village where the light could not be seen. I knew I had seen the pattern of the coming revival, and I turned to those who were involved in the ministry and said, "God said that the pattern would be America."

Harvest Glory

The week before the Second Inauguration of President Clinton in Washington, we were busy preparing for our Presidential Inaugural Prayer Breakfast. As before, I would be hosting it at the Sheraton Hotel the morning of the Inauguration. The nights that we didn't have church services in Richmond we were at the campground praying. We sang prophetically and were carried away in the Spirit. During this intense time of revelation, the Lord suddenly showed us that we did not have time. He told us to give our time and strength to the revival in America.

One night during that winter campmeeting I saw a vision of some cornfields and a lone country house in the middle of them. The Lord said to me, "The heartland of America." For some years, I had been jetting from big city to big city, all over the world, and it seemed odd that suddenly the Lord would bring me back to America and show me a cornfield and one country house in the middle of it. But I was willing.

Not long after that I received a telephone call from a pastor inviting me to Paris, Illinois. "Are there cornfields there?" I asked.

She laughed and said, "There's nothing but cornfields here."

"Then I'll come," I told her, and I explained why.

While I was in Paris, Illinois, I met a pastor who had a church right in the middle of a cornfield, and he was very receptive to our ministry.

Most of the churches in which I was led to minister that year were in towns of less than two thousand people. The total population of the town was less than the membership of many of the larger churches to which I had been invited. But God had chosen to send me to the heartlands, and I was loving every minute of it. It was God's hour for revival in America and for the ingathering of the harvest.

God had awakened me one night in Jerusalem, and I heard His voice saying, *"From sea to shining sea."* As I struggled to get fully awake, I was trying to remember which of our patriotic songs contained that phrase. Before long, it began to come to me:

> *America, America,*
> *God shed His grace on thee.*
> *And crown thy good with brotherhood,*
> *From sea to shining sea.*

God was about to shed His grace on America in a new way.

Earlier in 1996, my brother and I and Brother Dwight Jones had been talking about the revival coming to America, and we agreed that we needed to begin to do in America what we had been doing overseas for many years. After his passing, Brother Jones and I felt led to go ahead with those scheduled meetings — in New Orleans, Louisiana and in Caddo Mills, Texas. The people there were very responsive to us.

Rev. Floyd Lawhon who was in Atlanta, Georgia, called Marcus Lamb, the owner of Channel 29 in Dallas and said, "I've been reading a book called *Glory*. Let me read an excerpt to you from the postscript," and he read my statement that when revival in America is in full bloom, the Dallas Metroplex will be the center of the revival. Marcus Lamb was so excited that he quoted the statement on television every day for a while. He ordered a thousand copies of the book and challenged his listeners to get their own copy. When he discovered that I was coming to town, he arranged for Brother Jones and me to be on one of his programs. God had been using him for revival.

He interviewed us for an hour about revival and played it back three times that day and many times over the days and weeks to come. Since then I have returned as a guest on Channel 29 in Dallas several times. Brother Lamb and his wife Joni are busy promoting revival all over the Dallas–Ft. Worth area and graciously brought the mobile television unit and a crew out to Caddo Mills and filmed two services for us.

Later, Brother Buford Smith of Abingdon, Virginia, preempted everything in his television schedule for five hours, as we talked about revival two nights in succession on his television station.

A pastor called me from North Carolina. Someone from Atlanta had read my book and sent him a copy. He read it and began to experience violent shaking in his body. Before long, great revival had come to his church. Before I finished talking with him that day I felt revived myself. It was wonderful what was happening to him and his people.

We had seen God raise up large numbers of new converts in Asia, South America, Africa and the former Eastern Bloc countries, and now it was America's turn. I was so thankful to be part of the end-time harvest. ✳

≈ 125 ≈

"See the Good of America"

When we first went to Jerusalem to live, the Lord told us to "see the good of Jerusalem." He reminded us of the experience of the twelve men who spied out the land of Israel in Joshua's day. Ten gave a report that God called *"evil."* Although what they said was true, it caused a whole generation of Israelites to miss out on the promises of God. The two men who offered a *"good"* report were kept alive to lead the next generation of Israelites into the Promised Land. God told us that if we would see the good of Jerusalem and only speak good about Jerusalem, He would keep us in the land.

We had to cultivate this ability, and I remember failing one day. I nodded my head in agreement with someone who had made a negative comment about Jerusalem, and I had to go to that person afterward and apologize. God has helped us to concentrate on the positive aspects of Jerusalem and has kept us in the land as a result. Recently we celebrated the twenty-fifth anniversary of our ministry in the Holy City.

Having learned this lesson in Jerusalem, we now had to put it into action here in America. Instead of constantly speaking of the problems around us, we had to learn to speak positively about our people and about our cities and to release our faith for them. We had to declare God's glory over America and believe for revival.

We refused to have anything but optimism for the future of America, refused to speak anything but blessing to this country. We stood together in unity and believed God to bless us as He had promised. We knew that we were on the brink of the greatest visitation of God the world had ever seen, and we were determined to be part of it.

A sister from New England said to me, "Sister Ruth, I always felt bad when I would hear preachers talking about 'the frozen Northeast.' " The reason she felt bad, it turns out, was that God had given her a vision of a flame that was already burning in that part of the country. It was not a great flame, but it was a flame; and, by seeing it, she knew that not all the Northeast was "frozen."

She was so blessed when she attended our Second Presidential Inaugural

I Ask for America

Prayer Breakfast in Washington. When she heard me say that I saw flickering lights coming on all over the map of America, she realized that they were the same flickering flames she had seen coming in the Northeast, and she knew that God was going to send revival there.

It was my privilege to be involved with the Charismatic Renewal from the beginning, and most of the last forty years of my life have been spent in non-Pentecostal circles. I saw God reaching into every denomination. The only time I was with Pentecostal people was when I returned to the campground each year in Virginia.

Most of the people I worked with did not see their churches being thrown open to the move of the Spirit of God or their church leaders flowing with the river of God's glory. If they were truly hungry, however, they did not give up. Those who meant business with God started some type of midweek prayer meeting in their homes or in some other convenient meeting place, and God prospered those meetings. One of our spiritual sons, the Ethiopian brother whom I have already mentioned, Beta Mingistu, known to many as the Apostle of the Ethiopian church, started such a meeting in his home in Nairobi, Kenya. That meeting is now running about two thousand people each week. That is how hungry people are for God.

"I Will Lift You Up"

Before my brother had passed away, necessitating my moving back to Virginia from Jerusalem to assume his ministry, God had been telling me, "I will lift you up." My book *Glory* had been out for several years, and it had already blessed many, but I was still relatively unknown in America since I had spent most of my life in other countries.

Then, suddenly I was invited to speak at the Pastor's Conference in Pensacola, Florida, and after that, at two more such conferences there. In those three conferences alone, I ministered to approximately six thousand pastors.

I was invited, along with my brother, to the Revivalfest, hosted by the 700 Club and CBN, at the Founders Inn in Virginia Beach, Virginia, two years in a row. There we ministered prophetically to many people. One of them was Oral Roberts.

It was a wonderful word that the Lord gave him, and the opening sentence set the tone: "Your greatest days are just ahead." In the natural, that seemed like a strange word because his son Richard had more or less indicated the night before that his dad had retired and moved to California, but God was saying something else.

When I finished prophesying, Brother Roberts said something to the effect that he didn't have a word of knowledge ministry like Richard, and you could tell he was feeling a little awkward because of it. My brother spoke up and said, "There's not one person in the world who wouldn't be thrilled to have Oral Roberts lay his hand on their head." He was encouraging Brother Oral Roberts to use what God had given him.

Afterward Brother Roberts began to tell me what he was doing in connection with television, and I could see what God meant by saying that his greatest days were still ahead. Shortly after that, when I turned on the television, I saw Brother Roberts preaching at Rod Parsley's church, and how blessed I was to see how well he was doing. He looked to me as if he were twenty years younger, and he was moving out among the people in a way I had never seen him do before. I knew that God's word to him was being fulfilled in a very special way. It really doesn't matter how old we are. When God has ordained us to help bring in revival, He will work through us.

I was unable to stay for the full Revivalfest that first year and had to leave early to return to Jerusalem. My brother stayed on, and that night was invited to have dinner after the evening service with Pastor Benny Hinn. When Jackie Yockey, Guest Coordinator for the 700 Club, introduced him to Benny Hinn, Benny said, "I know your sister in Jerusalem. She prophesied over me many years ago that God would use me among the leaders of the world and would give me the ministry in which I am now flowing. Some of the things she prophesied are just now beginning to come to pass, and she said all these things years before I came into prominence."

The next day my brother called to tell me what had been said. My first response was, "I never prophesied over Benny Hinn," thinking of the Benny Hinn we all know now.

My brother continued, "Jackie asked him, 'Was that when you were still wearing a pony tail?' and he said it was. She asked, 'Was that when you were still stuttering?' and he said it was." The experience had been so life-changing for him that he had often told it to his staff, and they knew the details of it well. Through the years, however, I had prayed over so many people that I didn't remember it.

"Well, he has never forgotten it," my brother said. "He's grateful and wants to see you in person to tell you."

When we did meet again, Benny gave me an open invitation to be with him in his great crusades, and I have taken him up on that invitation whenever I have had free time. I attended meetings in Oslo, Norway; Richmond, Virginia; Raleigh, North Carolina; Atlanta, Georgia; and Miami, Florida, and each time Pastor Benny has graciously honored me publicly.

In three simple events God seemed to wipe out the obscurity of the past thirty-nine years of ministering overseas to facilitate my reentry into American ministry.

Suddenly my book *Glory* was in great demand, was on the Christian bestseller list, was moving into its ninth edition in English and was available in French, Spanish, German, Swedish, Finnish, Russian, Norwegian, Korean, Latvian and several Indian dialects, and was in the process of being translated into many other languages.

When I was writing *Glory*, God told me that it would be used to help bring in the last-day revival. Letters that poured in from those who read it over the past months and years seemed to prove the fulfillment of that promise. The effects people describe to me sound very much like what happened to me as a girl when Mother read to us from *A Man Sent From God*.

Harvest Glory

I received a fax from Jerusalem stating that a Kenyan brother who was attending an international conference on the environment in Netanya attended our daily prayer meeting in Jerusalem the day before. In Kenya he had read a photocopy of my book *Glory*. He said that no one seemed to know who had the original copy as everyone was reading photocopies. He felt he had to find our place of ministry in Jerusalem and did so with great effort. Our telephone had not been working for about a week, yet he wanted to tell us how much the Kenyans were being blessed by the book.

The same day I received another fax, this one from a mission in a remote part of Chile. The members of the church took turns reading the one copy of *Glory* they had (in Spanish), and they were so hungry for more that they were inviting me to come and teach them.

When I was in Oslo, Norway, in May 1997, I was aware that even in the Pentecostal and Charismatic churches, revival was several years away. I knew that if the pastors and their congregations would read *Glory* they would move into the revival quickly. I immediately sought out a person to translate *Glory* into Norwegian and a printer to print it, and the book is now available there. I believe that this same thing applies to nation after nation. I am desirous of having *Glory* published and distributed in all the nations of the world, as I believe it to be a powerful instrument of revival, and I trust that some of you who are reading these words will help to bring this to pass.

The people of Latvia translated the book, printed it and distributed it on their own. This revival will not only touch America "from sea to shining sea," but it will reach out to every nation. When we look at the vast numbers of people who need to be touched by this revival, we see that we need such a medium to carry the message.

All across the world, God was using *Glory* to cause barriers to come down in the lives of pastors and to bring their people into things that should be normal in the life of the Spirit but have not been taught.

Glory has now been translated into nearly a dozen languages, and many of those manuscripts are ready for printing. Ten thousand copies of *Glory* were printed and distributed freely to the churches across Russia.

As revival broke, God spoke to me to write my second book. We called it *Revival Glory*. It was published in January of 1998 and also became a bestseller. A third volume, *River Glory*, followed and is having similar success.

All it took was three events for God to begin to do what He said He would do, to make my name more widely known and to open doors more fully to me. I soon found that I had far more invitations than I could possibly fill.

This vision has been fulfilled through my appearances with Marcus and Joni Lamb on their Daystar Television Network out of Dallas, Texas.

I Ask for America

God had said, "I will lift you up," and He was doing it.

One night in Jerusalem, I was carried away in the Spirit and saw the last-day revival. I saw a large platform. It was the deepest platform I had ever seen. I have stood on very broad platforms, but never one so deep. On the platform there were at least a hundred hospital stretchers filled with critically ill people. I knew that they were there because of the miracles that were taking place in the meetings. I saw television cameras and reporters from all of the major networks and knew that they were there recording the great revival. I saw America ablaze with God, and I knew that when the revival had fully been ignited across America, Dallas, Texas, would be the center of it.

People often ask me if my ministry is continuing in Jerusalem, and I am happy to say that it is. In fact, it is doing very well under the leadership of Nancy Bergen. Nancy, who has been with us now for about nine years, is well-loved and respected in the city. She has also been well-received by the mayor of the city and by other political leaders in the country as well.

Nancy has a beautiful prophetic anointing and wonderful prophetic insight, and everyone who attends the services at Mt. Zion Fellowship is blessed by her ministry. She oversees at least six services there every weekend in the chapel: Friday morning, Friday night, Saturday morning, Saturday night, Sunday morning and Sunday night.

Nancy does far more than just oversee the services in the Miracle Prayer Chapel. She looks after guests who come from abroad to stay with us and still finds time to help out with meetings every Tuesday night at the End Time Handmaidens' prayer center in the city, with Christ Church and the Messianic Assembly on Monday nights and Saturday afternoons and with many other spiritual activities in the Holy City. Jerusalem is blessed to have such a faithful and anointed servant of God.   ✳

✍ 127 ✍

"Stuck in Place"

The first time I experienced being frozen or stuck in place was in April of 1997. I was in Mandan, North Dakota, a town that adjoins Bismarck, and it was the first night of a series of meetings at the Bethel Assembly of God church there. As the pastor introduced me, I rose from the first row of the auditorium where I had been sitting and started to walk toward the pulpit. Before I could get there, I found myself suddenly frozen in place. Not only was I frozen in place, but I was unable to speak. I could not tell anyone what was happening to me. The pastor was waiting on the platform for me to come forward, the entire congregation was expecting to hear from me, and there I was stuck between the front row and the altar.

I am not sure just how long I stayed there like that. Perhaps because of the circumstances, it seemed like eternity. Finally, the Lord released my tongue and I said, "I'm stuck. I can't move." Everyone broke into laughter. It was several minutes before the Lord released me to walk the rest of the way to the platform.

A man came by that night and told us that the night before he had been driving by and had seen from the highway a terrible fire in the city. He was in a hurry to get somewhere and was unable to stop to see what damage was done to the building he saw being consumed by flame, but that morning he was able to stop to see what damage had been done. To his amazement, it was the church in which he had seen the fire, and it had not been damaged at all. The people of the church had been gathered praying for revival, and God had allowed that great manifestation of fire to come forth. No wonder I had felt such glory there that I had been stuck in place! From that time on, I have been frozen in place many times, usually when I least expect it, sometimes several times in a single service, and always for at least a minute or two — and sometimes longer.   ✳

Daddy (bottom center) at a Prayer Conference in Washington, D.C., March 26, 1930.

With a White House security guard in front of The White House, 1972.

With First Lady Hillary Clinton in a reception, Jerusalem Reception, 1995.

With President George Bush, Birmingham, Alabama, 1998.

The First Inaugural Prayer
Breakfast, Grand
Ballroom, Washington
Sheraton Hotel, Washington,
D.C., January 20, 1993

With Carol Poulos, Dennis
Pisani, my brother, and Donna
Pisani

With Mother and my brother standing at attention as the
National Anthem is being sung.

With my brother at the swearing-in ceremony.

The Second Inaugural Prayer Breakfast, January 20, 1997.

Sister Jane Lowder leading prayer, behind her: Lila Terhune,
Betsy Tibbs and Merrie Turner.

Mrs. Geri Morgan and Dr. Elizabeth Vaughn.

With Senator Stewart Greenleaf, Pennsylvania
State Senate, 1996.

With Pastor Lee, Senator Greenleaf, the translator
and Bible woman, Pyongyang, North Korea,
December 1996.

With Bill and Connie Wilson, Congressman Tom Lantos, Annettte Lantos, Speaker of the House Newt
Gingrich, Eli Mizrachi, my brother, and Chaplain Ford, February 14, 1995.

Praying at the Pennsylvania State Senate, 1996.

With Ruth Carneal, Oral Roberts, my brother and Dwight Jones.

With Molly Young, my brother and Norm Mintle, CBN Revivalfest, 1996.

With Benny Hinn overlooking Jerusalem, 1996.

At The Feast of Tabernacles, Jerusalem.

With Joan and Michael Le Morvan, Director of
Catholic Bible School, Chichester, England.

With Nancy Bergen and Father Pixner,
recognized biblical archeologist, 1995.

With Monsignor Vincent Walsh, Presentation Church, Wynnewood, Pennsylvania, 1998.

In Ashland camp, summer, 1997.

Dr. William Arthur Ward and wife, (Uncle Bill and Aunt Margaret), 1996.

With my nephews in Jerusalem: William and Michael Henderson and James Douds, 1998.

With Rev. Bob Shattles at Christian
Renewal Center, Brunswick, Georgia, 1999.

With Silvana, 1999.

Praying with Chaplain Albert Isler and Dr. Eva Evans at
The Pentagon, Washington, D.C., June 1999.

At the Pentagon, June 1999.

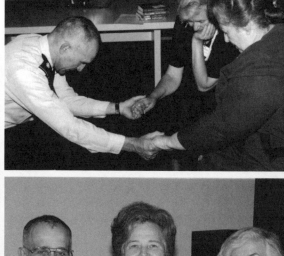

⚘ 128 ⚘

"The Sweetest Expression of Revival"

Our friends, Father Owen Lally and Sister Yvonne Zeller, spent thirty days during the summer of 1997 visiting places in America that were experiencing revival, enjoying being in the glory and evaluating what they were seeing for the benefit of the entire Catholic community. Father Lally is well qualified in the area of revival, as he was actively involved in the Philippine revival in the early seventies, when countless numbers of priests, nuns and laity were baptized in the Holy Ghost.

The two of them published an appreciation of the several present-day revivals they visited and sent it out to Catholic leaders and laity across America. This is what they wrote about what God was doing in Ashland:

> *Ashland, Virginia, was the sweetest expression of Revival that we saw. This community dates back to the great Revival at Azusa Street at the turn of the century. The Heflin and Ward families have been pioneers in Revival and their followers have evolved into a beautiful worshipping people. The music was gentle and calm though lively and filled with joy. Dancing in the Spirit was a strong feature of their gatherings. Ruth Heflin is now the leader of the Community and her book entitled* Glory *is truly a mystical gem. She has discovered the three archetypal steps into the experience of God's manifest presence. She herself is a very edifying witness to the beauty and importance of the Revival. She has a great love for the Catholic Church it seems and is most eager to help us in the birthing of the Revival. She has visited the Church of the Presentation in Philadelphia and is delighted to see what God is doing in our midst.*

The tide was rising, and it was affecting people of every religious background.

✺

⨓ 129 ⨒

"The Eyes of the Blind Shall See"

In November of 1997, during one of our weekend revival meetings in Ashland, I stepped up to the pulpit to preach one night and was suddenly carried away in the Spirit. I could feel myself being rapidly lifted upward. I must have been carried away for at least a half hour to forty-five minutes and during that time everything in the meeting just stopped.

When I came to myself there was a rhythm that was repeating itself over and over in my spirit. Very slowly I heard myself saying, "The eyes of the blind shall see; the ears of the deaf shall hear; and the dead shall be raised to life again." Again, "The eyes of the blind shall see; the ears of the deaf shall hear; and the dead shall be raised to life again."

The people had been sitting all this time in the glory, and some later said it was the greatest glory they had ever experienced. Still, it was a strange experience. One would naturally think that if the Lord had wanted to carry me away, why had He not done it while I was sitting on the platform earlier in the service? The fact that He had waited until I was at the pulpit showed me that He obviously wanted everything to come to a stop and for that great glory to come in.

Less than a week later we took several carloads of our camp people to the funeral of a pastor in Fredericksburg, Virginia. Just before the funeral service started, my associate, Ruth Carneal, who was seated next to me on the front row, turned to me and asked where the rest room was. I pointed it out at the back of the church.

"Would I have time to go before the service begins?" she asked.

"Please do," I answered her.

When she didn't return, I assumed that she had taken a seat farther back in the sanctuary.

I am not sure how much time elapsed. I had a part in the ceremony and several other pastors read scripture portions. After a time, however (probably fifteen or twenty minutes), someone tapped me on the shoulder and said, "Sister Ruth Carneal is on the floor at the back." I got up and went back quietly, not wanting to disturb the service. When I saw Ruth stretched out on the floor, I knew immediately that she was dead.

My first thought was not to interrupt the funeral, so I got two brothers to pick her up, one by the feet and the other by the shoulders, and to carry her into a side room. It was a small room, and there wasn't enough space to stretch her body out completely, so the men sat her up on a chair. Her head was falling to one side, so I reached over to support her head and neck.

Until that moment, my only concern had been to get her away from the funeral service so that it would not be disturbed. As I placed my hand on Ruth's neck, suddenly those rhythms from the week before returned to my spirit. The words came to me just as slowly and distinctly and powerfully as they had that night: "The eyes of the blind shall see; the ears of the deaf shall hear; and the dead shall be raised to life again." I was not saying the words out loud; they were going over and over in my spirit. "The eyes of the blind shall see; the ears of the deaf shall hear; and the dead shall be raised to life again." When I said it the second time within myself, she gasped and life came back into her.

Someone had called an ambulance and, by this time, it had arrived. The paramedics quickly placed Ruth into the ambulance and headed for the hospital. I was able to ride in the front seat of the ambulance with them. In the rear they were doing a preliminary examination of Ruth, and they found that all her vital signs were normal. When we arrived at the Emergency Room and doctors had thoroughly examined Ruth, they discovered that when she had gone to the rest room she had suffered a severe hemorrhage and lost fully a third of her blood. This had caused her to faint and die as she came out of the rest room.

It had been an awesome experience, when I was first carried away, and, again, that day when the rhythms of the river came to me, but the most amazing thing about this experience came to me later. I had never actually prayed for her to come back to life. The miracle happened in the flow of the river. ❋

⚜ 130 ⚜

"Let the River Flow"

During the summer of 1998, God gave us as the theme for our summer camp-meeting, "Let the River Flow." In reality, a new river had been felt in our midst from early that year.

Camp had been so blessed during that previous summer that the Lord spoke to us to continue the meetings on the weekends, to have revival meetings at the camp every Friday, Saturday and Sunday. We thought we would try it for one month and see what happened, but the response was so great that those weekend meetings continue to this day. We made a change in the camp schedule, eliminating the afternoon service and pushing lunch back an hour, so that we could all spend more time in God's presence.

That summer, as the campmeetings progressed and spiritually hungry people came from all over America and the world, we felt the waters rising, much as Ezekiel had experienced, and God began to give us, through the analogy of the river, a whole new consciousness of His Spirit.

People were coming to the campmeetings from all over the world and sitting willingly in our open-air tabernacle because they were so hungry for God, and they had heard that the river was with us. In earlier years, when we had conducted our women's conferences and our men's conferences, many were in the habit of calling to ask who the speakers would be, and they based their decision about coming on the answer to that question. Now, people were so hungry that they no longer cared who the speaker was. They just wanted to be in the atmosphere of the glory.

As the summer progressed, the flow of the river became so great that some people went home to get others and bring them back. Buses were chartered, and busloads of spiritually hungry people were brought to the camp. It was like that all summer long.

Earlier that summer, Monsignor Vincent Walsh of Wynnewood, Pennsylvania, a suburb of Philadelphia, invited me to speak at the Catholic priests' retreat in Malvern, Pennsylvania. About seventy-five priests from the East Coast and other parts of the country gathered. I had been privileged to speak at Catholic lay-leaders' conferences in England and in other parts of the world, but this was my first priests' conference. God poured out His Spirit upon us there in a most glorious fashion.

They had a little different flow than I was accustomed to, so I found myself in a new situation. The first night of the services, the Monsignor stepped up and took me by the hand. I had my eyes closed, and we were praising and worshiping the Lord, but when he took my hand, something wonderful happened. In the uniting of our hands, the individual flows were merged into one great flow. Rather than two separate flows, we now had one.

One of the priests who was a part of the ministry team was also a member of the Catholic/Pentecostal Dialogue. His comment the next day was this: "I wanted to see what is happening between Catholics and Pentecostals, and I take from here a picture forever embedded in my memory. It is of the Monsignor (representing the Catholics) and Ruth (the Pentecostals) as they were joined hand in hand, dancing, swaying, moving together by the Spirit of God. I will never forget it."

In another Catholic conference last summer, at Presentation Church in Wynnewood, Pennsylvania, every day the aisles and the altar area were full of people who were resting under the power of God. There was not a single open spot where another person could lie down. Priests were out of their seats, going up and down the aisles and in and out of the pews, laying hands on the heads of the people. It was a marvelous experience. We are seeing a sudden acceleration of spiritual activity because we are so near to the coming of the Lord. We found unity in the flow of the river of God. I was invited to speak at the same conference again the next year.　　　　　　　　　　　　　　　　　　　※

⚞ 131 ⚟

"Visible Flecks of Gold Dust"

Something else began to happen with us that year, something very unusual. Our Sister Jane Lowder had come back from South America at Christmas time the year before and was telling us about a lady who had gold dust appearing on her while she was worshiping the Lord. Jane brought a video to show us this sign. During a service, while the sister was worshiping, her face would suddenly be covered with visible flecks of golden dust. The first time Jane saw it she didn't know quite what she was seeing. She wondered why Silvana had put glitter all over her face. That didn't seem to be necessary. Was this some new cosmetic craze? She had prayed for Silvana about a year before, and she was baptized in the Holy Ghost. What was happening with her now?

As Sister Jane began to inquire, she discovered that the golden dust was something that God was giving the sister supernaturally. It seemed to flow from her scalp. On occasion, her Brazilian pastor would open his Bible, and she would shake the gold dust from her head onto the Bible. Little piles of gold dust would fall onto the open Bible. The pastor, recognizing how miraculous this was, took that golden dust and anointed the people with it, and great miracles were reported among them as a result.

We rejoiced when we saw the video, but we had no idea that soon God would be manifesting gold dust in our meetings in Ashland. It happened within a few weeks of viewing the video. During our winter campmeeting it happened ten or twelve times in our services.

One morning, during our Spring '98 Ladies' Convention, we showed the video from Brazil of the gold dust. After the service, one of the ladies went into the rest room to change her clothes for the drive home. She heard something fall to the floor and thought it must be the brooch she had been wearing. She stooped to pick it up, but to her amazement, what she picked up was a gold nugget. She brought it back into the meeting so that everyone could see what God had done and rejoice. Others experienced the gold dust as well.

In August of that year Silvana came from Brazil to visit us. There was such a presence of God with her that I instantly began to cry when I met her. Our people witnessed the miracle taking place in her, and others experienced it as they worshiped. God brought a new dimension of the miraculous into our lives, and before the summer was over, this phenomena was appearing more and more among us. Nearly every time I preached, gold dust appeared on my face and on the people who were attending.

In September, after campmeeting was over, I went to Jerusalem. Gold dust appeared in our services there with Nancy Bergen. I also spoke for the Messianic congregation that meets at Christ Church inside Jaffa Gate, and it happened there as well.

Two weeks before Thanksgiving in 1998 I got a call from Pastor Bob Shattles of Friendship Baptist Church in Austell, near Atlanta, Georgia. His secretary had attended one of my meetings a year before and told him that he should have me in his church. One day the Lord told him if he would have me in his church, He would bring him and his people into a new realm of glory.

I was scheduled to be in Atlanta the following Thursday, so I suggested that I could be with him on Tuesday night, Wednesday morning and Wednesday night. Although it was very short notice, he agreed.

I found Pastor Bob to be a very warm person and his members to be very warm as well. The first night in the service, he was carried away to Heaven, and he had supernatural oil on his hand. I would say it was at least a quarter of a cup of oil, and he had to cup his hands so that it would not run out.

The next morning he again had supernatural oil at the end of the service, and he began anointing people with this oil. On Wednesday night in the service, I looked and he had gold dust on his face and on his neck. I said, "Oh, Brother Bob, you have gold dust on you."

Those were wonderful meetings, and I should not have been surprised. That Sunday night the Lord had spoken to me to draw an imaginary line on the platform where I was ministering and to jump over it. He wanted us to be totally out of the old and into the new no later than November 15. Surely this was the new wave of revival of which the Lord spoke.

On Thanksgiving Day I called Austell to see how things were going, and I first got the church answering service. What I heard on the recorded message was so dynamic that it thrilled my soul: "This is Pastor Bob Shattles of Friendship Baptist Church. Come on over because we are in the midst of revival, the glory of God is falling upon us as gold dust and supernatural oil, and God is doing mighty miracles in our midst." I had never heard an answering machine message quite like it, and I called several friends, gave them the number and suggested that they call and listen for themselves. I knew that they would experience revival, just hearing what Pastor Bob had to say.

When I located Pastor Bob's home number and called him there, he began to tell me what had happened since I was with them. It was phenomenal. Gold dust had been raining down from Heaven upon his services, and his people had all seen it. That first Sunday night after I left, some of his members had found gold dust in their hair when they were getting ready to go back to church for the evening service. How exciting it all was for me, too!

Several months later, when I was in France, God spoke to me to go and spend several days with Pastor Shattles. Just as soon as we could arrange it, I flew in to be with him in the revival he had begun in Brunswick, Georgia, with Pastor Bill Ligon and his congregation at Christian Renewal Church. The first night, as I sat on the platform, I was amazed to see gold dust raining down upon the platform four or five times during the first twenty minutes of the service.

Since that time, Pastor Bob and I have been on several telecasts together, he has preached for us at our Men's Convention in Ashland, and we did a camp-meeting together at Caddo Mills, Greenville, Texas, near Dallas. He continues to move in revival fire and glory, and I sense that what is happening in his life and ministry is the new wave of revival, the new wave of God's glory among us.

The most wonderful thing about Pastor Shattles' experience is that he is bringing many other pastors and churches into the glory. The up-to-date story of how the manifestation of the glory of God has changed his life and ministry is told in his new book, *Revival Fire and Glory*. I highly recommend it.

One pastor who heard me speak at Mahesh Chavda's conference in Charlotte, North Carolina, later called to tell me that when he returned to the Nashville area, the children in his school had the gold dust on them. This new wave of the glory of God is spreading across America and the world.

On the way to a meeting the last evening I was in the Houston area, a pastor said he received a phone call in his car from his daughter. She said, "Daddy, you know the Spanish lady who cleans our church? She came into the office just a few minutes ago and had gold dust all over her face. I asked her where she had been, and she said, 'I only clean sanctuary. I only clean bathrooms.' I asked her again if she had put sparkles on her face, and she said, 'No, I only clean sanctuary,' but her face was covered in gold dust."

One of my associates reported, "Every place we went the gold dust came. The exciting thing was it didn't always happen while we were there, but sometimes came afterward. One lady from Hawaii, a Japanese sister, called her son from one of the meetings and was telling him about the gold dust on her.

"He said, 'Oh, those people are just manipulating that.'

"She said, 'No, they didn't come near me.'

"He said, 'They're putting it through an air-conditioning system. That's the reason it's coming on everybody.' She tried to tell him it wasn't so, but he didn't want to listen. Later, when she opened her purse, there was gold dust scattered around the inside of the purse.

"The pastor said that this Japanese sister is a giver and has been supporting a number of ministries. She had asked for prayer that God would enable her to give $100,000 a month, and then this wonderful sign of gold dust came on her and was scattered throughout her purse." How good the Lord is!

Another young sister came to one of the Aglow meetings where I was ministering. After the meeting that morning she went to Montgomery Ward to get herself a vacuum cleaner. As she was standing in front of the salesman, he noticed gold dust on her face and asked her about it. That gave her the opportunity to witness to him. He was backslidden, and before it was all over, he had come back to the Lord.

She went downstairs to the shipping dock to pick up her vacuum cleaner, but it had not yet arrived. A clerk from shipping dock went upstairs to see why. When he saw the salesman upstairs, he asked, "Where did all that glitter on you come from?" As a result of this manifestation, he got saved too.

The sister finally got her vacuum cleaner, and she went home very excited about what God was doing.

I have been watching this phenomenon and the most exciting thing I find about it is that God is doing it a little differently each time. He wants the sense of the unexpected to be in our spirits. We must believe Him, not only for the gold dust and the oil, but for other signs and wonders. He is about to do many great things for us.

When gold fillings began to appear in many people's mouths in our services, some questioned it. *Charisma* magazine, which did an article on my ministry in the spring of 1999, called me to ask if we were having it. I told them that we had experienced it in the sixties, in the seventies and in the eighties, and if this is the new thing God was doing, He would do it for us, too. He has.

In early June Dr. Eva Evans came to visit me. She has been teaching the Bible at the Pentagon for the past eighteen years, and she and the Pentagon chaplain had invited me to come there and speak. She had come to discuss my visit, but for the first thirty minutes we were unable to speak of anything except the miracles she and her friends are experiencing with gold dust and gold fillings.

She had brought a lady minister from Alaska to our ladies' convention. Since I prayed for that lady, she has been having gold fillings and the manifestation of gold dust in all of her meetings as well. My friend Brother Dwight Jones is having it happen in his meetings. Hundreds of people are calling and telling us that it is happening in their meetings as well. This is the new wave of revival. This is *Harvest Glory*. ✸

"Blessed Are the Merciful"

I have always prayed for our President, and in 1998/99 I prayed that President Bill Clinton would remain in office. I knew that for the sake of America and for the sake of revival, we needed a stable presidency. From January 1998 until February 12, 1999, when he was acquitted, much of my time was spent in prayer for him. It was nearly all-consuming. I prayed as if his future and the future of the nation depended on my prayers alone. I had learned years ago that the only way to pray is as if no one else is praying about that particular need or situation and that if our attitude is indifferent, our prayers are ineffectual.

I knew from the beginning that prayer would prevail. Along the way, there were many encouragements from the Lord. In one vision, I saw the Lord stoop and begin to write in the sand. In the story from the Scriptures, the woman's accusers slipped away one by one as Jesus wrote in the sand.

In another vision, I saw the Lord take the American flag and swish it back and forth in the pure crystal flow of the river of God. I knew that it would happen again.

During the impeachment process, I sent an editorial piece to newspapers across America. Later, I sent a copy of that piece, as well as a copy of a letter to Senator John Ashcroft, to members of the Senate. The op-ed piece read as follows:

September 2, 1999

Ruth Ward Heflin
Minister

As Christians, we are called to mercy and not sacrifice. It would be a great loss for us to sacrifice President Clinton and possibly the presidency because of our failure as a people to extend him mercy.
Christian leaders have been appallingly silent and, in general, those who have spoken out have emphasized the transgression, the transgressor and the penalty, without any mention of forgiveness and mercy. Could it be that God is trying our hearts? Could it be that God is asking us to go the extra mile?

I Ask for America

For twenty-five years I have pastored a daily prayer ministry in Jerusalem, where we pray for Jerusalem, the Middle East and the nations. In Jerusalem, we have lived under immense pressures of wars and rumors of wars. We found rumors of wars to be worse than wars. I cannot imagine the pressure our President, the First Lady and their daughter are experiencing, when even the smallest gesture or nuance is weighed and judged publicly from every angle.

Americans must not heed the voices that cry, "Impeach! Impeach!" or the more subtle voices that call for the President to quietly resign. Rather than being different voices, they are really one and the same. Both of these options would greatly rob the American people and the Judeo-Christian world of this unique opportunity to show mercy. As Jesus said in the Sermon on the Mount, "Blessed are the merciful for they shall obtain mercy." *Who among us, if he were our brother, son or father, would not extend mercy and want others to do the same?*

Moreover it seems that we as Christians are willing to offer the President as a sacrifice to purge us from our own guilt concerning the sins of our nation. We have our own sins of omission for which to answer. We have failed to pray for the President as we ought, and when we have prayed, we have often prayed according to our own will and understanding. President Clinton, will you forgive us? Perhaps in this, our "Garden of Gethsemane," we should follow the Lord's example and pray, "Not my will but Thine be done."

The real call is for us to humble ourselves before God and for no man to think of himself more highly than he ought. Otherwise, our uncontrite voices are heard demanding contrition on the part of the President. Let us offer God an acceptable sacrifice: our own broken spirits and our own contrite hearts. Let us fulfill our biblical responsibility to pray for those who are in authority.

Certainly our nation needs God's mercy now more than ever before. In the very act of sowing mercy, we as a people would reap the more from the Lord. "He that troubleth his own house shall inherit the wind" *(Proverbs 11:29). I fear that the very ones who are calling for the impeachment or resignation of the President may face very difficult situations in the days ahead in which they will be calling for mercy themselves.*

Revival is breaking across America. Since 1994, people by the hundreds of thousands have stood in lines for as many as twelve hours just to be admitted to revival meetings in our cities. Repentance abounds. Forgiveness and mercy follow. Revival is new. It is sweet and full of goodness. It makes people softer and kinder. It is "milk and honey." *Revival takes away the hard edge in relationships and the hardness of heart toward God and one another.*

President Clinton, in spite of every appearance to the contrary, will survive.

Harvest Glory

The generosity of heart and spirit which emanates from prayer will bring us a willingness to forgive and show mercy. Ultimately, the prayers of the American people will prevail, and God will heal our land.

Rev. Ruth Ward Heflin

The letter to Senator Ashcroft read as follows:

January 6, 1999

The Honorable John D. Ashcroft
U.S. Senate
316 Hart Building
Washington, D.C.

Dear Senator Ashcroft:

I'm writing at this late hour because of my great concern for our nation at this time. I feel that if the Senate continues in the present mode and is successful in impeaching the President that the Senate will have set in motion events to bring a total collapse of the American society as we know it. I believe that the only solution is for each Senator to see the larger ramifications of his actions and judge whether he wants to be part of the total destruction of America.

I am asking that God change your heart concerning the President and that you use your voice to temper others who see only the immediacy of the moment and not the far-reaching effects, as well as the dramatic and drastic changes for our nation subsequent to the President's impeachment. I believe every Senator who votes for impeachment will rue the day that his eyes did not have a more far-reaching vision. Our nation's economy and the world's economy are at stake and with them the whole American way of life, as you and I have known it. In addition, we must have stability for the coming revival at hand. Perhaps I may sound as an extremist and an alarmist, neither of which I am. I come from a similar background as yours. My uncle, Dr. William A. Ward, traveled with your father, and together they were greatly used of God to teach Full Gospel Businessmen across America in large conventions and auditoriums. My late brother, Rev. Wallace Heflin, Jr., and I have met you on several occasions.

If one errs, it is better to err on the side of mercy than of judgment. I am forwarding an op-ed piece I wrote and sent to newspapers across America in early September and am also forwarding a prophetic word given in our ser-

I Ask for America

vice this last Sunday morning, January 3, 1999. We are not "doom and gloom" people, but we do hear from Heaven. Our response at this time is found in the words of Moses from Hebrews 12:21, "I exceedingly fear and quake."

Sincerely,

Rev. Ruth Ward Heflin, Pastor
Calvary Pentecostal Tabernacle

The day before the hearings were to begin in the Senate, I was ministering in a retreat in New Jersey. That morning l had an amazing vision of Jesus. I saw the Lord's wounded, broken and bleeding body as it was taken from the cross. It was the first time I had seen it this way, and I began to weep. Moved with love for the Lord, as I was reminded afresh of His willingness to suffer, bleed and die for me, I knelt down in the vision and began to kiss His body, first on one side, from His toe to His head and then on the other side, from His head to His toe. I poured out my love for Him, weeping and crying all the time. That experience stayed with me as I was driving alone back home to Virginia. I had planned to stop in Washington, but a storm was fast approaching. I called my friends, Bill and Connie Wilson, and told them that I would be driving directly back to Ashland.

When I got to the exit for Washington, my car automatically turned, heading for Capitol Hill. Bill and Connie live on Capitol Hill, so I called them and asked them to be ready to come out of their house to meet me in a few minutes, as I would not have time to come in.

After Bill and Connie got in the car, we drove to the Senate side of the Capitol Building, stopped the car and began to sing to the Lord: "You are great. You do miracles, so great. There is no one else like You. There is no one else like You. You deserve the honor and the glory. Lord, we lift our hearts in worship, as we praise Your holy name." We continued to sing in that beautiful anointing that I had felt since morning, weeping in gratitude for the miracle for which we were believing God.

From there, we drove around each side of the Capital, where the lights were still burning late into the night, and stopped, sang and prayed. We drove up to the White House and did the same thing at several points around the White House, with broken and contrite hearts, which, the Lord says, He does not despise.

By this time, it was after midnight and we drove to the Senate office buildings, where the lights were still burning and people were evidently still working, and proclaimed our faith and worshiped again.

I took Bill and Connie home and headed back to Ashland, knowing everything would be all right.

One day during the hearings I found myself in a vision, standing before the Capitol, praying with my hands on the dome of the Capitol, as if they were on the head of a bald man. After praying for the Capitol, I stepped back and put my left hand on the Senate side and my right hand on the House of Representatives side. In the vision, I picked up the whole Capitol building, as if I were picking up a cake. At that moment, the phrase, "It's a piece of cake," came to me. The Scriptures say that the nations are as a drop in the bucket to God, and He was letting me know that this problem was easy for Him to resolve. It was "a piece of cake."

I never took the miracle for granted, however, and have thanked God thousands of times since then for hearing our prayer.   ✻

≤ 133 ≥

"Abundance! Abundance! Abundance!"

Some might wonder how so much international travel could be accomplished by a person from a small church with limited resources. I can only say that God is great, His resources are unlimited, and His methods of supply are varied. When we step forth to reap His harvest, He will always supply what we need to accomplish it.

Often when God has spoken to us to do something for Him, we have not had the funds with which to do it. Once, for example, in the early years of our traveling for the Lord, we were in Copenhagen and were momentarily frustrated to find that because of a devaluation of the dollar just as markets were closing on Friday, no one wanted to change dollars on the weekend. We had looked forward to seeing the sights of Copenhagen, but now we could not do anything.

We settled into the lounge at the SAS downtown terminal and tried to decide what to do next. Stretching, my associate put one hand absentmindedly behind her, and it went into a crack between the cushions. When she pulled the hand out, I saw that she had in it a large assortment of local change, Danish Kroner and Ore.

We were so excited by that miracle that we looked in other seats and other cushions to find more, but the seat she was in had been the only one with money in it. The Lord had put it there just for us, and it was enough for us to get a room at a youth hostel.

After we paid our room we had only 14 Ore left, and we went out to find something to eat. It was a snowy day in Copenhagen, and we were hungry. We found a bakery and spied a wonderful loaf of bread in the window. Surely we could afford that, but when we asked how much it was, we were disappointed to hear that it cost 17 Ore. That wasn't much, but because we had only 14 Ore, the fact that the bread was cheap didn't help us.

As we were standing there at the cash register, my eyes were drawn to three small coins on the floor. They were Ores, and that gave us just enough to buy the loaf of bread we wanted. How excited we were that God could put money in the airport seat and on the bakery floor just for us!

We have laughed at this story many times because we would need large sums of money in the future for God to take us to the nations, but we all have to start somewhere.

As our faith increases, things do not necessarily get easier for us. God gives us greater and greater challenges to stretch our faith. He wants us to be totally dependent upon Him. If things have become too easy for us, we may not be walking in the Spirit. His delight is that we live of His miracle provision.

On Christmas night in 1998, we were sitting around the Christmas tree in our camp sharing a bit, and one of the ladies present gave a prophetic word. It spoke of "abundance, abundance, abundance." At that moment, I had a vision. I saw myself reach out and taking hold of the West Coast of America with my right hand and the East Coast of America with my left hand. I brought the two hands together, gathering in the considerable abundance of the nation.

I then began to disperse this abundance with my right hand, from the Pacific Coast, into the nations of the Pacific rim and Asia, and, with my left hand, into Scandinavia and other areas of Europe, the Middle East and Africa. It went out as far as India and the rest of the subcontinent.

I knew in that moment that I had released all the wealth of America that would be needed for the ingathering of the last-day harvest. My understanding was not that it would necessarily come through my hands, but that I had released it in the realm of the Spirit for the whole Body of Christ for the future ingathering. It was one of the most amazing experiences I ever had, a Christmas gift from the Lord. This is *Harvest Glory*. ✳

☙ 134 ☙

"Thy Will Be Done"

In September of 1998, it was my privilege to be invited to the Pentagon for lunch and to walk through the corridors, praying quietly. As we walked, Dr. Eva Evans, who, as I said before, has been teaching the Bible at the Pentagon for eighteen years, said, "Ruth, you've got gold dust coming on your face, just walking through the Pentagon."

We had a full escorted tour of the Offices of the Joint Chiefs of Staff and the Offices of the Secretary of Defense, with Suzanne Stewart as our escort. We felt very special as we ate lunch in the Executive Dining Room of the Pentagon. We enjoyed the wonderful fellowship. It was an important day, and we knew that our prayers were effectual.

After lunch, as we walked back to the entrance lobby, it was suggested that we dance. In the corridor of the Pentagon we sang quietly and worshiped the Lord in the dance. The dancing was especially wonderful. When we all met together, we looked and several of us had gold dust on our faces, necks and hands.

In the early spring of 1999, when the daffodils were in bloom, the Lord spoke to me one day while I was sitting on the platform of our church in Richmond. He said that I had not even begun to perceive my destiny, nor did I know how to pray into it. He urged me to begin praying the part of the Lord's Prayer that says: *"Thy will be done on Earth as it is in Heaven."* Being from a non-liturgical background, I seldom pray the Lord's Prayer, unless I am visiting a liturgical church or attending a special event, but that day I purposed to begin praying this prayer. Throughout the next days I prayed: *"Thy will be done on Earth as it is in Heaven"* many times a day.

Then one evening I arrived at the evening service in the Ashland camp to find that a friend sent by Dr. Eva Evans had driven down from Washington, D.C. to tell me that I was being invited to speak at the Pentagon. Chaplain Albert Isler wanted me to send him several possible dates. From the dates I sent, Chaplain Isler chose Flag Day, June 14, 1999 for me to come. I was very excited and felt honored to be invited. There were aspects of the invitation that had been extended to only one other person, and that was Dr. Billy Graham.

On Flag Day we met Chaplain Isler and visited with him about half an hour before the service. This was his last official day before being posted to Europe.

Harvest Glory

As the service opened in the auditorium, the glory of God was manifested and remained with us for three hours. The heavens opened physically as well, and a fifty-nine-day drought in Northern Virginia ended as rain fell in a deluge. What a miracle!

We had been invited specifically to bring the river of God's glory into the Pentagon, and we were later told that the meeting had exceeded our host's hopes and expectations. Someone who had worked at the Pentagon for thirty-seven years said that never before had there been such high praise in the Pentagon. Never before had there been such anointed dancing. Never before had people rested in the Spirit on the floor. People spoke of the great music and the festive (party) atmosphere that came with the spirit of celebration. The river had come. God's glory was present.

The heart of my message at the Pentagon that day was the healing of our land that comes with the flow of the river, for it brings life wherever it goes. Great waves of healing were released, not only for the people who work in the Pentagon, but also for members of the American Defense Forces throughout the world. ✵

"The Field is the World"

When I was a young person in Hong Kong, I already had a vision for the nations. Just how early it was that God had put thoughts into my heart concerning the nations of the world I cannot say for sure. What I can say is that as children we sat around the table with preachers and missionaries from various parts of the world who were passing our way and overheard them telling their stories of God's grace among the nations. There was Brother Lichty from Kenya, Brother Cossey and Brother Sprague from Mexico and others.

We had the opportunity to sit on the front row of anointed meetings and hear all the great people who were flowing in God at the moment: Oral Roberts, A.A. Allen, William Branham, Jack Coe, T.L. Osborn, Katherine Kuhlman and many others. How blessed I was to have things sown into my spirit at that young age, things that have never left me, but have only continued to grow! In that anointing, seeds of greatness were sown into our lives.

But there was much more to my love for the nations. One year during the eighties when I was home in Virginia for my birthday, Mother planned a little celebration for me that night, with birthday cake and ice cream. During the daytime, however, I was trying to think of something exciting to do with a few friends who had come to celebrate with me. My options were rather limited because it was pouring down rain outside.

Finally, I decided we could go to Mother's house, dig out my baby book and look through it. I had seen it only once since childhood that I could remember, and I was suddenly curious.

Mother had saved absolutely everything relating to the year of my birth, so there was a wealth of interesting information in the baby book. She included announcements of the revivals that took place during my first year. I was able to look through them and know exactly whom God was using in evangelism in Virginia the year I was born.

Among all the photos and clippings that were neatly arranged in the scrapbook, two things caught my eye. The first was a group of photos of Chinese pastors and their wives. Excited by it, I asked, "Mother, who were Pastor and Mrs. Wu? And why are they here?"

"They were pastors that your daddy and I supported in China the year you were born," she answered.

The second thing that caught my eye was a group of postcards postmarked Tel Aviv (before that city became part of modern Israel). The year I was born Granddaddy Ward had gone to Tel Aviv and had sent back postcards.

The two countries that would become the major focus of my life for many years were represented at my birth. Sometimes we are not conscious of how wonderfully the Lord is leading our lives, for His ways are beyond our comprehension. My parents and grandparents had a vision for the nations, and that vision was imparted to me and grew until it became my life.

In Washington, D.C., in the great church that was raised up there, Grandmother Ward was the one to host all of the visiting missionaries. My parents continued that tradition. Grandfather Ward had traveled so widely that he could speak phrases of sixty-four languages he had picked up in his travels. He came to live with us when I was in high school. He was in his nineties. His body was beginning to fail, but his mind remained very sharp to the end. He read from morning to night.

I loved to hear Grandpa Ward recite poems. Still today, beside my bed in Jerusalem, I keep a thick volume of the poems of Edgar Guest. That love for poems was imparted to me by Grandfather Ward.

I can still hear Grandpa reciting: "It takes a heap of living to make a house a home" or:

> *I have to live with myself and so,*
> *I want to be fit for myself to know.*
> *I want to be able, as days go by,*
> *Always to look myself in the eye.*
> *I don't want to stand with the setting sun,*
> *And hate myself for the things I've done.*
> *I always want to be*
> *Self-respecting and conscience free.*

Mother always said that I was more like Grandpa Ward than anyone else in the family. He had the "faraway places" syndrome in his soul or, in religious terms, "the regions beyond." He and Grandmother Ward, when they were first married, crisscrossed America preaching. That's why Mother was born in Los Angeles (on November 4, 1910). Her parents had traveled to Los Angeles to be part of the Azusa Street Revival.

Even after they settled in Washington, D.C., Grandpa traveled as the director of a Chautauqua team, a government project for the cultural enrichment of the American people, and also as an evangelist. When he was home in Washington, he loved to dress up formally and attend official Washington receptions.

Grandmother Ward's mother's maiden name was Edwards, and she was a descendant of the famous New England revivalist, Jonathan Edwards.

Uncle Bill (Dr. William A. Ward) inherited that love of poetry from his father, and he can still (in his eighties) recite dozens of poems he learned in his youth. Dr. Ward is a great evangelist and has preached in every state of the union, in every major city and in more than eighty foreign countries. At one time he had the largest Gospel tent in the world. It seated more than twenty thousand, and he filled it.

I was not the first in our family to be sent by God to a head of state. During World War II, President Franklin D. Roosevelt called for Uncle Bill and enquired of him.

Of my grandfather Arthur L. Heflin I can say little, for I do not remember him. What I can say is that in colonial times the Heflin family was granted a four-hundred-acre tract of land in Fauquier County, Virginia, by King George. The grant was signed by Lord Fairfax. Mother always remembered that homeplace and the lovely one-acre plot set aside as a family cemetery and surrounded by an elegant wrought-iron fence. Unfortunately, the entire property was later swallowed up by an enlargement of the Quantico Marine Base, and the graves and salvageable tombstones were moved to another location. There remained, however, that undeniable seed of greatness that had been sown into our lives.

In the latter years of her life, Grandma Heflin lived with us in the summertime and with Uncle Leroy in Catlett, Virginia, in the wintertime. She chose to be with us in the summer because she developed a great love for the summer tent meetings, and every night, when it came time for the car to travel to the distant places for the tent meeting, she was always ready to go. She loved the miracle healings and loved Daddy's great faith preaching that brought changes to the lives of the people.

Today, Aunt Abilene is the only one of Daddy's immediate family still living. She was the baby of the family and all the brothers spoiled her.

Daddy's larger family of aunts, uncles and cousins were a great clan, hundreds of which salt and pepper the Northern Virginia countryside. More concerning the family story can be found in Mother's book, *I Serve a God of Miracles, 80 Years of the Miraculous.*

As I grew up, our church in Richmond, Virginia, was a missionary church, and many of the members of the church had a deep burden for the nations of the world. Some of them could only pray for the nations. Others gave sacrificially to bless the nations. And still others were able to go to the nations, taking the Gospel.

Sister Enid Morrison was typical of some of those fine believers. She had been a Presbyterian missionary in North India, and after she came back to this country she was filled with the Spirit and attended our church. She was a woman of great faith. She made a scrapbook of famous people and believed the Lord each day to save them. She also interceded for tribal groups.

Sister Morrison went further. Although she never had much money, she was a generous giver. When she heard that someone was translating the Bible into some new tribal language, she would send a few dollars to have a part in the spiritual harvest. She did not know any of the people involved, but she had a greatness of spirit that caused her to reach out and do what she could for every harvest effort. When the record was complete, she had contributed to harvest in more than a thousand languages and tribal groups.

When she read about a missionary couple in Burma who were translating the Bible into a new tribal language and saw that the missionary's name was the same as her brother's (Elmer Morrison), she decided to pay for the entire printing of Bibles in that language, in memory of her deceased brother. I later met those missionaries, who were with the Assemblies of God. What a privilege it was to know people like Enid Morrison!

Our family and our church had a very simple faith. We cherished and held dear the words of the Lord, and when He spoke, we not only believed, we sought a means of obeying Him. He taught us, beginning with small things, and working up to ever greater things, until His will for us included the hearts of the kings and rulers of the Earth.

The vision for the nations, imparted to me by my parents, my grandparents and my uncle, and reinforced by the faith of many other believers, became all-consuming and has caused me to live my life differently than many Americans. Early in life, I chose to trust God for my own personal needs and to spend my time asking Him for the nations of the world. I fell in love with maps and atlases because the tiny dots I found there represent millions of souls for whom Christ died. What a privilege it is to be called by God and sent to the ends of the Earth to help reap the end-time harvest.

When the Lord first gave us the song *I Ask For the Nations* during our prayer meetings in Bethlehem, we began to use it to bless the nations. As He led us, we would ask together for China, for Argentina, for Peru, for Zaire and for many other nations. Even though we had a burden for the nations, God had given us a song that was greater than our understanding at the moment. The total reality of it was vast, and we periodically called out the nations to Him in prayer, individually and collectively.

Through the years, God would take me to virtually all the nations and would

I Ask for the Nations

allow me to be a blessing to them. He would send people to Jerusalem and to our campground in Virginia to receive a vision for the nations and to go out and bless people everywhere. One summer, not long ago, we had people stand in our campmeeting service and call out the nations to which God had recently sent them. We heard: Fiji, Australia (to the Aboriginals), India, Indonesia, Guatemala, Haiti, Egypt, Dominican Republic, China, Israel, the Philippines, the Arctic, the Antarctic, Argentina, Chile, Ecuador, Canada, Denmark, South Africa, Greece, Afghanistan, Pakistan, Iran, Portugal, Mexico, Turkey, Uruguay, Norway, Brazil, Yugoslavia, Japan, Korea, Taiwan, Bolivia and Paraguay, and that was just one service.

God said to our father Abraham, *"In thee shall all the nations of the Earth be blessed."* We know that from the standpoint of the coming of Christ into the world, all nations were blessed, but when Jesus went back to Heaven, He again spoke to us of our obligation to the nations and said to us, *"Go ye into all the world."* The Great Commission is to *"all nations,"* for Christ's love extends to all.

I am continually challenged by the Holy Ghost concerning the greatness of the vision for the nations, and I am determined to continue to reach out in revival to help reap in *Harvest Glory.*

In retelling these stories, I have not mentioned the number of souls saved, healed or filled with the Holy Spirit in each place. I was blessed to preach to very large crowds on many occasions, but aside from the fact that it is difficult to remember exactly how many were blessed on each of thousands of occasions, we always believed that our ministry went far beyond the congregation to which we were ministering at the moment. We were sowing seeds for an end-time ingathering of *Harvest Glory.*   ✳

Epilogue

We are called for this day and this hour. Born for it. Destined for it. It is a time greater than the Day of Pentecost. Greater than the period of the first-century church. The end time. The time of the culmination of all things. The day of fulfillment. The day that the Apostles longed to see. The day that we are not only seeing, but the day we are experiencing. The time of the harvest. The time of *Harvest Glory*.

All things are ready. Everything is prepared, and you and I are making ourselves available to be instruments, threshing instruments, new sharp threshing instruments having teeth, to be used in bringing in the endtime harvest, the harvest of the world.

Harvest Glory is the day in which God pulls out all the stops on Heaven's organ, and Heaven and Earth cooperate in bringing in the precious fruit of the Earth. All of Heaven's preparations have been for this day.

We are not alone in this task. Angelic hosts assist us. Signs, wonders, healings and miracles confirm us. All that has happened through the centuries has been geared for this hour. We are laborers together with God. Brothers and sisters as yet unknown to us, scattered throughout the world, are joined with us in the task. We are wielding the sickle together. Their strength is added to ours. Strengthened together in God, we shall bring all the harvest into the barn. Not one grain shall be lost. This is *Harvest Glory*.

Behold, the husbandman waiteth for the precious fruit of the earth.

James 5:7

Ask of me, ...

And I shall give thee the heathen for thine inheritance,

and the uttermost parts of the earth for thy possession.

Psalm 2:8

He reserveth unto us

the appointed weeks

of the harvest.

Jeremiah 5:24

Come, my beloved,

Let us go forth into the field;
Let us lodge in the villages.
Let us get up early to the
vineyards;
Let us see if the vine
flourish, whether the tender
grape appear, and the
pomegrantates bud forth;
There I will give thee my
loves.

Song of Songs 7:11-12

A Sampling of My Journeyings Among the Nations

January 21, 1940	I was born in Richmond, Virginia.
September 10, 1949	I was baptized in the Holy Spirit.
July 1955	I was called to the Chinese people.
September 1956	I held my first revival.
March 25, 1958	I arrived in Hong Kong to begin my ministry there.
Summer 1960	I went home to Virginia for campmeeting.
January 1961	I traveled to India with Daddy and Mother.
February 1961	I returned to Hong Kong, fired up for the Lord.
Easter 1961	Revival broke out among the young people of Hong Kong.
Spring 1961	I received my first song from the Lord, "One Day by One Day."
November 1961	Revival broke out among the wealthy and the denominational missionaries in Hong Kong.
November 1961	I was called to a worldwide ministry.
January 1962	I traveled to India on my own.
June 1962	I attended the FGBMFI European Convention in Zurich and went on to Beirut, Damascus, Jerusalem, Cairo and Rome. In Jerusalem, God spoke to me about an endtime ministry there.
July 1962	During the annual meeting of the FGBMFI World Convention in Seattle, Washington, which I also attended, my brother was saved, and God spoke to me that whereas I had gleaned in a corner of the field behind the reapers I would now reap with them all over the world.
December 1962	I traveled on to India for six months of ministry.
December 1963	I traveled again to India for six months of ministry. I suffered heat stroke and was healed when I told the Lord that I was willing to remain in India.
December 1964	I ministered in Rome, Italy, on my way to India.
December 1994	I preached in India again.
July 1965	My ministry was changed. I would now go, the Lord told me, to people of position.
November 1965	I spent six months in Nepal and witnessed to members of the Royal Family.

I Ask for the Nations

August 1966	I went to Tarata, Peru, guided by a vision and a word from the Lord.
Early 1967	I began a six-month trip through Europe, the Middle East and Africa, guided by visions and revelations and blessed with the Lord's miraculous provision.
Fall 1967	I met and prophesied to Emperor Haile Selassie of Ethiopia.
1967	I was sent by the Lord to Devil's Island in French Guyana.
August 1968	President Lyndon Johnson introduced me to the King of Nepal at a Washington reception.
1968	My associate and I trekked in Nepal, distributing Gospels to every area of the country.
1969	We visited Sikkim at the invitation of the Queen.
December 1970	I arrived in the Philippines for the preparations for the Spiritual Fiesta.
January 22, 1971	The Spiritual Fiesta Crusades began.
April 1971	On the way home from the Philippines, I met an Israeli Ambassador in Rangoon and the King of Bhutan in New Delhi. I traveled overland from India to Lebanon, from there by ship to Italy and on home by air.
May 1971	I was sent by the Lord to a conference on Bible prophecy in Jerusalem.
June 1971	The living creatures came into my room, I received a revelation concerning my future work in Israel, and God gave me the song "The Flutter of Their Wings."
Fall 1971	We opened a missionary training center in the camp to prepare men and women for the world harvest.
September 1971	I was received the second time by Emperor Haile Selassie in Ethiopia.
Fall of 1971	We did our first *Ulpan* in Israel.
December 1971	We visited Bhutan at the invitation of the King.
Spring 1972	We made a trip down the Amazon River by boat.
June 1972	We were sent on a 55,000-mile journey to discover the Jewish diaspora.
July 1972	The Lord spoke to us to take a team to Israel for six months.
October 1972	On the way to Israel, we ministered in Russia.
November 1972	We conducted a Prophecy Conference in Jerusalem and afterward began our work there.

December 5, 1972	We began regular services in the Assumptionist Church of Saint Peter-en-Gallicantu on Mount Zion.
December 6, 1972	My father died.
Winter 1972-73	Our group visited and ministered to the Catholic communities of Israel.
May/June 1973	Our group left Israel and went home to Virginia before the Yom Kippur War.
August 1973	We took a group of thirty-four to London for ministry.
1974	I made a ministry trip to Ecuador and Bolivia.
August 1974	We began a praise ministry in Carros, France, and from there we reached out as "fishers" to all the Jewish communities in Europe.
Fall 1974	We did additional Hebrew language studies in Netanya, Israel.
September 1975	We resumed the ministry in Jerusalem, the Lord gave us a house there, Halcyon House in Sheikh Jarrah, and Jerusalem quickly became a launching pad to the nation.
June 1977	The Lord sent me to Hong Kong to study Mandarin.
1997	On the way back from Hong Kong, I was sent to Australia to declare open skies over the country.
July 1977	God gave us a vision of the rise of Deng Xiao Ping and the opening of China.
August 1978	We went to China for the first time.
September 1978	We met and ministered to Jashil Choi in Korea.
October 1979	We traveled extensively inside China.
April 1980	Sister Jashil Choi, mother-in-law of David Yonggi Cho, visited us for the first time in Jerusalem.
September 1980	We went to Tibet for the first time.
1981	We opened a work in Hong Kong.
1981	We conducted a series of yearly Prayer and Fasting Conferences in Jerusalem with Sister Jahil Choi.
1981	We traveled extensively and ministered inside China.
1982	The Lord sent me to Japan with the message *"Kabuki."*
1982	We traveled extensively and ministered inside China.
Spring 1983	Prior to the International Praise Conference, I traveled for three months in England, Ireland, Scotland and Wales, ministering daily and raising up praisers for the conference.
July 1983	I conducted an International Praise Conference in the Royal Albert Hall in London.

I Ask for the Nations

1983	We traveled extensively and ministered inside China.
1984	The Lord sent me on a trip to Lagos, Freetown and Rio de Janeiro, to prophesy to the heavens.
1984	We traveled extensively and ministered inside China.
1985	We traveled extensively and ministered inside China.
1986	We traveled extensively and ministered inside China.
August 1986	We visited Tibet again.
1988	The Lord sent me to the Philippines to command time for Cory Aquino.
1990	My book *Glory* was published.
1992	The Lord led me to anoint Yitzhak Rabin as Prime Minister of Israel
January 1993	We conducted our First Inaugural Prayer Breakfast in Washington, D.C.
1994	*Jerusalem, Zion, Israel and the Nations* was published.
February 14, 1995	I was Guest Chaplain of the U.S. Congress
1996	*Glory* was first published in Spanish.
December 1996	I traveled to Cuba and North Korea, the final countries I had not visited through the years.
December 27, 1996	My brother died, and God called me back to America.
January 1997	We conducted our Second Inaugural Prayer Breakfast in Washington, D.C.
1997	*Glory* was first published in French.
1997	*Glory* was first published in German.
September 1997	I first spoke at Presentation Church in Wynnewood, Pennsylvania.
June 1997	We made preparations for revival in our Ashland campground.
December 1997	We first heard of the appearance of gold dust.
January 1998	*Revival Glory* was published.
February 1998	Gold dust appeared in our Winter Campmeetings.
1998	*Glory* was first published in Swedish.
1998	*Glory* was first published in Finnish.
August 1998	Silvana visited us for the first time. Gold dust appeared in every service of Summer Campmeeting.
June 1998	We ministered to Catholics in revival.
January 1999	*River Glory* was published.
February 1999	The paperback edition *of Jerusalem, Zion, Israel and the Nations* was published.
June 14, 1999	I ministered at the Pentagon.
July 1999	*Harvest Glory* was published.

Churches Founded by My Parents in Virginia

Ashland, Virginia
Callao, Virginia
Bristersburg, Virginia
Falmouth, Virginia
Richmond, Virginia
Weems, Virginia
West Point, Virginia

The Campground Founded by My Parents in Virginia

Calvary Pentecostal Camp, Ashland, Virginia

Index

Index

Index

419

Index

Index

423

Index

Calvary Pentecostal Tabernacle

11352 Heflin Lane
Ashland, VA 23005

Tel. (804) 798-7756
Fax. (804) 752-2163
www.revivalglory.org

8 ½ Weeks of Summer Campmeeting 2000

Friday night, June 30 – Sunday night, August 27
With two great services daily, 11 A.M. & 8 P.M.

Ruth Heflin will be speaking nightly the first ten days and each Friday and Saturday night during Summer Campmeeting

Winter Campmeeting 2000

February 4 – 27

Ruth Heflin will be speaking nightly the first week and each Friday and Saturday night during Winter Campmeeting

Revival Meetings

Each Friday night, Saturday morning, Saturday night and Sunday night
with Sister Ruth Heflin in all other months

Ministry tapes and song tapes are also available upon request.

Mount Zion Miracle Prayer Chapel

13 Ragheb Nashashibi
P.O. Box 20897
Sheikh Jarrah
Jerusalem, Israel

Tel. 972-2-5828964
Fax. 972-2-5824725
www.revivalglory.org

Prayer Meetings:

2:00 – 3:00 P.M. Daily
Monday – Thursday

Services:
Friday, Saturday and Sunday
10:30 A.M.
7:30 P.M.
Pre-meeting praise 7:00 P.M.

Come and worship with us in Jerusalem!

Ministry addresses:

Calvary Pentecostal Tabernacle & Campground
11352 Heflin Lane
Ashland, Virginia 23005

Tel: 804-798-7756
FAX: 804-752-2163
e-mail: cpt@richmond.net

Halcyon House
13 Nashashibi Street
Sheikh Jarrah
P.O. Box 20897
Jerusalem, Israel

Tel: 972-02-582-8964
FAX: 972-02-582-4725
e-mail: mzf@netvision.net

On the World Wide Web
www.revivalglory.org

Books by Ruth Ward Heflin

Glory
Revival Glory
River Glory
Jerusalem, Zion, Israel and the Nations
Harvest Glory

Books by Wallace H. Heflin, Jr.

The Power of Prophecy
Hear the Voice of God
The Potter's House
Power in Your Hand
A Pocket Full of Miracles
The Bride

By Edith Ward Heflin

God of Miracles

Books by Dr. William A. Ward

Miracles I Have Seen
God Can Turn Things Around
On the Edge of Time
Get Off the Ash Heap
Christian Cybernetics

Visas

Visas

Entries

ENTRIES

HIGH COMMISSION OF INDIA
LONDON

AMBASSADE DE COTE D'IVOIRE ADDIS-ABEBA

NOM: HEFLIN
Prénoms: RUTH WARD
1. Numéro du visa: 8167
2. Genre de visa: court séjour
3. Date de délivrance: 4 mai 1967
4. Date d'expiration: 3 août 1967
5. Nombre d'entrées autorisées: une
6. Durée autorisée du séjour: un mois

R L Ambassadeur

ADDIS. ABABA

IMMIGRATION OFFICER
(94)
EMBARKED
17 APR 1968
LONDON AIRPORT

CCCP
У 21 0108
Транзит

IMMIGRATION DEPARTED
565
9 JUN 1996
A
565 SINGAPORE 565

ENTRADA
PUNTA CAUCEDO
Aeropuerto Internacional
República Dominicana

EMBASSY OF PAKISTAN
KABUL

EMBASSY OF THE REPUBLIC OF THE SO
CAIRO
ENTRY / TRAN

No. of Visa
Date of Issue
Validity
Period of Stay
Purpose of Visit   Tourism
Fees Collected   L.E. 2,
Receipt No. 15292

CONSUL GENERAL

8 MAI 1967

L'Ambassadeur.

IMMIGRATION DIVISION
BANGKOK THAILAND
A 280 DEPARTED
29 DEC 1991
SIGNED

1986